ALEXANDER FORBES OF BRECHIN

Alexander Forbes of Brechin

The First Tractarian Bishop

ROWAN STRONG

CLARENDON PRESS · OXFORD
1995

Oxford University Press, Walton Street, Oxford OX2 6DP

Oxford New York
Athens Auckland Bangkok Bombay
Calcutta Cape Town Dar es Salaam Delhi
Florence Hong Kong Istanbul Karachi
Kuala Lumpur Madras Madrid Melbourne
Mexico City Nairobi Paris Singapore
Taipei Tokyo Toronto
and associated companies in
Berlin Ibadan

Oxford is a trade mark of Oxford University Press

Published in the United States
by Oxford University Press Inc., New York

British Library Cataloguing in Publication Data
Data available

Library of Congress Cataloging in Publication Data
Alexander Forbes of Brechin : the first Tractarian bishop
Rowan Strong
Includes bibliographical references.
1. Forbes, A. P. (Alexander Penrose), 1817–1875.   2. Episcopal
Church in Scotland—Bishops—Biography.   3. Anglican Communion—
Scotland—Bishops—Biography.   4. Oxford movement—Scotland.
I. Title
BX5395.F58S77 1995   283'.092—dc20   94–3536
ISBN 0-19-826357-0

1 3 5 7 9 10 8 6 4 2

Typeset by Seton Music Graphics Ltd., Bantry, Co. Cork, Ireland
Printed in Great Britain on acid-free paper by
Bookcraft Ltd., Midsomer Norton, Bath

To Toni
who made it all possible

PREFACE

ALEXANDER FORBES, Bishop of Brechin in the Scottish Episcopal Church for nigh on thirty years has, according to the title of one modern hagiographical pamphlet, achieved the status of 'unofficial Patron saint of the Scottish Episcopal Church'. Most writers on Forbes since his death have expressed similar sentiments, fascinated by Forbes's slum ministry in Dundee, and his fight to propagate Tractarian doctrine in the Scottish Church. He was the first Tractarian bishop in the United Kingdom, and a leading figure of the Oxford Movement during his episcopate. His Tractarian leadership, his urban ministry in one of the most industrialized cities in Britain, his trial for heresy in 1860, his defence of Scottish Episcopal traditions, and his involvement in the campaign for Catholic reunion, made Forbes also a figure of note to many in the Church of England, and in European Roman Catholic circles.

Forbes's career sheds light on the effects of Anglicization in Scotland, the diffusion of the Oxford Movement beyond England, and the response of the Churches in nineteenth-century Britain to the development of an urbanized, industrialized society. This study goes behind the mask of sanctity which has shrouded Forbes to provide a critical history of the first Tractarian bishop within the context of nineteenth-century Scottish Episcopalianism, of which he was the foremost contemporary representative.

An explanation is necessary regarding terminology. The term 'high church' is used in two senses. When capitalized (High Church) it refers to that group of Churchmen, both in the Church of England and the Scottish Episcopal Church, whose existence pre-dated the Oxford Movement, and who continued as a distinct group both during and after it. These High Churchmen held to a Catholic theology deriving from English theologians of the seventeenth century, looked appreciatively upon the English Reformation, and regarded the Church of England as exemplary. There were, however, significant differences between High Churchmen in England and Scotland, the latter having a greater regard for the Nonjurors of the late seventeenth and eighteenth centuries. Where the term is used in the lower case (as in 'high church' or 'high') it is inclusive of High Churchmen proper, and also of Tractarians and Anglo-Catholics.

A distinction is also made between the earliest group in the Catholic revival and their successors. So 'Tractarian' is used to describe those directly influenced by the Oxford Movement proper (that is, the Movement centred on Oxford University from 1833 to 1845). Tractarians were more interested in developing Catholic doctrine and teaching than in liturgical ritualism. 'Anglo-Catholics' describes their younger successors who continued the revival after 1845 outside the university, in parishes and various organizations, predominantly through the promotion of Catholic ritual. To distinguish between these groups highlights the development of the Catholic revival and mitigates any tendency to regard the Catholic-minded in either Church as a monolithic or unified party.

Any research sustained over three years incurs a number of debts and I take this opportunity gladly to acknowledge mine. My earliest debt is to my mother who initiated in me a love of the past, although the present work is far from her beloved sixteenth-century Elizabethans. Two scholars who gave me initial encouragement and support and who have honoured me with their friendship are Professor John Macquarrie of Oxford University, and the Revd Dr Austin Cooper, Master of the Catholic Theological College, Melbourne. My greatest academic debt is to Professor Stewart J. Brown, a master of the ecclesiastical history of nineteenth-century Britain. As supervisor of my Ph.D. thesis, Professor Brown's keen interest and attention to detail taught me much about the science and art of history, and the importance of the social context of any ecclesiastical history. Dr Gavin White of Glasgow University, and Canon A. M. Allchin have kindly shared relevant material with me. The entire manuscript has generously been read by Drs Sheridan Gilley, Peter Nockles, Geoffrey Rowell, John Wolffe, and David Wright, who all made invaluable suggestions and saved me from a number of errors. But the responsibility for the final work and its interpretation is, of course, entirely my own. Dr James Jurich kindly gave permission to quote portions of Forbes's correspondence from his thesis on the Belgian Jesuit, Victor de Buck. Other manuscript material is used with the permission of the relevant authorities as cited in the notes and bibliography.

No historian would be able to function without the unstinting help of the staff of many libraries, and I have received more than my share of such assistance. To the librarians and archivists of St Andrews University Library, the British Library, the Theological College of the Scottish Episcopal Church, Lambeth Palace Library, the National Library of Scotland, and New College, University of Edinburgh, I would like to express my thanks. More particularly, I appreciated the assistance of Joan Auld and her staff in the archives of Dundee University Library; Dr Peter Doll of Pusey House Library; and Peter Vasey of the Scottish Record Office who all gave me patient and sustained help over many months. The General Secretary of the General Synod of the Scottish Episcopal Church kindly allowed me unlimited access to their records, as did the then Provost Peter Sanderson of St Paul's Cathedral, Dundee. The Very Revd Robert Breaden and the parish of St Mary's, Broughty Ferry, generously financed much of my time in Dundee for research purposes. Small research grants were also received from the Faculty of Divinity, University of Edinburgh; the General Synod Office, Scottish Episcopal Church; the Southdown Trust; and the Bishop of Brechin. But my greatest obligation is to my wife, Toni, who freely gave up her career in Australia, agreed to sell all we possessed, and to come half-way across the world so her husband could satisfy his yearning to test himself in doctoral research. It is out of that endeavour that this book has been born.

CONTENTS

ABBREVIATIONS

BHT	Brotherhood of the Holy Trinity papers, Pusey House archives
BL	British Library
BpF	Bishop Forbes correspondence, Pusey House archives
BrMs	Brechin Diocesan archives, Dundee University
DCL	Dundee Central Library
DNB	*Dictionary of National Biography*
DUL	Dundee University Library archives
EUML	Edinburgh University Main Library archives
IOR	India Office Records, British Library
Lathbury	D. C. Lathbury, *Correspondence on Church and Religion of William Ewart Gladstone* (1910)
KP	Keble to Pusey correspondence, Pusey House archives
LPL	Lambeth Palace Library
Mackey	Donald Mackey, *Bishop Forbes: a Memoir* (1888)
NLS	National Library of Scotland
Perry	W. Perry, *Alexander Penrose Forbes* (1939)
PH	Pusey House archives
PK	Pusey to Keble correspondence, Pusey House archives
PP	Pusey Papers, Pusey House archives
REC	Registers of Episcopal College, Scottish Episcopal Church
RSCHS	*Records of the Scottish Church History Society*
SAUL	St Andrews University Library archives
SEJ	Scottish Ecclesiastical Journal
SPC	Records of St Paul's Cathedral, Dundee
SRO	Scottish Record Office

I

An Anglicized Young Scotsman

IN 1817 Edinburgh was just coming to the end of its cultural golden age
in the years of the Scottish enlightenment. European figures such as
David Hume, Adam Smith, Robert Adam, and William Robertson were
already dead. Dugald Stewart, professor of moral philosophy at Edinburgh University, and the last leader of these eighteenth-century literati,
would die in 1828. But the most lasting legacy of the classical culture of
eighteenth-century Edinburgh was the building of the new town after
1767. For the remainder of the eighteenth century the middle and upper
classes migrated wholesale to this part of the city with its wide, straight
streets, Georgian crescents, and classical façades. They left to the lower
orders the wynds and tenements of the old town. But the break between
the two was never complete, for such necessary institutions as the law
courts, council chambers, and the Royal High School remained in the old
town. Edinburgh gave indications of a city moving confidently into the
nineteenth century, despite the economic recession in Britain following
the end of the Napoleonic wars in 1815. The Union Canal between
Edinburgh and Glasgow was begun in 1818 and opened in 1822.[1] Also
indicative of the industrialized society to come was the start in 1821 of a
steam-packet service between London and Leith.[2] The end of the
Napoleonic wars drew to a close a period of sweeping change for
Edinburgh society. Previously the social orders had intermingled in the
old town, competing for the centre of the street to avoid the dung, or
the contents of a chamber-pot thrown from an upper window, in a
manner hardly different from their medieval predecessors. The lower-
middle orders and the nobility even shared different floors of the same
tenement. The building of the new town not only expressed the greater
confidence of the middle orders, who were to be the most successful class
in the nineteenth century, but also the hardening of nineteenth-century
society into separate economic and social classes with increasingly
different values and aspirations.

[1] William Gilbert, *Edinburgh Life in the Nineteenth Century* (1901, repr. 1989), 26.
[2] Ibid. 29.

The more immediate changes in Edinburgh proceeded chiefly from the growth of the city.[3] The single circumstance of the increase of population, and its consequent overflowing from the old town to the new, implied a general alteration of our habits. It altered the style of living, obliterated local arrangements, and destroyed a thousand associations, which nothing but the still preserved names of houses and of places is left to recal [*sic*]. It was the rise of the new town that obliterated our old peculiarities with the greatest rapidity and effect.[4]

Alexander Penrose Forbes was born into this changing city on 6 June 1817.[5] The Forbeses lived in York Place in the new town and a few years later moved to 17 Ainslie Place, one of the more fashionable crescents in the west end. He was the second son of the family and had three brothers and seven sisters, although a brother and three sisters died in childhood.[6] His mother Louisa (a shadowy figure in the available evidence) was the daughter of Sir Alexander Cumming-Gordon of Altyre, in Morayshire, and had married John Forbes in 1802. The Cumming-Gordons were influential enough in the nineteenth century for his mother's father and eldest brother to be Tory Members of Parliament, for Inverness and Elgin respectively.[7]

Alexander was baptized one month later on 9 July at the Episcopalian St Paul's Chapel in York Place to which his parents belonged.[8] The congregation moved into this new chapel from their old one in the Cowgate in 1818.[9] St Paul's, in keeping with its former life as a qualified chapel, was a fashionable, Anglicized congregation, using the English Book of Common Prayer, and was predominantly middle and upper class. St John's, in the west end of Princes Street, where John Forbes's older brother William was a respected member of the congregation, was also built at the same time.[10] The erection of such prominent buildings illustrated a new confidence among the Episcopalians of Edinburgh.

Our episcopalians used to be so few that their two principal congregations met, the one in a humble place at the west end of Rose Street, the other in a chapel

---

[3] The population of Edinburgh grew from approximately 36,000 in 1755 (exclusive of the parish of St Cuthbert's and of Leith) to 59,000 in the 1831 census. T. C . Smout, *A History of the Scottish People 1560–1830* (1972), 343.

[4] Henry Cockburn, *Memorials of his Time* (1856), 28.

[5] From a transcript of his baptismal certificate made by William Marshall, treasurer of St Paul's Chapel and submitted with Forbes's application to the East India Company on 17 July 1834, IOR J 1. 52, fo. 247.

[6] See the genealogical appendices in William Forbes, *Narrative of the Last Sickness and Death of Dame Christian Forbes* (1875).

[7] William Anderson, *The Scottish Nation* (1859), i. 740.

[8] See n. 5.

[9] Gilbert, *Edinburgh Life*, 22.

[10] Anderson, *Scottish Nation*, ii. 232.

which, though handsome and spacious when got at, was buried in an inaccessible close on the south side of the Cannongate. Indeed it was only within a few years before this sect had got some of the legal vexations which had clouded it removed. They now raised their heads; and growing in numbers, and in aristocracy, erected their new chapels at the west end of Princes Street, and at the east end of York Place.[11]

As well as these two increasingly prosperous and respected congregations there was also a small, former nonjuring congregation, which met in Carrubber's Close on the north side of the High Street.

The son of a prominent lawyer usually has pleasant prospects, and in 1825 Alexander's father, John Hay Forbes, was appointed to the bench of the Court of Session, the highest court in Scotland. He marked his success in the usual way for established Edinburgh lawyers by buying an estate, at Medwyn in Peebleshire, and took his legal title from his new lands. As a Tory judge Lord Medwyn earned the respect of the Whig, Henry Cockburn, with whom he shared the bench. Cockburn remembered John Forbes as 'more of a monk in matters of religion or politics than any man I know, [he] is an excellent, judicious, humane, practical judge, with great integrity, and a deep sense of official duty'.[12] Medwyn was one of the majority on the bench of the Court of Session which decided in the Auchterarder case in 1838 that the Church of Scotland's Veto Act of 1834 was illegal, upholding instead the rights of patrons to appoint to parishes.[13] Medwyn's Tory opinions inevitably assisted his rise to the top of his profession as Scotland was governed by the Tories of the landed classes until the Reform Act of 1832. His decision in the Auchterarder case shows Medwyn strongly sympathetic to the interest of the landed classes, but his rise to legal pre-eminence was also supported by his own father's links to the government.

Sir William Forbes was senior partner in Forbes and Company, a leading Edinburgh banking firm which, in 1838, became the Union Bank. He was consulted by the ministry over finance and declined a number of invitations to stand for Parliament.[14] Sir William's rise to prosperity enabled him to restore the family to the status of landed gentry, through his purchase of the old ancestral estate of Pitsligo. This had previously belonged to the family of his maternal grandmother whose sister had married Alexander, fourth Lord of Pitsligo. As a Jacobite,

11 Cockburn, *Memorials*, 305.
12 Henry Cockburn, *Circuit Journeys* (1889), 91–2.
13 Henry Cockburn, *Journal* (1874), i. 167.
14 *DNB* (1899), xix. 412, 413.

Pitsligo's estates had been confiscated after the failure of the rising of 1715. Following some years of exile in France, where he maintained his Episcopalianism at the Roman Catholic court of the Chevalier, Pitsligo eventually returned to Scotland only to join the Jacobite rising of 1745 as a cavalry commander in Prince Charles Edward Stuart's army. Following the defeat at Culloden he ended his days living incognito in his son's house.[15] After the death of Pitsligo's son, William succeeded to the baronetcy, becoming Sir William Forbes of Pitsligo, baronet. As the late nineteenth-century biographer, Thomas Thomson, observed, William Forbes was 'a link between the old Scottish aristocratic families, to which he belonged by birth, and the rising commercial opulence with which he was connected by profession'.[16] In addition to his landed aspirations Sir William Forbes maintained a strong attachment to the civic life of Edinburgh and cultivated its literary society. He was very active in city charities, including the Charity Workhouse,[17] was prominent in the rebuilding of the Royal High School, and was a member of the Society of Antiquaries.[18] But he also felt the attraction of the English south, especially London to which he was a frequent visitor, 'being partial to its society'.[19]

From the beginning of Alexander Forbes's life there was therefore a tension inherited from his family background. The social position of his father and grandfather associated the Forbes family with Anglicizing forces in Scottish society, such as the St Paul's congregation, the Tory interest, and London society. Yet these two influential men in Alexander's life also had strong connections with native traditions such as the Scottish enlightenment, the Scots law, and, principally, a love for the nonjuring and Jacobite tradition of the Scottish Episcopal Church. Alexander derived his devotion to Episcopalianism principally from his father and grandfather, who were both leading figures in the Episcopal Church in their generation.

His grandfather combined his membership of an Episcopalian congregation which conformed to the reigning Hanoverians with an attachment to the former Stuart dynasty. In 1793 he undertook a belated grand tour of Europe for the sake of his wife's health. While in Rome he spent time with a friend of Cardinal Henry Stuart, the younger brother of Prince Charles Edward Stuart, who since the latter's death in 1788 was the

[15] *DNB* xix. 377–8.
[16] Thomas Thomson, *A Biographical Dictionary of Eminent Scotsmen* (1875), ii. 53.
[17] John Kay, *A Series of Original Portraits and Caricature Etchings* (1877), 129.
[18] Thomson, *Biographical Dictionary* , ii. 51.
[19] Anderson, *Scottish Nation* (1863), v. 243.

Stuart claimant to the British throne. Forbes wrote in his journal, 'it is impossible for me, nor indeed do I wish, to divest myself of a partiality, for the Count of Albany [Cardinal Henry Stuart] & his ill-fated house.'[20] Forbes availed himself of the chance of seeing the Stuart heir himself by going to St Peter's basilica to observe him saying mass, but was too embarrassed to accept an invitation to be introduced as he was uncertain how to address the royal cardinal. His dilemma as recorded in his journal reveals both his disposition to be generous towards the cardinal's royal lineage and his Scottish nationalism. He considered that to address him as 'his eminence' would be

short of what I considered him to be entitled to as the Grandson of King James the Second. *Royal Highness*, which, in politeness & courtesy at least, I should have thought due to him; as his Father had been recognised as king by the Pope, & by Louis the Fourteenth; would have done well enough when his Elder Brother was alive; but which he would probably have considered too little now that he had assumed the title & style of *Henry the nineth* . . . and to have called him *His Majesty*, I could not think altogether proper on my part who owed allegiance to the reigning Family of Britain . . . thus [I] lost the only opportunity I shall probably ever have of being in the Company of the last male descendant of our Antient Scottish kings for whom I do not conceal my having a strong & partial veneration.[21]

These thoughts of Sir William Forbes would have surprised the good burghers of Edinburgh for whom he was a solid member of the establishment of the city with its secure allegiance, at least since 1746, to the Hanoverians. But such thoughts would have been far less surprising to Forbes's fellow Episcopalians who, for most of the eighteenth century, were periodically persecuted for their Jacobite loyalty to the defeated and exiled house of Stuart. William Forbes's sympathy towards the Jacobite cause, however, contrasts with his practical decision to accept the Hanoverian dynasty. This contrast typifies the divisions among eighteenth-century Scottish Episcopalians, divisions that continued, despite formal union, into the nineteenth century.

Episcopalians were primarily motivated by Jacobitism from 1689 until at least 1715.[22] Yet while the majority of Episcopalians were unable to take the oaths to William and Mary in 1689, there were a number who were

[20] Sir William Forbes, 'Journal of European Tour 1792–3', NLS 1540, fo. 384.

[21] Ibid. NLS 1544, fos. 49–50.

[22] Bruce Lenman, 'The Scottish Episcopal Clergy and the Ideology of Jacobitism', in Eveline Cruickshanks (ed.), *Ideology and Conspiracy: Aspects of Jacobitism 1689–1759* (1982), 36–48.

willing to conform and these formed an increasingly separate and isolated group during the course of the eighteenth century. These conformists were always a minority and never included any of the Scottish bishops. Initially after 1689 they were penalized by those zealous for presbytery but were gradually able to take advantage of the lenient attitude of the monarchs. In 1712 an Act of Parliament gave legal toleration to those Episcopal ministers who would take the oaths to Queen Anne and pray for her and the Princess Sophia of Hanover by name in public worship.[23] From 1712 therefore this conformist group of Episcopalians 'qualified' for toleration. After the 1715 Jacobite rising, as the fever of the rebellion died down and they began to enjoy the fruits of tolerance, these qualified Episcopalians grew less political and became increasingly Anglicized, more especially after the penal Acts of 1719. These led to several Episcopal congregations appointing clergy who were willing to take the oaths to the Hanoverians and thus to qualify for toleration. As all the Scottish bishops were nonjuring these conforming congregations were supplied by clergy ordained in England or the Church of Ireland. Anglicization of the qualified clergy further increased after the 1745 rebellion when the penal acts decreed that only Episcopal ministers ordained in England and Ireland could be recognized in law. As only five nonjuring clergy qualified at that time, and two of these later repented of their action, obviously the source of Scottish clergymen for the qualified congregations had run dry.[24] Their Anglicization was further accentuated by the arrival into the south of Scotland of English immigrants who employed the English Book of Common Prayer for worship. Throughout the eighteenth century Episcopalians in the south of Scotland became increasingly Anglicized and cut off from their nonjuring brethren. This led to a disparity of outlook which remained and intensified through the last half of the eighteenth century.

For the majority nonjuring Episcopalians, it was because of the binding nature of their oath of allegiance to the Stuarts that they lost the battle for a legally established episcopacy in 1688-9. In 1705 the bishops agreed to continue the episcopal succession and consecrate bishops without title or jurisdiction to a diocese but only as members of the 'episcopal college', so as not to infringe upon the right of their acknowledged sovereign to nominate to dioceses.[25] In all matters, including internal Church government, the bishops in 1705 considered themselves answerable to their sovereign.

[23] George Grub, *An Ecclesiastical History of Scotland* (1861), iii. 364.
[24] Ibid. iv. 35-7.
[25] Ibid. iii. 346-7.

However, the Jacobite allegiance of the Episcopal Church became increasingly conditional in the period after 1715 as Episcopalian identity was more and more established upon uniquely theological foundations. The influence of James Stuart (known as the Chevalier, and the Stuart claimant to the British throne) with the bishops weakened after 1720 and gradually episcopal independence began to be asserted. This process can be seen particularly in the middle of the century, and was associated with Bishops James Gadderar and Thomas Rattray. Gadderar and Rattray desired the re-establishment of a diocesan episcopacy and the use of the Scottish liturgy based on the Scottish Prayer Book of 1637. In their struggle for these principles they were prepared to oppose the continuation of the royal prerogative in the Scottish Episcopal Church. But prior to the 1740s they were resisted in this desire by the majority of the other bishops known as the 'college party', who wanted the Church to be governed non-territorially by a college of bishops nominated by their king.

Both Gadderar and Rattray lived for a time in London and had extensive contact with the English Nonjurors while there.[26] English Nonjurors had more leisure and freedom to pursue scholarship than was possible to those in Scotland, and contact with this scholarship south of the border influenced the two Scots. Largely through an interest in and regard for the authority of the early Church, the Nonjurors in England formulated high theologies of the spiritual independence of the Church from the state. They believed this independence was enshrined and preserved in the apostolic succession of the episcopate and needed to be expressed through a richer, more Catholic liturgy than the contemporary English Book of Common Prayer.[27] It is not surprising that Gadderar and Rattray, given their years of contact with the English Nonjurors, should be protagonists for those things in their own Church which represented the theology they had come to value in the south; even if these things were moribund, like the Scottish liturgy, or antagonistic to their Jacobitism, like their claim to diocesan episcopacy against the wishes of the Chevalier. Gadderar, for example, republished and annotated some hundred copies of the Scottish Communion Office of 1637 for use in his diocese, which became extremely popular.[28] This liturgy formed the basis of the most widespread use in the Episcopal Church during the

---

[26] Henry Broxap, *The Later Non-Jurors* (1924), 61.

[27] See ibid., and J. D. Overton, *The Non-Jurors* (1902).

[28] See a letter of 18 May 1744 by Bishop Gerard of Aberdeen quoted from the original manuscript by Patrick Cheyne in his *The Authority and Use of the Scottish Communion Office Vindicated* (1843), 26.

eighteenth century.[29] Rattray also did a great deal to promote the Scottish liturgy, being primarily responsible for the most characteristic features of the Scottish Communion Office in its most authoritative form of 1764.[30] It was this liturgy that was to become a major source of controversy and division within the Episcopal Church during the nineteenth century, climaxing during the episcopate of Alexander Forbes.

But the major area of conflict between the two groups of nonjuring Episcopalians in the eighteenth century, however, was the re-establishment of diocesan episcopacy. When one or two bishops began to be elected to specific dioceses from 1727 against the wishes of the majority, the theological claim to diocesan episcopacy was beginning to drive the bishops into two camps.

Rattray formulated the best theological defence of diocesan episcopacy and the spiritual independence of the Church when, in 1728, he wrote *An Essay on the Nature of the Church*. The work was essentially an argument for an independent, authoritative episcopate drawn from the authority of the Church Fathers. He was applying the theological lessons learnt from the English Nonjurors. Among the claims he made in that essay for the episcopate were for monarchical, diocesan bishops as of the *esse* of the Church.[31] The communion between the bishops and the diocese or 'particular Church' constituted the unity of the Church.[32] Each diocesan bishop was independent because he had no higher 'Principle of Unity' above him, being himself immediately subordinate to Christ.[33] Only Christ might judge a bishop.[34] From an argument that the Catholic or universal Church was comprised of bishops who ratified one another's deeds[35] Rattray concluded that the consent of all bishops in one province was needed for a canon law;[36] only a diocesan bishop could have the authority of oversight to govern at a provincial level;[37] and a national Church without dioceses was thus contrary not only to the original purpose of episcopacy but also to the 'design of God'.[38]

While this was clearly written primarily to oppose theologically the 'college party' among the bishops, it is also obvious that the nature of the Church for Rattray had little or no place for the royal supremacy. Having asserted the independence of the Church Rattray went on to question the need for royal authority within it. He believed that the old form of

---

[29] John Dowden, *The Scottish Communion Office 1764* (1922), 69.
[30] Ibid. 74.
[31] Thomas Rattray, *An Essay on the Nature of the Church* (1728), 1–2.
[32] Ibid. 5ff.   [33] Ibid. 11.   [34] Ibid. 15.
[35] Ibid. 23.   [36] Ibid. 24.   [37] Ibid. 40.
[38] Ibid. 42.

episcopal election by royal nomination 'cannot take place in our present circumstances, when the Church must act upon her own original and inherent rights'.[39] First among inherent rights was the appointment of her own governors, the bishops. Not content with this dismissal of the royal supremacy Rattray went on to claim that the only reason for the Church's previous submission to civil authority was its recognition of the temporal advantages the latter could bestow; but when that civil protection failed the Church was bound to assert her inherent rights again, for her own survival in difficult times.[40] There could have hardly been a more assertive theology of episcopacy as an inherent spiritual authority of the Church, while the royal authority was reduced to a matter of convenience in good times and irrelevant in bad.

By the late 1720s the influence within Scottish Episcopacy lay increasingly with men of the mind of Rattray and Gadderar to the detriment of those upholding the prerogatives of the 'king over the water'. However, both parties were augmenting their numbers by new consecrations. The beginning of the end of this division among the bishops, and another step towards victory for the diocesan ideal, came in 1731 in a concordat subscribed to by all the bishops. They agreed to the following articles:

1. That we shall only make use of the Scottish or English Liturgy in the public divine service, nor shall we disturb the peace of the Church by introducing into the public worship any of the ancient Usages,[41] concerning which there has been lately a difference among us; and that we shall censure any of our clergy who act otherwise.

2. That hereafter no man shall be consecrated a Bishop of this Church without the consent and approval of the majority of the other Bishops.

3. That upon the demise or removal elsewhere of a Bishop of any district, the presbyters thereof shall neither elect, nor entrust to, another Bishop, without a mandate from the Primus, by consent of the other Bishops.

4. That the Bishops of this Church shall, by a majority of voices, choose their Primus, for convocating and presiding only, and that no Bishop shall claim jursidiction without the bounds of his own district.

Districts corresponding to the former dioceses were then allocated to all the bishops with the rider that 'by the aforesaid divisions of districts we do not pretend to claim any legal title to dioceses'.[42]

---

[39] Ibid. 62.   [40] Ibid. 65–6.

[41] These were principally the mixing of water with the wine at the Eucharist; prayer for the dead; the *epiclesis* or invocation of the Holy Spirit over the Eucharistic elements; the prayer of oblation in the Eucharistic Prayer.

[42] J. P. Lawson, *History of the Scottish Episcopal Church from the Revolution to the Present Time* (1843), 257–8.

This, of course, was a compromise. Dioceses were claimed only under
the provisional description of 'districts' with no legal title, and the agreement was still sent to the Chevalier. But it was sent as something already
decided and its provisions made no mention of his prerogative. The
bishops were now diocesans in all but name. The diocesan party grew in
influence in the bishops' meetings that followed. Gadderar died in
February 1733 but his vision continued under Rattray's leadership as primus, or senior bishop, from 1739. Although he died shortly before the
Episcopal Synod of 1743 which saw the triumph of the diocesan party's
principles, Rattray had in fact already drawn up the first ten canons
which, in addition to those of 1731, were then ratified.[43] These increased
the almost-diocesan authority of the bishop. No priest, for example, could
move from his district without dismissal of his bishop. The canons
affirmed the use of the Scottish liturgy as well as the English, with a
strong recommendation for the former.[44] One of the canons also encouraged that attention to the authority of the early Church which had been
so formative for the English Nonjurors. The clergy were encouraged not
only to study scripture but also 'the Fathers of the apostolical and two
next succeeding ages and . . . to instruct their people in the truly
Catholic principles of that pure and primitive Church'.[45] This was a
recommendation which could only bolster support for the authority of
the early Church among Scottish Episcopalian clergy. The diocesan party
had gained victory over the old seventeenth-century theology of royal
supremacy, passive obedience, and non-resistance represented by the
college party and the trustees of the Chevalier. More importantly for the
future of the nonjuring Church they had, whether they fully realized it or
not, fundamentally weakened the theological basis of Jacobitism.

Perhaps the bishops did realize this to some extent, which may
account for their lack of support for the 1745 rebellion. Only two
Episcopal clergy actually followed the Prince's army and both were
tried and executed.[46] A future bishop, Robert Forbes, had certainly
intended to do so but had been apprehended on the way.[47] But there
appears to be no record of the bishops giving overt support to the
Jacobite army or to the Prince, whereas in 1715 the Episcopalians,
including the bishops, had endorsed that uprising.[48] In 1745 they had

[43] Ibid. 268.
[44] W. Stephen, *History of the Scottish Church* (1896), ii. 512.
[45] Grub, *Ecclesiastical History*, iv. 16.
[46] F. Goldie, *A Short History of the Episcopal Church in Scotland* (1951), 58.
[47] Lawson, *Scottish Episcopal Church*, 288.
[48] Stephen, *Scottish Church*, 479.

an even better opportunity to offer the same support. The Prince's army this time had defeated its first opponents and entered Edinburgh. The outlook was certainly more hopeful than at the time of the Episcopalian loyal address in 1715 when the Jacobite army was already in retreat. Perhaps it was their reduced fortunes that produced the lack of response in 1745. Certainly since 1715 the Episcopal clergy were much diminished in numbers. It has been estimated that there were no more than 130 priests in communion with the Scottish bishops at this time.[49] The long years of persecution and uncertainty had taken a toll and probably engendered a spirit of caution into the reduced body of the faithful. Yet if ever there was hope for their long allegiance to the Stuarts it was surely in those days in Edinburgh after the Jacobite victory at Prestonpans, when others were not afraid, or considered it expedient, to wave a white cockade.

After the 45's spirit had been defeated and savagely repressed the theological and liturgical values of Gadderar and Rattray continued dominant within the Episcopal Church. The independence and power of the bishops had already been established in the Episcopal Synod of 1743. The Scottish Liturgy was reprinted in 1743 and used in those congregations which did not follow the English book, so that by 1764 an edition of the Scottish Communion Office could be published which became the recognized standard of this much varied liturgy.[50] By 1764, the Scottish Communion Office had become generally accepted among nonjuring Episcopal congregations.[51]

The 1740s were therefore a pivotal decade for the Scottish Episcopal Church. Prior to this most of the bishops had supported the old theological-political nexus of the seventeenth century, comprising the royal supremacy over the Church based on the divine right of kings, passive obedience, and non-resistance. It was a theological and political connection which had kept Episcopalians conscientiously obedient to their oaths to James VII in 1689. However, by 1743 some of the bishops were beginning to come to grips with the implications of a Church which was disestablished, periodically persecuted for its Jacobitism and, at times, for its episcopacy; and whose royal master was not only physically and religiously distant from its life, but after 1745 looked increasingly unlikely to be restored. Especially under the influence of Gadderar and Rattray the inherent spiritual life and authority of the Episcopalians as a

---

[49] Ibid. 514.
[50] Dowden, *Scottish Comunion Office*, 78.
[51] Ibid. 78.

distinctive Church was being argued for. It was argued for at times, as in Rattray's treatise on the Church, in ways that could only raise doubts about the old monarchical theology. When the college party bishops fought against the theology of these men they did so authentically representing the old seventeenth-century understanding of the Church. But the future belonged to the theology of the diocesan party. It was not that the eighteenth-century nonjuring Episcopalians ceased to be Jacobite. After all, it was only when Prince Charles died leaving a totally unacceptable successor (a Roman Catholic cardinal) that they formally renounced their allegiance to the Stuarts, and not before. But the theological basis of such allegiance was undermined in the 1740s. In its place came a viable tradition—of the inherent spiritual independence of the Church as represented in diocesan episcopacy, liturgical worship, and the authority of the early Church. This new theological basis for the nonjuring Episcopalians was increasingly consciously held in the later eighteenth century and made it possible for them to continue as a Church after 1788 when Jacobitism and the Stuarts were at last renounced and the auld song was ended.

After the formal declaration of allegiance to the Hanoverian dynasty in 1788, signified in a loyal address and the inclusion of the new sovereign and his family in public prayer,[52] the Episcopal Church was eventually granted legal recognition and toleration in 1792.[53] The most urgent remaining business for the Church was the reunion of the qualified congregations with those (formerly nonjuring) giving allegiance to the Scottish bishops. Since their separation in 1715, a number of new qualified congregations had been established, particularly in the south of Scotland. These had known neither the authority of the Scottish bishops nor the Scottish Communion Office. But the impoverished Scottish Episcopal Church was not well equipped to propose a union with congregations grown respectable and prosperous during a century of toleration and which looked south to the Church of England for legitimacy.

By 1792 the Episcopal Church was a tiny successor to the Episcopalians of 1689, and the Scottish bishops were mostly elderly, the exception being John Skinner of Aberdeen. As bishop of the most Episcopally populous diocese he was the leading influence working for union. In 1800 he wrote a revealing answer to a query about the state of the Episcopal Church. Skinner thought there were about eleven thousand adult members of the Church who regularly attended its services, and about four thousand in the qualified congregations. These two parties of Episcopalians were found

[52] T. Lathbury, *A History of the Non-Jurors* (1845), 477–8.
[53] Grub, *Ecclesiastical History*, iv. 109.

primarily in Edinburgh, Aberdeenshire, the Mearns, and Angus, but there were other scattered congregations in Moray and Ross, and the highlands of Perth and Argyllshire. There were six bishops and fifty ministers whose stipends came from pew-rents and collections at services. Skinner numbered the qualified clergy at twenty-three, supported in the same way as the clergy of the Episcopal Church, but these were usually engaged for a stipulated time 'having no superior Authority by which they are collated or tyed [*sic*] to their several Charges'.[54]

As primus since 1788 Skinner was in a good position to be reasonably accurate in his estimates. Skinner considered the former nonjuring Episcopalians to be just over twice the number of the qualified.[55] As his estimate was only that of adults the difference may have been even greater as the poorer north, where the qualified Episcopalians were fewer, had larger families than the richer south. With his dedication to Episcopalian union Skinner did not specify which group was stronger in which locality, but presumably the qualified congregations were stronger in Edinburgh and the old Nonjurors in Aberdeen, Angus, and the Mearns. The other qualified congregations were all in the south and eastern lowlands. There were small congregations of Scottish Episcopalians in the highlands but by that time they were very few. The Church was poor, with only a single endowed congregation. All the bishops needed to have congregational charges in order to draw an income. Skinner was hopeful of acquiring a government subsidy to alleviate this poverty and this made union all the more necessary as the most wealthy and politically influential Episcopalians, men such as Sir William Forbes, were necessarily members of qualified congregations.

The division between qualified and former nonjuring congregations was exacerbated by other differences of theology and geography. The north held firmly to the principles of the nonjuring eighteenth century. The south was more open to influences from England, strengthened by the presence of English clergy. The northern tradition of an independent diocesan episcopate based on a theology which exalted the power and status of the episcopate had resulted in almost unilateral control of the Church by the bishops. These alone could meet in synod and make the canons by which the life of the Church was regulated and organized. This control was suited to a small Church subject to periodic harassment during the eighteenth century. In the nineteenth, however, it would

[54] Letter of 27 June 1800, EUML La. IV. 17.
[55] William Walker, *Life of the Right Reverend Alexander Jolly and the Right Reverend George Gleig* (1878), 212.

become increasingly ill-suited to a growing Church and would lead to tensions over involvement in church government by the lower clergy, and later by the laity. However, the unchecked power of the bishops in the early nineteenth century did assist Bishop Skinner's efforts for union with the qualified chapels.

Sir William Forbes was a major influence supporting the plans of Skinner for union. He was well qualified to do so for he had direct, personal links with both groups of Episcopalians. Although a member of a qualified congregation, Forbes evidently did not in principle frown upon the nonjuring Episcopalians as he was a financial supporter of Bishop Alexander Jolly of Moray.[56] Forbes was instrumental in dissuading Skinner from affixing a preamble to the English Thirty-nine Articles of Religion refuting the Calvinism of some Articles which Skinner felt was necessary to make subscription to the Articles acceptable to the Scottish clergy.[57] At a convocation of bishops and clergy called by Skinner on 24 October 1804, the Articles of Religion were subscribed to, as the 1792 Repeal Act and any hope of Episcopalian union required. Sir William's Cowgate congregation was one of the first to unite with the Scottish Episcopal Church, although they continued to use the English Book of Common Prayer.[58]

After Sir William's death in 1806 his sons continued his devotion to the Episcopal Church, Lord Medwyn especially being a supporter of the old nonjuring tradition exemplified in its bishops and the Scottish Communion Office. Medwyn's support for the Scottish bishops was formalized through his leadership in establishing the Scots Episcopal Fund in 1838 (later the Episcopal Church Society) to provide for the stipends of the bishops and other needs.[59] As well as being a generous donor to various Episcopal causes, Medwyn was prominent in working towards healing the Drummond Schism, writing pamphlets supporting the claims of the Episcopal Church against so-called chapels of the 'Church of England in Scotland'. This splinter-group among Episcopalians was named after the Revd D. T. K. Drummond, an English Evangelical minister of Trinity Chapel, Edinburgh, who in 1842 was ordered by Bishop James Walker of Edinburgh to cease from extempore prayer in devotional meetings. He refused and began a separate so-called 'Church of England' congregation independent of the Scottish

[56] Letter of 24 Jan. 1809, SRO CH 12. 30. 97; and 27 Oct. 1825, SRO CH 12. 30. 151.
[57] Ibid. 340–3.
[58] Ibid. 363–7.
[59] William Perry, *George Hay Forbes* (1927), 20.

bishops' authority. His example was followed by a few other independent Evangelical congregations in Glasgow and Aberdeen. Although originally a clash between High Churchmanship and Evangelicalism both narrowly defined by Walker and Drummond, these schismatic congregations soon cited the Scottish Communion Office as the reason for continuing separation from the Episcopal Church. They acknowledged no authority of the Scottish bishops, and professed to come under the Church of England although none of the English bishops claimed them. They were essentially independent congregations using the English Book of Common Prayer, led by clergy ordained in England or Ireland who felt antagonistic to the Scottish Communion Office because of their Evangelicalism.[60] Against this schism Medwyn argued that the Scottish Episcopal Church was the true Church of Scotland, going back to the Reformation, and therefore it behoved Episcopalians in Scotland to be in communion with it. He regarded the former qualified chapels as justified only by prevailing political circumstances.[61] The nonjuring bishops, he argued, may have had their temporal advantages removed but the state 'could not take away their clerical character . . . for the Bishops . . . lost, [no] portion of their spiritual office'.[62] Medwyn also 'greatly admired' the Scottish Communion Office as closer to the worship of the early Church and a stronger defence against Roman Catholic doctrine than was the English Eucharistic liturgy.[63] He also commented upon the influence of Anglicization beginning to be felt within the Episcopal Church: 'it has unquestionably occurred that the love of uniformity, and the use of the English form by the chief congregations in our principal cities in the south of Scotland, has given the tone to other places, so as to have made our National Office less respected, less esteemed, than it was prior to the union of the English congregations.'[64]

Notwithstanding his father's anxiety about the effects of Anglicization in the Episcopal Church, from 1825 to 1832 Alexander attended the new Edinburgh Academy.[65] The Academy opened in October 1825, having been founded by a group of leading Edinburgh men who believed that the old Royal High School, under the control of the town council, was not providing the sort of English classical education they wanted. The

[60] R. Foskett, 'The Drummond Controversy 1842', in *RSCHS* 16 (1969), 99–101.

[61] John Hay Forbes, *On English Episcopal Chapels in Scotland* (1846), 9.

[62] Ibid. 8–9.

[63] John Hay Forbes, *Address to Members of the Episcopal Church in Scotland* (1847), 17–18.

[64] Forbes, *Address*, 17.

[65] *The Edinburgh Academy Register* (1914), 30.

school, therefore, was a force for Anglicization in the city and a break
with the more democratic ethos of Scottish education, as even the
sympathetic historian of the school acknowledges.[66] The new rector of the
school was Archdeacon Williams, an accomplished Oxford-educated
classicist.[67] Made rector of Edinburgh Academy in 1824, he stayed,
almost continuously, until 1847 modelling the Academy on the lines of an
English public school.[68] The school's historian describes him as 'firm for
standards of study and scholarship . . . He was unquestionably in
command from the very beginning: confident, imperious even, utterly
dogmatic when it came to the matter of his beloved classics.'[69]

The school suited Alexander. The rector's report says that every year
but one he was on the prize list. 'That during the whole of the period he
conducted himself with due attention to his studies and to the rules of
discipline established at the institution.' The rector also reported Forbes's
'great quickness of perception, and that were he to add to his natural
powers perseverance in study much might be expected of him, that his
scholarship is very fair, and that both in feeling and manners he is most
gentlemanly'.[70] The aims of the school were evidently fulfilled in
Alexander. He was a good scholar. This, in the opinion of a rector 'dogmatic' about the classics, meant primarily that he had a firm grasp of the
logic and principles of the classical languages. Alexander was a bright boy,
yet the rector felt he lacked perseverance and relied too much on his
natural talent. He was amenable to discipline and authority, and Archdeacon Williams's remark on Alexander's courtesy was an early indication of
the personal charm that many others later remarked on. Above all,
Alexander's education exposed him to greater English influence than
either his father or grandfather had experienced in their schooling. It
prepared him for a place in a wider world than theirs—for higher education in England, in the civil service at home or in the growing needs of
the empire. It did this at the expense of his attachment to much of what
was distinctive in Scottish life, such as that of his grandfather to
Edinburgh society or that of his father to Scots law. Alexander's early
education made him more British than Scottish and would have taught
him to value most the English contribution to that Britishness.

When Forbes left the Academy there was some thought that he might
obtain a nomination to the civil service of the East India Company. In an

[66] Magnus Magnusson, *The Clacken and the Slate* (1974), 52; George Davie, *The
Democratic Intellect* (2nd edn. 1964).
[67] Magnusson, *Clacken*, 70.
[68] Ibid. 93.   [69] Ibid. 91.   [70] IOR J 1. 94, fo. 95.

oration in 1875 to an Oxford society Alexander later joined as an undergraduate, the Master said he had accepted an Indian career in deference to his father's wishes.[71] Evidently, Lord Medwyn wanted to ensure that his second son, who would not inherit his lands, had a financially secure future in a lucrative and worthwhile career. A career in the civil service of the East India Company involved gaining a successful nomination to the Company's training institution, Haileybury College, which could only come from one of the members of the Court of Directors. Such a nomination was a valuable source of patronage for the directors and was much sought after, for appointment as an Indian civilian was regarded as providing financial security for life, and therefore was desirable despite the risks to health in the Indian climate. The necessary nomination required influence, which could have come from the family's banking firm, Forbes and Company, and its connection with the East India Company. By 1820 the bank had become one of the two most important of the East India Company's Agency Houses. These banking firms were responsible for remitting to England from India the monies of Company servants and other British merchants there. A lot of this money was consequently invested by its owners in East India Company stock. The votes then obtained in the Court of Proprietors were often put at the service of the Agency House, and the banking firm used them in elections for the Court of Directors to increase the interests of private trade and the City.[72] The family's banking firm was therefore in a powerful position, not only to secure a nomination to Haileybury College, but also to assist the career of any young Company servant in India. Later, in his written interview at the Company's London headquarters, Alexander stated that the actual nomination was gained through his maternal uncle, Sir William Cumming-Gordon, who knew the nominating director, a Colonel Toone.[73] As a Member of Parliament, Cumming-Gordon was in a good position to approach a Company director such as Toone, who would be reluctant not to nominate a youth so influentially connected on both sides of his family. The minimum age of entry to the Company's college was 17.[74] If it had been decided on leaving Edinburgh Academy that Alexander should pursue a career in India he would have been too young to enter Haileybury. His nomination had to come in 1834 at the earliest.

[71] Minutes of Chapters, 1874–1878, BHT.

[72] C. H. Philips, *The East India Company* (1940), 43.

[73] IOR J 1. 52, fo. 251.

[74] Imogen Thomas, *Haileybury* (1987), 14.

The interval was usefully employed by sending him to Thomas Dale at Beckenham in Kent, a clergyman who was a noted coach for boys preparing for entry into Haileybury. Dale's testimonial submitted with Alexander's Company application in 1834 states that he was with Dale from 11 August 1832 to 29 September 1833.[75] His year in Kent was spent widening his classical reading and also in studying Euclid and algebra. Dale testified that during this time Alexander's 'moral conduct was uniformly free from all reproach, and he evinced a competent diligence in the prosecution of his studies'.[76] During this time he lived with nineteen other boys, and his health, which had always been delicate, improved enough for him to join a rowing club, 'the only sport, except polo for a short time in India, for which he was ever fit'.[77]

The hoped-for nomination had not yet arrived when Alexander returned home at the end of September 1833 so in the interim he attended Glasgow University. Certificates of attendance were submitted with his Company application from Daniel Sandford, professor of Greek, and Robert Buchanan, professor of Logic.[78] These show that he attended the session of 1834. Glasgow University was possibly chosen over Edinburgh because of the reputation of Sandford, who was a man of 'somewhat similar Oxonian outlook to Archdeacon Williams', the rector of Edinburgh Academy.[79] It is likely that Williams knew of Sandford, at least by reputation, and may have recommended him to Alexander. Alexander's time with Sandford would further have reinforced the Anglicized classical education Alexander received at Edinburgh Academy and with Thomas Dale. Both professors expressed their satisfaction with his work, Buchanan describing him as 'a young man of amicable dispositions, gentlemanly manners & very promising abilities'.

The required nomination finally occurred in a letter from Colonel Toone to the East India Company on 15 February 1834.[80] After agreeing to abide by the regulations of the East India College, the forwarding of his academic testimonials and his baptismal certificate to the Company, Alexander went to London to sit the requisite three-day preliminary examination.[81] On 23 July 1834 he was finally in possession of official written acceptance of his nomination as a student at the college.[82]

[75] IOR J 1. 94, fo. 97.   [76] Ibid.   [77] Perry, 13.
[78] IOR J 1. 94, fos. 94, 96.
[79] Davie, *Democratic Intellect*, 28.
[80] IOR J 1. 52, fo. 245.
[81] Frederick Danvers, *Memorials of Old Haileybury College* (1894), 31; IOR J 1. 52, fos. 251–2.
[82] IOR J 1. 94, fos. 93–7.

The young Forbes entered Haileybury in July 1834 to begin his required two years. The college was one of two established by the East India Company in England—the other at Addiscombe, near Croydon, trained officers for the Company's military service. The college for the civil service was originally founded in 1804 at Hertford Castle but was moved to the new purpose-built site at Haileybury in Hertfordshire in 1809.[83] The East India Company considered that training its young civil servants, known as writers, in England rather than in India would see them arrive in India older, more mature, and better able to face India's rigours and temptations. The college course consisted of two streams known as 'Orientals' and 'Europeans'. By 1830 the students had to pass in at least three Indian languages and not suprisingly about a fifth of each new entering class failed the course.[84]

Haileybury developed a rigorous scholastic programme. The Company's aim was to attract distinguished staff by offering high salaries so that, not only would its future civil servants be competently educated, but it was also hoped, the college would become a centre for oriental studies.[85] The historian of the college claims that its oriental teaching put Haileybury thirty years ahead of any British university in this field.[86] Students faced monthly examinations in each subject and the oriental languages required weekly exercises. Graduation depended on passing four written examinations (two each year) in Greek, Latin, and mathematics; three Indian languages; law; political economy and history.[87] Forbes's own examination results show a continuously improving result during his four terms. From the start he excelled in classics, as expected from his previous education. Also in mathematics and law he came top of his class. Hindustani was apparently more difficult for him and he evidently dropped it for Arabic, in which he won prizes. In his final term he passed first of his class in all subjects, except Persian where he came third. He won a medal in classics and also the Arabic prize that year.[88] In his final report the principal concluded: 'The College Council in consideration of his Industry, Proficiency, & Conduct placed him in the First Class . . . and assigns him the rank of First on the List of Students now leaving College for the Presidency of Fort St. George.'[89] Something of the promise detected by Archdeacon Williams began to flourish, probably

[83] Ibid. 4–5.
[84] Brian Gardner, *The East India Company* (1971), 190.
[85] Anthony Farrington, *Records of the East India College* (1976), 8.
[86] Thomas, *Haileybury*, 8.
[87] Danvers, *Old Haileybury*, 30.
[88] IOR J 1. 99.   [89] IOR J 1. 104, fo. 136.

because the academic demands of Haileybury necessitated the perseverance his old rector felt had been lacking in his application to study. Forbes
could no longer coast along on his natural talents, but was one of the
'hard-reading men' and a talented scholar.

On 10 September 1836 Alexander Forbes signed the standard cove-
nant (number 3,198) between himself and the East India Company,
guaranteed by his father for £3,000. Alexander's bond of £1,000 to the
Company was signed by his uncle, William Forbes, and himself.[90]
Company servants on the overseas establishment had to enter into these
bonds, plus find the securities for faithful performance of their duties.
From this time he was officially a writer 'on the staff of the Madras
Establishment' with his service backdated to his entry into Haileybury.
In the same month Forbes sailed for Madras for what promised to be,
given his college record, a brilliant administrative career in the East India
Company's government of India.

The East India Company had been founded by royal charter in 1600
as a trading company. Its first territorial acquisition in India was made in
1640, at Fort St George, later Madras.[91] The Company's government in
India when Forbes joined it consisted of a governor-general appointed by
the parliamentary Board of Control, with a legislative council to advise
him. Under him were regional governors in various Company-controlled
areas such as Madras. There was a system of law whose writ ran
throughout the Company's territories, which by then equalled approximately half the subcontinent, with most of the rest controlled indirectly
by the Company through alliances with Indian princes.

Forbes landed at Fort St George on 27 January 1837 after a sea
voyage of four months around the horn of Africa.[92] All the evidence that
remains of Forbes's Indian service are the official Company records and
these are sparse, as Forbes was a very new and junior member of a large
and far-flung civil service. He remained at Madras for five months
learning the local conditions and duties of service.[93] Although just starting
his career, as a covenanted civilian Forbes was one of the Company's
élite. One Company civilian remembered that 'in "vulgar parlance" he
[the covenanted civilian] used to be described as an individual worth
£300 a year dead or alive, because of his prospects or his Civil Fund
payments if [he] died prematurely'.[94]

90   IOR O 1. 97.
91   Gardner, *East India Company*, 41.
92   IOR L AG 23. 8. 1.   93   Perry, 15.
94   C. T. Buckland, *Social Life in India* (1884), 81.

Forbes was posted on 4 July 1837 to the district of Rajamundry as assistant to the acting collector there.[95] On 9 January 1838 he was gazetted as assistant to the collector-magistrate of the same district.[96] The area was one of the oldest possessions of the Company and was north of Madras on the eastern seaboard, along the Godovari River.[97] The collector was equivalent to that standard imperial administrator, the district commissioner, but under the East India Company civilians retained the titles that reflected their commercial past. The collector combined judicial and administrative functions and was a general governor and inspector over his allotted area.[98] To this official Forbes came to serve his apprenticeship. As assistant Forbes could try and fine minor criminal cases; be put in charge of the treasury or matters of land revenue; and had to learn the local dialect and case law. He held fourth place in the local official hierarchy after the judge, the collector-magistrate, and the joint-magistrate.[99] A former Company civilian described this period of his career, which illustrates the sort of work Forbes would have been engaged in.

Whilst he is serving his apprenticeship for the higher offices of Government, he must be prepared to adapt his mind to the most humble and unintellectual duties. He must learn to obey, so that he may understand how to rule. He will have to look after scavengers who are occupied with the drainage and sanitation of the town in which he lives. He will have to count and deliver out postage stamps with his own hands, and woe betide him if his Treasury accounts and cash balances do not agree to the utmost farthing.[100]

Normally after a year, provided that he had passed his exams, the young writer was given charge of a sub-district and eventually became a joint-magistrate, then collector-magistrate, and finally judge.[101] However, at the beginning of 1838 Forbes contracted a persistent fever and was granted sick-leave at Cape Town, the Company's nearest 'health-resort', leaving for there in February 1838.[102] His health improved on the voyage but he stayed convalescing at the Cape for nine months.[103]

With his health restored, Forbes returned to Madras in the spring.[104] On 9 April he was gazetted assistant to the registrar of Sudderand

[95] Mackey, 24.   [96] Ibid. 25.
[97] George Chesney, *Indian Polity* (1894), 35.
[98] M. Edwardes, *Raj: The Story of British India* (1969), 80–1.
[99] Buckland, *Social Life*, 90–1.
[100] Ibid. 79.
[101] Ibid. 94–5.
[102] Perry, 15.
[103] Mackey, 25.
[104] Ibid.

Foujdarry. Commissioned to prepare a digest of laws for the guidance of
civil servants, he was probably singled out because of his excellent marks
in law at Haileybury and his having been listed as first among the new
writers of his year sent to Madras from the college.[105] During this period
he devoted his spare time to a study of Hinduism.[106] His cousin, Frances
Skene, in her little book of memoirs of Forbes, says he also studied
theology in his spare time and that friends there knew of his desire for
what he called 'Christian work'.[107] This is entirely possible given his
ordination just five years later. Certainly there is evidence for his interest
in theology during this time in his later controversial synod charge of
1857 where he mentioned that while in India he asked Arabic scholars
there the meaning of some scriptural phrases.[108] According to a later
intimate friend Forbes's 'first deep impressions of religion . . . came
through RCs'.[109] This contact was probably made during Forbes's time in
India. A young man like Forbes, from a devout Episcopalian family,
would have been unlikely to have made any contact with the small and
inconspicuous Roman Catholic Church as it existed in Britain prior to
the 1840s. But the situation was different in India. On the subcontinent,
where Europeans and Christians were a tiny minority, contact with
European Roman Catholic missionaries would have been both more permissible and more possible than at home where anti-Catholicism still
flourished. The area covered by the Madras Presidency was an established area of Roman Catholic missions. There were Franciscan missions
in the former French settlements, and a number of devoted Irish secular
priests as well in the region.[110] Priests from either of these missions
would probably have impressed Forbes given his later Tractarian opinions. Was it one of these Roman priests who initially attracted Forbes to
a more Catholic Christianity? His contact with the Oxford Movement
just two years later would then have enabled him to espouse many of the
same Catholic beliefs without the familial or social difficulties of a Roman
Catholic conversion.

Fever once more struck in his new station and in November 1839
Forbes again applied for furlough and this time sailed for two years' sick-
leave in England on 23 January 1840.[111] The fever was possibly malaria to

105 Ibid.
106 Perry, 17.
107 F. M. F. Skene, *Memoir of Alexander, Bishop of Brechin* (1876), 4.
108 A. P. Forbes, *A Primary Charge* (1857), 20.
109 E. B. Pusey to J. Keble, n.d. [3 May 1861], PK iv.
110 K. S. Latourette, *A History of the Expansion of Christianity* (1944), vi. 80–3.
111 Mackey, 26.

which his poor constitution could put up little resistance in the conditions of India. On arrival in Britain he returned to his parents' home and for the next four years was on paid sick-leave from the Company. Forbes's furlough was extended until he finally resigned the Company's civil service on 5 June 1844. During these years from January 1840 to January 1843 he received £250 a year from the Company's Civil Fund, and the appropriate part-payment in the final months of 1844.[112] So it was not until the year of his ordination that Forbes finally severed his links with the East India Company.

At the end of 1839 Forbes faced the likelihood that his chosen career was incompatible with his delicate health, and that he would have to reconsider his future. There is some evidence that he was thinking of ordination when he returned from India. In 1875, the year Forbes died, one obituary reported that he won his father's agreement to his going to Oxford to study for holy orders by asking the trenchant question, 'whether would you wish me a dead Indian judge or a living Scotch curate?'[113] Forbes's desire to be a priest was also recollected in his cousin's memoir of him.[114] Aspirations to priesthood notwithstanding, aside from his Indian experience Forbes was, in many respects, little different from many other scions of upper-class families. His education and wealth, Anglicized education, and personal contacts enabled him to fit almost anywhere into the upper echelons of British society. The major element of his life which cut across the prevailing English influence upon him was his family's attachment to certain Scottish traditions, particularly their Scottish Episcopalianism and its native nonjuring tradition. It would remain to be seen what effect this churchmanship would have on Forbes as he made plans for a change of career in the 1840s.

[112] IOR L AG 20. 1. 3–4.
[113] *Scottish Guardian*, 15 Oct. 1875, 191.
[114] Skene, *Memoir of Alexander*, 4.

An Oxford Puseyite

FORBES came up to Oxford on 23 May 1840 and was enrolled in Brasenose College as a gentleman commoner.[1] After the recovery of his health, following some months of convalescence in Italy, his move to Oxford University returned him to the usual career path taken by sons of the gentry, including the increasingly Anglicized gentry of Scotland, who finished their education at one of the universities of England. At 22 he was old for an undergraduate and, despite his previous academic success, his uncertain health prevented him from reading for an honours degree.[2] In 1841 he won the Boden scholarship for Sanskrit, which would not have been too difficult for someone of Forbes's successful East India Company education. The most important personal consequence was not the scholarship itself but the fact that it brought Forbes into contact with Edward Bouverie Pusey, who was on the examination board in his capacity as Regius Professor of Hebrew. In this way Forbes began a personal friendship with one of the leaders of the Oxford Movement, a friendship which would become the most influential relationship of his life. We know from Forbes's later correspondence that their early friendship was close. Unfortunately, lacking any letters from these crucial years at Oxford University, we must rely on the history of the Oxford Movement at this period to understand the profound effect of the Tractarians on Forbes. This impact centred on the importance of dogma, and shaped Forbes's awareness of the industrial poor, directing his ministry towards them.

Some measure of the impression the Oxford Movement made on Forbes can be gained from the preface he wrote to his edition of the *Remains* of the historian Arthur Haddan which was published the year after Forbes's death. Forbes had first met Haddan at Oxford when Haddan was curate to John Henry Newman at St Mary's, the university church (from 1841 to the following Michaelmas term).[3] Haddan also was

[1] J. Foster (arr. and ann.), *Alumni Oxoniensis: The Members of the University of Oxford 1715–1886* (1887), ii. 475.
[2] F. M. C. Skene, *A Memoir of Alexander, Bishop of Brechin* (1876), 5.
[3] A. P. Forbes (ed.), *Remains of the Late Rev. Arthur West Haddan* (1876), pp. xi–xii.

a lifelong proponent of the Oxford Movement, albeit a moderate one, so Forbes's preface included an encomium to the influence of the movement which had captured them both.

The great ecclesiastical movement, which has since made itself felt through the length and breadth of the land, was then at its height in the seat of its birth. Thwarted and persecuted by the purblind authorities, the very disabilities under which it rested, gave an additional charm to the young and enthusiastic minds which threw themselves into it. The great leader shewed no external signs of the coming defection. On the afternoon sermons at St Mary's men hung in rapt attention. Young men from the manor-houses and parsonages of the country, from the streets and squares of the city, (for Oxford then was still the privileged seat of the education of the upper classes,) came term by term under the charm of Oxford, and, in many cases, to Oxford owed their immortal souls . . . Real earnest self-denial shewed itself in the lives of the undergraduates. Not that they were without their foibles. The manners and dress of the great leader of the movement were imitated to the pitch of absurdity, and a great movement among the young men could not be without its side of unreality. If they assembled in each other's rooms to sing the Canonical Hours in Latin during the season of Lent, it was not a mere exhibition of religious dilettantism. It was the outcome of a real devotion, which made itself felt in many other and tangible ways,—in abstinence from hall on fasting-days, in conscientious attendance at Chapel, in personal assistance at the evening sittings of the Mendicity Society, in regular frequentation of the early Communion at St Mary's (then the only accessible service of the kind), in conscientious study, in plenteous alms-deeds.[4]

As an older undergraduate Forbes perhaps escaped some of the more boyish fads and imitations he attests to, but the remarks on singing the daily offices in Lent and membership of the Mendicity Society indicates that he probably embraced some of the devotional enthusiasms the movement engendered among the students.

The usual origin given to the Oxford Movement is John Keble's Assize sermon in 1833 directed against the parliamentary suppression of ten bishoprics in the Church of Ireland, a suppression he labelled as national apostasy. Keble was protesting against the failure of the reformed Parliament to defend the interests of the Church, and the collapse in Britain of the old certainties of Church and society. The repeal of the Test and Corporation Acts in 1828, the passing of the Act for Catholic emancipation in 1829, and the Reform Act of 1832 represented a widening of the political nation which had serious connotations for the Church of England. Dominated by Parliament since the Reformation, the Church of England could no longer look on that body with equanimity, since the

4 Ibid.

recent reforms had meant the end of Parliament as a theoretically
Anglican forum. Although the exclusion of Dissenters from public office
by the Test and Corporations Acts was purely nominal by the 1820s, the
revoking of these Acts was understood by Churchmen to be a relinquishing of a principle of the Establishment. An even greater change was
Catholic emancipation which allowed traditional enemies of the Church of
England into Parliament. For the Church of England this broadening of
the base of parliamentary representation posed a question as to the basis of
its authority.[5] One of the old answers had been that the authority of the
Church was grounded on its legal establishment in Parliament as an
expression of the will and consent of the nation. But with the widening of
the non-Anglican base of Parliament in the legislation of 1828-9 the
Church of England was faced with the question as to its legitimacy in a
nation that in principle was no longer understood to be completely Anglican. Could the Church continue to rely on its parliamentary establishment
as the basis for its authority; and if not, then what was the alternative?

Some answers had been attempted before the Oxford Movement.
Thomas Arnold, for example, proposed a broadening of the confessional
boundaries of the Established Church to embrace all Christians, except
Roman Catholics and Quakers who were regarded as subversive. But for
Dean Church, as for many other Churchmen, Arnold's proposal was too
unprecedented.[6] The Tractarian answer in 1833 was to assert unequivocally
the old High Church claims about the nature of the Church of England
through the publication of the famous *Tracts for the Times* (1833-40).
These declared uncompromisingly the Church's spiritual independence
from the state by virtue of its divine foundation as a branch of the Catholic
Church. This identity was based on the claim that the Church retained
substantial links to the early Church, and so to Christ, which had not been
broken at the Reformation. This old High Church theology gave the
Church of England an authority deriving from Christ and not from parliamentary establishment. Initially the Oxford Movement was a defensive
response to an immediate crisis for the Church's legitimacy and authority.
However, the Tractarians' argument for the independent existence of the
Church from the state very soon led them beyond mere reaction. The
Oxford Movement, although initiated by a political crisis, soon became a
distinctly religious movement seeking religious and not political answers.

One of the most fundamental religious answers of the Oxford
Movement which influenced many of its young adherents like Forbes was

    5 R. W. Church, *The Oxford Movement: Twelve Years 1833-1845* (3rd edn. 1892), 51-2.
    6 Ibid. 8.

the importance of dogma. The Oxford Movement had its immediate origins not only in reaction to the constitutional crisis, but also in the ferment of one of the most original intellects of the century. In John Henry Newman's mind concerns about the status of the Church of England had connected with his reading of the Fathers of the early Church occasioned by his transition from Evangelicalism to High Church views.[7] The consequence of Newman's Patristic studies was his *Arians of the Fourth Century* (1833). Not only does this book reveal evidence for Newman's concern about Church and state relations prior to his hearing Keble's Assize sermon, it also anticipated much of the theological agenda of the Oxford Movement.[8] The book is a historical work on the Arian heresy whose hero is Athanasius, Bishop of Alexandria, battling against imperial persecution and Arianism to uphold the Nicene Creed. For Newman heresy flourished when rationalism exceeded its own limitations which were at most 'to detect error, rather than to establish truth'.[9] Heresy developed when reason trespassed into the area of moral or revealed truth, and the Arians were the epitome of such uninhibited rationalism and its consequences. The correct attitude to revealed truth for Newman was one of reserve. This meant a withholding of the fullness of revelation until its hearers were properly prepared, morally and in submission to God, to hear and accept it, lest divine truth be rejected or even mocked by being paraded before unfit persons. Reserve followed from the nature of the truth being communicated. There had to be a reverence for its sacred mystery because it was God's truth. To communicate such truth the Church was the divinely authorized and necessary teacher. The creed demonstrated the Church fulfilling its teaching office by defining doctrine, which was thus an 'adequate symbol' of revealed truth. Doctrine was not simply a matter of intellect alone, Newman claimed, because it was connected to worship and morality in that it 'directly assists the acts of religious worship and obedience'.[10] In addition to upholding the dogma of the Church, the conflict between Athanasius and the emperor gave Newman a pattern for interpreting the contemporary predicament of the Church of England and its relation to the state.

Then as now, there was the prospect, and partly the presence in the Church, of an Heretical Power enthralling it, exerting a varied influence and a usurped

---

[7] J. H. Newman (ed. Martin Svaglic), *Apologia Pro Vita Sua* (1967), 39.

[8] S. Gilley, *Newman and his Age* (1990), 86ff; I. Ker, *John Henry Newman: A Biography* (1988), 48ff.

[9] J. H. Newman, *Arians of the Fourth Century* (3rd edn. 1871), 30.

[10] Ibid. 150.

claim in the appointment of her functionaries, and interfering with the management of her internal affairs . . . Meanwhile . . . we may rejoice in the piety, prudence, and varied graces of our Spiritual Rulers; and rest in the confidence, that, should the hand of Satan press us sore, our Athanasius and Basil will be given us in their destined season, to break the bonds of the Oppressor, and let the captives go free.[11]

The Arian heresy showed Newman that too close an alliance between Church and state could lead to a comprehension of incompatible views and a dilution of the Church's truth, because the state's demands for comprehension conflicted with the requirement of the Church to be faithful to God's truth. Doctrine, according to Newman, as a symbol of God's truth, must be exclusive of error, even if it proves divisive. Where Christians were members of both Church and state, their membership of the Church was superior.[12]

The first Tracts, published in September 1833, reiterated much of the theological agenda contained in Newman's *Arians*, with a more aggressive sacerdotal element. The Tracts reminded their readers of the divine basis of the Church, independent of the state. They located this basis in the apostolic succession and pointed to the bishops as the successors to the apostles; to the priesthood as a divine and awesome commission; to the need to take a stand when the state infringed the rights of the Church. They called on their readers to note that the Church was not a state creation but a part of the Catholic Church of Christ. Readers were urged to oppose attempts to alter the Prayer Book, because this would lead to a dilution or compromise of divine truth.[13] For the Tractarians dogma was, as Newman elsewhere succinctly put it, a 'Mystery', that is, 'a doctrine *lying hid* in language'.[14] These early Tracts therefore highlighted three fundamental issues for the Oxford Movement—the emphasis on dogma, the apostolic succession of the bishops, and the sense of contemporary crisis for the Church of England. Newman and the other Tractarians were all disposed towards a radically traditional response to the contemporary situation. They felt that the answer could be found in the reassertion of the Catholic nature of the Church of England and in the rediscovery of Catholic tradition. In this they were united with the older High Church tradition to which the Tractarians owed much.[15]

[11] Ibid. 406.
[12] Ibid. 264–5.
[13] Tracts 1–3 in *Tracts for the Times* (1834).
[14] A. Hardelin, *The Tractarian Understanding of the Eucharist* (1965), 32 n. 31.
[15] Peter Nockles, 'The Oxford Movement: Historical Background 1780–1833', in Geoffrey Rowell (ed.), *Tradition Renewed* (1986), 24–50.

The emphasis of the Tracts for most of the 1830s was broadly in accord with that of the old High Church tradition which had been prominent in the Church throughout the eighteenth century. Many emphases of the Oxford Movement during these years were primarily accentuations of central beliefs of this older High Church tradition including the Church of England as a branch of the Catholic Church, the authority of the Fathers, attachment to the Book of Common Prayer and its rubrics, a high theology of the Eucharist, even the valuation, within limits, of Roman Catholic devotional works.[16] This old High Church tradition was not uniform but divided into a number of strands. In its widest sense 'High Church' described those clergy and laity who were closely linked to Toryism in politics, ultra-Tories who were zealous for the legal privileges of the Church of England and alert for any threat to its establishment. More specifically, among clergy the description could mean a dedicated conservative attention to upholding the formularies, canons, and ceremonies of the Church. These two attitudes often went by the epithet 'high and dry' churchmanship. But there was also a specific and consistent High Church theology which derived in part from the Nonjurors of the late seventeenth and early eighteenth centuries. This theology upheld divine-right monarchy, asserted the apostolic succession of the Church of England as a defence against Dissent, and affirmed the 'mysterious element in religion' against Latitudinarian reasonableness and Evangelical enthusiasm.[17] At the beginning of the Oxford Movement this High Church tradition was dominant in the upper ranks of the Church of England, and was undergoing something of a renascence with the vitality of younger High Churchmen such as W. F. Hook and William Palmer of Worcester College. These younger men, and their older High Church colleagues such as Hugh James Rose and Bishops John Kaye of Lincoln and Richard Bagot of Oxford, welcomed the initiatives of the Oxford Movement in its first years because they saw it as reaffirming traditional High Church theology. This the Tractarians were glad to do, claiming they were merely declaring the true Catholic theology of the Church of England as it had come down to the High Churchmen from the Caroline divines of the early seventeenth century.[18]

[16] Richard Sharp, 'New Perspectives on the High Church Tradition: Historical Background 1730–1780', in Geoffrey Rowell (ed.), *Tradition Renewed* (1986), 9–14.

[17] F. C. Mather, *High Church Prophet: Bishop Samuel Horsley (1733–1806) and the Caroline Tradition in the Later Georgian Church* (1992), 304–9.

[18] Peter Nockles, 'Continuity and Change in Anglican High Churchmanship in Britain 1792–1850', D. Phil. thesis (University of Oxford, 1982), 430ff.

However, by the time Forbes went up to Oxford in 1840 most of the older High Churchmen were increasingly disturbed by the direction and tone of the new high churchmen from Oxford. Even younger High Churchmen like Hook and Edward Churton, who were more in sympathy with the spiritual dynamism of the Oxford Movement, began to voice privately their concern about developments in Tractarian thinking and writing. There was increasing tension between the High Churchmen and the developing Oxford Movement theology over attitudes to the state, the authority of the early Church in relation to the English Reformation, the independence of national churches, and the tendency of the Tractarians to look towards Rome for sacramental theology and spirituality.[19] But central to this growing divergence between High Churchmen and the Tractarians from their former continuity was the increasing generosity of the Tractarians towards Rome, and their consequent criticism of the Anglican tradition. High Churchmen took as their standard of catholicity the English Reformation and the theology of the Caroline divines, believing that the Reformation was a necessary reform that had not taken away the English Church's claim to be a branch of the Catholic Church. Consequently they esteemed the English Reformation and the tradition of the Church of England since that time as essentially reformed Catholic. Therefore, to High Churchmen, the characteristic of a true Churchman was that he placed the authority of the Church of England over his own private judgement. Walter Hook was typical of these High Church sentiments about the Church of England:

When I was called a High Churchmen, we meant by the word one who, having ascertained that the Church of England was reformed on the right principle, cordially accepted the Reformers. We meant by a High Churchman one who, thinking the Church wiser than himself, observed her regulations and obeyed her laws, whether we understood them or not.[20]

But by the late 1830s Tractarians were going behind the sixteenth and seventeenth centuries to the early Church as the ultimate authoritative standard of what was Catholic in Anglican theology and practice. While the old High Church tradition judged what was Catholic by the Anglican formularies and Anglican theologians from the sixteenth century onwards, the Tractarians increasingly judged the English Reformation and the consequent centuries of the Church of England by antiquity and found Anglicanism wanting. High Churchmen were becoming anxious about

[19] Ibid. chs. 1–3, 1–343.
[20] Quoted in Reginald H. Fuller, 'The Classical High Church Reaction to the Tractarians', in Geoffrey Rowell (ed.), *Tradition Renewed* (1986), 54.

the Anglican loyalities of the Tractarians, and Tractarians were growing increasingly dubious about the Catholic credentials of the High Churchmen, seeing that tradition as too cautious in its Catholicism and compromised by its affection for the Protestant Reformers. Even John Keble, who had been raised in the High Church tradition, could write to his sister by 1836 of his dislike of the English Reformers.

As to the Reformers, I certainly do think that as a set they belonged to the same class with the Puritans and Radicals and I have very little doubt that if we had lived in those times, neither my Father nor you . . . would have had anything to do with them. And I think we shall never be able to make our ground good against either Romanists or Puritans till we have separated ourselves and our liturgy from them.[21]

But High Churchmen believed that the Tractarians' elevation of the early Church as a standard above that of the Reformation formularies of the Church of England was an exercise of the same sort of private judgement over the teaching of the Church the Tractarians criticized Low Churchmen for.[22]

This primacy ascribed to antiquity by the Tractarians became of increasing concern to High Churchmen because they believed it was also leading the Tractarians in the direction of Roman Catholicism. High Churchmen viewed with increasing alarm the softening of the Tractarian attitude to Rome as giving credence to the traditional enemy which had always denied the label Catholic to the Church of England that the old High Church tradition had striven to uphold. Once the Reformation was devalued, or even regarded as contrary to Catholicism, High Churchmen maintained, then not only was the Church of England suspect as a Catholic Church but the Roman Catholic Church would have a greater attraction for Anglicans than their own Church. That attraction, according to High Churchmen, was towards a Church seriously in error and lacking the necessary correction supplied to the Church of England by the Reformation.

Forbes's years at Oxford coincided with this growing divergence and discontinuity between the Oxford Movement and its former High Church sympathizers. Just prior to his arrival at the university the publication of Hurrell Froude's *Remains* by Keble and Newman in February 1838 alarmed many High Churchmen by revealing Froude's warmth towards Roman Catholicism and his intense dislike of the

---

[21] Quoted in Brian Martin, *John Keble Priest, Professor and Poet* (1976), 25.
[22] Nockles, 'Continuity and Change', 125ff.

Protestant Reformation. The beginning of 1839 saw an attempt to test
Tractarian loyalty to the Reformation in a subscription for a memorial
to the Reformation bishops martyred in Oxford. For some of the younger
followers of the movement, the more assertive and authoritarian catholicity of the Roman Church was proving increasingly attractive. In 1840
Newman wrote Tract 90 to convince such followers that the Anglican
Church was just as Catholic as Rome, and that the Protestantism in the
Thirty-nine Articles was only in apparent contradiction to Catholic
teaching. But to many High Churchmen Tract 90 appeared a betrayal of
the Anglican Church to Rome. In 1841 the Tractarian leadership protested over the plan by the Church of England and the Lutheran Church
in Prussia jointly to send a bishop to Jerusalem. This demonstrated
clearly the divergence between most High Churchmen, and the Tractarians who intensely disliked this Anglican alliance with Protestantism.
High Churchmen however were largely behind the scheme as a means of
bringing continental Protestantism into closer conformity with the
reformed Catholicism of the Church of England.[23] The increasing fears of
High Churchmen were eventually realized on 9 October 1845 when
Newman was finally received into the Roman Catholic Church.

It was into the heart of this avant-garde movement that Forbes was
brought by his connection with Pusey after winning the prize for
Sanskrit. Forbes was one of the numbers of undergraduates enduringly
influenced in the search for holiness by Newman's four o'clock sermons
at St Mary's. But it was Edward Pusey who was the most intimate and
prolonged Tractarian influence upon him. By 1840 Pusey's views were
well advanced in his transition from High Churchman to full-blown
Tractarian, a change that had been progressing ever since his attachment
to the Oxford Movement in 1835 with his tract on baptism.[24] When
Forbes first encountered him, Pusey was disowning many of his former
opinions, especially his early liberalism manifest in his book *An Historical
Enquiry into the Probable Causes of the Rationalist Character Lately Predominant in the Theology of Germany*, published in 1828 (with a second
part in 1830). Pusey had reversed his earlier moderate appreciation of
German liberal theology under the influence of Keble and Hugh James
Rose, who believed such theology only encouraged doubt and disbelief.[25]
By the late 1830s Pusey's growing emphasis on the objectivity of grace in
baptism and the sacraments was forming for him an important defence

    [23] Ibid., 223ff.
    [24] David Forrester, *Young Doctor Pusey* (1989), 186ff.
    [25] Ibid. 78ff.

against the relativism of liberal rationalism. During the early 1840s Pusey
was moving into his final Tractarian position from his earlier positive
attitude towards the English Reformers.[26] By 1845 he had come to believe
that there was something 'fundamentally wrong' with the English
Reformation in allying itself with Protestantism, and he was now determined to keep a 'kind of neutrality' with respect to the Roman Church.[27]
It was precisely during Forbes's undergraduate years that Pusey moved
to the extreme wing of the Oxford Movement, among those Tractarians
sympathetic to Rome, who yet remained loyal to the validity of the
Anglican Church.

There remains little evidence for other friendships and intellectual
influences upon Forbes at this time. In 1842 he attempted to have an
article published in the high Tory *Blackwood's Magazine*, so his politics
probably remained those of his family's traditional link between High
Churchmanship and Toryism. According to Perry he knew W. G. Ward
and Martin Routh, the venerable president of Magdalen College. Forbes
himself, in a later letter, referred to a Heathcote as a 'dear friend' and the
'first of my Oxford set who has gone to his account'.[28] This may well
have been W. B. Heathcote who, as precentor of Salisbury cathedral,
signed the Tractarian protest against the Denison judgement in 1856. If
so, it suggests Forbes's set was a group of undergraduate Tractarians.
However, as a mature student, Forbes may well have been friendly with
the younger fellows as much as, if not more than, his undergraduate contemporaries. Passing references in Charles Marriott's letters to Forbes
helping him with his work on the *Library of the Fathers* confirms the
remembrance of James Nicolson, Forbes's colleague in Dundee, that
Forbes immersed himself at Oxford in the study of the Fathers.[29] The
contact with Marriott gave Forbes the friendship with one of the most
attractive personalities of the Oxford Movement. Marriott was a fellow
of Oriel and had returned there in 1841, having had to relinquish his post
as principal of Chichester Theological College because of his delicate
health. He was a thorough scholar, well read in the Fathers. He returned
to Oxford just at the time Newman was retiring from the university
scene. Marriott endeavoured to take his place among Newman's confused
undergraduate disciples, and he gave himself unstintingly to their needs

[26] Ibid. 205ff.
[27] Ibid. 207–8.
[28] A. P. Forbes to G. H. Forbes, n.d. [1863/4], SAUL 19. 2. 284.
[29] C. Marriott to E. B. Pusey, Feb. 1844, PP Lett. 134; and J. Nicolson, *In
Memoriam* (1875), 4.

and to the literary labours of others to the detriment of his own writing. In 1850 he succeeded C. P. Eden as vicar of St Mary's. John Burgon, as one who knew him well, considered 'his primary qualification for supplying Newman's place was his unswerving loyalty . . . his absolute and undoubting confidence in the Apostolicity of the Church of England'.[30] In forming an attachment with Pusey and with Marriott, Forbes came under the influence of two leaders of the Oxford Movement who remained convinced of the catholicity of the Church of England, and whose Tractarian thinking never led them to contemplate conversion to Rome, despite their undoubted sympathy for Roman Catholicism. Forbes's labours for Marriott indicate his usual attention to study, an application which led to his being awarded a fourth-class pass in classics on graduation in 1844. This was a rare distinction for one not reading for an honours degree.[31]

Another influence upon Forbes during these Oxford years was his continuing links with the Scottish Episcopal Church and its nonjuring High Church tradition. One of his very few letters surviving from this period is to John Alexander, the priest involved in the building of a new mission church, dedicated to St Columba, for the poor in the Old Town of Edinburgh. In it Forbes asks for more information about the subscriptions for the new church.[32] The church was also meant to provide a home for the Scottish Communion Office in Edinburgh, in conjunction with its existing use by the Carrubber's Close congregation, of which John Alexander was the pastor. This support for the Scottish Communion Office was a fundamental ingredient in the subscription of the Forbes family to the project.[33] But despite Alexander's fervent support the plan to use the Communion Office failed, because Bishop Terrot held him to a previous agreement to discourage any such usage.[34]

Forbes was ordained deacon by Bishop Bagot on Trinity Sunday 1844 and went as assistant curate to the parish of Aston Rowant. He was 27 years old. A small country living of about eight hundred people, the parish comprised the two villages of Aston Rowant and Kingston Blount. It was about twenty miles east of Oxford and about two hours on horseback from the city. Forbes began his ministry there the following

[30] John William Burgon, *Lives of Twelve Good Men* (1891), 163.

[31] Perry, 22.

[32] A. P. Forbes to J. Alexander, 15 Mar. [1844], SRO CH 12. 5. 34.

[33] A. P. Forbes, *Jesus our Worship: A Sermon Preached at the Consecration of St. Columba's Church, Edinburgh* (1848), 28.

[34] Ronald Johnson, 'A Short History of St. Columba's Episcopal Church 1843–1969' (typed and duplicated booklet 1977), SRO CH 12. 5. 81, 8–9.

Sunday, 9 June, and immediately found himself in sole charge because the vicar was ill.[35] A letter to his brother describes his work as typical of a country parson—visiting, replacing the schoolmistress, preaching, and marrying.[36] He must have found the quiet of the country a great change from India or Oxford. With the vicar absent he would have been virtually divorced from the intellectual companionship and stimulation he had found at Oxford. Perry quoted two other letters, which suggest a sense of isolation as they are more full of the news and gossip of Oxford and even of Scotland, than of his parish. He also sent his brother a self-mocking witticism, asking 'why do the Puseyites dislike pews so much in churches? . . . Because they are so much attached to forms.' Forbes's devotion to Pusey was evidently sufficiently mature at this time to allow him to disagree with his mentor about the indelibility of post-baptismal sin, which Pusey had argued for intensely in his tract on baptism (although he later modified his belief).[37] Instead, Forbes told his brother that penance and the Eucharist were surely sufficient to destroy the guilt of such sin.[38] Forbes's delicate health and his intellectual interests made him ill-suited to rural life. He seems to have taken a number of opportunities to escape to Oxford, to research his brother's queries on patristic or liturgical sources, or just to keep contact with old friends.[39] He was reprieved in October. Called back to Edinburgh where his mother was seriously ill, he resigned the title and told his father he could never stand another country living.[40] But, perhaps like all first appointments, the memory of Aston Rowant remained with him fondly enough for him to write to the vicar in 1868 and invite himself back for a Sunday 'to see all the improvements in the Parish in which I take so deep an interest'.[41]

It must have been Pusey who had the influence to get him his next position, at St Thomas's, West Oxford, whose vicar, Thomas Chamberlain, had been Senior Student of Christ Church and was deeply influenced by the Oxford Movement from its beginning. The living was in the patronage of the college, and Chamberlain was appointed to it in 1842 after having been vicar of Cowley. A man of 'strong convictions backed by a determined will', he was inspired with the idea of making St Thomas's a model of Tractarian piety and pastoral practice, the first such

[35] Perry, 24.
[36] A. P. Forbes to G. H. Forbes, postmarked 12 Sept. 1844, SAUL 19. 1. 10.
[37] Forrester, *Young Doctor Pusey*, 198.
[38] A. P. Forbes to G. H. Forbes, postmarked 12 Sept. 1844, SAUL 19. 1. 10.
[39] A. P. Forbes to G. H. Forbes, n.d. [1844], SAUL 19. 1. 12.
[40] Perry, 28.
[41] Letter of A. P. Forbes, June 1868, LPL 3417, fo. 101.

parish in the Church of England.[42] He succeeded so well that one of
Bishop Samuel Wilberforce's first acts on becoming Bishop of Oxford in
1845 was to remove Chamberlain as rural dean, on the grounds that he
was a party man.[43] Possibly it was Chamberlain's personal intransigence in
the face of any opposition to his Tractarianism which contributed to
Wilberforce relieving him of a position requiring greater understanding
towards his fellow clergy.[44] Under Chamberlain, St Thomas's became the
premier Tractarian parish in the city. It had suffered prior to his arrival
by not having a resident vicar, the living having previously been filled by
Students of Christ Church who lived in college. Chamberlain soon bought
two cottages near the church and turned them into a clergyhouse. There
he lived with his curates, an early model of the sort of community of celibate priests the Tractarians believed to be a means of providing pastoral
care for the unchurched masses of urban poor. Chamberlain remained
unmarried all his life. He introduced the daily offices and expected his
curates to attend, and there was a celebration of Holy Communion on
saints' and other holy days. He was a believer in incessant house-to-house
visiting in an area where there were large numbers of labouring poor,
delapidated housing, and many brothels. The brothels Chamberlain drove
out, by the simple expedient of targeting them for frequent visits, a
method requiring a certain amount of moral courage as it could easily
have led to public notoriety in Victorian Britain.[45]

Forbes was ordained priest in 1845 by Bishop Bagot, and at St
Thomas's was given particular charge of the Boatman's Floating Chapel.[46]
This was a barge moored on the canal which served as a chapel on
Sundays for boatmen and their families. On weekdays it became a school
for children.[47] He received the small stipend of £70 a year and must have
drawn from his own private means for, in 1846, Forbes financed renovations to the church which Chamberlain was preparing to make. These
included a new north aisle and chancel arch; the dismantling of a low
chancel ceiling which partially obscured the east window; and removal of
some old high box pews.[48] While most of the ritual innovations for which
the parish became famous (or notorious) were introduced after Forbes's

[42]   A. B. Simeon, *A Short Memoir of the Rev. Thomas Chamberlain* (1892), 10.
[43]   Thomas Squires (ed.), *In West Oxford* (1928), 23.
[44]   Peter G. Cobb, 'Thomas Chamberlain: A Forgotten Tractarian', in *Studies in Church History*, ed. Derek Baker, 16 (1979), 374.
[45]   Squires, *West Oxford*, 18–19.
[46]   Mackey, 38.
[47]   Squires, *West Oxford*, 24.
[48]   Ibid. 18.

time, these renovations, which must have brought the altar in to greater prominence within the church, prepared the way for them. One important friend Forbes met while there was Richard Benson who, in 1866, became the founder of the first permanent religious order for men in the Church of England.[49]

In 1846 Forbes published an article in the *Ecclesiastic*, a Tractarian journal edited by Chamberlain, on 'Parochial Work in France'.[50] Alongside the experience of St Thomas's the article provides further insight into Forbes's model for parish work. He drew attention to the valuable place of the confessional in French parochial work and commented that the practice was conducive to holiness. The place of the priest in the lives of his people and their growth in religion was furthered by administering the last rites, his daily visiting round, and the Sunday sermon. Forbes commended this form of parochial work as an example to the Church of England where clergy began with an advantage over their French counterparts in having greater wealth and social standing. The experience of the French parochial clergy may have been known to Forbes from his own European travels, or it may have come from Pusey who was the leading Tractarian exponent of sacramental confession. The article points to the influence of European examples on the formation of Forbes's Tractarian ministry. Both St Thomas's and the French example demonstrate that by 1846 Forbes had before him the example of the ministry of single priests, living in community, and being prepared to go out among their people with an active sacramental ministry. But it was Forbes's personal experience of St Thomas's, and the influence of Thomas Chamberlain, that was undoubtedly one of the major influences for his later parish work. Forbes continued to visit Chamberlain almost every year of his life, whenever he went to stay with Pusey.

At Oxford in 1846 Forbes joined the Brotherhood of the Holy Trinity, a move which indicates the influence of religious life upon him at this time. Perry claims that Forbes actually founded this as a devotional society for undergraduates, but the Roll of the Brotherhood records that he was not admitted as a member until 1846.[51] The society, according to the minutes, was originally founded as the Brotherhood of St Mary in December 1844 for the study of ecclesiastical art, with four members. Soon after it became a more devotional society named after the Holy Trinity, but the Master remained the same as before, Edwin

[49] M. V. Woodgate, *Father Benson* (1953), 33.
[50] A. P. Forbes, 'Parochial Work in France', *Ecclesiastic*, 1 (1846), 81–9.
[51] 'Roll of the Brethren 1844–1858', BHT 3.

Millard of Magdalen. As Millard remained in this position until he
retired it is reasonable to assume that he, not Forbes, was the founder.
The Brotherhood's original rule gives an indication of the sort of piety
Forbes found attractive by 1846, if not before. Members subscribed to a
simple rule of life—to rise early; be moderate in food; spend a part of
each day in 'serious reading'; to speak evil of no one; avoid drunkenness;
to recite the 'Glory be' first thing in the morning and on going to bed;
and to pray for the unity of the Church, the conversion of sinners, the
advancement of the faithful, and members of the Brotherhood.[52] The
society had many of the external signs of a quasi-religious order—the
officers were known by religious titles such as Master and Almoner, there
was a badge for members to wear, and it had monthly 'chapters'. Among
the membership were many names prominent either in the development
of the Catholic revival or in Forbes's later life. They include George
Boyle, Roger Lingard, Richard Benson, Edward King, Charles Lowder,
and Arthur Henry Stanton.[53]

It was death of his mother on 11 July 1845 that brought about the
termination of Forbes's ministry at St Thomas's. After spending some
time in Edinburgh following the funeral, he decided he was needed near
his father for the immediate future. He advised Chamberlain accordingly,
and his name appeared in the parish registers for the last time on 8
February 1846.[54] While in Edinburgh Forbes may have been stimulated
to offer his services to the Scottish Episcopal Church by the Tractarian
Marchioness of Lothian, who suggested he should work for his 'own
Church'.[55] Bishop David Moir of Brechin wrote to Forbes on 19 May
1846, and contacted him again on 10 June. He had not been able to find
a clergyman for the charge of Stonehaven so willingly accepted Forbes's
services. The parish had been vacant since 22 January, probably because
Moir admitted he could not offer a sufficient stipend. Only £60 a year
could be guaranteed as this was all the congregation could afford. Moir
understood that Forbes had offered his services for a limited time. The
bishop informed him that the number of the congregation was between
three and four hundred. 'There are several respectable families in the
town and its vicinity belonging to the congregation. The fishing village of
Cowie, in the immediate neighbourhood is inhabited almost exclusively
by members of the Congregation.'[56]

[52] Minutes of Chapters Dec. 1844–Oct. 1856, BHT 1–3.
[53] Ibid. 17–18.   [54] Perry, 31–2.
[55] Mackey, 41.
[56] D. Moir to A. P. Forbes, 10 June 1846, SPC.

The following July Forbes wrote to his father that he was not likely to
suffer from overwork in Stonehaven and that he was disappointed over
the lack of church attendance. 'The lower part of the town contains many
who never go near a church, who are worse than heathen.' There was no
use even building a school, he said, for the children simply would not go.
Forbes also encountered a lively opposition from the friends and family of
the previous priest who had been dismissed by the bishop for contumacy.
(He had been summoned to appear before the bishop's court to answer a
charge of drunkenness and had not attended.) Forbes was further annoyed
that the previous incumbent had 'totally neglected the poor here'.[57]

Stonehaven had had a continuous Episcopal congregation since the
days of the disestablishment of episcopacy in 1690 and its congregation
included a predominance of fisherfolk who kept themselves apart from the
town, were sometimes illiterate, and lived in simple but-and-ben cottages.
The congregation was used to the Scottish Communion Office, for which
quarterly communion tokens were dispensed and the liturgy celebrated with little ceremony. They kept their distance from the Church of
Scotland whose worship their services resembled except on Communion
Sundays, and they had a fear of popery. So Forbes's first pastoral contact
with the Scottish Episcopal Church was with a congregation tracing its
origins to the nonjuring days and which, unlike many in the south of
Scotland where he was raised, had a large proportion of the lower classes
among its adherents. Forbes made little changes in the short time he was
there but he did, like Chamberlain in Oxford, introduce the daily offices
which were attended by sufficient parishioners to be encouraging.[58] He
also found the practice of communion tokens so agreeable that he continued to use them for the rest of his life.

The nonjuring connection and the adherence of the poor were evidently important to Forbes, and he wrote a small romantic novella based
on the Stonehaven congregation during the illegal days of the eighteenth
century. *The Prisoners of Craigmacaire* (the Gaelic name for Stonehaven)
told of the occupation and 'pacification' of the town by the Hanoverian
troops after Culloden, and especially of the consequent suffering of the
Episcopalian fisherfolk there. The story has all the romanticism of a
Walter Scott novel—a dashing Jacobite laird who rescues imprisoned
Episcopal ministers, loyal and brave Episcopal countrymen, smugglers,
and women who assist the saintly suffering clerics. The story includes the
famous incident from Episcopalian folklore of the imprisonment of three

57 A. P. Forbes to J. H. Forbes, 17 July 1846, SPC.
58 William Palmer to A. P. Forbes, July 1846, LPL 1895, fo. 101.

Episcopal priests in Stonehaven gaol in 1746, where the fisherwomen held
their babies up to the gaol window to be baptized.[59] At this point the
story becomes a vehicle for Forbes's own Tractarian agenda regarding
Roman Catholicism. The three Episcopalian clergy find themselves
imprisoned with a Scots Roman Catholic priest from the Jacobite army
and discover a common ground of religion.

> He [the Roman Catholic] had hitherto classed all the reformed bodies under one
> category, of course varying more or less, but all built on a sandy foundation. He
> was now surprised to find principles boldly asserted, which though to his mind
> grossly misapplied were nevertheless true principles, and which they ratified by
> appeals to the early Church, an authority to which he gave due weight. The
> Scotch clergy on the other hand were agreeably surprised to find that a man of
> his opinions might yet be a good Christian.[60]

The novella indicates that the sympathy for the tradition of the
Scottish Episcopal Church Forbes had learnt in his family was
reinforced by his contact with living examples of that same tradition,
and that his imagination was stirred by his ministry in a locality which
witnessed some of the suffering of the Episcopal past. It is also sugges-
tive of a gap between the Tractarian Forbes and native Episcopalians
in their respective attitudes to the Church of Rome.

The same Episcopalian sympathy stirred him again in a more critical
fashion in an article published in the *Ecclesiastic* in 1846. 'The Revolution
and the Nonjurors' was a review of *Coniston Hall, or the Jacobites; a
Historical Tale,* a novel by W. Gresley. In the article Forbes revealed his
antipathy towards the Revolution of 1688 which, in Tory fashion, he
considered an unholy, violent overthrow of the 'constitutional order of
things'. It resulted in the Church of England succumbing to both
Latitudinarianism and the dominance of the state. He revealed his
qualified affections for the Nonjurors as being 'the energetic element in
the Church', but whose removal had meant the Church, while not losing
her supernatural power, gave up her claims to apostolic authority and
foundation. After the Revolution, Forbes thought the Church looked to
the state for her legitimacy, while the Nonjurors created a schism which
left the Church of England crippled and at the mercy of the state.

> They extort our respect while we regret their act. They carried with them
> most of the Catholic element of the Church of England, and then, quarrelling
> among themselves, rent it in pieces and cast it to the winds. Theirs is the only

⁵⁹ John Archibald, *A Ten Year's Conflict and Subsequent Persecutions* (1907), 157–8.
⁶⁰ A. P. Forbes, *The Prisoners of Craigmacaire: A Story of the '46* (1852), 42.

act of confessorship in ecclesiastical history that has been attended with no apparent good.[61]

The contrast with his novella is important. In the story Forbes reveals an emotional sympathy for the sufferings and witness of the nonjuring Scottish Episcopal Church. But in the article he reveals an awareness of the shortcomings of that nonjuring tradition as regards the Church of England, believing the Nonjurors left that Church debilitated in its Catholic claim and life and prey to the two evils identified by the Oxford Movement—Erastianism and Latitudinarianism. For Forbes the Nonjurors were a very mixed blessing.

Another article for the *Ecclesiastic* written that year exhibits Forbes's thinking about social problems and the loosening of the ties between the working classes and the Church. 'On Religious Guilds' lamented the suppression of the medieval religious guilds at the Reformation.[62] These, he argued, were conducive to the unity of society by their inclusion of members from all ranks of society, while their benevolence to members in need supported the work of the Church. These two aspects of the Church's outreach were now, in many cases, left inadequately in the hands of a single vicar. He felt the numerous membership of the guilds had been better able than a single priest to deal with the victims of large-scale unemployment or disease. Their revival would be a means of fostering attachment to the Church among the working classes who were more in the habit, he considered, of identifying their interests with Dissent. The article had a romantic view of the social cohesion of medieval society founded upon a common faith. But it does show that Forbes was concerned about the declining influence of the Church among the working classes, and was thinking about the unity of nineteenth-century society.

It was around the time he went to Stonehaven that there is evidence for his anxiety over Newman's secession, and he turned to William Palmer of Magdalen College for advice. Palmer was a theologian among the younger High Churchmen who were drawn to the vitality of the Oxford Movement. He had been a classics tutor at Magdalen when Forbes was at Oxford. Palmer had anticipated the argument of Tract 90 in a Latin preface to the Thirty-nine Articles for his pupils, but played little part in the Oxford Movement. He spent most of the 1840s seeking ways to bring about intercommunion between the Anglican and Orthodox Churches. While Forbes's letter to Palmer does not appear to have

[61] A. P. Forbes, 'The Revolution and the Nonjurors', *Ecclesiastic*, 1 (1846), 213–22.
[62] A. P. Forbes, 'On Religious Guilds', *Ecclesiastic*, 1 (1846), 49–53.

survived, Palmer's reply, written in July 1846, has.[63] In it Palmer made a
very lengthy reference to Newman's *Essay on Development*, opining it was
not widely influential and that Newman's theory of development was
unacceptable to the Roman Church. He went on to refer to an article in
the *Christian Remembrancer* by J. B. Mozley that Forbes had obviously
mentioned. He thought that Forbes had been 'rather hasty' in criticizing
Mozley for saying that 'argument from the Orbis terrarum' was no longer
applicable. Palmer said that Mozley 'did not mean that the consent of the
Orbis terrarum [i.e. the Catholic (universal) Church] against Britain now
if it existed would not tell just as conclusively as the consent of the Orbis
terrarum against Africa & the Donatists in the time of S. Austin'. Mozley
was not objecting to the argument from such a world-wide Catholic
consensus, Palmer asserted, but to the fact that it was not applicable in
the present because it did not exist. There was universal Christian
condemnation against the position of the Donatist schism in the fourth
century, but there was no such world-wide consensus existing in the
nineteenth century to use as an argument to condemn the Anglican
position. Palmer's reply indicates that Forbes apparently had two
anxieties. The first was the possible widespread effect of Newman's
conversion, and more particularly about Anglicans finding compelling the
argument of Newman's *Essay*. The second was that the consensus of
Catholic Christendom may have stood against the truth of the Anglican
position. What is most significant at this stage is that Palmer's letter is
evidence that Forbes had been unsettled in his understanding of the
Anglican standpoint by Newman's secession. Forbes's criticism of Mozley
seems to presuppose that he did think that there may exist the possibility
of a consensus of the Catholic Church, the Christian *orbis terrarum*,
denying the validity of the Anglican position. Palmer's use of the example
of the schismatic Donatists suggests that Forbes had used it in his letter
to him. It would appear therefore that Newman's secession caused Forbes
to think, however briefly, that the Anglican Church could be in schism.

   In May 1847 Pusey nominated Forbes to the Bishop of Ripon,
Charles Longley, as vicar of St Saviour's, Leeds, and said that he
hoped there would be no difficulty about it.[64] Pusey had cause to be
concerned. Just as St Thomas's, Oxford, showed how a Tractarian
parish could develop strongly when the vicar's Anglican loyalties were
secure, St Saviour's showed what happened when they were not. It
also revealed some of the pitfalls the Oxford Movement fell into when

   [63] W. Palmer to A. P. Forbes, 4 July 1846, LPL 1895, fo. 101.
   [64] E. B. Pusey to J. Keble, n.d. [May 1847], PK ii.

it moved beyond the confines of the university into the parishes of the Church of England. Pusey had financed the building of the church and was its patron. He had chosen Leeds because of his personal friendship with the vicar, W. F. Hook, and because it was an evident case of need. The whole of the recently industrialized city had, until 1844, constituted a single parish of over 150,000 people, and it was still a glaring illustration in 1847 of the inadequacy of the Church of England in meeting the needs of the new urban masses.[65] Pusey intended the parish to be an example of the effectiveness of Tractarian models of ministry in this new urban society, and of the power of Tractarian piety to attract the unchurched poor.

Pusey, of all the Tractarian leaders, was most aware of the destitution of the urban poor and consistently endeavoured to relieve their lot. He passionately believed the Church of England had a moral obligation to remind society that the poor had souls and therefore should not be exploited. He often drew attention to the social dangers of leaving cities without an adequate religious presence. In his *Cathedral Institutions* (1833) Pusey had drawn attention to the widespread squalor of England's cities where he believed the presence of the Church could bring a civilizing influence. Pusey also had a particular concern for the religious poor, and to assist them advocated the abolition of pew-rents and the development of religious education and parochial schools.[66] One scholar has drawn attention to Pusey's campaign for church extension in which Pusey advocated the building of churches where the Eucharist would be celebrated weekly, and he pawned his wife's jewels and sold his carriage to help finance such projects.[67] Pusey was, therefore, at the forefront of Tractarian plans to revive the parishes of the Church of England as Eucharistic communities.

Pusey intended St Saviour's to encapsulate some of his ideas on urban mission. It would be staffed by priests living communally. They would serve an area that in 1838 had a population of approximately 6,000. These were mostly poor, living in a district with few shops and many public houses on the eastern outskirts of the city, immersed in wretchedness and dirt. The foundation stone was laid on 14 September 1842 after the bishop had unofficially sanctioned the experiment of a college of priests for the parish. At the consecration of the church in October 1845,

[65] W. R. W. Stephens, *The Life and Letters of Walter Farquhar Hook D. D.* (1880), 377ff.
[66] Forrester, *Young Doctor Pusey*, 153–60.
[67] R. W. Franklin, 'Pusey and Worship in Industrial Society', *Worship*, 57 (1983), 386–412.

however, he objected to some of the signs of Tractarianism in the building and caused the dedication to be changed from that of 'Holy Cross' to
St Saviour's.[68] Disagreements soon emerged between Hook and priests of
St Saviour's over their ritualism. Hook was not intolerant of Tractarianism, nor of mild ritualism.[69] However, as a High Churchman Hook would
not tolerate teaching or ceremony which he considered outwith the
comprehension of the Church of England and which emulated Rome. In
January 1847 one of the curates of St Saviour's was received into the
Roman Catholic Church together with two lay assistants of the parish.
Following the curate's secession Hook had insisted on the resignation of
the vicar.[70] A new vicar was not easy to find because St Saviour's was a
poor living in squalid conditions with arduous pastoral work, and it was
also suspect as a breeding ground for conversions to Rome. Therefore
clergy who went there were regarded by Hook and the bishop as suspect in their loyalty to the Church of England. Hook's experience of St
Saviour's had completely reversed his former sympathies for the
Tractarian experiment.

Forbes began work there in April 1847 without a curate, the bishop
also having joined Hook in his condemnation of the parish as untrue to
the principles of the Church of England. Forbes lived on his own in
the vicarage and the wife of the schoolmaster kept house for him. Each
Sunday there was Matins with Holy Communion following and
Evensong. There was also Sunday School to be taught in the morning
and afternoon. The daily office was said publicly during the week. In
1847 there was a cholera epidemic in Leeds, and Forbes became a
regular visitor at hospitals. This was a risky practice as three Roman
Catholic priests and one of the Anglican curates died of the disease.[71]
Charles Marriott was anxious about the lack of assistance which was
causing Forbes's health to suffer, but as he told Pusey in a comparison
with the Irish Famine 'Curates are as scarce as potatoes'.[72] In July
there was some prospect of help although Hook was actively
discouraging prospective candidates.[73] By this time relations between
Hook and Pusey had reached an all-time low and Forbes was caught in
the middle. In August Hook bluntly told Pusey that St Saviour's

[68] John Pollen, *Narrative of Five Years at St. Saviour's, Leeds* (1851), 33–6.
[69] Nigel Yates, *Leeds and the Oxford Movement* (1975), 15–16.
[70] Nigel Yates, *The Oxford Movement and Parish Life: St. Saviour's, Leeds, 1839–1929*,
Borthwick Papers, no. 48 (1975), 8–9.
[71] Pollen, *Narrative*, 57–8.
[72] C. Marriott to E. B. Pusey, 18 June 1847, PP Lett. 134.
[73] C. Marriott to E. B. Pusey, 20 July 1847, PP Lett. 134.

would remain an object of suspicion as long as Pusey continued to be patron, and he asked Pusey and his fellow trustees to resign. 'We could', he added, 'manage to get on with Mr Forbes, if he were to appear to me as a substantive character.' However he suspected Forbes was merely an agent to acquire and send penitents to Pusey for oral confession. Hook went on vehemently:

You will not be able to carry into effect the object you have in view. Not while I am Vicar of Leeds, for I am uniting myself with the moderate Evangelical Party under the conviction that it is by them, improving as they are in Church Principles, and not by your Friends, dissenting from Church Principles as they do, that the Glory of God will be promoted in the Church of England . . . I am ready for war, if it be the Lord's will that I maintain the cause of His Church here against you—but I desire that peace which will ensue by your retreating from ground which you are unable to occupy.[74]

Hook's vitriolic demands and accusations stirred Pusey to defend Forbes and himself. Hook, he thought, was overestimating the office of patron, and if he were to give that office up it would not alter the present circumstances. He believed that his resignation as patron would render Forbes's position untenable. 'Forbes is my friend; he would not cease to be so. My relation to him is not as patron, but as friend.' Pusey's resignation as patron would only 'encourage those who suspect Forbes, &, as you say "watch his every movement & report it to the Bp." to weary him out of holding St Saviours'. If he remained as patron these opponents would realize the futility of their efforts because Forbes would only be replaced by someone similar. Pusey claimed, somewhat artfully, that once his appointment of the vicar was made he had no more to do with St Saviour's than with any other parish in England, save for his financial grants which were necessary because of its poverty. He questioned Hook's credentials to criticize Forbes as lacking character, and he assured him that it would be a mistake to 'hold aloof' from Forbes simply on account of his connection with Pusey. He denied that Forbes was a vehicle to send Pusey penitents.[75]

The argument demonstrates some of the pressure Forbes was under in Leeds. St Saviour's was helping to confirm in the minds of many in the Church of England a connection between the Oxford Movement and Romanism, a suspicion that began with the publication of Froude's *Remains* and Tract 90. Deeply shaken by the previous Roman Catholic

74 W. F. Hook to E. B. Pusey, 3 Aug. 1847, PP 5. 4.
75 E. B. Pusey to W. F. Hook, 14 July [1847], PH Hook correspondence, 426.

conversions among the St Saviour's clergy Hook was ready to listen sympathetically to those who accused Forbes of leaning that way. These opponents kept the parish and the vicar under close scrutiny for any false move. Alongside the difficult living conditions and the lack of curates Forbes had to minister in an atmosphere of distrust. The argument between Hook and Pusey exemplifies the rift between some High Churchmen and the Tractarians which had developed apace since Newman's conversion. The number of similar Roman Catholic conversions since then made High Churchmen like Hook join the Evangelicals in their distrust of Tractarianism as a breeding ground for popery.

Forbes's appointment to St Thomas's and St Saviour's connected him with two of the earliest attempts of the Oxford Movement to move from an academic environment into a parochial one. It was a move partly associated with urban parishes situated among the poorer working classes, and Forbes's friendship with Pusey would have directed his thoughts and ministry in this direction. While St Thomas's undoubtedly gave him an example to emulate, St Saviour's gave him one to avoid. The Leeds parish demonstrated how people were alienated by Catholic ritual and practice when it was too far in advance of their understanding or prejudices. This was especially true when, by too close an emulation of Roman Catholic ritual engendered by naïve enthusiasm on the part of some inexperienced Anglo-Catholic clergy, such ritual evoked the traditional anti-popery of the British. When that happened, potential allies like Hook were alienated and the work of the parish disrupted. It is difficult in these early years of Forbes's ministry to determine exactly what his own priorities in such parish work were. As a curate he had been assisting the initiatives of others, and his time in Stonehaven and Leeds was too short for his own plans to emerge. The shape and initiatives of his own Tractarian priesthood, influenced by these experiences, only fully emerged when Forbes embarked on his long ministry at Dundee.

3

The Tractarian Bishop

WHEN Alexander Forbes was consecrated Bishop of Brechin in 1847 he was the very first Tractarian to become a bishop. During his episcopate Forbes began to express in his diocese the ideals of the Oxford Movement he had espoused earlier, in a Tractarian ministry influenced by the heavily industrialized environment of Dundee. In Dundee Forbes reinvigorated an Episcopal congregation which, like the Episcopal Church generally, had been largely introspective. He worked to develop a congregation that was inclusive of the urban poor, and focused around the Church as a Eucharistic community. Forbes also set a powerful example to his own clergy and to the Episcopal Church of responsiveness to the labouring poor and of civic involvement. As a bishop Forbes soon demonstrated he was a staunch supporter of the old nonjuring tradition, although he remained criticial of nonjuring theology. In these years Bishop Forbes encountered again the low level of church attendance among the labouring poor and the working classes, and he began to propose the formulation of a dogmatic theology which, coupled with sacrificial living among the poor, he believed could reawaken confidence in the spiritual realities taught by the Church.

The process by which Forbes came to be nominated as Bishop of Brechin illustrates one of the important reasons for his influence as a bishop. His nomination was the result of support for his candidacy by influential figures within the Episcopal Church, the chief of which was William Gladstone. In August 1847 William Gladstone was on his annual visit to his father[1] at his country estate of Fasque, in the Mearns in the east of Scotland. While there he heard of the death of David Moir, the Bishop of Brechin. On 27 August, the day Gladstone attended the bishop's funeral, he wrote to Alexander Forbes.[2] There is no record of this letter but on 1 September Gladstone wrote to Walter Goalen, the

---

[1] Contrary to what Mowat and Perry state, Gladstone was visiting his father and not his brother. Thomas Gladstone did not succeed as baronet until his father's death in 1851.
[2] M. R. D. Foot and H. C. G. Matthew (eds.), *The Gladstone Diaries*, vol. iii: *1840–1847* (1974), 644.

Episcopal priest at Laurencekirk and his first cousin, to ask his opinion of
Forbes.[3] He wrote to Lord Medwyn the next day and to Forbes again on
7 September.[4] On 8 September he recorded in his diary that he had seen
Forbes 'on the bishopric'.[5] Gladstone was, therefore, the instigator behind
the proposing of Alexander Forbes's name for election as Bishop of
Brechin. He was able to do so because of his own involvement with the
Scottish Episcopal Church and because he knew the Forbes family.

   Gladstone's own knowledge of the Episcopal Church came as a result
of his father's move to Fasque. Sir John Gladstone was himself a Scot, of
Presbyterian stock, who had joined the Church of England after moving
to Liverpool. He was a successful merchant in Atlantic and North Sea
trade and the West Indian sugar plantations, so that he was worth more
than half a million pounds by 1828.[6] The country seat of Fasque,
acquired in 1830, was an expression of his rise in society.[7] By then
William, his fourth son, was at Oxford, but he took an active interest in
the new family home and especially in the Episcopal Church. In doing so
Gladstone was probably realizing an interest he remembered from his
mother's family background. Anne Mackenzie Robertson was John
Gladstone's second wife and came from a minor line of highland Jacobite
Episcopalian gentry. Gladstone later recalled his maternal grandmother as
'stoutly Episcopalian and Jacobite'.[8]

   Gladstone's contact with the Episcopal Church led to his scheme for
the establishment of Trinity College, Glenalmond, in Perthshire, as a
combined theological college and public school. Gladstone first mooted
the idea with Henry Manning in 1840; and with James Hope, another
Tractarian layman, he circulated a formal proposal for subscriptions the
following year. The foundation stone was laid in 1846 and work began in
1847. The institution was inspired by the Oxford Movement, being concerned to educate boys in Church principles and also to train candidates
for ordination in a system akin to Roman seminaries.[9] Under its first
warden, Charles Wordsworth, later Bishop of St Andrews, the school was
modelled on an English public school and was another agent of Anglicization among the Scottish middle class. It was the Trinity College project
that brought Gladstone into contact with the Forbes family. The first
mention of them in Gladstone's diary was on 3 September 1845 when he
wrote to Lord Medwyn and his sons 'on College and Church matters'.[10]

   [3] Ibid. 646.   [4] Ibid. 646–7.   [5] Ibid. 648.
   [6] H. C. G. Matthew, *Gladstone* (1988), 3.   [7] Ibid. 4–9.   [8] Ibid. 4.
   [9] Marion Lochhead, *Episcopal Scotland in the Nineteenth Century* (1966), 79–80.
   [10] *Gladstone Diaries*, iii. 479.

This could not have been the first contact however as the following day Gladstone dined at William Forbes's, Medwyn's oldest son, at what he familiarly described as 'a College and Ch. party'.[11] William Forbes became a member of the board of trustees of the college and kept Gladstone informed about the battles over the use of the Scottish Communion Office in the college chapel. For the next two years Gladstone corresponded regularly with both Medwyn and William Forbes in connection with Trinity College. His first recorded meeting with Alexander was at a dinner party at Fasque on 26 October 1846 during the time Forbes was at Stonehaven, and Gladstone recalled a conversation with him about Dante, to whom both men were devoted. Gladstone wrote of Forbes that he liked him 'particularly'.[12] Alexander was apparently a house guest at this time, for the day after the dinner party Gladstone shared a walk with him.[13] Keeping in touch with his slightly younger contemporary, in May 1847 Gladstone read Forbes's commentary on the penitential psalms,[14] and later that same month met him in London.[15]

Gladstone's personal religion predisposed him towards using his influence in Forbes's favour in the Brechin nomination. His religious position had undergone a severe disruption from his experience of practical politics. By 1847 Gladstone had already discovered that his theory of a revived Anglican confessional state (as set forth in his *The State in its Relations with the Church*, published in 1838) was impractical. He had come to understand that such a revival was an unreal expectation in the increasingly pluralistic Britain of the mid-nineteenth century. In 1845 he had resigned from the Conservative cabinet over the proposed government grant to the Roman Catholic seminary of Maynooth. But he supported the grant from the backbenches however, reflecting his awakening to the religious plurality of the British state. Against growing government support for undenominational Christianity Gladstone increasingly thought the Church of England needed to be free of its ties to the state which, he felt, shackled its ability to uphold a Catholic Christianity with a distinctive dogmatic content. This was the kernel of his commitment to religious liberty after the 1840s. None the less, if he could never again be a public upholder of the state as an Anglican entity (as demanded by his Tory and High Church constituents of Oxford University), in his private religion he remained very sympathetic towards Tractarianism.[16] Gladstone had developed his own High Church theology independent of the Oxford

[11] Ibid. 480.   [12] Ibid. 579.   [13] Ibid. 580.
[14] Ibid. 618.   [15] Ibid. 623.
[16] Matthew, *Gladstone*, 68–9.

Movement by the mid-1830s. This theology centred on the Church as a divine institution, having its own *magisterium* as a consequence of retaining its apostolic links. It was a theology that did not reject his Evangelical upbringing but built upon it. For Gladstone the Oxford Movement complemented, not contradicted, the Evangelical revival and consequently he abhorred those who turned these two streams of Anglicanism into antagonistic parties. Gladstone disliked the factionalism in the Church of England because, after the 1840s, they were incompatible with his emerging ideas of an inclusive catholicity in religion. He therefore strongly disagreed with the pro-Roman Catholic radicals in the Oxford Movement, but defended them publicly as a matter of justice because ultra-Protestants in the Church were not similarly persecuted. By the mid-1840s, however, these radical elements had destroyed Gladstone's hopes of the Oxford Movement capturing the Church of England and transforming it into a more devout and truly national Church. Gladstone was a Tractarian in so far as his spirituality was based on the Church and particularly on the Eucharist—he was religiously most at home in the devotional atmosphere of Margaret Street chapel for example. But he was not a Tractarian if by this is meant adherence to a particular ecclesiastical party. One historian of his religious opinions considered that, 'Scottish episcopalianism with its Caroline ethos, and its communion office based on Laud's Scottish Liturgy probably approximated most closely to his own ideal of Anglicanism as both Catholic and reformed'.[17] The Scottish Episcopal Church was also attractive to Gladstone as an Anglican Church free of state restrictions, unlike the Church of England.

Forbes himself conformed to Gladstone's attitude to the Oxford Movement. As well as his personal affinity with Gladstone, Forbes's ministry in Leeds demonstrated he was not disposed to the unbridled pro-Roman enthusiasms of his predecessors. This can only have enhanced Forbes's candidacy for the statesman. Gladstone also knew of and respected the Forbes family's history of support for the Episcopal Church, which meant he was proposing a candidate with solid Episcopalian credentials.

The election of the bishop was solely in the hands of the priests of Brechin diocese, therefore it was important for Gladstone to find one of them to support his candidate. Perry claims that Gladstone visited Robert Thom, the priest at neighbouring Drumlithie and a senior figure in the diocese, and that Thom became an enthusiastic supporter of Forbes's candidacy.[18] At the later electoral synod it was certainly

[17] Perry Butler, *Gladstone: Church, State and Tractarianism* (1982), 164.
[18] Perry, 38.

Thom who proposed Forbes, but there is no mention of Thom, or a visit to Drumlithie, anywhere in Gladstone's diary between Bishop Moir's death on 21 August and Forbes's election on 15 September. It seems unlikely that some such visit would have been omitted when Gladstone was punctilious in recording other visits and correspondence undertaken during his visit to Fasque. In fact the earliest mention of a visit to Thom by Gladstone comes much later, in Donald Mackey's *Memoir*, published in 1888. Certainly Gladstone must have made some connection with one of the Brechin clergy to secure a nomination to the bishopric, and Robert Thom would not have proposed Forbes at the electoral synod without agreeing to the suggestion beforehand. But the only contemporary source, Gladstone's diary, is silent about any connection between Gladstone and Thom. What the diary does record is a lengthy conversation between Gladstone and Bishop Samuel Wilberforce of Oxford on 26 August, the day before Gladstone wrote to Forbes.[19] Wilberforce was at Fasque for the consecration of the new chapel two days later. There were also a number of letters written to Lord Medwyn, and a conversation with the primus, Bishop Skinner of Aberdeen, 'on several immediate questions', at a dinner party on the night of the consecration.[20] Did Gladstone simply forget to enter a visit to Thom in his diary, or omit it as insignificant? Or, following his usual practice of wide consultation on important matters, did he first sound out the opinions of Bishop Wilberforce, Lord Medwyn, and the primus before approaching one of the Brechin electors? That elector was his first cousin, Walter Goalen. Was it Goalen who then approached Thom who, being unrelated to Gladstone, was a better nominator to the electoral synod? For all the Gladstone influence, William, being resident in England, was only indirectly connected to the Scottish Episcopal Church. This construction of events seems likely, and it demonstrates the important personal connections Forbes's candidacy could muster. It included Forbes's father, a judicial lord and the head of one of the most important Episcopal families with a proven record of support for the Church; William Skinner, the leading bishop; Samuel Wilberforce who, while having no official voice within the Episcopal Church, as a bishop of the Church of England represented an important influence for many Episcopalians; and finally Gladstone himself. Forbes's candidacy could be presented to the priests of the small Diocese of Brechin as having the support of significant figures in

[19] *Gladstone Diaries*, iii. 644.
[20] Ibid. 645.

the Church. This support illustrates the weight of influence Forbes
himself, as Bishop of Brechin, could hope to bring to bear on important
issues and projects.

The electoral synod was convened at St Mary's, Montrose, on 15
September. Dean Horsley of the Dundee congregation was too ill to
attend, which left nine priests entitled to vote. There were two candidates, Forbes and William Henderson, the incumbent of St Mary's,
Arbroath. Henderson was proposed by Torry Anderson, the joint
incumbent of Dundee. The vote was six votes for Forbes and three for
Henderson. Forbes's supporters included Goalen and John Moir, the
son of the previous bishop.[21] Gladstone heard the news that same
afternoon and declared it to be a 'great mercy'.[22]

Forbes wrote to Pusey with the news of his election and told him that
his first thought was 'lest the Church suffer from my life and secondly
the awful responsibility: yearly decreasing congregations: a house divided
against itself: all things apparently against us'. He asked if he could come
to Pusey to prepare for his consecration as he thought 'a fortnight's
retreat at Oxford wd. help me'.[23] No one from his family could be
unaware of the contemporary state of the Episcopal Church and these
comments of Forbes point to his realization that divisions continued
within the Episcopal Church. They had not been solved with the formal
grounds for union between the qualified and nonjuring congregations in
1804 and strains between the two groups continued into the middle of
the century.

The continuing tension between northern and southern Episcopalians
since 1804 had focused on the most visible difference between the two,
namely the Scottish Communion Office in preference to the English
Eucharistic liturgy of the Book of Common Prayer. After 1804 Bishop
John Skinner of Aberdeen and the northern bishops, who were
predominant at this time, revealed a nervousness about the emerging
power of the south with its links to the attractive establishment of the
Church of England, and they feared their northern tradition would be
overwhelmed. Skinner devoted his charge to the clergy of Aberdeen in
1806 to this subject and to the need to retain their own Scottish
traditions in worship. According to his son, Skinner had 'reason to
suspect that there were, among the junior clergy of Scottish ordination,
some whose ambition it was to be considered Clergymen of the Church

[21] Brechin Diocese Synod Minutes, BrMs 4. 1. 2, 187–8.
[22] *Gladstone Diaries*, iii. 649.
[23] A. P. Forbes to E. B. Pusey, n.d. [Sept. 1847], PP 5. 40.

of England, and who, if they had not already abandoned the use of the Eucharistic service of the Scottish Church, were ready to do so,—for no other reason but that it was Scottish!'[24] The intimation by Skinner of the possible republication of the Scottish Communion Office complete with doctrinal explanation caused concern in the south, where there was anxiety that such a step would revive the acrimony of the last century over liturgy, and that the Book of Common Prayer would be reduced to a subordinate role. The former qualified and English clergy also felt nervous and insecure about their position so soon after the union of many of them with the Scottish Episcopal Church. The tension surfaced again in 1816 over the election to the diocese of Aberdeen. The election of William Skinner to succeed his father was not regarded favourably by the southern bishops and clergy. They argued that the north had more than half the bishops and that someone from the south should be elected to keep the balance. More particularly, they did not want someone from the Skinner family for, despite John Skinner's work for union, the Skinners were thought too wedded to northern traditions to work well with the south.[25]

The nineteenth-century northern bishops were conscious of being inheritors of a definite theological tradition from their nonjuring past and all had a strong attachment to the Scottish Communion Office. Having a majority in these early decades of the nineteenth century they managed to secure the place of the Communion Office. At the General Synod of 1811, in Aberdeen, the fifteenth canon gave this liturgy 'primary author- ity' over the Book of Common Prayer and dictated that it was to be used at all consecrations of bishops. The new canons further stipulated it could not be dropped from use by a congregation without the approval of all the bishops.[26] But a sign of the increasing influence of the south surfaced during the General Synod of 1828, when the clause in the canon for- bidding the relinquishing of the Scottish Office without the consent of all the bishops was changed. Henceforth the permission of the diocesan bishop alone was all that was required.[27]

The northern bishops also revealed themselves as conscious inheritors of their nonjuring past with regard to the episcopate. Like their eighteenth-century predecessors they upheld the tradition of powerful, monarchic bishops. In his first charge to his clergy, on the need for

[24] John Skinner, *Annals of Scottish Episcopacy* (1818), 434.
[25] W. Walker, *Life of Alexander Jolly and George Gleig* (1878), 296–7.
[26] W. Stephen, *History of the Scottish Church* (1896), ii. 572–3.
[27] George Grub, *An Ecclesiastical History of Scotland* (1861), iv. 185.

liturgical uniformity, Bishop George Gleig of Brechin used almost identical language to that of Thomas Rattray. Gleig maintained that party spirit could not

> be *widely* spread among us, if we keep constantly in our recollection the unques-
> tionable truths, that the Clergy of one diocese have nothing whatever to do with
> the affairs of another; that every diocese, under its own Bishop, is a particular
> church . . . and that the union of dioceses into National Churches is maintained
> only by the union of several Bishops under the Divine Shepherd and Bishop of
> our souls, and by Canons enacted for the government of the several dioceses thus
> united in one body.[28]

Other northern bishops also identified with this tradition of exalted diocesan episcopacy. At the General Synod in 1811 the clergy were given the vote for the first time and canons were passed requiring that both houses—bishops and clergy—approve all legislation.[29] Bishop Alexander Jolly of Moray considered that this synod diminished the episcopal prerogative.[30]

The attitude of the northern bishops towards their own episcopal authority retarded the inclusion of the laity in the councils of the Church. John Skinner, pastor of Forfar and son of Bishop John Skinner, had early become aware of the need for the representation of the laity in synods. Stimulated by the visit of Bishop Hobart of New York in 1823 he suggested an emulation of this practice of American Episcopalianism.[31] But his bishop, Patrick Torry, feared that the inclusion of laity in synod would erode episcopal authority and was 'too hazardous' an experiment.[32] This issue, like that of the Communion Office, was not resolved at that time, although some steps towards wider government were taken. In the 1828 General Synod a canon was passed providing for annual diocesan synods and a General Synod every fifth year.[33] This removed the initiating of synods from the bishops and made them a regular event. But because of the influence of the northern bishops David Low and Alexander Jolly, and the weakness of the elderly Gleig as primus, another General Synod was convened the following year which repealed both the canon instituting a regular General Synod and that giving the clergy a veto on acts of General Synod through their own diocesan synods.[34] Jolly had objected to the canons of 1828 because they implied that the

---

28 Walker, *Alexander Jolly*, 270.   29 Grub, *Ecclesiastical History*, iv. 128–30.
30 Walker, *Alexander Jolly*, 80.
31 J. M. Neale, *The Life and Times of Patrick Torry, D. D.* (1856), 112–13.
32 Ibid. 115.   33 Grub, *Ecclesiastical History*, iv. 182ff.
34 Walker, *Alexander Jolly*, 356.

apostolic authority given to the bishops to govern the Church was diminished. Jolly's concern was partly justified as the laity were unlikely to have the theological ability necessary for the synodical formulation of doctrine. But much of this opposition to the laity in synod came from the bishops' understanding of the episcopate as holding the plenitude of spiritual authority and power, a view which reduced the clergy and laity to passive recipients of episcopal decisions.

The early nineteenth century also witnessed the advent of Evangelicalism in the Episcopal Church for the first time. The Calvinist theology of some Evangelical clergy who appeared in the south was something of a shock to the bishops as Calvinism had been rejected among Scottish Episcopalians after 1689.[35] Evangelicalism arrived in the form of a visit to Edinburgh in 1822 by Gerard Noel, a Church of England Evangelical. Noel's disciple, Edward Craig, minister of St James's chapel, Edinburgh, later attacked James Walker, professor of the Theological College, in 1826 over Walker's upholding baptismal regeneration. The concern of the bishops and clergy at this attack, on what was unanimously regarded as the doctrine of the Church, prompted the calling of an Episcopal Synod in 1826. In the event the synod did nothing because the bishops did not want to prejudice their authority by attempting to impose on Craig a discipline he was likely to repudiate or ignore. They did, however, commend a declaration from over thirty clergy criticizing Craig and upholding Walker for his 'true doctrine'.[36]

In the first half of the nineteenth century the Episcopal Church concentrated on its own internal unity and organization. This was a consequence of the Church adjusting to the transition from its illegality of the eighteenth century to its legal existence in the nineteenth. Despite Forbes's comment to Pusey about declining congregations there was growth in real terms. Before his death in 1830 Bishop Daniel Sandford of Edinburgh had seen six new churches built in the south, including two in Edinburgh. His clergy in the diocese of Edinburgh had grown from seven to twenty-five, of whom five were formerly clergy of qualified congregations and seven were for newly-formed congregations.[37] Since 1792 churches could be built for the first time in years, clergy could be openly recruited, and worship offered publicly. The Episcopal Church needed time to adjust to this new situation before attempting anything by way of evangelization, or an involvement in wider society. These years

[35] Grub, *Ecclesiastical History*, iv. 174.
[36] Ibid. 180–1.
[37] R. Foskett, 'The Episcopate of Daniel Sandford', in *RSCHS*, 15 (1966), 152.

were spent putting its own house not just in order, but fashioning it on the scanty foundations of the previous century. This caused tension and argument, particularly between the northern and southern portions with their different emphases and theological nuances; and between bishops used to running the small body without interference and competition. Reluctantly, the bishops began to share the government of the Church with the clergy in synods which met with greater frequency and dealt with more and more business.

By the 1840s a major shift in the theological and geographical basis of the Episcopal Church was beginning to be noticeable. As a result of the pull of industrialization and, to a lesser extent, the push of the Highland emigration, the south was fast becoming the area of greatest population and Episcopal growth was most rapid there. This meant that the predominance of the north and the nonjuring tradition in the Church was coming to an end. The increasing strength of the south meant also the greater influence of the Church of England, as clergy of English birth or Scots of Anglicized disposition took it for their model. It was not that the southern clergy were diametrically opposed to those of the north. In fact most of them were High Church as this was understood in the Church of England and therefore had much in common with the northern tradition. But there were significant differences between the two. William Walker remarks on this difference of southern Churchmanship in his reminiscence of Bishop Michael Russell when Russell was Bishop of Glasgow and pastor of the congregation at Leith after 1809.

In his 'form of doctrine' and style of services he was a man of his age and of his diocese; resembling a clergyman of the eighteenth century English type, rather than the Keiths and Forbeses—those ardent Jacobites and Usagers—who had preceded him at Leith. There was, so far as the writer remembers, little if any difference in the mode in which the service was conducted in the Edinburgh churches in the early 'Forties'. It was the old moderate High Church style.[38]

It was the same High Churchmanship that, in England, was initially favourable to the Oxford Movement but parted company with it during the 1840s. On the other hand Evangelicalism, which stood in opposition to both, played little part in these tensions as it was represented throughout the century by only one or two independent chapels in Edinburgh, Glasgow, and Aberdeen.

Despite the problems Forbes mentioned to Pusey he retained his personal appreciation for the Episcopal Church. He particularly respected

---

[38]　William Walker, *Three Churchmen* (1893), 20.

its witness to Catholic truth and Patristic tradition during its penal suffering of the eighteenth century. Forbes regarded this witness as being more complete than that to be found in the Church of England at the time, although he accepted that there was very little in Episcopal services of worship that could evoke an emotional or imaginative response to this truth. As he commented in his novella *The Prisoners of Craigmacaire* in 1852:

In her [the Episcopal Church] there is no aesthetic charm nor much food for the imagination. Her ritual is meagre, her services few and tasteless, her outward form loveless and unattractive, but she has the higher and more ennobling poetry of earnest endurance and patient suffering for the conscience sake. Her past history has been one of temporal misfortune borne unflinchingly in a noble cause . . . . who shall deny that when England was lost in the distressing lukewarmness of the last century, hearts further north responded to the harmonies of Catholic truth, and sighed after Catholic unity? Who knows not that a fuller and purer service obtains in her public litugies, that the mixed chalice, the invocation of the Holy Spirit on the hallowed gifts, the express oblation of the same . . . still remain to her, and that tradition asserts that even nearer approaches to the Apostolic model from time to time obtained?[39]

But while appreciative of the Episcopal Church Forbes did not completely identify with either the northern or the southern groups. His election cemented the place of Tractarianism within the Episcopal Church and Tractarianism stood at a critical distance from both older groups. It looked at both sympathetically but with reservations. English High Churchmen, like the Nonjurors, were applauded by Tractarians for their history of upholding of Catholic doctrine, but not for their moderation, their appreciation of the Reformation, or their support of the principle of establishment. The Nonjurors were also questionable for their schism and for the vagueness of some of their teaching. In the Scottish context that meant the Tractarian Forbes favoured the Scottish Communion Office and the authority of the episcopate as evidences of Catholic teaching, but also criticized the northern tradition for its Eucharistic doctrine and lack of ritual in worship. But nor did he like the unquestioning perfection ascribed to the Church of England by some among the southern High Churchmen. As the first Tractarian bishop, Forbes became a focus within the Episcopal Church for those sympathetic to the Oxford Movement and thus was the centre for a smaller Tractarian third force within the Church. Although a minority compared to the northerners and southerners, in Alexander Forbes Scottish Tractarianism possessed invaluable

[39] A. P. Forbes, *Prisoners of Craigmacaire* (1852), 4–5.

English connections among the Tractarian leadership which ensured that Forbes's actions would not be lacking in support south of the border.

Alexander Forbes's election was confirmed by the bishops and he was consecrated Bishop of Brechin on 28 October 1847 (the Feast of SS Simon and Jude) by Bishops Skinner, Russell, and Charles Terrot, in St Andrew's, Aberdeen. He was consecrated along with Alexander Ewing, the first Bishop of Argyll and the Isles, whose diocese had been separated from Moray and Ross.[40] Immediately prior to his consecration Forbes signified his adherence to the eighteenth-century concordat between the bishops which was the basis for episcopal collegiality. This promised he would not consecrate anyone as bishop without the prior consent of the majority of the bishops, and that 'in all matters relating to the Church, Worship, and Discipline thereof, we shall be determined by the same majority'. Originally the agreement of the bishops of the eighteenth-century diocesan party, this concordat had been adhered to by all bishops since 1741.[41] It gave expression to the centrality of episcopal authority and solidarity which had been won free from royal control in the 1740s. At the consecration service Forbes was in such ill health that few thought he would be capable of much work and would only last five years.[42]

Dean Horsley, the joint incumbent of St Paul's, Dundee, had died that October and Forbes was elected in his place, since Scottish bishoprics still needed the income of a congregational charge. There had been an Episcopal congregation in Dundee since Robert Rait and Robert Norrie had been deprived as the Episcopalian parish ministers in 1689. The history of the congregation during the eighteenth century reflected the wider divisions between Episcopalians during that century. There had been a schism over the Scottish Communion Office and the usages and another congregation was formed which lasted until 1745, when the two reunited. In 1749 there was another schism when some of this reunited congregation broke away to form a qualified congregation. These two groups remained separated until 1829 when they merged under joint incumbents and met in the Castle Street chapel, which had been built in 1812 for the congregation in communion with the bishops.[43]

When Forbes arrived in Dundee in 1847 St Paul's congregation numbered around 1,000, with 350 communicant members. It included

[40] REC II, 28 Oct. 1847, SRO CH 12. 60. 3, 149–50.
[41] REC I, SRO CH 12. 60. 1, frontispiece.
[42] J. Nicolson, *In Memoriam* (1875), 5.
[43] Draft of an article on St Paul's, Dundee, for the *Scottish Churchman* by Dean Christie, Mar. 1930, SPC.

some of the leading families in the area, a number of English middle-class immigrants, some hereditary lower-class Episcopalians, and a number of Ulster Irish.[44] The congregation maintained some contact with the poor and the artisans of the city. Of 137 marriages celebrated in the Castle Street chapel between 1817 and 1847, fifty-six, or approximately one third, were illiterate and made only a mark as their signature in the register.[45] Occupations were rarely listed in the marriage registers before 1848, being given partially in only nine years during this period. Among these were three labourers, a weaver, mason, blacksmith, and an army corporal.[46] The congregation Forbes found was emerging from former obscurity and growing in middle-class membership and respectability since its merger in 1829 with the former qualified congregation. In Castle Street the chapel itself was surrounded by the masses of labouring poor, but the richer and more influential members lived elsewhere. Forbes chose not to follow the example of other members of the Dundee upper classes. He moved into the city centre, to a house in Springfield Place, where he lived until moving in 1853 to Burnfield House off the Seagate.[47] In February 1853 the vestry of St Paul's agreed to the offer from one of their number to sell a site on Castlehill for £1,255 in order to build a clergyhouse on it, and borrowed the cost from Forbes.[48] The building of this clergyhouse enabled Forbes to live with his assistant curates and other priests in a form of celibate priestly community—the sort of collegial life that Pusey advocated for ministry to the urban poor. As well as the curates the basic household consisted of a cook-housekeeper and a maid, while James Nicolson, incumbent of St Salvador's and later Dean of the Diocese, also lived there. Guests more often stayed in a hotel at Forbes's expense because of the limited accommodation. Forbes did not entertain in the usual sense of giving dinner parties. He seldom accepted invitations to dine, except by close friends in the area, and occasional luncheons were the usual mode of entertaining at the clergyhouse.[49] The house was a place of privacy for Forbes where he could relax among close associates and pursue his scholarship. Although he thought the house gloomy it was his refuge from the demands and squalor of the city. Forbes's move into Dundee was a conscious decision to place

[44] Perry, 40.

[45] This figure includes only those who actually made a mark. In some entries no one other than the officiating minister signed the register or only the witnesses did.

[46] SPC Registers of Marriages, Scots Episcopal Chapel, Castle St, 1817–47.

[47] *Dundee Directory* (1850), 35; (1853), 92.

[48] SPC 'Vestry Minute Book, St Paul's Episcopal Church, Dundee, 1852– ', 30 Mar. 1853.

[49] G. Grub, *My Years in Dundee with Bishop Forbes* (1912), 55.

himself at the population centre of his diocese, and among the crowded
tenements and slums of the poor. His previous experience at St
Thomas's, Oxford, and at Leeds, had undoubtedly convinced him that
there was nowhere else he could live and reasonably expect to pastor the
poor. His move was indicative that the poor of the city would be of
particular concern to him. In doing so Forbes set an almost unique example among Episcopalian clergy, and one that was still uncommon even in
the Church of England. It was certainly unique among bishops in either
England or Scotland and set a powerful and attractive example to Anglican clergy and laity in both countries. Forbes was the only one of the
seven Scottish bishops to live in such surroundings. The Bishop of
Glasgow, the only equivalently industrialized city in Scotland, pleaded his
wife's health for his frequent residence in Tunbridge Wells, and his successor chose to live in the more salubrious conditions of Ayr. To understand the radicalism of Forbes's choice of home it is only necessary to
consider the comment of a social historian of mid-Victorian Britain.

The slums of the cities terrified respectable mid-Victorians. Unless strongly
motivated by philanthropy, public service or the spirit of adventure, they never
went into them if they could help it. Often they had little idea what the city
slums were like inside. It was one thing, a perfectly manageable thing, to visit
the homes of the rural poor . . . Town slums were, reputedly, unsafe to visit
without a police escort.[50]

Forbes chose not only to visit the slums but to live among them,
separated later from the surrounding tenements and dark closes only by
the gentle rise of Castlehill.

The presence in Forbes's congregation of Irish and English immigrants
was a reflection of Dundee's growth. Dundee was one of the Scottish
towns most affected by the industrialization of Scotland during the
nineteenth century through its rapidly growing linen industry, and later
from the jute industry which began effective production around 1850. Not
all urban growth was as a result of industrialization, but where industrialization and urbanization went together such large towns were in the
forefront of the change towards a modern, industrialized society. For the
first half of the century this was particularly true of the spinning mills of
the textile industry. These have been described as 'the advance guard of
the factory system' and therefore as 'the birthplace of the industrial
proletariat'.[51] Although Dundee's linen industry generated significant
outwork the jute industry was a factory production from the start. By the

---

[50] Geoffrey Best, *Mid-Victorian Britain* (1971), 60.
[51] F. M. L. Thompson, *The Rise of Respectable Society* (1988), 22–3.

1850s the textile industry generally ceased to expand and was surpassed by metal-working and engineering as the leader in industrial change. But in Dundee, because of the new jute industry, industrialization continued to contribute directly to urbanization after 1850. Therefore the connection between industrialization and urbanization kept Dundee at the forefront of the emerging industrial society, which placed Forbes at the cutting-edge of the transformation of British society.

In Dundee in 1811, even with the boost of the Napoleonic wars, there had been only four spinning mills.[52] The real change came in the 1820s with the arrival of large-scale steam-powered machine spinning, which meant mills were no longer limited by accessibility to water-power nor by the amount of power a water-mill could provide. It also made economic sense to be in close proximity to markets and shipping, so mills began to be located in the town itself and to grow in size.[53] This in turn led to greater urbanization as mill-owners began to need an increased labour force, living within walking distance of the mill. By 1832 there were upwards of thirty flax-spinning mills in Dundee employing some three thousand persons.[54] The population of the town had risen accordingly, from 12,000 in 1766 to 30,000 in 1821, 45,000 in 1831,[55] and in 1841 it reached 63,000.[56]

Such extensive industrial growth and population increase produced widespread changes in the society of the city. There were very few hereditary noble families in Dundee and so the mill-owners became a sort of local aristocracy.[57] By the middle of the century these owners and the rest of the upper classes had left the city itself for the cleaner air and better sanitation of Broughty Ferry, three miles to the east. Influenced by the new industrialists, Dundee became a stronghold of the Liberal party, like much of Scotland during the nineteenth century before the rise of the Labour party. From 1832 until 1902 the city returned solely Liberals to Parliament for its two-member constituency. Liberals also predominated on the town council, the Parish Council and, later, the School Board. The city's Liberalism has been characterized as 'cautious, limited, but genuinely progressive' on social issues.[58]

While the middle classes grew to provide such services as clerks and managers for the mills and shipping, by far the biggest change in society

[52] *New Statistical Account of Scotland*, xi (1845), 26.
[53] Enid Gauldie (ed.), *The Dundee Textile Industry: 1790–1885* (1969), p. xx.
[54] *New Statistical Account*, xi. 26. [55] Ibid. 19.
[56] Sydney and Olive Checkland, *Industry and Ethos: Scotland 1832–1914* (1984), 46.
[57] *New Statistical Account*, xi. 20.
[58] W. W. Walker, *Juteopolis* (1979), 52.

was the immigration into the town of unskilled labourers and semi-skilled workers needed for the factories. In 1832 the thirty spinning mills had a working population of three thousand, of which over 50 per cent were children. These, and their adult co-workers, worked a twelve-and-a-half hour day, excluding meals, from 5.30 a.m. to 7.00 p.m. The wages of these mill workers ranged from the skilled millwrights receiving 14–18s. per week, to women on 5–8s. and children on just 3–6s.[59] The Dundee work-force was largely female and the mill girls were characteristic of the city.[60] Coarse of language and exhibitionist in behaviour the mill girl was 'instinctively committed to a rigorous hedonism', constituting an identifiable subculture on the city streets.[61] In Dundee women were commonly found occupying prestige jobs such as weaving and spinning. Weavers, men and women, were the superior echelon of an industrial caste system because their work in the factory was cleaner, more skilled, and more permanent than the spinners, next in the hierarchy. The position of women in the work-force in such large numbers was the result of the policy of the mill-owners, as they regarded women as more manageable than men. Dundee was not a city where men were the normal bread-winners among the working classes. They were often unemployed, and dependent on the wages of their women.[62]

The growth in manufacturing brought an influx of Irish. In 1840 there were 7,000 Irish in Angus, most of them in Dundee. By 1861 their numbers had doubled, boosted by the Irish Famine of the 1840s.[63] The jute industry's historian argued that the city only attracted Catholic Irish and that there was no effective Orange movement.[64] But the statistical returns of Brechin diocese for 1847 estimated that the numbers of Irish who attached themselves to the Episcopal Church in the diocese was approximately 2,000.[65] It is likely that these Irish immigrants congregated mostly in Dundee itself where there was work in the mills, rather than in the smaller towns and countryside. In an Episcopal congregation in Dundee estimated in the same return as just 1,000 members this would have been an overwhelming proportion, even if most of the Irish did not attend worship. There was widespread anti-Catholic prejudice in Dundee even to refusing the Irish poor relief to which they were legally entitled, although once again not as vociferous as that in Glasgow.[66]

The arrival of such large numbers of workers, either from other regions of Scotland or from Ireland, meant fundamental changes in social conditions in Dundee. Housing them all produced overcrowding in the central areas close to the mills.[67] The insalubrious tenements produced disease and there was a typhus outbreak in 1819, cholera outbursts in 1832 and 1833, and smallpox in 1833.[68] The poor and the manual labourers of all sexes and ages sought solace not so much in religion as in drink. In the eighteenth century drunkenness had been mainly an upper-class phenomenon because alcohol was expensive. But in 1794 cheap licences were instituted for shops selling only whisky, and after 1832 lower duties made spirits even cheaper and easier to buy.[69] One minister of the Church of Scotland in Dundee commented that 'the whisky shops are most numerous and pernicious'.[70]

All this could not fail to have some effect on the Churches in Dundee, although at this time their attitude was largely approving and complacent towards the new industrial and urban conditions. The Revd James Thomson, minister of the Cross parish of Dundee, was hardly critical of these fundamental social changes, and certainly not of the mill-owners whose paternalism he commended. Writing of Dundee's industry in the *New Statistical Account of Scotland* in 1845 he believed that: 'generally speaking, there does not appear to be any operation connected with it [linen manufacture] particularly prejudicial to health, unless it be too long hours of labour, to which some of the youth of more tender years are no doubt exposed.'[71] He then contradicted his optimism by suggesting the establishment of a fund from employees and masters for those whose livelihood was threatened by severe accident 'for not a year passes by without accidents occurring to both old and young persons employed about machinery'.[72] But aside from this implied criticism the mill-owners were commended for their concern. The blame for any misfortune and lack of morals fell mostly on the workers themselves, or on parents for sending children into the mills.[73] If this leading minister of the Established Church is a reliable guide the Churches in Dundee at the middle of the century supported the city's industrialization and the benefits of *laissez-faire* capitalism. Thomson complimented the mill-owners on their educational initiatives although the *New Statistical Account* gave the

[67] *New Statistical Account*, xi. 20.
[68] Ibid. 2.
[69] Checkland, *Industry and Ethos*, 83.
[70] *New Statistical Account*, xi. 52.
[71] Ibid. 28.   [72] Ibid. 29.   [73] Ibid.

number of mill schools as just five, teaching reading, writing, arithmetic, and 'sometimes geography' to what the *Account* estimated were about five hundred pupils.[74] Thomson concluded: 'after every drawback, however, persons visiting the mills and manufactories will see with pleasure the appearances of health and cheerfulness every where exhibited.'[75] If this was the response of one of the ministers of the Church of Scotland with his wider access and knowledge of Dundee society at all levels, then it is unlikely that the pastors of the small Episcopal chapel would have been any different.

The Church of Scotland in Dundee had begun to respond to conditions in the growing city. In 1830 it established a City Missionary Society and raised £160 for its work, employing four missionaries in daily house-to-house visiting among the poor.[76] The Episcopal Church had no such involvement. Internal matters, such as the building and financing of their chapel, took up most of the energy of the Dundee Episcopalians. Certainly their poor relief was comparatively low. In 1831 St Paul's congregation gave £30 for relief of their own poor which compares unfavourably with the £75 from the Old Baptist congregation with approximately one hundred people less in their congregation.[77]

Forbes therefore endeavoured to raise the profile of the Episcopalians in Dundee. Within two years of his arrival in Dundee Forbes's Tractarianism motivated him to propose the building of a new church to his congregation, in a sermon preached in 1849. This was probably delivered in February, as by early March William Forbes was already informing Gladstone of the project which, he said, would be cathedral-like and have schools attached to it.[78] Forbes advocated raising a 'real, consecrated church'. He was obviously unhappy with the Castle Street chapel with its furnishings indicative of the liturgy of the eighteenth century and not of the centrality of Eucharistic worship so important to the Tractarians. The chapel was upstairs from a bank and furnished in accordance with the contemporary sparse ceremony of the Episcopal Church. There were green baize-covered pews, the pulpit and the prayer desk were as prominent as the altar which was covered in red velvet all the year round, while the service was conducted by the priest in the usual black preaching gown.[79] Forbes said in his sermon that the meanness of the chapel had been appropriate to the position of the Episcopal Church

[74] Ibid. 45.   [75] Ibid. 29.
[76] Ibid. 43–4.   [77] Ibid. 43, 49.
[78] W. Forbes to W. E. Gladstone, 5 Mar. 1849, Gladstone Papers, BL 44154, fo. 369.
[79] Perry, 40.

during the previous century when it had been a scattered remnant of its former self. But since their legal toleration, Forbes asserted, there had grown up a lethargy among them. 'Is not the Church regarded as an easy religion, very creditable to belong to, the faith of the aristocracy of the country, not making any great demands upon our comforts, our purses, or our principles?' Forbes proposed to make such demands by building a new church which would be 'a standing creed', testifying to orthodox doctrine by the very form of its architecture and evidence of the sincerity of the congregation's religious convictions. As such the church would also be 'the great mart where all men meet as equals, and where the just and natural distinctions that exist outside are merged into equality before the omnipotence of God'. Forbes went on to testify to the importance he attached to Eucharistic worship and the sacraments, by describing the proposed church as an acknowledgement of 'the great doctrine of the blessed Presence of Jesus Christ within the Church . . . communicating to us His sacred manhood in the Sacraments of the new law'.[80] He finished with a caution to the congregation not to allow the financial demands of the new building to lead to neglect of present duties towards their poor.[81] The link between orthodox belief and Christian practice to be expressed in the new church was one Forbes had made even more explicitly the year before, when he preached the sermon at the consecration of St Columba's in Edinburgh.

It has pleased God, in some way to us unknown, to bind together holy living and right believing. However different the sources in the soul, whence these spring, they are nevertheless united in their consequences. They act and re-act upon each other; either tends to produce the other. Thus, an orthodox faith finds its co-relative on a high and exalted standard of practice; while lax views, with regard to what Christians believe, are in general accompanied by low notions of what they should do.[82]

A holy life and a true faith were, for Forbes, intimately connected in a 'golden bond'. While the building of a new church was an expression of right belief, that belief would invariably lead to serious and demanding Christian action. The process also worked in reverse. Holy worship would lead to holy belief and to holy lives. He evidently hoped that the congregation, rich and poor, would find within the walls of the church during worship a common identity as members of the Church. As the son of upper-class Tories Forbes accepted that in

[80] A. P. Forbes, *Haggai's Mission: A Sermon* (1849), 8–9.
[81] Ibid. 14.
[82] A. P. Forbes, *Jesus our Worship: A Sermon* (1848), 5–6.

mundane society there were right and proper differences of degree. But these, he hoped, could be set aside during worship when membership of a higher, divine society was expressed. Forbes implied that if such an ideal could be realized it would attract the surrounding poor to worship. Once they became church attenders the emotional and aesthetic impact of the worship and their surroundings would cause them to become regular, orthodox believers. It was the same connection between worship and evangelism expressed later in the more famous slum ministries of English Anglo-Catholic ritualist clergy in the 1850s.[83]

Money began to be raised after the preaching of this sermon, which was printed by the vestry to assist the cause. By March 1852 George Gilbert Scott had been commissioned as the architect and William Forbes was telling Gladstone that his brother considered Scott's designs 'most beautiful and that it will be the finest building in Scotland of modern times'.[84] Gilbert Scott at this time was becoming renowned as the greatest exponent of the gothic revival in architecture, and the decision to employ Scott was apparently Forbes's for later the same month he was being complimented on his choice.[85] The original tender for the new church was £8,500, but this proved too rich for the vestry's blood and a lesser one of £6,033 was finally accepted from Scott which involved deferring work on the tower and the interior.[86] However Forbes was asked to write to Scott for further modifications to enable the cost to be reduced to £5,000. A compromise was reached and the foundation stone was laid on 21 July 1853.[87] Funds towards the new church were also raised at the vestry meeting on February 1853 by agreeing to the sale of the existing chapel to the Princes Street Independent Congregation for £1,250.[88] There was a dispute between the two congregations later that year over the proposed position of the organ in the new church. The Congregationalists objected to the organ being put into the west-end gallery as this would enable it to be heard by them in the old chapel. An agreement that September repositioned the organ in the north transept.[89] Forbes had his aesthetic sensibilities offended by the clash between the new gothic church and the eighteenth-century church plate of the congregation. He told the vestry

[83] L. E. Ellsworth, *Charles Lowder and the Ritualist Movement* (1982).
[84] W. Forbes to W. E. Gladstone, 12 Mar. 1852, Gladstone Papers, BL 44154, fo. 393.
[85] A. B. Hope to A. P. Forbes, 14 Mar. 1852, Eeles Papers, LPL 1543, fo. 81.
[86] SPC 'Vestry Minute Book, St Paul's Episcopal Church, Dundee, 1852– ', 12 August 1852.
[87] Ibid., 27 Sept. 1852.
[88] Ibid., 30 Mar. 1853.
[89] Ibid., 14 Sept. 1853.

much of this was 'almost useless' being poorly designed, and he obtained
their agreement to recast much of it to 'obtain vessels better suited for
Divine Service'.[90] In May 1854 Forbes delightedly reported to the vestry
that he had accepted from Dr Anderson of Newburgh an old font which
had supposedly been in the medieval church there.[91]

The new church was finally ready to be opened at the end of
December 1855 by which time it had cost £11,000, exclusive of the land
itself. It was built on Castlehill, the site of the old medieval castle, so that
it towered over the city and was reportedly the highest church in
Scotland at the time.[92] Compared with the eighteenth-century liturgical
furnishing of the old chapel the new gothic church highlighted the altar.
In company with other Tractarians like Thomas Chamberlain Forbes had
striven to erect a church where the liturgical space reflected the prominence of the Eucharistic celebration. The new church was to be the place
where the Eucharistic presence of Christ was communicated to the
congregation, and where all were equal in the sight of God, if not in the
eyes of each other. It was a physical expression of Pusey's ideal of parishes as Eucharistic communities which could reach out to embrace the
urban poor. It was an ideal realized not just in the new building, but also
in the more frequent celebrations of Holy Communion Forbes instituted.

In preparation for the opening service Forbes wrote to Walter Kerr
Hamilton, the Bishop of Salisbury, to invite him to be the preacher.
Hamilton was the second Tractarian bishop to be consecrated, and the
first in the Church of England. Forbes felt the presence of a bishop of the
Church of England would assist in overcoming Episcopal divisions. He
explained: 'there is a class of persons who neglect to hear the Church in
this country on the plea of our not being identical with the Church of
England.'[93] This description suggests that it was those who separated
themselves into so-called chapels of the 'Church of England in Scotland'
that he hoped to encourage into the Episcopal Church. If a bishop of the
Church of England were present at the opening of the new church and
thereby testified to his recognition of the Episcopal Church, Forbes hoped
these Evangelicals would realize the futility of their objection to the
Episcopal Church. But Hamilton was evidently unable to come and
instead Bishop Robert Eden of Moray was the preacher for the service on
13 December 1855.

90 Ibid., 5 Sept. 1853.
91 Ibid., 3 May 1854.
92 *SEJ* (Jan. 1856), 19.
93 A. P. Forbes to W. K. Hamilton, 7 Aug. 1855, PH Hamilton correspondence 6. 59. 1.

The cost of the building, and the consequent indebtedness of the congregation, necessitated the continuance of pew-rents in the new church. There is no evidence of how Forbes felt about this but it is probable he agreed with Pusey that pew-rents were undesirable as a barrier to church attendance by the poor. Nevertheless Forbes acknowledged that the fabric was the responsibility of the vestry and so rents were set between five to forty-two shillings a year.[94] It is difficult to see how else the vestry could have met the cost incurred as there were no endowments or other sources of income save that of the giving of the congregation.

Forbes's concern for the poor was also emphasized by his pastoral visiting. Living where he did meant he became a familiar figure in the area and therefore he was unlike the usual middle- or upper-class philanthropist who visited the poor, but lived elsewhere in more congenial surroundings. No doubt this made Forbes's ministry more authentic to the labouring poor. While he visited every member of the congregation his greatest task was visiting the masses of unchurched poor in the city's tenements. His cousin, Frances Skene, believed he became popular with the city's poor through his practice of visiting patients in the infirmary regardless of their denomination, and the records of admissions to the Royal Infirmary give some idea of the scope of Forbes's contact with the poor.[95] For the first ten years of his ministry Forbes, or one of the other clergy at St Paul's, made 188 recommendations of admission, some of whom were readmissions. Of these 114 patients were born in Ireland, fifty-nine in Scotland, ten in England, and six were born elsewhere or their place of birth was not recorded. Most lived around the centre of the city but a number came from outlying Lochee. Predominantly the patients were weavers or millworkers but there were significant numbers of winders and domestic servants. Other workers included washerwomen, factory workers, labourers, shoemakers, loom workers; also a watchmaker, schoolmistress, cutler, tailor, turner, housewife, seaman, and a sailmaker. There were also nine children. Of the total referrals ninety-eight were women, most of whom were employed.[96] These numbers represent only those ill enough to be hospitalized, but they indicate that Forbes and the St Paul's clergy had extensive connection with the labouring poor. If this contact derived from their pastoral visiting and was not initiated by the poor themselves, as seems likely, then the clergy's work took them all

[94] SPC 'Vestry Minute Book, St Paul's Episcopal Church, Dundee, 1852– ', 8 Nov. 1855.

[95] F. M. C. Skene, *A Memoir of Alexander, Bishop of Brechin* (1876), 14.

[96] Dundee Royal Infirmary Registers, 1848–1857, DUL THB 1. 4. 1–2.

over the city. The high proportion of Irish among those referred by the
Episcopal clergy suggests that Forbes and his clergy in Dundee were in
the habit of visiting the poor and working classes irrespective of their
denomination. Certainly some of the Irish would have belonged to the
Church of Ireland; but many of those referred were among the poorest,
unskilled workers among whom the Church of Ireland had little support.
It is likely therefore that a number of the Irish referred to the infirmary
were Roman Catholics. Such contact contrasts with the anti-Irish feeling
and Catholic prejudice common at the time. But his visiting down filthy
streets and in unsavoury tenements cannot have come easily to Forbes
who read Dante with Gladstone, whose sensibilities were heightened by
gothic architecture, and whose health was always delicate. For those who
knew him this substantial personal involvement with the labouring poor
made Forbes's example all the more powerful. His sister Elizabeth,
undoubtedly in admiration of her older brother, testified to the impact
his life in Dundee made on her. Writing of her visits to Dundee she said:

When I used to be there after a day of district visiting in the slums of Dundee
his great refreshment was a Canto of Dante—which we read together. He was
an excellent linguist both ancient & modern & he had the greatest pleasure in
Antiquarian lore & with it all surprised us by keeping up so much with the
literature of the present day. What I admire so much in his character was the
self-sacrifice, for his love of refinement & beauty . . . would never have fixed
upon the money making town of Dundee for a home.[97]

In October 1855 Forbes's close friend and frequent holiday companion, John Mason Neale, paid a brief visit to Dundee. Neale was the
Anglo-Catholic warden of Sackville College, East Grinstead, and a
leading liturgical authority. His account of the visit is chiefly interesting
for its detail about Forbes's daily work. After Sunday services Forbes
took Neale with him to the St Paul's school while he spoke to a class of
mill girls. Then Forbes went to speak with a condemned murderer in
gaol, returning for choral Evensong. Neale remembered the church as
'*crammed* with poor' for this service. Afterwards there was an evening
class for schoolmistresses. Forbes finally collapsed on the sofa after tea at
the clergyhouse. The next morning, after school again, they went around
the hospital wards. 'The ministers of the Establishment never go near,'
claimed Neale, 'the Roman priests are only allowed to visit their own
people, so that the whole comes back on the Bishop.' When their
infirmary rounds were over Forbes took Neale to show him one of the

[97] E. Forbes to W. Skene, 5 Nov. [?1875], SAUL 19. 5. 152.

model lodging houses for mill girls 'of which the Bishop seemed very proud' remarked Neale.[98]

However, despite these pastoral labours among the city's poor they do not appear to have translated their respect for Forbes into sustained church attendance throughout his ministry. By the 1870s one of his curates, George Grub, remembered that the congregation consisted chiefly of wealthy families from the outer areas of Dundee and that it was the 'better class of Church folk throughout the town' who mostly made up the worshipping congregation.[99] Perhaps Forbes's sermons were partly to blame as he tended to make these more learned than was the wont of the labouring poor because of his concern for doctrine. His younger brother, George, teased him about his frequent quotes from Aquinas.[100] In 1857 Forbes confessed his bewilderment to George about the weak hold the teaching of his Church had on his people. He felt 'the native Scotch mind looks upon us as a sort of illogical popery'; and he was unhappy at the increase in the congregation due to mixed marriages which seemed to him to be growth through marriage and not necessarily conviction.[101]

Like his father and grandfather before him Forbes became actively involved in the civic affairs of the city he lived in and did not confine himself to strictly congregational concerns. Forbes's involvement with the infirmary was not limited to referring the poor. He was periodically appointed as the infirmary's official house visitor and served on its weekly committee. St Paul's also supported the infirmary with annual donations and in 1851 Forbes was appointed a life governor.[102] As well as the Royal Infirmary, in April 1848 he was present at a meeting in the town hall for those interested in the establishment of model lodging houses for the labouring poor. The meeting resolved that existing conditions for the accommodation of the labouring poor were wretched, crowding together men, women, and children in ways injurious to their health and exposing the respectable among them 'to many risks and temptations'. Therefore a subscription would be raised to support lodging houses which would be comfortable, economical, run by 'strict superintendence' so as to exclude 'disorderly persons', and be models for the common lodging houses. It was thought that the labouring poor who were 'industrious and respectable' would use such model lodgings in preference to existing unsanitary accommodation, and this would force inadequate lodging houses to

[98] *Letters of John Mason Neale D. D. Selected and Edited by his Daughter* (1910), 256–8.
[99] G. Grub, *My Years in Dundee with Bishop Forbes of Brechin 1871–1875* (1912), 12.
[100] G. H. Forbes to A. P. Forbes, 18 Oct. 1862, BrMS 1. 3. 667.
[101] A. P. Forbes to G. H. Forbes, 20 Aug. 1857, SAUL 19. 2. 157.
[102] *Reports of the Dundee Royal Infirmary*, 1849–1876, DUL THB 1. 1. 3–5.

improve their physical and moral conditions.[103] It was as much the danger to the moral life of the respectable, deserving poor as the threat to their physical health that the meeting had in mind. By 1850 two model lodging houses were established, one each for men and women. A second house for women was added in the mid-1850s but only lasted a few years. Forbes served on the committee of management of the Model Lodging House Association from 1856 until the end of the 1860s.[104]

Another major social project of the early years of Forbes's episcopate was the establishment of the Baldoven Institute. This was a mental asylum for children built on the estate of Sir John Ogilvie and modelled on the work of Dr Guggenbühl of Interlaken. Ogilvie was the senior Liberal member of Parliament for Dundee and a member of St Paul's congregation. Forbes had been associated with his wife, Lady Jane Ogilvie, in the foundation in 1848 of a rescue home for prostitutes in the city known as the Home. In December 1855 the Ogilvies called a meeting at Baldoven of those interested in the asylum. Work had already begun on the building and they desired to make it known publicly and to decide on its future management. As well as the Ogilvies, the meeting included Forbes and five others. These formed themselves into a committee of management to which were added four others, including Professor Alison of Edinburgh and Thomas Erskine of Linlathen. An appeal for funds was launched and a board of directors formed, of which Forbes was a permanent *ex officio* member by virtue of the feu disposition of Sir John Ogilvie. In addition to the mentally disturbed children the institution also included provision for orphans and other destitute children of the Episcopal Church, who were housed in the same building but under different care. 'The advantage of having such children to be companions for the imbecile children during their play hours, when they have advanced to a certain stage of cure, need hardly be pointed out,' claimed the prospectus.[105] The Institute opened in January 1854 and by March had seven patients.[106] Forbes was very much involved with it, and subscribed annually. He searched out suitable house-keepers, prepared the directors' reports, frequently chaired their meetings when Sir John Ogilvy was absent, and was annually elected one of their Visiting Committee.

It is difficult to ascertain to what extent these projects originated with Forbes. Whether or not he was the author of these schemes it is

103 *Dundee Lodging House Association* (1848), DCL 308 (19).
104 *Dundee Directory* (1850–75).
105 Baldoven Minute Books, 1853, DUL THB 8. 3. 1., 11–12.
106 Ibid. (1854), 14.

certain his civic involvement was enhanced by the support of the influential Liberal establishment of the city, as represented particularly by Lord Kinnaird and Sir John Ogilvie, both Episcopalians. George William Fox, ninth Baron Kinnaird, was an agricultural reformer and a philanthropist. He established schools, reading rooms, and libraries on his estates and assisted in the foundation of industrial schools throughout the county. A Liberal peer and a free-trader he was a friend of David Ricardo and also of the Radicals Richard Cobden and John Bright.[107] His younger brother, Arthur Kinnaird, was the Liberal MP for Perth and a fervent Evangelical. Both men were on the board of the Royal Infirmary and Forbes probably owed his early appointment as a life governor to their influence. These important figures must have been extremely helpful in attracting support for the various philanthropic projects the bishop was concerned with. Forbes was a close friend of both families, but his influence may well have owed most to their wives. Lady Ogilvie's philanthropy has already been mentioned. Lady Frances Kinnaird was a supporter of some of the more Tractarian projects of Forbes, such as the sisterhood he founded in 1871. She also had the billiard room at Rossie Park converted into a chapel along Anglo-Catholic lines, complete with a stone altar.[108]

Forbes's involvement with the social needs of Dundee was underpinned by his concern for social cohesion. This can be illustrated from a sermon he published in 1853 called the *Duties of Society*. He emphasized the basic bonds of human society as the brotherhood of all mankind by virtue of their being children of God, having a common creation. More importantly, the unity of all humanity in society was to be found in Christ who, as the incarnate Word, united to himself all human nature.[109] While the mission of the Church was not, for Forbes, primarily a civilizing one, such an effect was an important consequence of the preaching of the gospel.[110] The natural weakness of mankind meant a necessary mutual dependence but, he asserted, there had been a perversion of this 'holy principle' in the egalitarian principles of the French Revolution which went beyond Christianity. However, the French Revolution did bear witness to one great principle in that it 'asserted in the most open terms, that every man has claims upon his fellow,—that mutual support, and comfort, and sustentation is a right of existence,—that each one is

[107] *DNB* (1892), xxxi. 191–2.
[108] Grub, *My Years in Dundee*, 58–62.
[109] A. P. Forbes, *The Duties of Society* (1853), 7–8.
[110] Ibid. 10–11.

his brother's keeper'.[111] Claims to a levelling of social differences did not meet with Forbes's approval, clashing as they did with his Tory upbringing and also with his Tractarian sense of hierarchy. However he did strongly object to those philosophies, such as political economy, which denied or curtailed the sense of philanthropy by the well-off towards the disadvantaged. Socially, Forbes retained the Tory paternalist outlook of his father. Like most of his contemporaries Lord Medwyn was influenced by political economy, and he advocated savings banks as a means of reducing dependence on the poor rates.[112] But even more fundamentally he was a representative of the old eighteenth-century 'moral economy'[113] where poverty was regarded as a natural condition, which the wealthy in a Christian polity had an obligation to relieve because the poor were equally members of society. Alexander Forbes shared these views in which wealth and social position were part of the natural order of things, but believed these privileges brought with them an obligation towards the poor. Almsgiving was the 'duty and end' of the rich and without it riches would lead to damnation.[114] Christian society was interconnected by bonds of dependence and moral obligation, and its members therefore should appreciate their common unity as creatures of God and as members of the Church. His membership of the Model Lodging House Association was an indication that Forbes, like the prevailing political economy, was concerned for the deserving poor. But his readiness to visit the impoverished poor in Dundee and to refer them to the infirmary is evidence of his willingness to relieve the non-deserving as well. Nowhere was Forbes's distance from the principles of political economy, with its disdain for the non-deserving poor, demonstrated more clearly than in his practice of the indiscriminate giving of alms. Beggars were wont to gather around the front door of St Paul's in the confident expectation of money from the bishop when he emerged after morning prayer. When one of the clergy remonstrated with Forbes's almsgiving on the grounds that the beggar was a 'humbug', Forbes merely replied, 'If I were as poor as he is, I should be a humbug too.'[115]

---

[111] Ibid. 13.

[112] J. H. Forbes, *A Short Account of the Edinburgh Savings Bank* (1815); *Observations on Banks for Savings* (1817).

[113] The phrase is used by Gertrude Himmelfarb in *The Idea of Poverty* (1984) and derives from E. P. Thompson's, 'The Moral Economy of the English Crowd in the Eighteenth Century', *Past and Present* (1971).

[114] A. P. Forbes, *Suffering* (1853), 113.

[115] T. Ball, 'Recollections of Bishop Forbes and of Dundee Two and Thirty Years ago', in *Scottish Standard Bearer*, 9 (1898), 116–17.

Coming from a Tory family Forbes was a steady supporter of Gladstone, at this time still a Peelite Conservative, in his Oxford University constituency. In 1853 he made a trip to Oxford from Aberdeen specially to vote for Gladstone.[116] But Dundee was a Liberal city and Forbes's ability to get on with the leading figures of the Liberal establishment was partly testimony to his personal charm, which was often remarked upon by those who met him. But it must have been congenial to Forbes that some of the Dundee élite were aristocrats, for he had a Tory attachment to the importance of aristocracy in a civilized society.[117] Forbes was also mindful of the rising middle classes, considering that since the 1830s they had incited the upper classes to become more public-minded. Such increased regard for 'the duties of their station' had caused the aristocracy to rise in public estimation, Forbes believed.[118]

Forbes was never very radical in his social criticism, except when he thought the rich were deserting the social obligations their privilege entailed. When this occurred Forbes could express the anger of a paternalistic Tory Christian at the desertion of the moral economy. Then Forbes could be very scathing indeed towards the wealthy, as he had no illusions about the combination of wealth and spiritual zeal, nor about Victorian respectability.

The rich are even more apt to neglect Him [Christ] than the poor, though they may not violate the outward decencies, and may think some profession of religion to be necessary to their station. You know what the SAVIOUR has said about the danger of riches. It is easier to be damned in a drawing-room than in the flats of a factory. There is more peril to the soul in the refinements of polite society, than in the heated atmosphere of the crowded workshop, or in the coarse relaxations of the village green.[119]

Forbes shared the familiar Tory paternalist outlook of many of his contemporaries among the bishops. Two things, however, distinguished Forbes from both the English and Scottish bishops. First was his Tractarianism. Secondly, there was his first-hand involvement with the labouring poor. Both of these mitigated his sense of satisfaction in the present hierarchical order of society. His Tractarianism taught him that the Church was a divine society not always in agreement with the surrounding secular society. As Forbes mentioned to his congregation when building the new St Paul's, there was an equality of membership within

[116] W. Forbes to W. E. Gladstone, 12 Jan. 1853, Gladstone Papers, BL 44154, fo. 417.
[117] A. P. Forbes, *A Commentary on the Litany* (1855), 109–10.
[118] Ibid. 120.
[119] A. P. Forbes, *Sermons on the Grace of God* (1862), 227.

the Church. This understanding of ecclesiastical society was at variance with the values of secular society expressed in pew-rents. Forbes's involvement with the poor also helped him realize that the undeserving poor could not be ignored. It taught him that assistance towards the poor could not simply be on the level of private charity but needed a more organized approach. His involvement with such organized help was aimed at alleviation rather than change, but this level of aid was perhaps the most common and immediate reaction engendered in mid-Victorian Britain by the plight of the poor.

Forbes's acceptance of hierarchy in society was mirrored in his belief in hierarchy within the Church. Ecclesiastical society had its own hierarchy in which the clergy predominated over the laity, and the clergy themselves were ranked from the bishop downwards. Forbes was not expressing anything new in this belief; it was a commonplace among Episcopalians as demonstrated by the anxiety of the northern bishops over the possibility of lay representation in synods earlier in the century. To Forbes, as to most Episcopal clergy, the crucial difference between clergy and laity lay in the authority over spiritual matters given to the clergy by virtue of their ordination. Forbes's exaltation of ordained authority was revealed in a clash with the vestry of St Paul's in 1853. The congregation had been experiencing difficulty over the repeated absence of the joint incumbent Torry Anderson. Anderson had been one of the supporters of the other candidate at the episcopal election in 1847 and Forbes evidently found him difficult to work with for he used to refer to Anderson as his 'moral hairshirt'.[120] Eventually, in October 1853, the vestry passed a minute expressing 'pain' at Anderson's continual long absences and also at his residence outside Dundee. They agreed this was inconsistent with someone who had no duties other than to the Dundee congregation. The whole matter had been brought to a head by the absence of both Forbes and Anderson the previous Sunday so that there had been no morning service.[121] A copy of the vestry minute was sent to both incumbents. This prompted such a reply from Forbes that it moved a meeting of lay members of vestry in January 1854 to pass a motion expressing regret 'that any act of theirs could bear the construction of being an interference on their part towards government in Spiritual things'.[122] Forbes's attitude to the division between the work of the laity and the

[120] G. H. Forbes to A. P. Forbes, 3 Aug. 1859, BrMs 1. 1. 178.
[121] SPC 'Vestry Minute Book, St Paul's Episcopal Church, Dundee, 1852– ', 7 Oct. 1853.
[122] Ibid., 19 Jan. 1854.

authority of the clergy is made even clearer in a letter he wrote to the
vestry in October of the same year, regarding the bishops' decision for a
national collection to raise money for the education fund. Forbes sought
the vestry's approval for the collection to be taken up in St Paul's. He
did so, he explained, because 'I am always most scrupulous in recognizing
an office of the Vestry in that which pertains to them, viz in regulating
the temporalities of the Congregation'.[123] In Forbes's theological understanding the laity could not trespass into the area of spiritual authority
which pertained solely to the clergy. The laity had a role in temporal
matters of building, finance, and the like, but it was ordination which
gave authority over doctrinal and other spiritual matters. For Forbes this
also meant the laity could not challenge the clergy except in mundane
matters. His attitude to the respective roles of the clergy and laity was
one area where Forbes's Tractarianism reinforced the tradition of the
Episcopal Church. But his view of the role of the laity in the Church
came under increasing pressure as more Episcopalians became supporters
of greater lay involvement in the affairs of the Church.

Forbes already had cause to oppose William Gladstone on the issue of
lay representation in synods. By 1850 Gladstone had relinquished his
former hopes for the Church of England and settled for it being given
sufficient freedom from parliamentary control to pursue untrammelled its
mission of converting the nation. He also looked to the non-established
Episcopal Church as being freer than the Church of England to give a
Catholic lead to Anglicans. But he thought it would be a stronger
Church, with greater support, and a better defence against Erastianism, if
it included the laity in its counsels.[124] In his *On the Functions of Laymen
in the Church* published in 1852, Gladstone proposed that a third chamber of laity be added to the General Synod consisting of communicant
laymen, but with the initiation of all legislation remaining in the hands of
the bishops. Bishop Forbes got wind of this proposal before it was
published and in January expressed his fears about it to Gladstone. 'I
confess', he wrote, 'I dread it much in a body where there is so little dogmatic faith—and tho' I should have less difficulty about the apportioning
of monies, or even the judicial trial of scandals etc, yet I see much risk in
the attempt.'[125] Forbes's anxiety was for doctrine, fearing the effects of
an untheologically educated laity voting on questions of dogma. Forbes
also was not prepared to have the laity trespass into what he regarded as

[123] Ibid., A. P. Forbes to Thomas Nicolson, 3 Oct. 1854.
[124] Richard Shannon, *Gladstone 1809–1865* (1982), 221.
[125] A. P. Forbes to W. E. Gladstone, 8 Jan. 1852, Gladstone Papers, BL 44154, fo. 204.

the spiritual prerogatives of the clergy. This attitude owed much to the sacerdotalism of the Oxford Movement but, in Forbes's case, it was motivated more by a concern for the maintenance of dogmatic truth than by a sense of clerical privilege. Forbes told Gladstone he was prepared to countenance the laity judging the clergy in non-spiritual matters such as conduct and finance. But this contrasts with his rebuke of the vestry of St Paul's the following year when they drew attention to Torry Anderson's absence from the congregation. This was surely the sort of area for lay involvement Forbes was theoretically conceding to Gladstone, but in practice he was not willing for his vestry to exercise a similar responsibility. It suggests that Forbes was not really comfortable even with the degree of lay involvement he surrendered to Gladstone, but was only reluctantly willing to compromise with those over whom he had no control, as long as it did not endanger the clerical monopoly over doctrine.

William Forbes told Gladstone that his brother was 'very strong' on this matter.[126] So emphatic did Forbes feel about this issue that he wrote a pamphlet on Gladstone's proposal in the form of an open letter to the primus, William Skinner of Aberdeen. It was published under the pseudonym of 'Cantus', and demonstrates Forbes's skills as a controversialist.[127] He criticized Gladstone's proposal as motivated by expediency and proposed a more principled answer. The crux of this answer was that spiritual authority was invested in the principle of hierarchy and was incompatible with democratic government. Spiritual authority, he argued, was personal, deriving from the person of Christ. Even the present government of the Episcopal Church realized this personal spiritual authority only imperfectly, because its hierarchy lacked an archbishop. Although as a Tractarian he was less than enamoured with the Reformation, he was not above suggesting Gladstone's proposal intimated that the English Reformation had been deficient with regard to lay representation and episcopal government. If the synods of the Church were opened up to the laity it would be only those with the necessary means who could attend. This, according to Forbes, would leave the Church at the mercy of the better-off, an undesirable repetition of the situation of the sixteenth century when the Church of Scotland was controlled by nobility, the so-called Lords of the Congregation. Forbes was attempting to create a fear of lay involvement leading to lay control and so to the end of episcopacy. Further, Forbes claimed that Gladstone's proposal

---

[126] W. Forbes to E. B. Pusey, 8 Oct. 1852, Gladstone Papers, BL 44154, fo. 401.
[127] Mackey, 224.

would undermine the legitimacy of the Scottish Episcopal Church which
he saw as rooted in the practices of the early Church, an early Church
which, he argued, had no such lay involvement.[128] The controversial
aspects aside, the pamphlet illustrated that Forbes considered the
Anglican Church had its own *magisterium*. This teaching authority was
given only to the clergy by virtue of the authority imparted to them by
their ordination and safeguarded by their theological training. Like most
Tractarians, Forbes divided the Church into the discerning and instruct-
ing clergy (*ecclesia discens*), and the passive receiving laity (*ecclesia docens*),
but he believed lay assent to the doctrine taught was a necessary and vital
component of the assurance of its truth.

In August 1852 Forbes ensured that his own diocese opposed
Gladstone's plan by using his casting vote to pass a motion against any
alteration in the present constitution of the Church.[129] Only Aberdeen was
also opposed to the proposed change, although other dioceses wanted it
referred to a General Synod. The bishops, however, did not see fit to call
one and the issue lapsed for the present. Forbes's brother, William,
remained convinced that economic stringency would force the Church to
look for wider lay support. 'We have too long been looking to the £10 of
Dukes' & Earls'', he wrote, '& this plank has notably failed & we feel that
the earnest middle class is the body to whom the temporal affairs of the
Communion is to be entrusted.'[130]

As a diocesan bishop Forbes was not always an upholder of the status
quo but encouraged his diocese to meet other contemporary challenges.
When he became Bishop of Brechin his diocese consisted of eleven
charges totalling 3,069 members, with church sittings for nearly 3,000.
The largest of these was St Paul's, while the new church at Fasque was
the smallest with only 55 members. The numbers of those attending
Holy Communion each year were even less. In 1847 there were just 1,710
for the diocese overall.[131] With the increasing population one of his priorities as bishop was supporting church extension, and his first involvement
in this area was the consecration of a new church at Catterline in 1849.[132]
By 1851 Forbes had initiated and licensed a new mission in Dundee out
of his own congregation, which later became St Mary Magdalene's,

[128] Cantus [A. P. Forbes], *A Letter to the Right Reverend Father in God, William Skinner,
D. D., Bishop of Aberdeen, and Primus of the Church in Scotland, on the Subject of the Rt.
Hon. W. E. Gladstone's Proposal to Admit the Laity into the Synods of that Church* (1852).
[129] Brechin Synod Minutes, 4 Aug. 1852, BrMs 4. 1. 3., 28.
[130] W. Forbes to W. E. Gladstone, 23 Feb. 1857, Gladstone Papers, BL 44154, fo. 436.
[131] Statistical returns 1847, Brechin Diocese Synod Minutes, BrMs 4. 1. 2, 193.
[132] Brechin Diocese Synod Minutes, 1 Aug. 1849, BrMs 4. 1. 3, 1–2.

Blunshall Street, with a new church built in 1854.[133] Along with church extension went the establishment of church schools. These were opened at a faster rate than new churches as most existing congregations lacked their own school. By March 1854 Forbes had ensured there were four Episcopal schools in Dundee and seventeen day schools throughout the diocese.[134] The following month another was opened at Lochee, a large manufacturing area on the south-western edge of Dundee where Forbes had established another mission congregation.[135] The Dundee schools included two at St Paul's, one attached to St Mary Magdalene's, and one at Bonnet Hill, as well as that at Lochee.[136] By 1851 the diocese had appointed three clergy as its school inspectors.[137] In 1855 Forbes opened an Episcopalian training centre for schoolmistresses in Dundee.[138]

Another of Forbes's diocesan projects was the foundation of an agricultural college. In 1851 he wrote to Arthur Gordon of Aberdeenshire, a potential benefactor, about his hopes to establish such a college in the diocese or at Aberdeen. Forbes planned to bring in boys from two or three neighbouring congregations, or even from further afield. The bishop was obviously thinking of the state of Episcopal poor in agricultural areas for he went on to explain, 'their habits are little better than those of the presbyterians & when they go out to service & encounter the ridicule which their profession exposes them to, they too often fall away from all religion.' Forbes was concerned not only with the piety of Episcopalian agricultural labourers, but also that their poverty and poor social standing led them to shun church-going and to become detached from Christian faith. What Forbes wanted was to 'found an institution which shall combine practical instruction in agriculture with a sound education in Christian principles'.[139] The college was eventually opened at Drumlithie in November 1853 on two sites under the care of Robert Thom, the local priest. The part known as the Home was a house in the village near the church and parsonage. Here the younger boys did light work on the farm or in the garden during summer. They were also taught reading, writing, arithmetic, grammar, geography, history, and the basics of farming and gardening. At another site on ten acres of land, known as the Temple, the older boys farmed eight acres and practised gardening on the other two. All boys went to daily service and received moral instruction. Boys were charged between £6 and £10 a year depending on their ages. In

---

[133] Ibid. 22.   [134] *SEJ* (Mar. 1854), 71.   [135] Ibid. 95.
[136] Brechin Diocese Synod Minutes, BrMs 4. 1. 3, 24, 35.
[137] Ibid. 23.   [138] Perry, 74.
[139] A. P. Forbes to A. Gordon, 28 Oct. 1851, Aberdeen Papers, BL 43247, fo. 231.

reporting the opening of the college (so-called from its communal nature) the *Scottish Ecclesiastical Journal* reported that the establishment was undersubscribed by £300 and only two boys came from homes that could afford the fees. At that time there were eight boys enrolled, aged 10 to 17.[140]

For all his social concern undoubtedly the pet project of Forbes in his first years as bishop was the Diocesan Library. The library had opened in 1792, following a motion for its establishment at the diocesan synod of that year. The clergy were to pay two shillings and sixpence a year for its upkeep, and it was originally housed in the home of the priest at Laurencekirk until a dedicated room was built in the chapel there in 1819.[141] By 1847 the library had received some valuable accessions, including seven hundred volumes from William Abernethy Drummond, Bishop of Edinburgh, at the turn of the century.[142] In 1821 another collection was begun at Brechin, as part of the Diocesan Library, following a bequest of six hundred volumes.[143] By the time Forbes became bishop the library was described by its historian as 'in a very flourishing and active condition . . . which says a good deal . . . for the quality and intellectual calibre of the Episcopalian clergy at this time'.[144] Forbes had borrowed from the library during his appointment at Stonehaven and he was keen to see it continue to grow. In 1849 he gave the library the works of William Maskell, the High Church antiquarian, and those of Alexander Knox, the precursor of Tractarian theology who died in 1831.[145] Forbes desired that the two collections of the library should come together under one roof, in a library financed by himself to be built at Brechin. This scheme eventually went ahead and work was finished in 1854. The completed buildings, which still stand, included a combined library and chapter house for the meeting of the Diocesan Synod, a church school, and a school house costing Forbes £500.[146] The following year the synod met for the first time in the new building. When the dean reminded them that they were 'solely indebted to the Bishop's generosity' grateful thanks were unanimously passed.[147] The library's historian suggests Forbes, by building the library at Brechin and by holding his diocesan synods there, was demonstrating his attachment to the medieval

[140] *SEJ* (Mar. 1854), 63–4.
[141] 'The Brechin Diocesan Library: Its History and Collections'. Talk given on the Brechin Diocesan Library by John Barker, Librarian of the University of Dundee, to the Abertay Historical Society in January 1988. BrMs 4. 2. 14 (8), 1–3.
[142] Ibid. 4. [143] Ibid. 7. [144] Ibid. 8.
[145] Brechin Diocese Synod Minutes, 1 Aug. 1849, BrMs 4. 1. 3, 1–2.
[146] Ibid. 2 Aug. 1854, 35–6. [147] Ibid. 1 Aug. 1855, 41.

centre of the diocese from which it derived its name, and perhaps intended Brechin to become its intellectual centre. By the end of the century the library was recognized by the Stationery Office as an important national collection of scholarly material when it donated one of its surplus sets of state papers to it, in company with other major research libraries throughout the country.[148] Forbes maintained his generous support of the library by a further donation of £100 in 1857, the interest of which was to be used in paying its running expenses. He also gave to its collection that year the works of Gaudentius, Gregory the Great, and Anselm.[149] Other accessions recorded in the diocesan minutes included works of Robert Wilberforce, William Palmer of Worcester College, Thomas Aquinas, an edition of the Scots Prayer Book, and various histories of the Scottish Church. Forbes did not donate all these works, but as a scholarly bishop library accessions would surely have had to meet with his approval. He was evidently concerned that his clergy be well read, particularly in patristic and scholastic theology, contemporary Anglican theology in the Catholic tradition, and in the history of the Church in Scotland.

As Bishop of Brechin Forbes was one of the most powerful individuals in the Episcopal Church. In addition to his congregational and civic duties his work also involved him in the almost unfettered governing of the Church in association with the other six bishops. Since the securing of episcopal control during the eighteenth century the Episcopal Synod continued firmly to resist any perceived threat to its authority from within or without the Church. Forbes upheld episcopal authority because he believed the bishops of the Episcopal Church to be the successors of the medieval Catholic hierarchy. Therefore in 1850 he protested against the possible reintroduction into Scotland of a Roman Catholic diocesan hierarchy. He claimed, upon the principle of the catholicity of the Episcopal Church, that it was contrary to the order of the Church for a second Catholic hierarchy to be superimposed upon an already existing one and that 'all bishops, whether of great or small sees, are of one order and rank'.[150] This understanding of episcopacy expressed by Forbes—of the equality of all bishops regardless of their see—was a central point of the Scottish nonjuring theology of the episcopate developed under Bishop Rattray. Unfortunately, given this threat to Forbes's fervent belief in the Episcopalian claim to be the Catholic herarchy of Scotland, nothing exists about the possible restoration of Roman dioceses among his personal

[148] Ibid. 17.   [149] Ibid. 50.
[150] Grub, *Ecclesiastical History*, iv. 272.

correspondence. In the event, the Roman Catholic hierarchy in Scotland was not restored until 1878.

The same year brought a further opportunity for Forbes, as a member of the Episcopal Synod, to uphold the episcopate according to the nonjuring tradition. In April the synod heard the appeal of Charles Wagstaffe, incumbent of St Andrew's, Aberdeen, against the sentence of Bishop William Skinner. Wagstaffe had been ordered by Skinner to desist from making changes in the liturgy, including the addition of an anthem. The priest continued his liturgical deviations and had consequently been tried by Skinner before his diocesan synod. Contrary to the opinion of the majority of the synod Skinner had found Wagstaffe guilty of disobedience. The Episcopal Synod upheld Wagstaffe's appeal, although it censured him for his lack of 'filial respect' towards Skinner and found that he had erred in supposing that his own discretionary power over the conducting of services enabled him to ignore his bishop's directions. Wagstaffe was also told to avoid being a stumbling block to the weaker members of his congregation.[151] The exact details of Wagstaffe's alterations in the liturgy are not given in the Episcopal Synod's records, but his inclusion of an anthem suggests that they were mild forms of ritualism. If this is correct then the case represents one of the first occasions in Scotland when ritualism was pursued in defiance of the wishes of the diocesan bishop. This was exactly the sort of tension Forbes had encountered during his brief time at St Saviour's, Leeds. However, unlike the Church of England, the authority of the Scottish bishops was sufficient to exercise real control over troublesome clergy.

The bishops understood that this case had focused particularly on the jurisdiction of the bishop, so they appended a lengthy Note to the minutes of the appeal to further clarify their position. In it they asserted that the authority of the diocesan bishop over his clergy consisted in 'enforcing the observance of Canons & Rubrics, but also in superintending, and, if need be, controlling their conduct in such ecclesiastical matters as Canons & Rubrics have either not touched at all, or have touched upon imperfectly'. The bishops recognized that their own power was regulated by the canon law passed by General Synod. However, they claimed that the diocesan bishop was the initial interpreter of the canons and that further appeal could only be made to the episcopal college. With regard to a bishop delivering sentence against the wishes of the majority of his synod the bishops declared the jurisdiction lay with the bishop and that

[151] REC II, 17–19 Apr. 1850, SRO CH 12. 60. 3, 194.

the clergy were present only to give their opinion and advice. The bishops concluded their Note with a vote of thanks to the Anglo-Catholic lawyer, James Hope, whose opinion had been sought at Forbes's suggestion.[152] But unrest among the clergy at the monarchical power of the bishops was evidently growing. Forbes had previously written about the Wagstaffe case to his colleague, Bishop Torry of St Andrews, explaining that it would not do for the bishops to settle it upon their 'preconceived notions' for, 'when I was last in the north I found a profound jealousy existing with respect to the justice of our awards'.[153] This was probably the reason for Forbes suggesting the outside opinion of Hope, although Hope's own Tractarian theology and personal inclinations (he became a Roman Catholic in 1851) would also have led him to exalt the bishop's office. Forbes sided with the bishops against the mild ritualism of Wagstaffe partly because the priest had upset the 'weaker' members of his congregation and, perhaps more importantly, because Wagstaffe had flouted episcopal authority.

Caution on matters of liturgy and ritual was characteristic of Forbes's ministry throughout his time as bishop and pastor of St Paul's. By 1871 the Sunday services during the morning featured Holy Communion at 8.00, and at 11.00 Matins, Litany, and sermon, while once a month there was a choral celebration of Holy Communion. At 3.00 in the afternoon there was a choral Evensong with a sermon and catechizing, and during the winter a full choral Evensong and sermon. Matins and Evensong were said daily and there was a celebration of Holy Communion on Thursday mornings and on saints' days.[154] This was a similar regime to that of many Tractarian parishes in England, but it fell short of the daily Holy Communion and Sunday Sung Eucharist with elaborate ceremonial which was becoming the norm in leading ritualist parishes in England by 1870.[155] Forbes's caution about ritual was also evident in the furniture and ceremonies of St Paul's. There were no candles on the altar and the black gown was used by all preachers except Forbes who, as a bishop, presumably dressed in his lawn rochet. He was keeping to a promise to retain the black gown for sermons made when he had first come to Dundee.[156] One of the projects dear to Forbes was the installation of a marble reredos of Christ in glory which was added to the interior of the

[152] Ibid. 194–8.
[153] A. P. Forbes to P. Torry (copy), 21 Feb. 1850, SRO CH 12. 12. 2409.
[154] Ibid. 24–5.
[155] Ellsworth, *Charles Lowder*, 38–9.
[156] Grub, *My Years in Dundee*, 26.

church in 1867. Like a number of Tractarians he blamed the lack of
beauty in churches on the Reformation, commenting to his intimate
friend and chaplain Roger Lingard 'what a vandal clearout there was in
the Reformation'.[157] The installation of the reredos suggests that Forbes
would have liked more ritual if he could have got it, but was determined
to go no faster in liturgical innovation than was likely to be understood
and accepted by his congregation. Unlike the priests of some Anglo-
Catholic slum parishes Forbes was not creating a parish out of virtually
nothing. In a non-established Church he had also to take into account the
membership subscriptions at St Paul's, funds which he could not afford
to alienate lightly. In fact his caution over ritualism and his appreciation
of the native Scots dislike of anything that smacked of popery caused
him to be wary of the younger generation of the Catholic revival—the
more ardent ritualists found in the Church of England and represented in
Scotland principally by the English clergy of St Ninian's cathedral, Perth.
In 1859 Forbes enquired about the possibility of having a young ordinand
from the Tractarian Cumbrae College come to Dundee as his curate.
However, he stipulated that he 'could not endure a grand English
Puseyite & the very simple way in which we are here rather vitiates
against any Englishmen'.[158] Presumably, in view of his own Puseyism at
Oxford, Forbes realized since coming to Scotland that the militant
ritualism of the Anglo-Catholics only antagonized many High Church
Episcopalians, or possibly he was not willing to import ritualism if, like
Wagstaffe, it resulted in a flouting of episcopal authority. Forbes was also
willing to be more restrained about ritualism in the Episcopal Church
because he considered Catholic doctrine more important than Catholic
ceremony. This caution about ritualism could, at times, be severe, and he
once ordered an incumbent to return a pair of candlesticks given for the
altar to their donor.[159] He positively forbade Eucharistic vestments in the
diocese because he considered that after the 1863 revision of the canons
they were illegal in the Episcopal Church, but he did wear them in
England where he believed they were permissible use.[160] His respect for
the law of the Church derived from his father and his own legal training
in the East India Company. Unlike many Anglo-Catholic sympathizers
the ritual Forbes did allow was not necessarily a copy of continental
Roman Catholicism. To the end of his life he retained the practice of

[157] A. P. Forbes to R. Lingard (-Guthrie), n.d., SPC.
[158] A. P. Forbes to G. F. Boyle, 23 July 1859, BrMS 1. 6. 74 (ii).
[159] W. Perry, *The Oxford Movement in Scotland* (1933), 84.
[160] Skene, *Alexander Bishop of Brechin*, 20.

giving communion tokens to those of the congregation intending to go to holy communion, distributing them at the chancel step of St Paul's. Forbes said he retained this old Episcopalian practice 'as a last relic of church discipline'.[161]

Forbes's prudence about ritualism contributed to the conversion to Roman Catholicism of one of his young Dundee clergy. William Humphrey, ordained in 1863, was incumbent of St Mary Magdalene's, a Dundee mission church with a largely Orange Lodge Irish congregation. He became a Roman Catholic in 1868 and was later ordained a Jesuit. All his life Humphrey retained a vivid memory of Forbes and in 1896 wrote a short book entitled *Recollections of Scottish Episcopalianism* giving his recollections of his time in Dundee, of Forbes in particular, and of the events leading to his conversion. Although a partisan apologetic for Roman Catholicism it is the only extended account of Forbes from someone who respected him personally, but was hostile towards his position and beliefs.[162] After his appointment to St Mary Magdalene's Humphrey saw a good deal of his bishop, remembering him as 'a fascinating man, with most charming manners. His conversation was refined, instructive, and somewhat cynical.' Forbes's cynicism was illustrated in a visit of Dean Ramsay's which coincided with Humphrey's stay at the Dundee clergyhouse prior to his induction. Afterwards, Ramsay wrote to thank Forbes for his hospitality but commented that he had observed one of the curates 'foully murdering' a grouse at breakfast. When Humphrey took this personally he was consoled by Forbes sardonically remarking, 'I fancy that good Mr. Dean values carving more than he does theology as a clerical accomplishment.'[163]

Humphrey portrayed Forbes as a 'timid man' who was a secret admirer of Roman Catholicism but too fearful to act sincerely on his beliefs. As an indication of this he told the story of his collaboration in Forbes's consecrations of altar stones and holy oil which were then supplied to various Anglo-Catholic clergy elsewhere. Humphrey said he would buy the marble and the oil which Forbes would then bless according to the Roman rite. Humphrey remembered that:

Dundee was at that time regarded as an emporium of these sacred luxuries, by the more advanced members of the Puseyite party. Like Dr. Pusey himself, his disciple Dr. Forbes had not the most rudimentary conception of ecclesiastical jurisdiction. Their idea of all that was necessary for the doing of

[161] J. Dowden, *The Scottish Communion Office* (1922), 225.
[162] W. Humphrey, *Recollections of Scottish Episcopalianism* (1896), 15–18.
[163] Ibid. 38.

episcopal or sacerdotal acts was possession of power of order, episcopal or sacerdotal, as the case might be. Just as Dr. Pusey was in the habit of making confession tours throughout the length and breadth of England, and giving absolution without receiving any faculties to do so from the Protestant Bishops within whose diocese he was sojourning, so was Bishop Forbes in the habit of exporting his holy oils and altar-stones into the dioceses of Bishops who would have regarded them as contraband.[164]

Humphrey condemned Forbes for a practice he himself was only too happy to participate in at the time, but which later proved a useful stick to beat Scottish Episcopacy with. But his criticism was valid, for it was uncanonical in the Episcopal Church, and contrary to its tradition of episcopacy developed in the eighteenth century, for a bishop to exercise his episcopacy outside his own diocese. However it seems Forbes was content to usurp what properly belonged to other diocesan bishops in some matters of ritual where the respective bishop was unlikely to be favourable.

Humphrey's own ritualism soon antagonized his congregation of Orangemen. They were scandalized, for instance, when in 1867, on a Sunday that coincided with the anniversary of the battle of the Boyne, he dressed the altar in a green frontal.[165] Inevitably this confrontational approach, and Humphrey's extravagant ritualism, divided the congregation. A deputation from the congregation called on Forbes who asked for their forbearance, promising to speak with Humphrey. Eventually Forbes decided that Humphrey should become priest of a new mission church, and his resignation was announced in St Mary Magdalene's in December 1867. But Humphrey made so many conditions about this new charge that Forbes ceased to continue the matter and the priest unilaterally rescinded his resignation. Humphrey's officiating at St Mary Magdalene's the following Sunday morning caused a disturbance and those objecting to him formed themselves into a separate congregation which met in the Kinnaird Hall. Forbes was deeply hurt by it all and had sleepless nights.[166] Humphrey at last resigned his charge on 12 March 1868 having, according to his own account, abruptly converted while on a visit to London to see a friend who had previously become a Roman Catholic.[167] He left behind him a permanently divided congregation because those who had separated themselves refused to return to St Mary Magdalene's, so that in August 1868 Forbes was compelled to license their existence as

[164] Ibid. 39–40.
[165] Ibid. 36.
[166] J. Nicolson to A. F. Irvine, 'New Years Day' 1868, BpF.
[167] Humphrey, *Recollections*, 40–4.

a mission congregation.[168] Forbes was clearly acting on his early parochial experience which had convinced him that confrontational ritualism could only alienate a congregation and harm the Catholic cause in parishes. The difference in the attitudes to ritualism of the two men is best explained by Forbes's greater pastoral experience and sensitivity.

One of the matters to come before the Episcopal Synod soon after Forbes became a member illustrates his continuing connection with important English Churchmen. An old Oxford acquaintance, William Palmer of Magdalen College, in his concern for reunion with the Orthodox Church approached Forbes in 1849. Palmer had been in Russia where he had been asked by the Orthodox to repudiate various heresies they alleged were contained in the Thirty-nine Articles and he was seeking support for his action. He made an appeal to the Scottish bishops because he held letters commendatory from Bishop Luscombe, who had been consecrated by the Scottish bishops in 1825 as a bishop for those in communion with the Church of England living in Europe.[169] However the bishops cordially declined to hear his appeal as being outwith their jurisdiction, Bishop Luscombe not being a member of the Episcopal Synod.

These two factors, episcopal authority and influential connections, came together during 1850 in a clash among the bishops over an edition of the Scottish Book of Common Prayer. It had been compiled by clergy and others sympathetic to the northern tradition, who sought and gained the authorization of Bishop Torry for the new edition.[170] They had used the 1764 version of Robert Falconer but amended it, making explicit reference by rubrics to the old liturgical usages revived the previous century. Forbes had known about the preparation of the edition since 1849, and it was eventually published the next year under the title of *The Book of Common Prayer . . . According to the Use of the Church of Scotland*. Included in the published edition was a notice from Bishop Torry stating that it was in 'strict conformity with the usage of the Church of Scotland; and I accordingly recommend it to the use of the clergy of my own diocese'.[171] Patrick Torry was one of the last survivors of the Episcopal Church from its penal days. He was born in 1763 in Aberdeenshire and had been ordained priest in 1783. In 1789 he had gone to the congregation at Peterhead where he remained incumbent

---

[168] Brechin Diocese Synod Minutes, 16 Sept. 1868, BrMS 4. 1. 3, 142–3.

[169] REC II, 4 Sept. 1849, SRO CH 12. 60. 3, 183.

[170] Letters of R. Campbell to A. P. Forbes, May–Sept. 1849, SAUL 19. 1. 64–5, 69–79.

[171] Grub, *Ecclesiastical History*, vi. 266.

until his death. Consecrated Bishop of Dunkeld in 1801 he later became
Bishop of St Andrews, Dunkeld, and Dunblane.[172] A firm adherent of
the Scottish Communion Office, Torry was a living representative of the
nonjuring traditions of the eighteenth century and it was those very
traditions which were at the heart of the ensuing struggle over the new
Prayer Book.

In April 1850 Forbes told his brother George that he had received a
letter from Charles Wordsworth, warden of Trinity College, asking about
Forbes's involvement with the Prayer Book. Forbes commented that
Wordsworth intended to make a row about it.[173] Wordsworth had been
raised in an English High Church household and his father was a vehe-
ment proponent of the principle of establishment.[174] The son continued
in the same faith, remaining a High Church supporter of establishment all
his life. Wordsworth even considered established Churches to be an article
of faith consistent with the mind of Christ.[175] His advocacy of established
Churches contributed to his positive attitude towards the established
Church of Scotland and he was a staunch advocate of union between it
and the Episcopal Church.[176] Despite Wordsworth's High Churchmanship
and his espousal of moderate ritual in church, his Establishmentarianism
and warmth towards Presbyterianism made him the enemy of Tractarians
such as Forbes and Episcopalians in the northern tradition like Forbes's
brother George. Wordsworth disliked the 1850 Prayer Book because it
represented to him an extreme party among Episcopalians. If the book was
held to be permissible it would presumably also have made his hopes of
greater *rapprochement* with the Established Church more difficult.

Wordsworth referred the matter to the Episcopal Synod and the
meeting in April passed a majority motion directing Bishop Torry to
withdraw his 'imprimatur'. They resolved that the publication of a
Prayer Book calling itself the use of the Church of Scotland, without
any sanction from General Synod, was 'an instance of High presump-
tion' on the part of the publisher and those who employed him, 'and
that the Sanction of a single Bishop, which has been obtained does not
extenuate the offence'. Forbes's dissent from this action was recorded
in the minutes. The synod also resolved to request the publisher of the
Prayer Book to recall all copies and to suppress the remainder.[177] For

172 Lochhead, *Episcopal Scotland*, 63–4.
173 A. P. Forbes to G. H. Forbes, postmarked 10 Apr. 1850, SAUL 19. 1. 99.
174 Owen Chadwick, *The Victorian Church*, Pt. 1: *1829–1859* (1971), 93.
175 John Wordsworth, *The Episcopate of Charles Wordsworth* (1899), 15.
176 Ibid. 56.
177 REC II, 19 Apr. 1850, SRO CH 12. 60. 3, 203–4.

the next five months there was a struggle, ostensibly about the right of a single bishop to issue a Prayer Book which claimed the authority of the Church. Underlying this issue, however, was a deeper tension about the place of the Scottish Communion Office. Bishop Walter Trower of Glasgow in particular argued that the liturgical usages had been bartered away at the end of the eighteenth century in return for the Church's legal status.[178]

The struggle saw the influence of the Forbes family used on the side of the newly published Prayer Book because they were afraid that an attack on it could become a threat to the Scottish Communion Office. Lord Medwyn proposed to Bishop Terrot of Edinburgh that while the bishops could not recognize the book as an official publication, they should not request Torry to withdraw it and should say nothing against the usages. Medwyn thought that if this was done Torry could be persuaded to alter the title-page and even his terms of recommendation. He also recognized that the issue drew attention to the differences between the Episcopal Church and the Church of England and that this acted as a disincentive to many prospective lay supporters 'who otherwise might befriend a Church using the same Liturgy & Rites'.[179] The printing of the Prayer Book and consequent highlighting of the Scottish Communion Office as a major difference between the two Churches was to Medwyn a 'false move' which could pave the way for its complete abolition as being a 'ground of division'.[180] One of the book's compilers was in touch with his fellow protagonist, George Forbes, expressing the hope that because of the letters he had received from Bishop Forbes 'the issue may be pretty safe'.[181] He pinned his hopes on Bishop Torry standing firm and Bishop Forbes speaking out.[182]

In May 1850 William Forbes was militantly suggesting the circulation of the Prayer Book regardless, and considering the possibility of a secession.[183] Later that month Alexander Lendrum, the priest at Crieff and another of the book's compilers, wrote to George Forbes about his recent conversation with Bishop Forbes. The bishop had assured him he would prevent any discussion on the Prayer Book (presumably at the regular Episcopal Synod in September) 'by refusing his sanction to

[178] R. Campbell to G. H. Forbes, 26 Apr. 1850, SAUL 19. 1. 106.
[179] W. Forbes to P. Torry, 13 Sept. 1850, SRO CH 12. 12. 2411.
[180] J. H. Forbes to G. H. Forbes, n.d. [1850], SAUL 19. 1. 115.
[181] R. Campbell to G. H. Forbes, 14 Apr. 1850, SAUL 19. 1. 101.
[182] R. Campbell to G. H. Forbes, 24 Apr. 1850, SAUL 19. 1. 105.
[183] W. Forbes to G. H. Forbes, 5 May 1850, SAUL 19. 1. 108.

open it up'.[184] At the Brechin Diocesan Synod in August, William Henderson and Torry Anderson proposed a motion thanking the bishops for their 'timely declaration' against the Prayer Book and asking them to take further measures to make it known that the book had no authority. An opposing amendment was proposed thanking Bishop Torry for sanctioning the book 'embodying the traditions and customs of the Church in Scotland', lamenting its censure by the bishops but expressing the synod's regret at the present form of the book and its lack of adequate authority. The Prayer Book had become a test of strength between two parties within the Diocese of Brechin. On the one hand were people such as Henderson and Anderson, who were opposed to Forbes personally and to the Scottish Communion Office because it distinguished the Episcopal Church from the Church of England. On the other hand were those who were proud of the distinctive traditions of Scottish Episcopacy. For the present the Anglicizing party was slightly stronger and Henderson's motion was carried by a majority of one.[185]

If Forbes hoped to prevent discussion of the Prayer Book at the Episcopal Synod that September he failed miserably. The bishops first issued an address to all Episcopalians dealing with three areas. Regarding the Episcopal Synod as a court of appeal, the bishops lamented the increase of legal argument which complicated questions. They next uncompromisingly reaffirmed episcopal authority which, they said, resembled 'that of a Parent over his children'. From their point of view one of the 'least encouraging symptoms of the prevailing religious excitement' was 'the disposition to forget this essentially fatherly character of the Bishop's office'. They reaffirmed the jurisdiction of the bishops over the meaning of the canons, subject only to General Synod, and the jurisdiction of each diocesan bishop over his clergy as 'the guardian of Christian Doctrine and Discipline'. Thirdly, the bishops concerned themselves with the ritual of the Church, calling attention expressly to the rubrics of the recent Prayer Book which they argued had no sanction, and they directed Church members against using it. They deplored the raising of divisive issues by the Prayer Book as 'likely to lead the mind rather to discussions of a ritual and ceremonial character than to the Eternal Realities which are the subject of Divine Revelation'.[186] The bishops next composed a letter 'to all the bishops of the Anglican

[184] A. Lendrum to G. H. Forbes, 19 May 1850, SAUL 19. 1. 150.
[185] Brechin Diocese Synod Minutes, 7 Aug. 1850, BrMs 4. 1. 3, 18–19.
[186] REC II., April 1850, SRO CH. 12. 60. 3, 212–19.

Communion' repudiating the 1850 Prayer Book.[187] Finally, they wrote to
Bishop Torry recalling him to the concordat he had signed at his
consecration agreeing to abide by the wishes of the majority in matters
relating to the Church, worship, and discipline. They again urged him to
withdraw his sanction of the Prayer Book.[188] Once again Forbes had his
dissent from all these measures recorded in the minutes, but he had been
unable to prevent their passing. He remained in a minority of one as
Torry was too aged to attend the synod.

Forbes did not think the Prayer Book could survive this repudiation.
He felt Torry had a right to publish the book, though not, to be sure,
under the authority claimed on the title-page. He wondered at Bishop
Trower's attitude and asked his brother George, 'how is it that every high
churchman who comes down here in love with the Sc. Office goes over to
the *enemy* in 18 months?'[189] William Forbes thought that Trower's antagonism to the book was guided by Wordsworth. As Englishmen, he
believed neither of them could understand Scots. This is a significant
comment coming from a member of the Forbes family who was one of
the upper classes in Scotland that were so often raised to look favourably
upon English life and influences. It is a further indication that, despite
Anglicizing influences, the Forbes family retained a sense of the distinction
between Scots and English in a way not always favourable to the latter.
William further commented to Bishop Torry that it was 'hard however
that [those] who come among us, like Bp. Trower, discontented with the
position of the English Church, shd. desire to tye [*sic*] us hand & foot to
that establishment'.[190]

As in the Brechin synod, the wider struggle over the 1850 Prayer
Book was between those who valued the links with the Episcopalian past
and those who valued conformity with the Church of England. It identified Forbes early in his episcopate as someone sympathetic to the
northern tradition in its most contentious form, the Scottish Communion
Office. To the tension over the Scottish Communion Office was added
the bishops' concerns about 'religious excitement'. Their allusions to this
excitement in their September synod address was connected with controversies surrounding ritual. Their restatement of episcopal authority in
the Wagstaffe case also suggests that the bishops were increasingly
concerned about the effects of Anglo-Catholic ritualism in the Scottish

[187]   Ibid. 219.
[188]   Ibid. 220.
[189]   A. P. Forbes to G. H. Forbes, n.d. [1850], SAUL 19. 1. 114.
[190]   W. Forbes to P. Torry, 13 Sept. 1850, SRO CH. 12. 12. 2411.

Church. They felt that the religious fervour created by the Oxford Movement was having a detrimental effect on the peace of the Church. Tractarian support for the nonjuring liturgical usages in the Episcopal Church exacerbated the differences over the Scottish Communion Office, while the tendency among clergy like Charles Wagstaffe, and others influenced by Anglo-Catholicism, to ignore their bishops in pursuit of ritualist goals was beginning to appear threatening to episcopal control of the Church.

Bishop Torry died in 1852 and this doughty supporter of Forbes in the counsels of the bishops was replaced by an equally vigorous opponent. Charles Wordsworth was elected Bishop of St Andrews, Dunkeld, and Dunblane, by a majority of one after he had controversially voted for himself.[191]

In response to the varied issues that arose during his first years as a bishop Forbes began to formulate his own theological understanding. His renewed contact with the nonjuring tradition had not caused him to diminish the dissatisfaction with nonjuring theology he had previously expressed in his article in 1846. In 1851 he wrote to his brother George referring to the classic Episcopalian writer on the Eucharist, Bishop Alexander Jolly, and to Jolly's devotional manual on the sacrament. Forbes said he thought what Jolly had written was true 'but not the whole truth'.[192] This dissatisfaction with the incompleteness of nonjuring theology was reinforced for Forbes by the celebrated Gorham judgement of 1850. In March 1850 the Judicial Committee of the Privy Council had upheld the appeal of a Low Church clergyman of the Church of England against his bishop, for refusing the clergyman induction into a parish because he denied baptismal regeneration. The decision created widespread anxiety among High Churchmen and Anglo-Catholics that the Church's doctrine was being defined by a secular court in contradiction of the Catholic faith, although the judicial decision was confined to the permissibility of Low Church baptismal belief in the Church of England. But to Anglo-Catholics a judgement on a doctrinal issue by a secular tribunal made the Church of England appear to be an Erastian institution instead of an independent, apostolic foundation. The Gorham judgement proved to be the catalyst that sent a number of Tractarians and Anglo-Catholics into the Roman Catholic Church, including Henry Manning, James Hope, and the Marchioness of Lothian. Forbes wrote to various English bishops, presumably to encourage them to speak out against the

[191] Wordsworth, *Charles Wordworth*, 6ff.
[192] A. P. Forbes to G. H. Forbes, n.d. [1851], SAUL 19. 1. 127.

judgement, but found they would do nothing. He applied to Wilberforce of Oxford, Blomfield of London, and Bethel of Bangor, but only Edward Denison of Salisbury was interested in Forbes's letter.[193] As ever, Forbes's concern was to safeguard doctrine and he was grateful that at least on this issue the doctrinal concern was clear. 'A Church *really* committed to laxity on such a point', he wrote, 'cannot be a true one. Then it is a great comfort that the controversy is not on the other Sacrament [the Eucharist], & so one's heart is not torn out of one by the mad impiety of our opponents.'[194]

The Gorham judgement came before the Episcopal Synod after having had resolutions passed against the Privy Council decision by the synods of Glasgow and St Andrews. The bishops unanimously passed a resolution expressing their sympathy with the concern of the clergy regarding the judgement. They asserted that the judgement had no authority in the Episcopal Church, and were content to limit their action to enjoining the clergy to teach baptismal regeneration in a series of five specific points.[195] A remaining worry about the possibility of the Church's formularies being thought inadequate brought together two strange allies. Forbes and Trower were united for the only time in an alternate resolution in which they affirmed: 'that the Doctrine of Holy Baptism is so clearly expressed in our Formularies, that although the fact of the late Decision has given occasion to the Present Declaration, we do not hereby mean to assert that the language in those documents is not precise & sufficient'.[196] Trower was obviously concerned that the formularies held in common with the Church of England should remain unquestioned. Forbes was afraid lest it be thought that the Thirty-nine Articles were inadequate expressions of Catholic truth and therefore increase Anglo-Catholic anxiety about the Anglican Church.

The matter stimulated Forbes to further reflection, in response to the crisis of confidence in their Church among many of the more Catholic members of the Church of England and the Episcopal Church. Forbes believed this lack of confidence in the Church could be met if there was a re-emphasis on the truth and definition of doctrine within the Anglican Church. In a book on the Nicene Creed in 1852 written in the light of the Gorham judgement, Forbes acknowledged that the Oxford Movement had taught 'deeper views of God's

[193] E. B. Pusey to J. Keble, 1850, PK iii.
[194] A. P. Forbes to G. H. Forbes, 10 Apr. 1850, SAUL 19. 1. 99.
[195] REC II, 19 Apr. 1850, SRO CH 12. 60. 3, 199–202.
[196] Ibid. 202.

Truth', which had resulted, he thought, in 'a desire for a more systematic theology' among Anglicans. This book was the most substantial work of theology he wrote in the first ten years of his episcopate. It was intended as a textbook for those beginning the study of theology and dedicated to John Keble in 'profound reverence and affection'. Probably because of this purpose Forbes merely rehearsed traditional scholastic theology. He nowhere made any mention of John Stuart Mill or other contemporary sceptical thinkers who were questioning the possibility of supernatural knowledge in the first place. Those contemporary writers who were acknowledged were mainly historians, including the German Ignaz von Döllinger. Faith, for Forbes, was assent to dogma, divinely revealed, but proposed to the would-be believer 'on competent authority', that is, the Church. In keeping with the Tractarian emphasis on the Church as a necessary and divine institution in the economy of salvation, Forbes believed it had an essential role in transmitting the content of revealed truth and that it had the authority to declare what is necessary to be believed for salvation. In the preface he explained how he believed the Church could best do this:

Such a theology is at once the most reverent and the most satisfying; the most satisfactory, because a strict dogmatic theology tells us in very plain language, that after the human intellect is exhausted, it has not reached God. Men also have felt, that in an exact theology is the only sure guarantee for a theology of faith. Where matters have not been defined, men have greatly contented themselves with the lower view . . . And we ourselves have seen how the faith of our own Church, on the subjects that were left as open questions, has shrivelled and withered away. A definite expression of doctrine embodied in the symbolic books of a Church becomes the institution by which the idea is preserved and perpetuated. Had a dogmatic teaching been then prevalent, the movement in the last century would in all probability have taken a more satisfactory direction.[197]

Forbes attributed the failure of the Church of England in 1850 in upholding the Catholic doctrine of baptismal regeneration to its weak hold on Catholic doctrine during the eighteenth century. This resulted, he felt, in the Evangelical revival of that century being captured by Protestant theology. Forbes desired the development of what he called 'an exact theology', meaning by that a precise and dogmatic Catholic teaching by the Church. This he considered to be not only an antidote to the Protestantism that denied baptismal regeneration, but also to what he referred to as taking the 'lower view' of religious truth. He believed that

---

[197] A. P. Forbes, *A Short Explanation of the Nicene Creed* (2nd edn. 1866), pp. vi–vii.

unless people were taught the truth of supernatural revelation exactly and plainly as being the teaching of the Church they would opt for more naturalistic, non-supernatural, rational explanations. These explanations, for Forbes, could not penetrate into the fullness of divine truth, and were far less capable of leading Christians into awe and holiness as they realized what God had given to his Church. Forbes feared that people would come to treat Christianity as a 'philosophy, as an opinion, as an idea'.[198] Exact theology was his response to the Gorham judgement, but Forbes also proposed it as a means to combat the increasing indifference in society towards the Church. One reason, he believed, why the Episcopal Church was not more successful in its mission to the Scottish people was because there was a lack of confidence that the doctrines taught by his Church were true and accurate expressions of divine realities. 'I believe that one of the many reasons why the true faith, in regard to the Church and the Sacraments, has not found the acceptance it ought among our countrymen, is this, that in asserting the right doctrine concerning them, we have not sufficiently dwelt upon their heavenly nature.'[199] In this sermon delivered in 1849 Forbes was already responding to the lack of church attendance, and even of Christian belief, he encountered among the urban poor. Awareness of this also lay behind his criticism of industrial society in another sermon he published in 1862.

Upon what a fearful substructure of practical atheism is the commercial success of this country founded! The creation of a God-forgetting, God-despising class seems the condition of our social advancement . . . None but the Clergy and those conversant with the poor can tell you the awful need there is of something to be done; how sin and guilt generate themselves in new and astounding forms and shapes; how the present generation of workers is really worse than that which went before . . . O what a duty this imposes on those whom GOD, by a special mercy, has not numbered among these classes![200]

Forbes was advocating that the Church recapture the adherence of the labouring poor by sacrificial living among them, coupled with a greater definition in Christian doctrine.

Forbes's confidence in, and support for, dogma was the major influence of the Oxford Movement upon him. He had an almost sacramental view of doctrine as being, in Newman's words, 'a Mystery . . . *lying hid* in language'. Like the English Tractarian leaders, Forbes believed that Catholic dogma conveyed supernatural truth. One

[198] A. P. Forbes, *Commentary on the Litany* (1855), 105–6.
[199] A. P. Forbes, *The Christian's Foundation* (1849), 12–13.
[200] A. P. Forbes, *Sermons on the Grace of God* (1862), 226–7.

consequence of this high view of doctrine was to give Forbes a horror
of heresy. The connection he made between truth and morality meant he
regarded heresy not only as sinful, but as immoral. It was, according to
Forbes, 'a dishonour to God to think of him other than as he has
revealed himself'.[201] The centrality of truth and error in his theology
could have unhappy consequences. One of the most obvious was that it
led Forbes into traditional Christian anti-Judaic, and even anti-Semitic,
expressions. Like other contemporary Churchmen, he regarded the Jews
as among those whose error caused them to be rejected by God for their
obstinate rejection of the truth of Christ. The harshness towards the Jews
in the Church's history Forbes accounted for by the increasing awareness
of the Church of the 'heinousness of the guilt of the Deicides'.[202] The
error of the Jews was an example of their 'stiff-necked Jewish nature,
ever intense, ever bigoted'.[203]

By the end of the 1850s Forbes's anxieties about the lack of confidence in the Church's teaching among its members, and the indifference
towards the Church among the labouring poor, were increased by an
emerging awareness of the effects of biblical criticism and science. Forbes
drew attention to these issues in two sets of sermons he published in
1857. He must surely have been aware of biblical criticism before this
through Pusey, but the appearance of it in a homiletic form indicates
that, by this time, Forbes felt sufficiently disturbed to be warning about
its effects among ordinary church-goers. He said that modern theories
which regarded scripture as culturally conditioned, or applicable only to
the period of history it was written in, were not to be listened to. The
knowledge of God in revelation, he said, could not be 'improved upon'
(that is, undergo development) like a steam-engine or a telegraph. The
closer his hearers were to the letter of scripture, he advised, the closer
they would be to divine truth.[204] Concerning science and the Bible, he
cautioned that scripture was not given to teach scientific but moral truth,
and the ways of God to men. Nevertheless, scripture was infallibly true.
He considered that science and the Bible could not contradict each other,
proceeding as they both did from the same divine source of all truth.
However, if any conflict did arise Christians 'must unreservedly succumb
to the latter'.[205]

---

[201] A. P. Forbes, *Litany*, 61.

[202] Ibid. 138.

[203] A. P. Forbes, *Are You Being Converted?* (1857), 71.

[204] Ibid. 75.

[205] A. P. Forbes, *Amendment*, 143.

As a complement to what he considered were the negative influences of doubt and indifference towards the Church's teaching, some of Forbes's other publications at this time were intended to deepen devotional life. He particularly wanted the clergy not simply to be devout but also to exercise the characteristic Tractarian ministry of confession and spiritual direction. His concern for devotional life was a facet of the usual Tractarian link between belief and holiness that Forbes had elaborated in his sermon at the opening of St Columba's in Edinburgh in 1847. Some of these devotional works were translations of Roman Catholic works with the more explicitly Roman content removed, and there was an emphasis on self-examination, preparation for Holy Communion, plus mention of ascetic practices. The use of Roman Catholic manuals and attention to confession points to the influence of Pusey, who pioneered the use of both in Tractarian spirituality. Pusey regarded asceticism as a necessary preliminary to sanctification, but as he had no one to guide him in the traditional ways of Catholic ascetical practice his personal grief at the death of his wife in 1839 increased the strain of mortification in his spirituality. Pusey's was a theology of the cross, meditating particularly on the passion of Christ. But his spirituality relied too heavily on minute personal examination and an acute awareness of personal sinfulness which encouraged the use of corporal penance and voluntary humiliations.[206] It was indicative of this scrupulous strain of spirituality that Pusey had begun to translate devotional material from seventeenth-century France when the French Church had been influenced by Jansenism. The same tendency in Forbes towards excessive scrupulousness and worry over his self-worth had already been marked by Pusey himself. When Forbes was elected bishop he had produced a paper expressing sentiments which may simply have been traditional expressions of spiritual humility. However Pusey was anxious enough about Forbes's strong condemnations of himself to ask Keble what he thought of them. Pusey was particularly concerned that his own 'general confessions of sinfulness' might have been unduly influential upon Forbes.[207]

The later years of Forbes's episcopate were those of the greatest growth in Brechin Diocese. Among the new churches built after 1857 were Broughty Ferry, Drumlithie, a chapel at the Kinnaird's estate of Rossie Priory, St Salvador's Dundee, and Laurencekirk. Even more schools or chapel-schools were erected. By 1871 St Paul's, Dundee, had a

---

[206] G. O'Donnell, 'The Spirituality of E. B. Pusey' in Perry Butler (ed.), *Pusey Rediscovered* (1983), 231–54.
[207] E. B. Pusey to J. Keble, n.d. [23 Oct. 1847], PK ii.

day school, a night school for working-class boys, and a Sunday school.[208]
Forbes was constantly endeavouring to extract more money for the schools
from his vestry.[209] The diocesan statistical returns also demonstrate this
growth during Forbes's episcopate, which of course coincided with large-
scale emigration into Dundee and surrounding areas resulting from the
industrialization of the city. During 1875, the last year of Forbes's life,
returns came from nineteen congregations including five from Dundee
itself, compared to the eleven congregations in 1847. Whereas membership
totalled 3,769 in 1847, by 1875 it was 11,363. Communicant numbers
were 1,710 in 1847 and 3,929 in 1875. But this later figure is, in part,
accounted for by the increase in the frequency of services of Holy
Communion by 1875. Whereas in 1847 only one congregation—St Paul's,
Dundee—celebrated Holy Communion more than quarterly, by 1875 all
congregations had a service at least monthly. In 1847 there were no
returns made for schools. Such returns did not commence until 1855
when there were schools in all but one of the twelve congregations. By
1875 schools existed in fourteen congregations—four had Sunday Schools
only, nine had day schools, and three also had night schools.[210] In his concern for church extension Forbes frequently turned to his wealthy friends
for financial help, partly because he believed Brechin was the poorest of
the seven dioceses, and partly because, as he once told Gladstone, he did
not get much help from the landowners in the diocese.[211]

Forbes's involvement in the civic affairs of Dundee also continued to
grow through the 1860s and into the 1870s. He was keen to establish a
convalescent hospital.[212] He joined the Society for the Prevention of
Cruelty to Animals in 1864, and became a director of the Albert Institute
(the forerunner of the city's museum and art gallery) in 1870.[213] The
same year he also became a committee member of the Free Library,
zealously soliciting books for it from his friends and acquaintances, such
as the historian John Hill Burton.[214] During August 1872 Forbes was
present at a meeting to establish the Prison Aid Society in Dundee and
was elected to its committee.[215] The following year he became concerned

---

[208]   Grub, *My Years in Dundee*, 35.
[209]   SPC 'Vestry Minute Book, St Paul's Episcopal Church, Dundee, 1852– ', 25 Sept.
1869.
[210]   Brechin Diocese Synod Minutes, 1847–1875, BrMS 4. 1. 3.
[211]   A. P. Forbes to W. E. Gladstone, 8 Apr. 1859, Gladstone Papers, BL 44154, fo. 234.
[212]   A. P. Forbes to G. F. Boyle, postmarked 14 Sept. 1860, BrMS 1. 7. 125.
[213]   A. H. Millar, *Jubilee of the Albert Institute 1867–1917* (1917).
[214]   A. P. Forbes to J. H. Burton, 21 Jan. [1873], NLS 9399, fo. 217.
[215]   *Dundee Advertiser*, 5 Aug. 1872.

that the Society address the great increase in juvenile crime in the city.[216] In 1873 Forbes also became a member of the Dundee School Board, and formed the Association of Church Choirs in the city.[217]

But this later growth and involvement in diocese and civic affairs only built upon the fundamental characteristics of Forbes's Tractarian-inspired ministry which were already established by 1857. His ministry was largely shaped in an engagement with urban society, adhering to the Church as a Eucharistic community which included the poor, worshipping in a church where the design of the church building and the layout of its furniture clearly demonstrated its Eucharistic emphasis. Forbes actively encouraged the development of an active, theologically well-read, yet prayerful clergy. He desired priests to be responsive to the needs of the poor, but also to the spiritual needs of their congregations, and to be examples of holiness. His most powerful instrument in implementing these plans was the attraction of his own example of living among the poor and the energy of his pastoral work both within his own congregation and his diocese. Forbes's Tractarian ministry gave a lead to those Episcopalians influenced by the Oxford Movement, and by virtue of his position, energy, and commitment to the poor, he became the *de facto* leader of a new force in the Episcopal Church. In doing so he demonstrated an appreciation for the nonjuring tradition, being particularly enthusiastic for the central authority of the bishops and the Scottish Communion Office. But Forbes remained critical of the vagueness of nonjuring theology which did not, he believed, go far enough in teaching explicit Catholic truth. It was this concern for Catholic truth that was fundamental to his outlook. The Gorham judgement in 1850 was the catalyst that led Forbes to express his belief in dogmatic theology as a solution to the doubt among Church members in the Church's teaching, and to the lack of church attendance or even of Christian belief among the labouring poor. Fundamentally, when confronted by the challenges to Christian belief that were growing from mid-Victorian intellectual doubt and urban indifference Forbes responded by appealing to authority. It was the 'development of the dogmatic element in the Church's teaching' which would act as the 'strongest bulwark against rationalism and infidelity'.[218] The instrument of this bastion against these contemporary threats to a secure Christian belief was the authoritative Church and her authorized teachers, the clergy. By a combination of holiness of

[216] *Dundee Advertiser*, 17 Sept. 1873.
[217] Mackey, 198.
[218] A. P. Forbes, *An Explanation of the Thirty Nine Articles* (1867), i, p. iv.

life and clear knowledge of an exact and dogmatic doctrine the clergy
would be able to stem the tide of doubt, disbelief, and indifference that
Forbes had encountered among the tenements and drawing-rooms of
Dundee. Such an appeal to authority placed Forbes among the most conservative in reaction to nineteenth-century difficulties of faith. However,
as a Tractarian, Forbes's appeal was to the authority of the Church rather
than the usual Protestant appeal to the infallibility of scripture.

4

Controversy and Trial

FORBES gave his first episcopal charge to his clergy at his diocesan synod of 1857, on the theology of the Eucharist. He had chosen this subject for his primary charge out of a desire to uphold Tractarian doctrine on the Eucharist at a time when similar teaching was on trial in the Church of England. But he was also motivated by a concern to continue to present the Church as a trustworthy guide to religious belief. The charge initiated what became known among Victorian Episcopalians as the Eucharistic controversy. The controversy ran for three years, until Forbes was presented for heresy by one of his clergy and eventually tried before the Episcopal Synod in March 1860. The opposition to Forbes's teaching drew in the other bishops, and large numbers of the clergy and influential laity. One of the fundamental reasons for the opposition was High Church suspicion of Tractarian Romanism. This opposition was itself exacerbated by the Scottish bishops' fear of alienating sympathy within the Church of England if the Tractarian teaching of Forbes was allowed to go unchallenged. Links with the Church of England were also valued by the Anglicized laity of the south and the bishops feared a split within their own Church. But neither Forbes's supporters, nor the opposition, were a cohesive group. At Forbes's trial the argument depended on a difference over what were the Anglican theological authorities, but underlying it was the question of a theologically tolerant Church. It is one of the ironies of the Eucharistic controversy that Bishop Forbes, the leading Tractarian figure in Scotland, should have directly caused the Episcopalian Church to become theologically more tolerant when, in fact, he desired it to be more dogmatic.

On Wednesday 5 August 1857 the clergy of the diocese gathered in St Mary's, Brechin, for what would be their most significant synod of the nineteenth century. Bishop Forbes celebrated Holy Communion and told them that there would be no sermon as he intended to deliver a charge. He explained that it was too long to read in full, but gave its leading points and said it was with his publisher who had instructions to send a copy to all his clergy. Forbes began by asking the question was Christ 'really present' in the Eucharist or not? The question, he maintained, was answered by the Church in the affirmative: the bread of the Eucharist was the flesh of Jesus. It was answered by 'the world', however, in the negative, denying any supernatural virtue and asserting the sacrament was merely a memorial. These two explanations, he said, had recently come into conflict in the Church of England.[1] To establish the position of the Anglican Church on this question of the real presence of Christ he proposed to consult all the 'authoritative documents' and not just the Thirty-nine Articles. These authoritative documents he listed in five groups: (i) the Articles and the catechism; (ii) 'the whole language of public prayers', that is, the liturgies of the Church; (iii) the exhortations, directions, and rubrics of the Prayer Book; (iv) the early Church; (v) scripture as interpreted by the early Church, which he called the 'paramount rule of faith' of the Anglican Church.[2] Only official statements of faith so derived from all these authorities could be morally binding on Church members.[3] He then proceeded to demonstrate, according to these documents, his claim that the Anglican Church taught the doctrine of the real objective presence of Christ in the sacrament of the Eucharist.

In upholding this understanding of Eucharistic presence Forbes was conscious of three possible attacks. First, that contrary to Article 38 of the Thirty-nine Articles, he taught transubstantiation. Forbes sought to fend this possible accusation off by maintaining that the real presence could not be effected through transubstantiation, because it contradicted the very nature of a sacrament. Forbes believed transubstantiation meant there was no longer any natural part in the Eucharistic elements but that the bread and wine ceased to be. In this, Forbes reiterated the classic Anglican objections made to transubstantiation since the seventeenth century. Basically he thought transubstantiation to be a theory which went beyond the limits of rational thought.[4]

A second possible criticism was that Forbes's teaching departed from the prevalent theory of Eucharistic presence among Scottish and English High Churchmen, namely virtualism.[5] This was the belief that there is a real presence, but only of the virtue or power or grace of the body and blood of Christ to the believing communicant, while the Eucharistic elements remained unchanged in substance. Although, Forbes acknowledged, this was the theology of the Nonjurors and some of the significant figures of the Episcopalian past, he regarded it as inadequate. It did not

---

[1] A. P. Forbes, *A Primary Charge* (1857), 6–7.   [2] Ibid. 7–11.
[3] Ibid. 12.   [4] Ibid. 23.   [5] Ibid. 12–13.

do justice to the substantial or objective presence of Christ distinct from the faith of the individual communicant. The conflict between the High Church defenders of virtualism and those, like Forbes, in favour of what they called the 'Real Objective Presence' was to be one of the key tensions in the ensuing controversy.

Thirdly, Forbes commented on Article 29 which asserted 'the wicked which eat not the Body of Christ in the Lord's Supper'. As against Forbes's argument that the Anglican Church maintained an objective Eucharistic presence irrespective of the communicant's faith, this article could be interpreted in terms of receptionism. This was the belief that the body and blood of Christ were present in the Eucharist, but only to those who received the sacrament with faith. The presence of the Christ was therefore determined by the communicant's faith and not by the independent action of God's grace. Forbes quoted St Paul in 1 Corinthians 11 who considered unworthy reception to be a serious matter, and he asked how this could be so if the wicked did not receive Christ but merely bread and wine.[6]

Having defended the real objective presence as acceptable Anglican doctrine Forbes went on to consider, as its logical consequence, the adoration of Christ, really present, in the Eucharist. 'The worship is due not to the gifts, but to Christ in the gifts', he affirmed.[7] 'Either Christ is present, or He is not. If He is, He ought to be adored; if He is not, *cadit quaestio*' [the question falls].[8] He argued that the Anglican formularies only condemned worship addressed to the outward parts of the Eucharistic sacrament, the bread and wine, or to a material presence of the human Jesus, but not the worship of the ascended Christ really present.[9] But he did not think that worship of Christ sacramentally present permitted the extravagant ritual introduced by some Anglo-Catholic priests. He maintained that while the 'truly pious mind delights in magnificent ritual, finding therein the expression of many high dogmatic verities, yet we must remember that there must always be a certain proportion to be kept between the ritual and the religious life of a congregation'.[10]

The next consequence of the real presence of Christ for Forbes was that the Eucharist became a sacrifice. Again he defended this through patristic evidence, claiming 'the ancient doctors teach that the Eucharistic Sacrifice is the same substantially with that of the Cross'.[11] But lest he be charged with teaching the Eucharist as a repetition of Calvary, and therefore blurring the sufficiency of Christ's sacrifice, he argued that

[6] Ibid. 26–9. [7] Ibid. 30. [8] Ibid. 31.
[9] Ibid. 32–4. [10] Ibid. 35. [11] Ibid. 38.

the sacrifice of Christ was not limited solely to Calvary but rather was the whole offering of himself in obedience to the Father, from incarnation to ascension. He also asserted that the Eucharist was not a repetition of the sacrifice of Christ but its re-presentation, made possible by the presence of the ascended and eternal Christ.[12]

Lastly he took up the contemporary debate on the Scottish Communion Office. After expressing his inability to appreciate the argument against having two liturgies in the one Church, the Eastern Orthodox living harmoniously with two, he acknowledged the 'very strong prejudice' against the Scottish Communion Office from some members of the Episcopal Church. For his part he had

no sympathy with those few earnest men who scruple to use the English Office, nor with those who look upon the question as a national one. I use the English Office constantly myself; I believe its consecration is valid, and in validity there can be no question of degree. As it stands at present, I regard it as a sad mutilation of the first Office of the Reformers; and an Eucharistic service 'more marred than any', but still, thanks be to God, preserving all the essentials of a true Sacrament.[13]

He considered there was a duty towards using the Scottish Communion Office as the embodiment of the faith of Episcopalian forebears. It was necessary to uphold it despite its present unpopularity, and he pointed to the frequent scriptural references to what he called the 'deadly antagonism' between popularity and truth. However, for Forbes the Scottish Communion Office was principally important because it represented a closer conformity with the practice of the patristic Church than did the English liturgy in the Book of Common Prayer. Thus the Scottish Office was more faithful to the belief of the apostolic Church, the period when, according to him, the Christian revelation was perfectly and completely delivered by Christ. In this way the Scottish Office was an example of his understanding of religious truth, that historically earlier was better than later in so far as Christian truth went.

I believe that the Scottish Office embodies the principle of Primitive Christianity; that, coming, as it does, confessedly nearer to the ancient Liturgies, it bears witness not only to the two great Christian doctrines of Eucharistic Sacrifice and Real Presence, but to the whole Vincentian theory—that Christianity is a final revelation, not a progressive philosophy; thus preserving us against all those theories which are prevalent in the present day, of a supplemental revelation, which exhibit themselves so offensively in Mormonism, less coarsely in Irvingism, and in that school of the Roman Catholic Church which not only rests on the

[12] Ibid. 39–42.   [13] Ibid. 43.

theory of development, but which lays so much store by that additional religion drawn from the visions and experiences of the saints.[14]

Forbes was, on the one hand, opposing the theology of a historical unfolding of original revelation particularly associated in Britain with Newman's *Essay on the Development of Doctrine* (1845). On the other he challenged any claim to what he considered new or further revelation given to the Church in mystical or personal experience, such as the charismatic phenomena associated with the preaching of Edward Irving in London, or, for example, the arguments drawn by the papacy from the history of piety for the 1854 definition of the dogma of the Immaculate Conception. His understanding of religious truth was more closed and static—all Christian truth was delivered once and for all in the event of Jesus Christ, and only interpreted thereafter. To abolish the Scottish Communion Office would not, he felt, bring the Scottish Episcopal Church any closer sympathy from the Evangelical party in the Church of England, as some in Scotland hoped, but merely serve to alienate its High Church members and give the Scottish Church a reputation for inconstancy.[15] Forbes believed that the Scottish Communion Office would make an important contribution to the future of the Anglican Church. As the liturgy of a non-established Church it demonstrated that Anglicanism need not be Erastian. This was particularly important as Forbes envisaged Anglicanism becoming increasingly significant through-out the world, as the religion of the 'present imperial race', and also as a catalyst for possible Christian reunion with its 'hierarchy and valid sacraments' on the one hand and 'open Bible' on the other.[16]

Such was the substance of Forbes's charge, the first he had given to his diocesan synod since his consecration as bishop. This gap was not unusual as it was not customary for Scottish bishops to give a charge to their synods on each annual occasion. They regularly gave an account of the year's events in their diocese, but restricted a formal charge to those years when definite theological teaching was required by con-temporary developments. Forbes's break in 1857 with the practice of his first ten years was significant. Significant also that it should have been such a weighty piece of theology on this particular topic for such a tiny gathering—in that year the synod of the diocese of Brechin numbered just fourteen clergy. What then was Forbes's motivation for such a charge at that particular time?

[14] Ibid. 44.   [15] Ibid. 46.   [16] Ibid. 48.

Perry considered the principal reason for the charge to have been Forbes's distress at the impoverished conception of the Eucharist and the lack of reverence among Episcopalians in Dundee.[17] But the evidence in the charge shows that Forbes had a wider concern than simply the shallowness of Episcopalian piety. In the charge, Forbes referred to the contemporary controversy on the Eucharist in the Church of England. This concerned the prosecution of George Anthony Denison, Archdeacon of Taunton, for his Eucharistic teaching of the real objective presence and Eucharistic sacrifice, in three sermons preached in Wells cathedral in 1854. Although a prosecution by one of the clergy of the diocese of Bath and Wells, it was supported by the Evangelical Alliance.[18] Denison's teaching was found contrary to the 28th and 29th Articles by Archbishop Sumner's court at Bath on 12 August 1856 and Denison was sentenced to deprivation. The judgement was reversed on a technicality after appeal to the Court of Arches on 23 April 1857. An appeal to the Judicial Committee of the Privy Council by the prosecution was rejected, again on a technicality, on 6 February 1858.[19] In his charge, Forbes commented on the case. He regretted that a doctrine not defined by the Church should be made a test for communion, and that something so sacred was brought before the civil courts 'to a tribunal so constituted from the intermixture of laymen, as to exceed the powers given it by God, when it attempted to define a doctrine'. But he thought the chief misfortune was the harm the case had done to the faith of Church members, being 'a blow struck at the whole sacramental system, as an attack upon one great supernatural element in religion'.[20] Forbes had been following the Denison case and had drawn the attention of his episcopal colleagues to it at the meeting of the Episcopal Synod on 25 September 1856.[21]

Forbes's charge was delivered while the Denison case was still going through its judicial process, and the case posed particular problems for Tractarians. The archbishop's was the only court to address itself to the substantive issues involved and it found against Denison's claim that his teaching was that of the Church of England. It was also uncomfortable to have the teaching of the Church brought before the civil courts. In this way the Denison case threatened two fundamental claims of the Oxford Movement—that the Church was spiritually

[17]   Perry, 76.

[18]   Owen Chadwick, *The Victorian Church*, pt. 1 (1971), 492; Kenneth Hylson-Smith, *Evangelicals in the Church of England 1734–1984* (1988), 126.

[19]   *DNB First Supplement* (1901), ii. 128.

[20]   Forbes, *Primary Charge*, 13.

[21]   REC II, 25 Sept. 1856, SRO CH 12. 60. 3, 323.

independent of the state; and that the Church of England was Catholic in practice and doctrine. Forbes's charge was in fact part of a general Tractarian response to the challenge of the Denison case, a response instigated by John Keble. In two letters to Forbes, written in 1859, Keble said he had 'played the Trumpeter in this fight'.[22] Later that same year Keble wrote that he desired to share Forbes's trouble 'were it only that I was instrumental (whether mistakenly so or not) in the manner of what I did in bringing the trouble upon you'.[23] Keble had encouraged the publication of three works on the Eucharist explicitly designed to refute the verdict of the archbishop's court that Denison's teaching was contrary to the teaching of the Church of England. These publications were his own *On Eucharistical Adoration* (1857), Pusey's *The Real Presence* (1857), and Forbes's charge. Pusey and Keble were acknowledged leaders in the Catholic revival, but Forbes also was an important figure to Tractarians. He was, apart from Hamilton of Salisbury, the only Tractarian bishop in 1857. From its very beginning, in Tract 1, the Oxford Movement had exalted the episcopate as an expression of the spiritual independence of the Church. It was only to be expected that the first bishop espousing the aims of the Oxford Movement should therefore be a prominent figure for Tractarians. Forbes was no doubt glad to be included in the defence for he considered Denison to be an unhappy choice of victim, believing he did not have 'a theological head'.[24] All three works argued, like Denison, that the doctrine of the 'real, objective presence' of Christ in the Eucharist was the teaching of the Anglican Church. It had been Robert Wilberforce who had been the first among Tractarians to argue for a 'real objective presence' in Eucharistic theology, in his book *The Doctrine of the Holy Eucharist* (1853).[25] Before then Tractarians had been content to speak, like High Churchmen, of a real, but spiritual presence, or a 'virtual' presence. Pusey, and especially Keble, were at first reluctant to see any weakness in the former virtualist language. It was the trial of Archdeacon Denison that pushed them into asking what exactly such a 'virtual presence' was, and into adopting Wilberforce's language, whose theology had influenced Denison. They could not defend Denison if they did not also subscribe to the theological terms he had used in his condemned sermons, for the case against the

[22] J. Keble to A. P. Forbes, 12 July 1859, BrMS 1. 1. 158.
[23] J. Keble to A. P. Forbes, 12 Oct. 1859, BrMS 1. 1. 203.
[24] A. P. Forbes to G. H. Forbes, 27 Oct. 1856, BrMS 1. 5. 2.
[25] A. Hardelin, *Tractarian Understanding of the Eucharist* (1965), 165–6.

archdeacon was precisely about such language. But if they did not defend Denison, or uphold his theology, it would have appeared to be a denial of his Eucharistic teaching and an acquiescence in Erastian interference in the teaching of the Church. Denison's trial forced the original Tractarian leaders to greater definition in their Eucharistic theology, adopting that of the younger generation of the movement.

As well as contributing to a defence of Denison, Forbes was also motivated in his charge by an opportunity to address the religious doubt of his time and to propose his remedy for it. The present he regarded as an age of 'restlessness and uncertainty' where old truths were being 'irreverently called into question'. He pointed to the inspiration of scripture being increasingly questioned by what he called 'a self-sufficient and fearless criticism'. New divine revelation was being claimed, he said, by the rise of Mormonism among the poor and Irvingism among the upper classes. There was doubt about hell, and the people were looking for truth in the divine spirit immanent in nature and personal experience, rather than in Christian doctrine. He questioned the effects of empirical science with its concentration on the physical universe. There was also what Forbes called Nestorianism (the heresy that there are two separate persons, human and divine, in the incarnate Christ) by which he probably meant such free-thinkers as Francis Newman and J. A. Froude. These had relinquished belief in Jesus as God while maintaining respect for him as a historical figure and great moral teacher. According to Forbes it was all leading to 'a vague spiritualism and religion of sensations . . . taking the place of the old orthodox Christianity'. Forbes's remedy was to appeal to tradition because clarity of Christian revelation he believed could be found in the first centuries of the Church.

In such a state of the human mind we must have something to rest upon, and where shall we find that save in an appeal to the universal tradition and consent of the Christian Church . . . To what ages shall we refer but to those in which they spoke who had drunk in knowledge from the lips of the Apostles of God, and learnt doctrine from those who had heard the 'voice of Wisdom crying in their streets'.[26]

Already concerned that the social conditions of the newly urbanized poor were contributing to declining church attendance and belief, Forbes now expressed anxiety about the intellectual aspects of the erosion of orthodox religious belief.

---

[26] Forbes, *Primary Charge*, 45.

By the 1850s British Christianity was having to contend with increasing domestic challenges to orthodox belief from science and social change.[27] Walter Houghton's examination of the literature of the Victorian middle and upper classes confirmed this period as increasingly conscious of its own religious doubt. He traced the breakdown of the old orthodox certainties, beginning in the late 1820s and early 1830s. Such things as railways producing a sense of mobility and speed, industrial development and wealth, and increasing knowledge, caused the Victorians to think of their society as one in transition. For them it was changing towards an ill-defined but better future, separated from its medieval past. But while the old certainties were passing, by the 1870s there were still no replacements. It was an age of doubt, although Victorians at this time never doubted their intellectual capacity to arrive, eventually, at truth, and Victorian confidence in reason made doubt a fluctuating experience for most.[28] However, for the majority of Victorians their doubt was not a liberation, and most retained the yearning to believe.

Forbes elaborated in his charge the remedy of exact or dogmatic theology he had proposed in previous books and sermons. He held that in an age of uncertainty there was the need for the mind to rest upon something secure. Forbes was not addressing the doubts of those who had already rejected the divinity of Christ. His audience were members of the Church who believed in God and in God revealed in Christ, but were prey to doubts. He therefore took such belief for granted, wanting to provide the desired security of belief by reinforcing the sufficiency of the Christ-event for salvation and truth. Divine knowledge was given definitely, certainly, and completely by Christ. This revelation could be known assuredly through a combination of scripture interpreted by the early Church. The task of the Church since the apostles, according to Forbes, was simply to explain the fullness of revealed doctrine they had received for contemporary Christians, without addition or change; or to remind the Church of those parts of revealed truth it may have lost sight of. This was the basis for Forbes's charge—to remind the Church of the doctrine of the 'real, objective presence' of Christ in the Eucharist, and to affirm for Forbes's Christian audience the certainty of the original deposit of truth given by Christ to the Church.

According to Perry the first intimation of opposition to the charge came after Forbes's return from a summer holiday in the south of

---

[27] B. M. G. Reardon, *From Coleridge to Gore* (1971), 252.
[28] W. E. Houghton, *The Victorian Frame of Mind* (1957), 21.

France. At the meeting of the Episcopal Synod in September 1857, Bishop Walter Trower of Glasgow denounced the charge but full discussion was postponed until the following December meeting.[29] By the December meeting Trower had made a formal objection to Forbes's Eucharistic teaching in a letter to Bishop Charles Terrot of Edinburgh.[30]

Notice of Trower's intention was communicated to the bishops prior to the convening of the synod, so Forbes had prepared a protest against the synod having jurisdiction in a matter he regarded as lying within his diocesan autonomy. After Forbes had read this protest the meeting resolved by majority that it could not be sustained. Trower however withdrew his notice of motion in favour of a paper prepared by the primus, but the bishops could not agree to Terrot's script.[31] Charles Terrot had succeeded William Skinner of Aberdeen as primus only that year, so perhaps was constrained at the December meeting by his new role as chairman of the synod. But he openly declared himself a few days later when he, with Ewing and Trower, issued on their own authority a declaration against the charge.

Terrot was regarded by the nineteenth-century Episcopalian biographer, William Walker, as one of the ablest primuses of that century.[32] But, as primus, Terrot had a serious deficiency in that his background gave him little sympathy for the northern, nonjuring tradition of the Episcopal Church. Born in 1790, as a boy he spent his holidays with his uncle, who was minister of the qualified congregation of Haddington. After graduating from Trinity College, Cambridge, and ordination in England in 1814, he went back to Haddington as minister of the congregation, and the following year led them into union with the Episcopal Church. Walker commented that Terrot was 'much in sympathy with the Edinburgh clergy of the time, and the moderate High Church views which they professed—views, which, with slight modification, he held and taught to the last'.[33] Terrot was ordained Bishop of Edinburgh in 1841. Walker perfectly captures this careful, moderate High Churchman as one who looked upon himself as a 'Scottish rather than an English Churchman, but it was a Scottish Churchman of the Edinburgh or trans-Forthian type—one who had no sympathy with the Scotch Office or any of the Non-juring traditions.'[34] Terrot saw the Episcopal Church as

[29] Perry, 84.
[30] REC II. 11 Dec. 1857, SRO CH 12. 60. 3, 335.
[31] Ibid. 335–6.
[32] William Walker, *Three Churchmen* (1893), 95–6.
[33] Ibid. 106.
[34] Ibid. 120.

very much made in his own image, as comprised largely of moderate Anglicized High Churchmen like himself. This was not surprising, given that his pastoral experience was confined to the south of Scotland. In writing to Bishop William Skinner of Aberdeen in 1844 he said, 'I may mention that the impression on my mind is that the great majority of the laity are not in heart Scotch Episcopalians, but Church of England men, and I have heard from many, most of them Edinburgh people, some from Aberdeenshire, great stress laid upon the desireableness of perfect conformity [with the Church of England]'.[35]

The declaration by these three bishops highlighted conformity with the Church of England when it was published in the December 1857 edition of the *Scottish Ecclesiastical Journal*. It did not mention Forbes or his charge, but instead spoke of 'recent statements' on the Lord's Supper which appeared to be contradictory to the teaching of the Scottish Episcopal Church and the Church of England. The bishops declared their belief in five points, basically opposing Eucharistic adoration and sacrifice.[36] The declaration was an affirmation of High Church theology sympathetic to the Reformation, by three bishops with one eye on the Church of England.

Like all High Churchmen the three bishops were antagonistic to Rome, and to Tractarianism for its increasing Roman sympathies. A couple of months after Newman's conversion in 1845, Terrot criticized the few in Scotland who had followed Newman's example in seceding from the Episcopal Church as expressing 'no sort of horror at their apostasy'. Terrot, like High Churchmen generally, disliked religious extremism, considering the Episcopal Church was 'sadly harassed in Scotland by a few men who go into the extremes of Puritanism and Puseyism, and that have a bone of contention in our Scotch Communion Office'.[37] Similar concern, by the High Churchmen, about Tractarian Romanism, surfaced repeatedly throughout the controversy, as did High Church confidence and affection for the Church of England.

It was High Church partiality for the example and authority of the Church of England which provided the most immediate reason for opposition to Forbes. The Scottish bishops had long been seeking the removal of the legal disqualification of Episcopal clergy ordained by Scottish bishops to hold a living in England. This was a part of the Act of 1792 which had removed the illegal status of the Scottish Episcopal Church. In response to submissions by the Episcopal Synod

35 Ibid. 125.   36 *SEJ* (Jan. 1858), 17–18.
37 Walker, *Three Churchmen*, 126.

begun in 1837, an Act of 1840 relaxed this disqualification by permitting Scottish-ordained clergy to officiate in England, but only for
up to two days.[38] In 1853 the bishops pressed for further alleviation
when Forbes, William Skinner, and Charles Wordsworth prepared a petition for presentation to Parliament. Forbes had for some years been
opposed to the removal of the disqualification because he felt it would
draw the best clergy south into the more lucrative livings of the Church
of England. He changed his mind, however, when Episcopalian stipends
improved. In 1857 a clerical deputation was sent to London, consisting of
Terrot, Trower, and Wordsworth, all men ordained in England. In a
statement dated 24 July 1857 Terrot reported the failure of their efforts
in London to win influential friends to their cause. They were unable
even to secure a seconder for their proposal in the House of Commons.
This must have surprised the Scottish deputation, considering the record
of assistance for their Church by English High Churchmen going back to
the late eighteenth century.[39] For Terrot, the lack of success had two
causes—fear of the effect on the principle of establishment in assisting a
non-established Church in Scotland; but principally, opposition from
English Evangelicals.

Among those who we expected wd. favour us, we find that our proposition is
considered as subversive of the Establishment principle, & hostile to the supremacy of the crown. But the strongest opposition is from the Low Church—from the
party represented by the Record, by Exeter Hall, & considered as headed by
Lord Shaftesbury. A Society of this party called the Protestant Defence Society,
have issued a course of papers directed against the Scotch Epl. Church; and
though many of their misrepresentations are so gross as to disgust those who
know us, I regret to say that they have been too successful in persuading many,
that we ought not to be received into any nearer communion with the Ch. of
England.[40]

By the late 1850s Evangelicals could draw on their previous experience
with the anti-slavery movement, and later in support of Shaftesbury's
factory acts, so that they knew how to organize politically in support of
their desired ends. They were united in hostility to any closer ties
between the Church of England and the small, but more uniformly high
Church north of the border. When Terrot suggested a petition from

[38]   3 and 4 Victoria, cap. xxxiii.
[39]   F. Mather, *High Church Prophet: Bishop Samuel Horsley (1733–1806) and the
Caroline Tradition in the Later Georgian Church* (1992), 130 ff.
[40]   Unlisted papers: Bishop Terrot's report on the 1857 deputation to London in
regard to the legal disabilities, dated 24 July 1857, in Scottish Record Office, to be
added to CH 12.

Scotland supporting Episcopal relief, he was reminded by Wordsworth and Trower that they 'wd. be met & overwhelmed by a much larger mass of petitions from a well-organized party hostile to us'.[41]

After Terrot's report in July 1857 it must have been clear to the bishops just how formidable an obstacle the Evangelical party in the Church of England constituted. The bishops would either have to overcome that resistance or relinquish their hopes of legal alleviation. Terrot, Trower, and Wordsworth were convinced by their visit to London that the Evangelical opposition could not be beaten, so the other alternative was to mollify them. This meant stressing what the Episcopal Church had in common with Evangelical views, and playing down any High Church belief which could further alienate Evangelical suspicions. It was probably in reaction to such suggestions among his episcopal brethren that Forbes, in his charge, had dismissed the idea that abolishing the Scottish Communion Office would bring about closer sympathy between the Episcopal Church and English Evangelicals.

The Scottish bishops were not Evangelicals but they looked on conformity with England as a thing to be desired and sought to remove whatever within the Episcopal Church stood in the way of such conformity. Of the seven bishops, all but Alexander Ewing had been ordained priest in England, and all but Ewing and Forbes had been born there. Ewing, however, had no sympathy for the native traditions of Scottish Episcopacy. To be sure, Ewing had been born in Aberdeen, and had spent all his clerical life in the north of Scotland. But he had also been sent to school in Chelsea where he was deeply influenced by an Evangelical schoolmaster.[42] Although he had a romantic love for the highlands and their Celtic past, he too looked south and desired conformity with the Church of England. Unlike the Scottish Episcopal tradition and the Oxford Movement, Ewing did not regard episcopacy as being of the *esse* of the Church, and he was an advocate of union between the Episcopal Church and the Church of Scotland.[43]

Ewing and Terrot then had their own good reasons for issuing their declaration against Forbes's charge. In the same month of December this declaration was followed by a statement from Charles Wordsworth of St Andrews and Bishop Robert Eden of Moray and Ross which, they claimed, was issued to avoid any 'misunderstanding' at not having

[41] Ibid.

[42] M. Lochhead, *Episcopal Scotland in the Nineteenth Century* (1966), 161.

[43] J. Tulloch, *Movements of Religious Thought in Britain during the Nineteenth Century* (1885, repr. 1971), 324.

signed the earlier declaration. These two bishops stated they were
withholding their opinion for the present because of the prospect of
charges being brought against 'one of their brethren', and because the
matter was due to be discussed at the next Episcopal Synod anyway.[44]
Eden and Wordsworth evidently considered the declaration by the
other bishops premature and hasty, involving them in moral and judicial dilemmas should they be called on to act as judges over Forbes's
charge. At the same time they too were anxious lest silence be interpreted as approval for the charge.

Eden, at least, did not think the charge actually heretical. In a letter to
Terrot on 28 October 1857, he said he did not care for some of Forbes's
expressions, and particularly for the attempt in the charge further to
define doctrine. But Eden did not consider that Forbes went beyond 'the
latitude & opinion which the Church allows'. He also thought that any
adoption of judicial proceedings by the bishops against Forbes would
'work injury in our own Church, & in the Church of England'.[45]

Greater approval for the three bishops' declaration was more forthcoming in other quarters. Dean Ramsay and nineteen of the clergy of
Edinburgh diocese sent an address to their bishop giving their 'respectful
and grateful acknowledgement of the Declaration', and had it published
in the *Scottish Ecclesiastical Journal* in January 1858.[46] No doubt many of
these clergy were also troubled by the thought of an important distinction
between themselves and the Church of England. It has already been
observed how Anglicized the southern clergy had become by this time.
By 1860, of fifty-eight clergy in the two southernmost dioceses, thirty-
nine had been ordained in England.[47]

Opposition to Forbes's charge was gathering force and organization.
Following a meeting in Edinburgh on 23 January 1858 a memorial
opposing the charge, signed by 103 laymen headed by the Earl of
Wemyss, was presented to the three bishops. In this memorial Forbes
was mentioned by name for the first time in the controversy. The memorialists spoke strongly of 'pain and alarm that the Bishop of Brechin . . .
has promulgated doctrines repugnant to our convictions, and inconsistent
with what we have hitherto believed to be the tenets and the teaching of
the Church'. If Forbes's doctrines could claim his episcopal authority,
they feared there would no longer be adequate security for 'the teaching

[44] *SEJ* (Jan. 1858), 18.
[45] R. Eden to C. H. Terrot, 'Ss. Simon & Jude' [28 October] 1857, BrMs 1. 5. 3.
[46] *SEJ* (Jan. 1858), 18.
[47] *SEJ* (Jan. 1860), 13–18.

of the Protestant Faith which we profess'.[48] Like the southern clergy, many leading Episcopalian laity, especially among the upper classes, valued links with England, and desired conformity with the Church of England. They accepted that their Church was a Protestant body, and feared for its unity if Tractarian teaching like Forbes's were to prevail. One such lay opponent was Sir John Ogilvie, of Forbes's own congregation. He later wrote to Forbes reminding him that he had disapproved of the charge when it was first delivered. Ogilvie, a Member of Parliament and a Scottish landowner, admired Forbes's pastoral work among the poor of Dundee and disliked the manner and spirit of the bishop's opponents, but he could not support Forbes's teaching on the Eucharist.[49] He wanted to see the controversy over with as soon as possible so that Forbes and the Church could get back to the more important business of ameliorating the lot of the poor.

Forbes replied to Lord Wemyss in a public letter on 6 February 1858, respectfully questioning the theological competency of the laity to judge 'such abstruse subjects as are in the charge'. Further, he pressed for a canonical trial instead of such 'agitation' and, in conclusion, claimed his teaching was within the usual doctrinal toleration of the Anglican Church.

> If my doctrine is not the doctrine of the Church of Christ from the beginning, if it exceeds the wise latitude which the Anglican Church has ever allowed her children, I am quite prepared to take the consequences. I have the deepest conviction that what I have taught is the Truth of God, and therefore, I feel sure that eventually that truth will vindicate and assert its supremacy, even though at the cost of my personal comfort.[50]

So attitudes were hardening. The south, influenced by its proximity to England, and by English High Churchmanship, was increasingly against Forbes. Forbes on the other hand was actively pursuing the programme in defence of Tractarian Eucharistic teaching initiated by Keble. By courting the possibility of a trial, he was following Keble's suggestion that those who agreed with Denison could likewise publish the same teaching and so be liable to the same 'molestations and penalities'.[51] Forbes informed Gladstone in February 1858 of the 'terrible mess we have got ourselves into as a result of my charge' and told him that the declaration of the three bishops was being sent to congregations 'like a fiery cross'. He was now, he said, waiting for a further move against

---

[48] *SEJ* (Feb. 1858), 36.
[49] J. Ogilvie to A. P. Forbes, 24 Feb. 1860, BrMS 1. 2. 369.
[50] *SEJ* (Feb. 1858), 36.
[51] J. Keble, *On Eucharistical Adoration* (1857), 172.

him. The bishops were being led by Bishop Trower who was 'quite fanatical against me—the others are timid & very sorry for themselves. Hints at disruption & extensive Drummondizing have terrified them.'[52]

Forbes, though, did not wait for further opposition moves. On 16 January 1858 he told his nephew-in-law George Boyle (his 'Son in Xt', later the sixth Earl of Glasgow) that the second edition of his charge was being printed and that in it he had 'pretty well disposed of the Three Bishops' paper'. At this stage Forbes was feeling confident, even over-confident given that the public opposition already included most of the leading figures in the Episcopal Church. Remarking on the interest in the newspapers, he commented wryly, 'it is proof that the Presbyterians feel the hidden reality of our Church & the searching values of Catholic truth, that the charge of a single Bishop should set all Scotland in a commotion'.[53] Forbes seemed to be preparing himself to become a northern Denison and a Tractarian martyr for dogmatic truth.

Up to this point Pusey had not read Forbes's charge, but the possibility of judicial proceedings now made him do so. Pusey intervened in an attempt to mollify Trower, in the faint hope of their previous acquaintance in Oxford giving him some influence with the bishop.[54] Trower, who had been elected Bishop of Glasgow in 1848, was the first Englishman to be appointed a bishop in the Episcopal Church who had not previously worked in Scotland. Forbes doubted Pusey would change Trower's mind, suspecting there was deep personal feeling behind it, for he was 'a lapsed high churchman, and they are always the most rabid opponents'.[55] On 26 February Trower wrote a long letter in reply to Pusey which forcefully set out his position, defending the declaration of the three bishops as a personal statement of faith and not a formal theological definition. He thought that a formal trial was now almost inevitable and that if the result of that trial was to permit a diversity of teaching on Eucharistic adoration, he would resign. Forbes, Trower believed, should have known better than to teach his doctrine '*ex cathedra*', given that Forbes's knowledge of Trower's beliefs should have made him aware that Trower was likely to object strongly to the teaching of the charge. Trower then blamed Pusey's teaching for destroying his own hopes for a theological consensus among 'moderate men on both sides'. Pusey could not therefore complain, he wrote, about this

[52] A. P. Forbes to W. E. Gladstone, 14 Feb. 1858, BL 44154, fo. 220.
[53] A. P. Forbes to G. F. Boyle, 16 Jan. 1858, BrMs 1. 5. 14.
[54] E. B. Pusey to J. Keble, n.d. [19 Feb. 1858], PK v.
[55] A. P. Forbes to E. B. Pusey, 25 Feb. [1858], PP 5. 40.

'Theological reaction which has now set in'. Trower said he did not believe in winking 'at such approximations to Romish practices and doctrine as you and the Bp. of B. put out, but to oppose them firmly at whatever cost to personal comfort'. Explaining that he desired a judgement by the Episcopal Synod against Forbes's teaching, Trower maintained he had the 'strongest and gravest disapproval of your cause since the very early days of the Oxford Movement'.[56]

Trower, like many of Forbes's opponents, believed Forbes was claiming an *ex cathedra* status for his teaching. But nowhere in his original charge did Forbes explicitly claim that the doctrines he expounded were the sole authorized teaching of the Anglican Church. In fact, he specifically acknowledged that the Church of England had not defined any doctrine on Eucharistic presence.[57] But some of Forbes's expressions certainly lent themselves to Trower's interpretation. Forbes claimed to say only 'what she [the Church] says'.[58] He also asserted that 'Holy Church . . . has with one voice [throughout history] declared . . . that the bread of the Eucharist is the Flesh of the Incarnate Jesus'.[59] He did however recognize that differing interpretations were not excluded by the Church. No doubt Forbes viewed this as a blurring of Catholic truth, but he accepted it as a fact of Anglican history. In his original charge, however, he was not sufficiently clear about this, and some of his expressions, combined with the fact he was speaking as a bishop to his clergy, gave opponents the impression he taught these doctrines as definitive. In this impression they were probably correct in so far as Forbes's inmost understanding went, even perhaps regarding his intention in the charge. But they were incorrect about his public statements, and by February 1858 Forbes was already following Keble's advice to claim only toleration for his teaching.

But Trower admitted that he was motivated by a long-standing dislike of the Oxford Movement which stretched back to the days when he was a tutor at Oriel College.[60] Forbes could have been right about Trower's sense of personal grievance as Trower may have found life difficult at Oxford during the years of Tractarian ascendency. Whatever the personal bias, however, Trower clearly objected most of all to the Roman Catholic tendencies he saw in the Oxford Movement.

---

[56] W. Trower to E. B. Pusey, 26 Feb. [1858], PK v.
[57] Forbes, *Primary Charge*, 12.
[58] Ibid. 6.
[59] Ibid. 7.
[60] H. P. Liddon, *Life of E. B. Pusey*, i (1893), 140.

He was stirred into action by Forbes's charge because it seemed to give Oxford Movement teaching an episcopal imprimatur, and he was anxious to secure an authoritative denial of Forbes's teaching, lest its influence grow within the Episcopal Church.

To what extent was Trower right in blaming Forbes for the ensuing controversy? Trower argued that the cause of the controversy was Forbes setting forth his teaching as definitive in a diocesan charge. Forbes, on the other hand, pointed to Trower's opposition as the instigation of opposition, which until then had been silent. Forbes certainly provided the issue for the controversy by choosing to propound Tractarian teaching on the Eucharist, which he must have known would have been contentious, given the Denison precedent and his knowledge of the High Church views of the Scottish bishops. Forbes also extended the audience for his charge by having it published. Although it may have been true for Forbes to say that there was no opposition to his teaching until Trower's formal complaint to the Episcopal Synod, the degree of support for the three bishops' declaration demonstrates the existence of widespread dissent from Forbes's teaching. Forbes must therefore bear the responsibility for initiating the resulting controversy. However, until the declaration of the three bishops, the controversy was carried out entirely within the confines of the Episcopal Synod. It was the publication of that declaration, and the letter of Wordsworth and Eden, which turned the disagreement among the bishops into a public one. Forbes had already published his charge twice, but that was a theological document of some fifty pages likely to appeal to a restricted audience. The declaration on the other hand was a short and direct appeal to public sentiment, published in the *Scottish Ecclesiastical Journal*, the Episcopalian newspaper. It was this declaration which instigated the memorials by the Edinburgh clergy and Lord Wemyss and the laity. Led by Trower's fervent opposition, and their anxiety about offending the Church of England, it was the five bishops who took their theological differences into the public arena.

Yet Forbes was finding himself somewhat isolated. Not only was opposition hardening among the bishops, and the more Anglicized southern clergy and laity, but also among the northern clergy, who were not entirely happy with his teaching. Suspicions of Roman Catholic tendencies in Forbes's teaching accounted for the opposition from some not raised in the English High Church tradition. John Alexander, for example, was one of the Edinburgh clergy who had signed the memorial to Bishop Terrot, supporting the declaration of the three bishops. Alexander was an authentic representative of the

northern tradition working in the south, where he was priest at the
newly built St Columba's in Edinburgh. He had been educated at
Marischal College, Aberdeen, and on his mother's side was descended
from a Jacobite executed after the battle of Culloden.[61] Alexander said
he understood the bishops to be claiming Christ was present in the
consecrated elements in 'virtue and efficacy: but He is not present in
the very substance of His flesh and blood, so that they can be worshipped there. Their proposition presents no difficulty to me.'[62] This
was the same virtualism in Eucharistic doctrine that Forbes and the
Oxford Movement regarded as inadequately specific and insufficiently
objective. In keeping with that northern tradition Alexander was
strongly anti-Roman Catholic. He wanted to spread the influence and
use of the Scottish Communion Office in the south and was therefore
anxious to distance himself and the Office from any apparent Roman
tendencies, which would be prejudicial to that aim. Alexander's fear
that the doctrine Forbes was teaching would lead to secessions to
Rome lay behind his concerns that the 'new views' may claim to be
'the true Catholic doctrine', but those who held them 'have been slowly
leaving the Church'. William Bright at Trinity College, Glenalmond,
reported that the Aberdeenshire clergy generally were not favourable
towards any doctrine which departed from the expressions used by
Bishop Jolly in his books on the Eucharist earlier in the century.[63] The
northern clergy, unlike the Tractarians, did not feel the old theological
language of virtualism was in any sense inadequate and were therefore
content to use it. It was understood in the north that Forbes was not
upholding this traditional virtualist language in his charge, and that left
him with few supporters among Episcopal clergy.

Forbes's most fervent supporters were those Anglo-Catholics who
wrote for the *Union Newspaper*. The *Union* was the organ of the Association for the Promotion of the Unity of Christendom, which was
dedicated to the corporate reunion of the Anglican and Roman Catholic
Churches, and its support could only increase suspicions of Forbes's
Roman sympathies. Included among these supporters were the clergy
of St Ninian's Cathedral, Perth. Provost Fortescue and Canon Henry
Humble were ardent English Anglo-Catholics who had declined to
moderate their ways at the request of Wordsworth, their bishop. As a

---

[61] R. Johnson, 'A Short History of St. Columba's Episcopal Church 1843–1969'
(typed booklet, 1977), SRO CH. 12. 5. 81, 12.
[62] J. Alexander to W. Brand, 24 Feb. 1858, SRO CH 12. 5. 74.
[63] W. Bright to G. F. Boyle, postmarked 27 Feb. 1858, BrMs 1. 5. 15.

Tractarian foundation, the St Ninian's clergy were among the few in Scotland to belong to the younger, ritualist generation of the Catholic revival.

Support was also forthcoming from Forbes's diocesan clergy. Some, like Robert Thom of Drumlithie, were personally sympathetic towards the Tractarians. But many had become loyal to Forbes personally, through admiration for his pastoral energies and through his personal charm. In March 1858 the Brechin clergy published an address of sympathy and support for Forbes, stating their 'entire confidence' in his teaching. It was signed by fourteen clergy. William Henderson of Arbroath published a separate declaration stating that he disavowed the Eucharistic doctrines within Forbes's charge.[64]

An extraordinary meeting of the Episcopal Synod was called in May 1858. A Pastoral Letter was moved, addressed 'to all faithful members of the Church in Scotland', and was prompted, the bishops claimed, by the degree of opposition to the charge and particularly by its republication in a second edition. This second edition had been prompted by Forbes's need to refute the declaration of the three bishops. At this time in the controversy there was little preparedness for compromise by any party in their search for self-justification. For the first time the bishops referred to Forbes and his charge by name. At the heart of their objection was the bishops' belief that Forbes's teaching would lead inevitably to 'corruptions and superstitions', that is, to Roman teaching and Eucharistic devotions. The bishops called upon the clergy to teach the essential mystery of Christ's Eucharistic presence, and affirmed: the Episcopal Church had no requirement for its faithful to believe this presence was a substantial one; that the Eucharistic sacrifice was one of praise and thanksgiving, the sacrifice of the cross being all-sufficient for salvation; while the consecrated elements of the Eucharist were to be treated with veneration, these gestures of reverence did not imply the corporal presence of Christ.[65] Forbes protested the competency of the synod to issue such a letter because he believed the canons of the Church gave responsibility for the declaration of doctrine only to the General Synod.[66] The motion for the pastoral passed with all the bishops but Forbes voting in its favour.

The bishops then considered various memorials sent to the synod. The first was from fifty clergy of all seven dioceses. These regretted the issuing of what they called 'quasi definitions of faith by individual

[64] *SEJ* (March 1858), 50.
[65] *SEJ* (May 1858), Supplement, 1–2.
[66] Ibid. 2–4.

prelates' when there was a canonical procedure of discipline that could be used. The clergy also asked the bishops to discourage 'all unauthoritative definitions of faith' and to refrain in future from 'putting-forth extrajudicial opinions or rules of Discipline tending to curtail the liberty the Church has allowed'. To this attempt to restrain them by impartially criticizing both Forbes and his episcopal opponents, the bishops replied that it was not open to the clergy to petition the Episcopal Synod directly, but only through their various diocesan synods. The bishops also received a memorial signed by nearly six hundred laymen, who protested the charge as teaching doctrines inconsistent with the Protestant faith. The bishops merely referred those who signed them to the Pastoral Letter. The synod concluded by agreeing to communicate the Pastoral to each of the diocesan synods.[67]

As far as Forbes was concerned the Pastoral Letter was a 'fearful document', and he did not see how his position and that of his supporters in his diocese could remain tenable. But he promised Pusey that he would hold on as long as he could.[68] He could derive some comfort from the support of English friends, who were now becoming increasingly interested in these Scottish developments. Richard Benson, at a meeting of the Brotherhood of the Holy Trinity on 2 June 1858, proposed a motion of encouragement.[69] More publicly, there was Keble's *Considerations Suggested by a Late Pastoral Letter on the Doctrine of the Most Holy Eucharist*, written to show the Pastoral Letter did not possess synodical authority. Forbes also informed his brother George that he had a long talk with Gladstone 'who is heartily with us'.[70]

At this time George Forbes was beginning to be extensively consulted about the controversy by Bishop Wordsworth. Wordsworth wrote on 31 July to say he had read, and been encouraged by, George's theological opposition to his brother's teaching, which he had published as an appendix in his own privately printed periodical, the *Gospel Messenger*.[71] Despite having contracted polio as a child which left him permanently crippled, George Forbes was ordained in 1848 and given charge of the small mission at Burntisland. His physical handicap did not prevent

[67] Ibid. 5.
[68] E. B. Pusey to J. Keble, 29 May 1858, PK v.
[69] BHT Minutes, Nov. 1856–June 1859, 103.
[70] A. P. Forbes to G. H. Forbes, 17 June 1858, BrMs 1. 5. 36.
[71] These appendices were later collected and published by Forbes in a concurrent publication known as the *Panoply*. The appendix Bishop Wordsworth was referring to in his letter to George Forbes (dated 31 July 1858) must have been that originally published in the *Gospel Messenger* between 20 June and 25 September 1858, later republished in the *Panoply* as 'Eucharistical Adoration'.

him from becoming an erudite liturgical scholar, whose work has been
ranked alongside Jean Mabillon's, the great seventeenth-century French
liturgist.[72] Devoted all his life to the native Episcopal tradition represented
by the Scottish Communion Office, George was the most learned representative of that northern tradition. His article was ostensibly written
to refute Keble's *Considerations*, but there is little doubt that George had
his brother's charge clearly in mind. As opposed to those he called
'Adorationists', he did not think Eucharistic adoration a doctrine of the
early Church. Its appearance in the Anglican Church he attributed to the
devotional poverty of the Book of Common Prayer of 1552. This resulted,
he said, in devout Anglicans seeking 'new and unauthorized' rituals to
satisfy their feelings about the Eucharist.[73] According to George Forbes
the Oxford Movement doctrines of his brother were an understandable,
but wrong and illegal departure from the teaching of the early Church,
and hence of the Episcopal Church as well. He blamed their appearance
on the lack of use of the Scottish Communion Office, and on the comparative devotional deficiency of the English liturgy.

The appearance of this article presented Bishop Wordsworth with a
fortuitous weapon. Not only was it written by a capable scholar and
leading representative of the northern tradition, but also by Alexander's
brother. At the end of July Wordsworth wrote to George Forbes, com-
plimenting him on his article which he thought would give Keble, 'or
any of that School, much ado to answer it satisfactorily'. He explained
that he was himself preparing some 'Notes' on the controversy for private
circulation and for his clergy, making use of one or two references from
Forbes's article.[74] George assisted Wordsworth with these *Notes*, and also
with his *Opinion*[75] published later that year.[76] This assistance to the man
who was rapidly succeeding Trower as Alexander's leading opponent
among the bishops incensed their sister Helen. Not only was she
mortified at the open knowledge of their division among people she met,
she also considered George unfaithful to the brother to whom he owed
his ordination. 'He [Alexander] alone induced my Father to consent . . .

    [72] J. B. Primrose, 'The Pitsligo Press of George Hay Forbes', in *Edinburgh
Bibliographical Society Transactions*, iv (1962), 56.
    [73] George Hay Forbes, 'Eucharistical Adoration', in the *Panoply*, 2. (n.d.), 264–5.
    [74] C. Wordsworth, *Notes to Assist towards Forming a Right Judgement on the Eucharistic
Controversy* (1858); and C. Wordsworth to G. H. Forbes, 31 July 1858, SAUL 19. 2. 192.
    [75] C. Wordsworth, *Opinion of the Bishop of St. Andrews on the Appeal of the Rev. P.
Cheyne* (1858).
    [76] C. Wordsworth to G. H. Forbes, 5 Oct. 1858, SAUL 19. 2. 198; and 15 Nov.
[1858], SAUL 19. 2. 201.

when my Father objected to his ordination George feigned a sort of madness—Dr Smith was in attendance. He said it was not real madness but a disappointment!! Since that time a great soreness has remained & extreme jealousy of Alexander, of the great influence he has over us in these matters, whereas George has none.'[77] Helen was evidently very much under the influence of her older brother.[78] Yet her mention of this story to an old family friend supports its veracity, which suggests that George had ambivalent feelings towards his brother. To a man determined to succeed despite his serious disability, George may have found it galling to know he owed his sought-after ordination to the brother who was more successful in their common profession. Even in scholarship, where George was more brilliant, Alexander produced more, being less hampered by George's near-obsession to consider everything available before publication. George's ambivalence must have been increased by Alexander's evident care for his brother, and his deference towards George in the correspondence they shared on matters of scholarly collaboration, such as the editing of the Arbuthnott Missal. It may be that the Eucharistic controversy gave George an opportunity to oppose his brother publicly on a matter of principle, without incurring too much odium, except among his family to whom Alexander was a favourite and a leader. But George was also led to assist Wordsworth by the bishop's apparent support for the Scottish Communion Office. Writing to George in November, Wordsworth must have encouraged him when he said, 'People, I find, are beginning to discover the value of the S. Office.'[79] Expressing such sentiments, Wordworth could have given George Forbes the impression he had found another supporter of the Scottish Office among the bishops, a supporter free of the dubious Tractarian doctrines of his brother.

The Brechin Diocesan Synod met on 4 August 1858. Forbes tabled the bishops' Pastoral, and in his charge deplored 'the acrimony and excitement' by which the controversy was carried on. Included in such deplorable things for Forbes was the involvement of 'men of the world [laymen] unlearned in the nice distinctions of Theological study'. But he was especially perturbed by rancorous divisions among the clergy. He drew a characteristic Tractarian connection when he said that divine truth would only prevail according to the 'earnestness and holiness of its propagators'. He made another claim for toleration of

[77] H. Forbes to W. Brand, n.d., SRO CH 12. 5. 45.
[78] H. Forbes to G. H. Forbes, n.d. and incomplete, SAUL 19. 2. 205.
[79] C. Wordsworth to G. H. Forbes, 15 Nov. [1858], SAUL 19. 2. 201.

his teaching. 'On the profound mystery, such as is the Holy Eucharist, there must be an infinite variety of ways in which the Truth presents itself to our acceptance, and therefore we must ever try . . . to make the best of the imperfect belief of those we have to do with.'[80]

For the rest of 1858 Forbes's charge took a back seat in the increasing controversy, as his own case became entwined with the fortunes of two like-minded clergy—Patrick Cheyne, priest of St Andrew's, Aberdeen, and William Bright, theological tutor at Trinity College, both of whom held the same Eucharistic theology as Forbes. Cheyne, who had spent all his life in the north, had given a series of sermons on the Eucharist during Lent of 1857 emphasizing the real presence. He had published them early in 1858, although Forbes had counselled him against it.[81] The Eucharistic teaching of his sermons resulted in his presentation to Bishop Thomas Suther, and to his trial by the bishop before the diocesan synod in June 1858. In a trial described by its historian as biased and partisan, with the bishop determined to understand Cheyne's teaching to be as similar to Roman Catholic doctrine as possible, Cheyne was found guilty of false teaching. The sentence was delayed until after his appeal to the Episcopal Synod.[82] On 21 July, the bishops dismissed the appeal on the grounds that Bishop Suther had acted within his prerogative, despite the protests of a number of Aberdeen clergy and some laity over the fairness of the trial proceedings. Forbes was the only bishop to uphold the appeal, opining that Cheyne was not guilty of subverting the teaching of the Episcopal Church by teaching Roman Catholic doctrine. Forbes thought Cheyne had deliberately set out to be controversial, but considered that if Suther's judgement were upheld it would result in the exclusion of Episcopalians who agreed with Cheyne's theology.[83] Cheyne appealed again to the Episcopal Synod and this was heard on 30 September, after which the synod adjourned to 4 November to deliver its judgement.[84]

Concurrently with this judgement against Cheyne for his Eucharistic teaching William Bright, a close associate of Forbes, was dismissed from his post at Trinity College in August 1858, for some remarks also in favour of the real presence. According to Forbes the attack on Bright had followed a 'friendly' letter to Bright from Bishop Trower, who had

[80]   Brechin Diocese Synod Minutes, BrMs 4. 1. 3, 53–62.

[81]   *Opinion of the Bishop of Brechin, in the Appeal of the Rev. P. Cheyne, against the sentence of the Bishop of Aberdeen* (1858), 3.

[82]   Gibb N. Pennie, 'The Trial of the Rev. Patrick Cheyne for Erroneous Teaching on the Eucharist in Aberdeen in 1858' in *RSCHS*, 23 (1987), 77–93.

[83]   *Opinion of the Bishop of Brechin*, 1–2.

[84]   REC II, 30 Sept.–1 Oct. 1858, SRO CH 12. 60. 3, 361–77.

referred to Keble's book on Eucharistic adoration. Bright in reply had expressed his agreement with Keble. Trower then told Bright he would be urging his removal.[85] Dr Hannah, warden of Trinity College, had dismissed Bright for not retaining a neutrality in the Eucharistic controversy. But Forbes was certain that the real cause of the sacking was Bright's sympathy with his charge.[86]

After the September Episcopal Synod a formal presentment for trial was made against Forbes. William Henderson, Forbes's old opponent and a High Churchman who valued conformity with the Church of England, with two of his vestrymen, lodged a presentment on 3 October 1858. The presentment charged Forbes with teaching doctrines contrary to the Thirty-nine Articles, the Book of Common Prayer, and the Scottish Communion Office. Specifically, the presenters alleged three unsanctioned doctrines. First, Forbes undermined Article 31 on the all-sufficiency of Christ's sacrifice by teaching the substantial unity of the cross and the Eucharistic sacrifice. Secondly, contrary to Article 38 Forbes called for adoration of Christ in the Eucharist. Thirdly, Forbes contradicted Article 29 by teaching that those without a living faith who receive holy communion do receive Christ.[87] Proceedings on this presentment however had to wait until the matter of Cheyne's appeal was completed. The Episcopal Synod reconvened in Edinburgh on 4 November to deliver its verdict. Cheyne's teaching was again adjudged erroneous, and subversive of the doctrines of the Church. The priest was given until the court met again on 2 December to retract. Forbes asked that his protest against the judgement be recorded in the minutes.[88]

The judgement of the bishops prompted a clerical reaction. A number of priests met at Stonehaven on 18 November, including some impetuous younger clergy. At least a few of these junior priests were considering schism, and one of them asked Forbes if he would lead them.[89] Forbes backed more moderate counsels and was relieved when the meeting decided upon a declaration of belief rather than a protest to the bishops.[90]

The reconvened Episcopal Synod on 2 December 1858 dismissed Cheyne's appeal in its entirety, and Forbes reiterated his protest. The sentence against Cheyne, passed previously by Bishop Suther, now came

[85] A. P. Forbes to W. E. Gladstone, 22 Feb. [1858], Gladstone Papers, BL 44154, fo. 230.

[86] A. P. Forbes to W. E. Gladstone, 29 Aug. 1858, Gladstone Papers, BL 44154, fo. 226.

[87] Presentment, BrMS 1. 1. 198.

[88] REC II, 4 Nov. 1858, SRO CH. 12. 60. 3, 383–4.

[89] D. Sandford to A. P. Forbes, 18 Nov. 1858, BrMS 1. 1. 12.

[90] J. Moir to A. P. Forbes, 19 Nov. 1858, BrMS 1. 1. 13 (i).

into effect and he was suspended as a priest until he retracted his published *Six Sermons*. Forbes considered that the bishops' judgement established
the theological leadership of Charles Wordsworth among his opponents.[91]

Forbes attempted to resolve William Bright's position at this time by
offering him a licence in Brechin diocese. Bright was touched by the
offer, but felt he could not accept as he was not resident. Instead he
asked if he might be made one of Forbes's chaplains as he had decided to
accept the offer from George Boyle of unofficial residence at the cathedral and college at Cumbrae (another Tractarian establishment financed
by George Boyle).[92]

During the Episcopal Synod on 2 December Forbes evidently
approached Wordsworth about the Eucharistic controversy. Wordsworth,
in a letter to Forbes on 21 December 1858, referred to his inability 'to
take any step in the direction which you mentioned when you were in
Edinburgh'. What these steps were, and whether they referred to
Cheyne's case or to his own presentment, it is impossible now to discern
as Forbes's letter initiating them no longer seems to exist. But from
Forbes's description of his letter as 'eirenic' it would appear it was the
beginning of an attempt to find some sort of theological compromise.
However, on the same day Wordsworth returned unopened Forbes's
communication because he had been stung by a letter in the *Guardian*
from Pusey critical of himself.[93] Forbes considered publishing his letter to
Wordsworth, believing 'it will do damage to the enemy'.[94] Boyle encouraged this so as to make it known that Forbes desired peace.[95] Henry
Humble, who wrote for the *Union*, also encouraged publication because
he characteristically saw things in militant terms—Anglo-Catholics versus
Protestant High Churchmen. Humble wrote, 'we are at war, when all
arrangements applicable to a state of peace are at an end.'[96] A bitingly
polite exchange of letters followed between the principal protagonists.
Wordsworth sent Forbes a copy of his *Notes* and their Supplement, the
writing of which he claimed to be a 'distasteful' task, undertaken
reluctantly at the request of others. Wordsworth considered he had said
nothing invidious, although he did not expect it to appear that way to
Forbes.[97] Forbes responded with the caustic politeness he sometimes used

91 E. B. Pusey to A. P. Forbes, n.d., BrMS 1. 1. 82.
92 W. Bright to A. P. Forbes, n.d., BrMS 1. 1. 38.
93 C. Wordsworth to A. P. Forbes, 'St. Thomas' Day' [21 Dec.], BrMS 1. 1. 49.
94 A. P. Forbes to G. F. Boyle, 6 Jan. 1859, BrMS 1. 6. 60 (ii).
95 G. F. Boyle to A. P. Forbes, 6 Jan. [1859], BrMS 1. 1. 63.
96 H. Humble to A. P. Forbes, 7 Jan. 1859, BrMS 1. 1. 65.
97 C. Wordsworth to A. P. Forbes, 8 Jan. 1859, BrMS 1. 1. 66.

to criticize others, and said he was 'glad' of the opportunity presented by their correspondence to let Wordsworth know he had informed Keble and others that his letter had been returned unopened.[98]

Wordsworth's *Notes* were the most succinct expression of his position in all his pamphlets on the controversy, so it is worth while examining it as a presentation of his case against Forbes. The pamphlet was first printed in September 1858 for the use of his clergy. Wordsworth had it reprinted in January 1859, to include a Supplement written as a rebuttal to extra theological authorities offered in Keble's *Considerations*, and by Cheyne in his appeal. The need for a second printing makes it questionable whether its circulation was as restricted as Wordsworth claimed. As well as seeking to refute Forbes and Keble, Wordsworth was primarily concerned to uphold the authority of the bishops' Pastoral Letter, which he described by the authoritative title of a 'Synodal Letter'. Most of the pamphlet was concerned to demonstrate that, according to Wordsworth, the patristic and Anglican divines Forbes and Keble used did not support their theological claims for the Eucharist. But it was in the last two chapters that Wordsworth set out his own arguments and where his language was strongest. He accused Forbes of disloyalty and denigration towards the theologians of the Episcopal past, such as the Nonjurors, encouraging insubordination, and promoting 'a conspiracy against Episcopal and Synodical authority'.[99] In the final chapter Wordsworth defended the Pastoral Letter against the accusation of having narrowed the terms of communion in the Episcopal Church. He claimed that the fundamental question at the basis of the controversy was: 'has the Church the power simply to censure a Publication which it considers *offensive* and *dangerous*? And if so, who are the Parties to exercise this power, according to the existing constitution of our own Church?'[100] Wordsworth answered his own question by saying that censorship was necessary, because some disputed questions could only be settled by authority. He then claimed it was the bishops to whom the existing constitution gave 'the chief ordinary powers of administration and jurisdiction'. Forbes, he said, was guilty of insubordination in conspiring against this constitutional authority. The Pastoral Letter, therefore, was not merely the 'letter of six bishops' as Forbes's supporters claimed, but a 'Godly admonition' of synodical authority. Wordsworth claimed that the Pastoral was also issued

---

[98] A. P. Forbes to C. Wordsworth, n.d., BrMS 1. 1. 67.
[99] C. Wordsworth, *Notes to Assist towards forming a Right Judgement on the Eucharistic Controversy* (1858), 51.
[100] Ibid. 54.

to restate the 'anti-Roman position' of the Episcopal Church. Otherwise Forbes's charge would lead the Church back to the corruption and superstition from which the Reformation had delivered it.[101]

Who was right? As to the correct exegesis of patristic and Anglican theologians, both Forbes and Wordsworth used these writings simply as proof texts, without regard to the historic context in which the various theologians were writing. Therefore they both tended to read into them the theological arguments they themselves wanted to uphold. But the crux of Wordsworth's accusations was that Forbes, in not accepting the censure of the Pastoral Letter, was guilty of denying the properly constituted authority of the Episcopal Church that he, as a bishop, was sworn to uphold. So Wordsworth's case hinged on the exact authority of the Pastoral. Was it simply the considered opinion of the majority of the bishops, or had it the synodical authority Wordsworth claimed? Wordsworth alleged the existing constitution of the Church gave the bishops the authority to issue the Pastoral. This constitution could only be the legislation enacted in the canons, and those in effect at the time had been passed by the General Synod of 1838. Forbes argued that in pronouncing on a matter of doctrine the Episcopal Synod exceeded its authority and trespassed on the preserve of General Synod. Canon 38 of the 1838 canons described a pastoral letter as 'containing an account of all the circumstances and occurrences, adverse as well as prosperous, which they [the bishops] think it may be for the benefit of the Church to be generally known'. It said nothing about doctrine. The canons did describe the Episcopal Synod as the final court of appeal in matters of ecclesiastical dispute (canon 35), which obviously could include disputes about doctrine. But the May synod, which issued the Pastoral, had no such appeal before it to give the bishops jurisdiction. In fact the canons made no mention of doctrine, the defining or explanation of it, whatsoever. The only business of an Episcopal Synod mentioned by the canons was the receiving of appeals (canon 34). The Introduction to the canons did mention doctrine as 'fixed and immutable' because founded on scripture, but it did not say who or what defined it. There was therefore no canonical, that is, no constitutional, authority for the bishops to issue a pastoral letter pronouncing on doctrine; indeed no constitutional authority for them to make any binding judgement on doctrine at all, save by way of acting as a court of appeal, or in the trial of a bishop. On the basis of the constitutional authority Wordsworth appealed to, Forbes was not compelled to accept the bishops' Pastoral Letter, even if it was issued by the majority at an

[101] Ibid. 57–9.

Episcopal Synod. The only document that did seem to bear upon any requirement of Forbes to accept the Pastoral as a binding authority was the eighteenth-century concordat he had signed on his consecration as a bishop. According to this, all bishops promised 'that in all matters relating to the Church, Worship and Discipline' they would be 'determined' by a majority of the bench. But this concordat was not mentioned by Words-worth, who instead insisted on the 'synodal authority' of the Episcopal Synod as exercising 'the chief ordinary powers of administration and jurisdiction'. But these powers did not include the definition of doctrine. Indeed that power was not explicitly given to any body by the constitu-tion, unless the General Synod elected to do so by framing a canon. Authority over doctrine, except by way of judicial appeal to the Episcopal Synod, was constitutionally in a vacuum, a vacuum the Episcopal Synod was trying to fill, being the oldest, continuing, authoritative body in the Episcopal Church. Those doctrinal disputes which had arisen in the past, such as the authority of bishops and of the Scottish Communion Office, had been jurisdictional. The Eucharistic controversy was a more purely doctrinal dispute, and much of the confusion in the controversy arose because, until Forbes was legally presented for trial, it remained uncertain just who had authority to pronounce on doctrinal matters and could require the obedience of the disputants. Such confusion was only made worse when the one group claiming such authority, the bishops in synod, were also parties to the controversy through their various publications.

A follow-up to the Stonehaven meeting took place among the clergy on 20 January 1859 at Laurencekirk. Forbes asked George Boyle to attend as a check on the more extreme.[102] The meeting passed three resolutions, which essentially agreed to do nothing regarding the Cheyne judgement except to assert the right of the clergy to 'hold & teach all such doctrine as was taught from the beginning by the undivided Church'.[103] While content with the meeting's moderation Forbes was feeling less confident than some about its consequences. One of the signatories to the Laurencekirk resolutions, James Smith, Dean of Moray and incumbent of Forgue in the Diocese of Aberdeen, was to be dismissed by Eden of Moray as his dean and tried by Bishop Suther for his signing what Suther believed to be an act contumacious to his judgement in the Cheyne case. Forbes asked Boyle on 11 February 1859 to be a support for the dean as he himself could not, because if

[102] A. P. Forbes to G. F. Boyle, postmarked 13 Jan. 1859, BrMS 1. 6. 62.
[103] Excerpts from the minutes of the Laurencekirk Meeting, notes in the hand of George Boyle, BrMS 1. 8. 166 (ii).

the case went to appeal Forbes could find himself one of Smith's judges.[104] Boyle responded on 21 February with a crucial assessment of the situation that revealed how much in the minority Cheyne (and therefore Forbes also) was in his theological opinions. According to Boyle most of the northern clergy did not support Cheyne's doctrines, and were content with a virtualist theology. Cheyne, wrote Boyle, was experiencing a 'sad awakening; he fancied he had more nonjuring support & that a large number really held "the doctrines", he finds that while *many* with true Scottish caution "decline to commit themselves" to such a document [as the Laurencekirk declarations] or are fully prepared for a conflict between the "Second Order" & the First, the proportion of those who *really* hold the doctrines he taught is not great.'[105] That was also true, said Boyle, of Dean Smith who *'barely approves'* of Cheyne's teaching, but was prepared to stand trial for 'constitutional liberty'. Boyle concluded that the dean, 'like most of our friends has a somewhat loose hold of the dogma'.[106] Boyle had already advised Forbes in a letter the previous day that 'very few even of the most zealous clergy wd. hold with Mr Cheyne . . . we are in a very complex state, our friends are *fewer and less consistent* than was once hoped'.[107] Even after his charge and subsequent elucidations, Forbes therefore learned from Boyle that most of the northern clergy held to the old High Church virtualism rather than his innovative Tractarian Eucharistic theology. With such a pessimistic but knowledgeable informant, it is not surprising that Forbes's hopes were fading, and so Keble was once again the recipient of Forbes's 'sad thoughts'.[108]

There was a change at this time in the episcopal bench when Trower tendered his resignation in February. In his place the dean of the diocese, William Scot Wilson, whom Boyle described as a low churchman, was elected.[109] Yet Wilson was entirely a Scottish Churchman by birth, education, and ordination, having personal links with prominent northern Churchmen of an earlier generation like Bishop David Low of Moray and Ross. But, from his many years of working in the south, he also disliked the Scottish Communion Office as an obstacle to conformity with the Church of England.[110] Forbes wrote to Wilson congratulating him on

[104] A. P. Forbes to G. F. Boyle, postmarked 11 Feb. 1859, BrMS 1. 6. 65.
[105] G. F. Boyle to A. P. Forbes, 17 Feb. [1859], BrMS 1. 1. 96.
[106] G. F. Boyle to A. P. Forbes, 'Wedn. morning' [Feb. 1859], BrMS 1. 1. 99.
[107] G. F. Boyle to A. P. Forbes, 17 Feb. [1859], BrMS 1. 1. 96.
[108] J. Keble to A. P. Forbes, 25 Feb. 1859, BrMS 1. 1. 97.
[109] G. F. Boyle to A. P. Forbes, 17 Feb. [1859], BrMS 1. 1. 96.
[110] Lochhead, *Episcopal Scotland*, 223–4.

his election, and commented that, 'in a small community like ours, our difficulties are much increased'.[111]

Forbes had experienced 'a solitary and trying Winter'. His delicate health never found winter in Dundee easy at the best of times, and his doubts and difficulties had grown since the bishops' decision went against Cheyne. He told Gladstone on 8 April 1859 that he thought he had maintained his ground and was now trusting 'to the truth and beauty of the doctrines I have so imperfectly advocated, for their final triumph'.[112] But this was small comfort when approval for those doctrines, either as expressed by himself or Cheyne, was so poor. Apart from the watered-down Laurencekirk resolutions, most of his own clergy, one or two highly placed friends like Boyle, or uncompromising Anglo-Catholic militants such as the St Ninian's clergy, Forbes had little support to show for his Tractarian teaching. Gladstone himself supported Forbes less for the cause of dogmatic truth, than because he believed the Cheyne judgement had changed the terms of communion. To have this change accomplished by 'two or three men meeting together' was, according to Gladstone, 'in reality a wild excess of the principle of private judgement although those men are bishops'. For such a change to have occurred in the tiny Scottish Episcopal Church—'in a corner of a corner of the Christian world'—only compounded the offence for Gladstone.[113]

Now that the flurry of action over the Cheyne judgement had died down, internal diocesan divisions over Forbes's stand began to occupy his attention. One of his senior priests was proposing a supportive motion at that year's synod, partly to forestall even more extreme supporters creating greater discord.[114] Dean Moir at Brechin was having to cope with his vestry withholding his stipend and William Henderson visiting his parish to drum up support.[115] At Fasque, Sir Thomas Gladstone, the older brother of William and an Evangelical, was actively opposing Forbes by arranging to have his domestic servants confirmed by Bishop Suther in Aberdeen.[116] Forbes consequently gave notice that he intended to raise the Fasque matter at the Episcopal Synod that October.[117] It

---

[111] A. P. Forbes to W. S. Wilson, 26 Mar. 1859, BrMS 1. 1. 111.
[112] A. P. Forbes to W. E. Gladstone, 8 Apr. 1859, Gladstone Papers, BL 44154, fo. 234.
[113] W. E. Gladstone to A. P. Forbes, 9 Apr. 1859, BrMS 1. 1. 125.
[114] H. S. Howard to J. Moir, 8 July 1859, BrMS 1. 1. 155; and J. Moir to A. P. Forbes, 16 July 1859, BrMS 1. 1. 161.
[115] J. Moir to A. P. Forbes, 15 June 1859, BrMS 1. 1. 147.
[116] *SEJ* (October 1859), 66; and George Foxton to A. P. Forbes, 14 Oct. 1859, BrMS 1. 1. 207.
[117] A. P. Forbes to T. Suther, draft letter n.d., BrMS 1. 1. 114.

must also have pleased him that as one of his opponents, Suther had laid himself open to criticism on a matter Forbes could present as distinct from the Eucharistic controversy. At Montrose the local patron, also an opponent of Forbes, was preventing the congregation's choice of priest from being inducted.[118]

Against the background of these diocesan divisions the Brechin synod met on 3 August 1859, with thirteen clergy and the chancellor present. But Forbes was conscious of a wider audience, because he permitted the admission of a reporter in order 'to procure a full and correct report'.[119] In his lengthy address Forbes first touched upon Cheyne's appeal. While he considered the sentence excessively severe and lacking in logic, 'in a small Communion like ours', he told his audience, 'men are led to take sides in every question that may arise'. More words, he felt, would not alter the convictions on either side. Robert Thom then moved that the synod confessed its faith that in the Eucharist there was 'a Presence, not of power and efficacy alone, but moreover a real and essential, though at the same time Spiritual, ineffable, and sacramental presence of our Lord'. It was an attempt at compromise, encompassing both virtualist and Tractarian Eucharistic theologies. The motion concluded that while the clergy were ready to be obedient to the Church's highest authorities, they deprecated any action which narrowed the interpretation of the formularies, or attempted to secure the monoply of a single interpretation. It was carried, with Henderson as the sole objector.[120] The voting on this motion demonstrates the extent to which Forbes's standing in his diocese had improved since his early years. In a similar contest of strength in the synod, over the Prayer Book of Bishop Torry in 1850, opponents had been able to muster sufficient votes to defeat a motion supporting the book, which Forbes and his family favoured. This time, eight years later, Forbes's support in the synod was overwhelming.

The Episcopal Synod in October had to come to grips with various issues which, while subsidiary to Forbes's presentment for trial, were a consequence of the greater dispute as the protagonists became more firmly divided. Aside from Forbes's unread 'eirenic' letter to Wordsworth the previous December, there had been little attempt to find a compromise or resolution over his charge. The long-running argument was generating further ill will and dissension, as the parties scored points off one another. Terrot commented on the 'almost personal estrangement

---

[118]   E. B. Ramsay to A. P. Forbes, 11 May 1859, BrMS 1. 1. 142.
[119]   Brechin Diocese Synod Minutes, 3 Aug. 1859, BrMS 4. 1. 3, 68.
[120]   Ibid. 69–78.

among us'.[121] At the October synod a motion was passed to erase from the minutes Forbes's protest over the Cheyne judgement on the grounds that it set a poor legal precedent for a judge to protest at the majority's decision in addition to giving his own minority judgement.[122] Regarding Suther's confirming Fasque parishioners, Terrot said Suther was wrong both in not communicating beforehand with Forbes, and in interfering at all, which Suther reluctantly accepted.[123] The synod also attended to the presentment against Forbes. He was directed to lodge his response with the clerk of the synod by 7 January 1860. Parties to the trial were to attend the synod on 7 February. Forbes asked for a delay of six months because he said his parochial work in Dundee was, next to Aberdeen, the heaviest in the Episcopal Church. Bishop Wordsworth said the agitated state of the Church did not warrant the extra interval, and as Forbes had republished his charge he could surely master the subject in three months. Having made his protest, Forbes accepted the decision.[124]

Forbes now began to make preparations to answer the presentment. On 11 October 1859 the historian George Grub agreed to be his legal counsel.[125] Grub was then lecturer in Scots law at King's College, Aberdeen. He had been born in Aberdeen in 1812 and came from a nonjuring Episcopalian family. His biographer remembers that he was equally learned in patristic theology as in history. While the only contemporary theology he read was Tractarian, like other northern Churchmen 'he stopped short of the Eucharistic views of Bishop Forbes and Mr. Cheyne'.[126] In his brief to Grub, Forbes stated he did not want to resort to any 'legal subtlety' to clear himself of the presentment. He said Grub could state the injustice Forbes felt at being tried two years after his supposed offence, and that he considered the bishops had already prejudged him, but he was not to press this. Forbes did not want anything to come in the way of 'the freest ventilation of the subject'. The bishop went on to say that from legal advice he had already received these doctrines were within the toleration of the Church. This advice seemed good to him though, personally, he would wish to claim them as the revealed and Catholic truth. Forbes was, however, willing to argue for them before the bishops on this lesser ground, but he desired Grub 'to keep this distinction in view'.

[121] C. H. Terrot to A. P. Forbes, 27 Aug. [1859], BrMS 1. 1. 183.
[122] REC II, 6 Oct. 1859, SRO CH 12. 60. 3, 405-9.
[123] REC II, 6 Oct. 1859, SRO CH 12. 60. 3, 409-10.
[124] *SEJ* (October 1859), 174.
[125] G. Grub to A. P. Forbes, 11 Oct. 1859, BrMS 1. 1. 200.
[126] W. Walker, *Three Churchmen* (1893), 269.

As for the theological argument against the presentment, Forbes divided the preparation of this among various friends.[127] Bright and Henry
Liddon would cover the Anglican theology and the liturgical objections, while Pusey took the patristic parts. They would consult with
Forbes by post from Oxford, or by the new electric telegraph. The
remainder would be left to Forbes himself.[128] But Pusey was worried
about Forbes's penchant for scholastic terminology, which he thought
would not help make his defence easily intelligible.[129]

At this stage Pusey thought the likely outcome of the presentment
would be Forbes's condemnation.[130] Keble was counselling Forbes against
those who believed a schism to be the only way of upholding the Eucharistic doctrine. He commented that such a schism, 'for such as believe as
we do' would require a bishop to head it, and as he understood it Forbes
would 'hardly think it right to be that bishop'. Keble's advice was that if
sentenced to deprivation Forbes should submit and continue to work in
the Church under protest, at least until such time as the formularies were
altered.[131] Forbes was considering his options, which did include what he
called 'setting his diocese against the Church'. By this Pusey understood
him to mean that most of his clergy in Brechin diocese would remain loyal
to him if he resigned, so that no other Bishop of Brechin could be elected
if he decided to hold the see despite being condemned or deprived by the
Episcopal Synod. This is a measure of how desperate Forbes was becoming. In effect, he was now considering leading a schism of his own clergy,
although he had previously warned hotter heads than his own against it.
He usually thought that a simple resignation was a more effective and
dignified protest. As for resigning, Pusey advised him not to commit
himself until he had consulted with Keble and himself.[132] At first Pusey
did not think Forbes serious about the schismatic option, but a further
letter from the bishop that October made him less sure. Forbes had written that his heart 'revolts from schism', but that no orthodox bishop in
the fourth century would have given up his see to an Arian heretic. This
was one of the many allusions Forbes made to the Arian heresy, in which
he identified his cause with the defence of the Nicene faith by the
orthodox Bishop Athanasius, who suffered deprivation and exile but was
ultimately triumphant. At this time, Forbes evidently also thought his

[127] A. P. Forbes to G. Grub, n.d., BrMS 1. 1. 202.
[128] E. B. Pusey to A. P. Forbes, n.d., BrMS 1. 2. 313.
[129] E. B. Pusey to A. P. Forbes, n.d., BrMS 1. 2. 314.
[130] E. B. Pusey to J. Keble, 11 Oct. [1859], PK v.
[131] J. Keble to A. P. Forbes, 12 Oct. 1859, BrMS 1. 1. 203.
[132] E. B. Pusey to A. P. Forbes, [Oct.] 1859, PK v.

condemnation the most likely outcome of the trial. The moral pressure on him may have been increased by Pusey suggesting his defence was also important for the Tractarian cause in England. Pusey mused to Keble that possibly a successful 'persecution' of Forbes in Scotland would become a ground 'for persecution in England, so that he [Forbes] might think of himself as fighting the battle of the Faith in England'.[133]

Forbes decided to go south to make a start on his defence, where he could be away from congregational duties and consult personally with Keble and Pusey. He arranged to spend nearly two weeks with Keble and then move to Pusey at Christ Church on 24 October, where he intended to stay until the Episcopal Synod reconvened over another appeal by Cheyne on 9 November.[134] Soon after he had arrived at Keble's vicarage at Hursley, Forbes had news that the primus had intervened directly in the controversy for the first time since the declaration of the three bishops in December 1857. Terrot made an informal approach to the Brechin chancellor, Alexander Forbes Irvine, through a private letter, to see if there was a possibility of Forbes and the bishops agreeing to a compromise theological formula. He had been prompted to make the approach, Terrot said, because a large proportion of Church people believed the continuation of the controversy was dangerous to the peace of the Church. Terrot would therefore welcome any 'reasonable overture' that could give the bishops an opportunity to decline to pursue the presentment. He claimed he was not the only bishop to wish for a peaceful resolution. While he did not think Forbes's opinions were heretical Terrot objected to them being taught as the official teaching of the Episcopal Church. To do so, he thought, would be to call into suspicion the beliefs not only of the present bishops, but of their predecessors as well. He explained in his letter to Forbes Irvine that he was not asking Forbes to recant, but queried if Forbes could agree to the following: to express regret that the form in which his opinions were published (that is, a diocesan charge) had caused misunderstanding as to their authority; he repudiated transubstantiation and consubstantiation; and he would henceforth 'abstain from claiming for such statements as have been repudiated by the College of Bishops, the authority of the Scottish branch of the reformed Catholic Church'. Terrot said he was not 'prescribing' a particular form to be adopted, but only indicating what he thought would prevent judicial proceedings and disruption in the Church.[135]

[133] E. B. Pusey to J. Keble, 13 Oct. 1859, PK v.
[134] E. B. Pusey to G. F. Boyle, 24 Oct. [1859], BrMS 1. 6. 88.
[135] C. H. Terrot to A. Forbes Irvine, n.d., BrMS 1. 1. 213.

Forbes Irvine forwarded a copy of the primus's letter to Forbes on 18 October, without revealing Terrot's identity. The chancellor said he was anxious to keep it quiet lest their uncompromising 'Perth friends' from St Ninian's found out, and the whole thing became public in the *Union*.[136] Forbes showed the letter to Keble who thought the overture a satisfactory one, understanding it as an agreement to let each party retain their opinions. Keble told Pusey that if this approach of Terrot's was unsuccessful, Forbes was thinking of submitting to suspension, as Pusey did when his university sermon was condemned in 1843, but remaining in Dundee and working privately.[137] When Forbes arrived at Christ Church a few days later Pusey found him in 'pretty good spirits', comforted by his visit to Keble.[138] Forbes was having difficulties with his defence—in keeping it concise—but he found time to write to Forbes Irvine that he did not see any 'insurmountable difficulty' in what was asked of him, as Terrot did not press for a recantation. He was willing to say, as his charge did, that he rejected transubstantiation and consubstantiation, he adhered *ex animo* to the formularies of the Church, and he regretted anything in the form of his charge, as distinct from its content, which had caused offence. Finally, he explained that he neither made his doctrines mandatory in his diocese, nor did he put them on a level with those required for salvation. But he personally believed they were sanctioned by the Church, although he acknowledged that other divines had not thought so, and neither did the Episcopal Synod.[139]

In one of his draft replies to Terrot during this negotiation Forbes used words which indicate, even more clearly than in his actual first reply, that his major concern was to avoid a formula which suggested he repudiated the doctrinal authorization of the Church for his teaching. He wrote:

of all I have taught some points are expressly sanctioned by the letter of the said formularies—others are but the logical consequences of the same. I therefore must claim for my various propositions such authority as is consistent with this view. There is, besides, the sanction which I believe my teaching possesses as a whole from those 'Catholic Fathers and Ancient Bishops' to whose judgement the Anglican Communion confidently defers.[140]

This question—the sanction of the Church for his teaching—was paramount in Forbes's mind to retain in his debate with Terrot. Failure

[136] A. Forbes Irvine to A. P. Forbes, 18 Oct. 1859, BrMS 1. 1. 212.
[137] J. Keble to E. B. Pusey, 23 Oct. 1859, KP iv.
[138] E. B. Pusey to G. F. Boyle, 24 Oct. [1859], BrMS 1. 6. 88.
[139] A. P. Forbes to A. Forbes Irvine, n.d. [Oct. 1859], BrMS 1. 1. 214.
[140] A. P. Forbes to A. Forbes Irvine, draft reply n.d., BrMS 1. 1. 215.

to realize it became the sticking point of the whole negotiation, as the primus gradually retreated from his first position of not insisting on a particular form of words and pressed Forbes to repudiate his claim to the authority of the Church, to which Forbes tenaciously clung.

George Boyle had suggested to Forbes that public opinion in the Church was mostly against him, and perhaps mindful of this the bishop published an open letter to his congregation. Written from Oxford on 5 November 1859, he said he believed he was writing in such a way as would 'induce men to look upon the most mysterious and blessed doctrine of the Holy Eucharist in a devotional and uncontroversial way'. He finished by thanking his congregation for their calm and their consideration.[141] When a partisan supporter reviewed this letter in the *Ecclesiastic* in December 1859, Forbes wrote to the journal to remonstrate against the reviewer's criticism of Wordsworth. The reviewer had accused Wordsworth of jealousy over the success of Forbes's work in Dundee which, the review claimed, was the only part of Scotland where the Episcopal Church had made any progress among the native Scots and the poor.[142] Forbes replied that it was 'one of the evils of controversy that we become inclined to undervalue the good in those to whom for the moment we are opposed'.[143] But, to Gladstone, Forbes expressed his opinion that Wordsworth not only dominated and controlled the other bishops, but that his dislike for Forbes had become a fixed idea with him. Privately, Forbes was prepared to acknowledge to trusted friends he thought Wordsworth a pernicious influence upon his opponents, but in public Forbes probably did not want to harm Terrot's negotiation by further antagonizing the influential Wordsworth. Forbes also explained to Gladstone that he had little hope of the negotiation succeeding, but he thought it was right to make as much explanation as possible, consistent with his beliefs. To do so could be a way of demonstrating his tolerance if it came to a trial. He went on:

I am much at a loss what to do in the event of condemnation. So far as regards my own comfort I should be thankful to be out of this, for I find it a great mistake to belong to a small religious community, but then I think of the poor souls entrusted to me in this large manufacturing town and the still considerable numbers of clergy of straitened means who might feel called upon to follow whatever example I might set them. All this rather points at resistance—but perhaps it is unwise to anticipate evil.[144]

---

[141]   A. P. Forbes, *Letter to the Congregation of S. Paul's, Dundee* (1859).
[142]   *Ecclesiastic and Theologian*, 21 (1859), 584–9.
[143]   Ibid. 22 (1860), 48.
[144]   A. P. Forbes to W. E. Gladstone, 12 Nov. 1859, Gladstone Papers, BL 44154, fo. 246.

This is the first hint of Forbes's dissatisfaction with the Episcopal Church, although on a number of previous occasions he had mentioned that its smallness exacerbated divisions. What prevented him from taking some drastic action in regard to this dissatisfaction was his work in Dundee, and his clergy. He strongly believed he was responsible for both before God, and that his clergy, most of whom (unlike himself) were married and had no income independent of their stipends, were less able than he was to leave their livings.

The reconvened Episcopal Synod on 9 November 1859, judging the appeals of Dean Smith and another from Cheyne, interrupted the progress of the negotiation. All the bishops but Forbes dismissed Smith's appeal, agreeing that Eden had acted within his prerogative. Cheyne's final appeal was also dismissed by all except Forbes. Cheyne was not willing to retract his teaching and was again pronounced 'to be no longer a clergyman of the Episcopal Church' until such time as he asked for restoration in accordance with canon 41.[145]

On receipt of Forbes's first reply to Terrot, Forbes Irvine, as intermediary, had an interview with the primus on 15 November. He reported to Forbes that Terrot liked much of Forbes's letter, but thought it fell short of being able to secure agreement. Terrot reminded Forbes Irvine that he had to answer to Henderson, as well as the bishops, and that some of these were 'less disposed to be friendly than himself'. Forbes Irvine enclosed a form of words which alone, he said, would satisfy Terrot.[146] Pusey however dismissed the formula because it said nothing about Forbes not retracting, but even more because it looked like a submission.[147] Pusey explained to Keble that the core of the problem was that Forbes 'could not bear saying that he had not the authority of the Scotch Church'. Pusey also told Keble that when he had suggested to Forbes he could only claim such authority for his teaching in so far as the Episcopal Church was 'a branch of the Church Catholic' Forbes could not bear it, got 'excited', and said, 'It is all that unhappy Reformation'.[148] This was a significant incident. Forbes became unhappy and agitated when Pusey suggested that the basis for Forbes's claim to the dogmatic authority of the Episcopal Church for his teaching lay in that Church being a part of the Catholic Church. Forbes's reply was to become excited and blame the Reformation, presumably for what he considered as the non-Catholic and Protestant theology of the other bishops. Did Forbes's agitation spring from the feeling that the presence of such diverse theological views was beginning, for him, to cast doubt on the claim of his Church to be a branch of the Catholic Church? This possibility is supported by Keble's reply that 'the worst of it is the way in which our friend seems predisposed to throw it [the failure of Forbes's response to Terrot] on the Anglican Divines'.[149] Keble seemed to be saying that Forbes blamed the Anglican Divines for being able to be claimed by both sides by their not being explicit enough in favour of his own, supposed Catholic, teaching. If this was so, then this period of the controversy was the beginning of a major shift in Forbes's outlook. Previously Forbes, like Keble and the Tractarians generally, believed that the Anglican Caroline divines could be appealed to as upholders of Catholic doctrine. The controversy was now slowly eroding Forbes's confidence in the Episcopal Church, and perhaps in the Catholic position of the whole Anglican Church as well. Pusey's comment that Forbes was 'so very sensitive about authority' indicates a personal, and not just a theological, involvement with this particular concern. Keble opined that Forbes be encouraged not to give way to his fear of apostasy, or what Keble called his 'marked fear of offering up incense to Jupiter'.[150]

Forbes sent his second reply to the primus on 23 November. It was much shorter than his first one, but still longer than Terrot wanted. Forbes began by explicitly disclaiming any retraction, believing his teaching conformable to scripture, the Fathers, and Anglican formularies and divines. He did agree to regret that the form in which he expressed that teaching had led to misapprehension about its authority, and again denied transubstantiation and consubstantiation. Finally, he said that while his doctrine of sacrifice flowed from that of the real presence as 'the natural meaning of the Scottish Office' and the Eucharistic adoration of Christ as the 'legitimate consequence of the Real Presence', he neither desired to force these beliefs on others, nor had he done so.[151] But Terrot found this response even less satisfactory than the first. He now presented Forbes with virtually an ultimatum. Unless Forbes was prepared to sign the formula Terrot had given, or something 'substantially' the same, the negotiation would cease. Terrot particularly desired to have Forbes's words about claiming the support of the formularies omitted.[152]

[149] J. Keble to E. B. Pusey, 18 Nov. 1859, KP iv.
[150] J. Keble to E. B. Pusey, 21 Nov. 1859, BrMS 1. 1. 260.
[151] A. P. Forbes to A. Forbes Irvine, 23 Nov. 1859, BrMS 1. 1. 262.
[152] A. Forbes Irvine to A. P. Forbes, 28 Nov. 1859, BrMS 1. 1. 266.

On 21 December Forbes sent his third response to the primus. He wrote to Gladstone the same day that he had 'less hope' than Gladstone did of his receiving 'friendly treatment'. Forbes could not accept all the suggestions Gladstone had made (in a long letter following Gladstone's visit to Edinburgh on 10 December for installation as rector of the university). He did agree to exclude a disclaimer of retraction, and to omit his explanations of transubstantiation and consubstantiation. But he wanted to retain the claim that his teaching was agreeable to Anglican authorities, as 'a *residuum*' of the degree of authority he alleged for his teaching. His desire was not just to make peace, he said, but to do so in a way compatible with the consciences of his supporters.[153] Forbes Irvine was happy to report that with this last paper 'there was now some prospect of peace'. The primus, he said, thought it 'would answer the end for which it was asked', with a few small textual alterations. There exists, in the Brechin Diocesan Archives, a draft in Forbes's hand, including Terrot's desired changes, with a note by Forbes that 'this was the paper finally agreed on with the Primus—in the abortive negociation'. This paper, as ultimately sent, read as follows:

The Bishop of Brechin regrets that the *form* in which his opinions were published has given occasion to misapprehension of his real meaning on certain points in the doctrine of the Holy Eucharist. He disbelieves and rejects the Tridentine Doctrine of Transubstantiation, and the alleged Lutheran Doctrine of Consubstantiation, which has been described as holding Christ really but invisibly moulded up with the substance of the *Elements*. While he firmly believes what he has taught, rightly understood, to be in conformity with the Word of God, and with our own Formularies, as interpreted by the light of the early Church, and that it is sanctioned by divers of our own esteemed Divines, he has never claimed for it the dogmatic sanction of the Scottish Branch of the Reformed Catholic Church, in the sense that that Church required it to be received as Terms of Communion, nor has he required it as a condition of ordination or communion, nor will he hereafter so require it.[154]

Forbes was now suffering from insomnia, which was not helped by the thought of what his radical supporters, such as those writing in the *Union*, would think when news of the negotiation became known. But Keble believed these would never be satisfied with anything less than a statement which would even exclude Hooker from the Catholic Church.[155] Boyle said he would do his best to 'gag' the *Union*, having

[153] A. P. Forbes to W. E. Gladstone, 21 Dec. 1859, Gladstone Papers, BL 44154, fo. 264.
[154] A. P. Forbes, n.d., BrMS 1. 2. 302.
[155] J. Keble to A. P. Forbes, 26 Dec. 1859, BrMS 1. 2. 298.

previously been a proprietor of the paper.[156] Pusey, Bright, and Boyle
were all hopeful of Forbes's final statement bringing an end to the threat
of a possible trial, although they were unhappy about Forbes calling the
teaching of the charge his 'opinions'. Keble wrote again, as so often, to
calm Forbes's troubled spirit over what he had done. 'I know something
of your sensitive heart', he wrote, '& your very tender conscience; & my
own heart aches to think of what you may be suffering at any moment
from a sort of indistinct fear that you may have inadvertently conceded
too much, & so far been wanting to the cause to wch. your heart & life
are devoted.'[157] But Forbes was hearing such reports of Wordsworth's
'bitter animosity' towards him that he told Gladstone he would not be
surprised if something upset this hope of peace, although Forbes thought
the primus had behaved 'very well'.[158] Terrot, meanwhile, had forwarded
a copy of Forbes's paper to all the bishops, asking if it could be received
as an interim defence. On 30 December 1859 he wrote to Forbes to say
he was sorry, but he had received 'very decided letters in the negative'.
Terrot explained that the opinion of the other bishops was that the
college could not 'by private correspondence' set aside a legal presentment. The bishops were also not as favourable as Terrot had been
towards Forbes's statement. The primus concluded that it was 'impossible for me now to say what would satisfy them', but to do so would
require far more from Forbes than he had agreed hitherto.[159] Forbes
drew the right conclusion; advising Gladstone of the outcome of the
negotiation he commented, 'the Trial must now take its course'.[160] But
Forbes himself was not completely disappointed at this prospect. He confessed to Boyle that he had 'a sort of feeling of relief, for I do not like
these negociations on matters of faith'. While he thought he was now
facing possible suspension, he said he had to consider if he had 'a duty to
the souls in Dundee antecedent to all Canons & Formularies'.[161] Forbes
was evidently planning to continue working in Dundee should he be
suspended because Bright reported that in such an outcome Forbes said
he would stay 'and work the hospital'.[162] At the same time Forbes wrote

[156] G. F. Boyle to A. P. Forbes, 'Xmas Eve' [24 Dec.] 1859, BrMS 1. 2. 295.
[157] J. Keble to A. P. Forbes, 'St. Stephen's Day' [26 Dec.] 1859, BrMS 1. 2. 298.
[158] A. P. Forbes to W. E. Gladstone, 27 Dec. [1859], Gladstone Papers, BL 44154, fo. 268.
[159] C. H. Terrot to A. P. Forbes, 30 Dec. [1859], BrMS 1. 2. 304.
[160] A. P. Forbes to W. E. Gladstone, 31 Dec. [1859], Gladstone Papers, BL 44154, fo. 270.
[161] A. P. Forbes to G. F. Boyle, 31 Dec. 1859, BrMS 1. 6. 99 (ii).
[162] W. Bright to G. F. Boyle, 23 Jan. 1860, BrMS 1. 7. 108.

a letter that Keble described as 'agonized' with remorse at having assented to the proposed arrangement.[163] Pusey wrote to Forbes to assure him that

there is no fear of your being like Liberius.[164] This is the mere tension of nerves, a mere phantom . . . . You really must either not have read, or have forgotten the miserable history of Liberius to think that anything you do would be like him. But is it not after all, that you are torn between the love of your people at Dundee on the one side, and the wish to get free altogether of the Scotch Episcopate?[165]

Pusey also wrote to Keble on 4 January 1860 that he had much the same sort of letter from Forbes, and that he thought it might be due to a 'deep wound that after teaching for his eleven years of most strength, so few of his people really do go along with his belief'.[166]

In January 1860 there came another attempt to prevent a trial, this time by influential laymen. Twenty-three such men, headed by the Duke of Buccleuch, signed a memorial to Forbes. They proposed that the presentment not be prosecuted if Forbes could agree to abide by the words of Bishops Taylor, Ken, and Wilson, whom he had quoted in his congregational letter the previous November. If he accepted the ultimate authority of these High Church divines over his teaching, and publicly denied opposing the Episcopal Synod, the memorialists were confident the presenters would withdraw. Essentially the conditions of the memorial were the same as Bishop Wordsworth had set out in his *Proposals for Peace*, published in December.[167] Both proposals had seized on Forbes's claim in his letter to St Paul's that in his charge he had not gone beyond the words of these three bishops. Wordsworth considered this meant Forbes affirmed that he restricted his teaching to that of these three divines. From that premiss Wordsworth sought to show Forbes had

---

[163] J. Keble to E. B. Pusey, 'New Years Eve' [1 Jan.] 1859, KP iv.
[164] Liberius was pope from 352 to 366. In 357 he submitted to the Arian emperor Constantius and signed an Arian formula of faith in order to be permitted to return to his see after two years of exile. He had been exiled for initially refusing to condemn Athanasius.
[165] E. B. Pusey to A. P. Forbes, n.d., BrMS 1. 2. 311.
[166] E. B. Pusey to J. Keble, 4 Jan. 1860, PK v.
[167] In his *Proposals for Peace* Wordsworth also inferred that a cause of the controversy was Forbes's sympathy towards Roman Catholicism: 'I do not ask the Bishop of Brechin to show himself as plain-spoken respecting the errors and corruptions of the Church of Rome as Bishop Taylor, Bishop Ken, and Bishop Wilson showed themselves in their respective times; for some persons now-a-days appear to think that the spirit and policy of the Church of Rome are changed, and that our policy, therefore, ought to be changed toward her. For my own part, I confess I see no sufficient reason for this opinion; rather I see the contrary.' C. Wordsworth, *Proposals for Peace* (1859), 24–5.

indeed gone beyond what these bishops taught on the Eucharist. Whether Wordsworth was correct or not, his was an unwarranted interpretation of the congregational letter. In his reply to the memorialists Forbes said he had quoted the three divines simply because they exactly expressed his beliefs. He acknowledged that the divines had written modifications of the particular passages he quoted, but this, Forbes suggested, was surely an argument for the toleration of differing views.[168]

Forbes lodged his formal reply to the presentment by the due date of 7 January.[169] In this he raised questions about the impartiality of the bishops as his judges. He argued that the issue at trial was whether the specific passages of his charge referred to in the presentment were contrary to the Thirty-nine Articles, and also, by consequence, to the authorities the Articles referred to—scripture and the Prayer Book. Unless this could be proved, Forbes said, the presentment had to be dismissed. As in his charge, Forbes was maintaining his argument that the Articles were not the sole 'authoritative documents' for Anglican doctrine. With regard to the first accusation, that he taught the Eucharist was a sacrifice substantially the same as the cross, Forbes drew a distinction between 'active' sacrifice, which was the actual 'act of sacrifice or offering', and 'passive' sacrifice or 'that which is offered'. The former, he said, was Calvary, the historical act of Christ's sacrifice which was perfect and unrepeatable; the latter was Christ's continual offering to the Father. 'I do not mean that the *acts* are identical, but the *Thing Offered* is identical, even the One Body of the Holy Lord; and that, on the Cross, in its natural mode of being, in the Sacrament truly and substantially present, but not after the natural mode of the existence of a body.'[170] Forbes argued that the active sacrifice of Christ on Calvary was passively perpetuated as an atoning offering by the memorial of the Eucharist Christ commanded his disciples to make. He repeated his understanding of memorial as the continual making-present by the Eucharist of that which is offered (Christ)—this passive sacrifice deriving from Christ's active sacrifice (the historic and unrepeatable act of the cross).[171] Against imputations of teaching Roman Catholic doctrine, Forbes said he taught a '*real though not a local, Objective Presence, not by way of Transubstantiation*'.[172] Referring to objections that he had dis-par-

---

[168] A. P. Forbes, n.d., BrMS 1. 2. 334.
[169] W. S. Wilson to A. P. Forbes, 9 Jan. 1860, BrMS 1. 2. 332.
[170] A. P. Forbes, *Theological Defence* (1860), 14.
[171] Ibid. 75–80.
[172] Ibid. 14.

aged the teaching of the Nonjurors, and therefore of important Episcopal divines, he reiterated his usual critical appreciation of this group.

I am not the person to undervalue their testimony to truth and honesty. Brought up as I have been from an early youth with an hereditary veneration for the House of Stuart, and, as I believe, being the only Bishop in the College who, from family associations, has an historical connexion with that unfortunate House, I am not likely to depreciate their testimony . . . but it is no true kindness to their memory to place their testimony in an unduly prominent position. They are but one school of opinion within the Anglican Church, though a school that deserves much consideration from the piety, learning, and self-sacrifice of its adherents.[173]

Forbes was reminding the bishops and his opponents that his personal connections with the nonjuring Episcopal past were stronger than theirs, and at the same time reducing the importance of the nonjuring virtualist theology.

Forbes then turned to the second accusation, that in upholding the Eucharistic adoration of Christ he was contravening Article 28.[174] Forbes maintained that the article was actually directed against Roman Catholic devotional practices such as the Corpus Christi procession, and said he had condemned these in his charge. He therefore claimed toleration for his teaching. 'I can readily understand . . . . a strong fear of paying, or seeming to pay, to this outward symbol a reverence due to God Alone . . . I condemn no one, and desire only that they who, with myself, follow what I believe to be an instinct of our spiritual natures, should not be condemned.'[175]

Regarding the third charge, that he had contravened Article 29[176] by teaching that 'in some sense' the unfaithful receive Christ if proceeding to Holy Communion, Forbes argued that to be or not to be 'a partaker of Christ' must refer only to a beneficial reception of Holy Communion,

---

[173] Ibid. 112.

[174] The relevant part of Article 28 reads: 'Transubstantiation (or the change of the substance of Bread and Wine) in the Supper of the Lord, cannot be proved by Holy Writ; but is repugnant to the plain words of Scripture, overthroweth the nature of a Sacrament, and hath occasion to many superstitions. The Body of Christ is given, taken, and eaten, in the Supper, only after an heavenly and spiritual manner. And the mean whereby the Body of Christ is received and eaten in the Supper is Faith. The Sacrament of the Lord's Supper was not by Christ's ordinance reserved, carried about, lifted up, or worshipped.'

[175] Forbes, *Theological Defence*, 211.

[176] 'The Wicked, and such as be void of a lively faith, although they do carnally and visibly press with their teeth (as Saint *Augustine* saith) the Sacrament of the Body and Blood of Christ, yet in no wise are they partakers of Christ: but rather, to their condemnation, do eat and drink the sign or Sacrament of so great a thing.'

and this was perfectly compatible with his teaching that the unworthy receive a detrimental reception, to their judgement.[177] He shrewdly turned the bishops' fears of alienating the Church of England against them. Forbes said his opinions were held by many in the Church of England, including some in high places, and they went unmolested. His condemnation would therefore make it evident that the two Churches had different terms of communion, asserting it was 'quite needless for the respondent to point out the fatal consequences of such a state of things.'[178] He finally concluded his massive defence in ringing tones.

The difference between the Presenters and myself is that they, I fear, do not believe what I with my whole heart believe—the real, supernatural Presence of the Body and Blood of CHRIST, yea, of CHRIST Himself, my Lord and my COD, in that Holy Sacrament . . . I have not attempted to force upon others this my belief, dearer though it is to me than my life itself . . . This is the hope for which I am this day called in question . . . *credidi propter quod loquutus sum.* 'I believed, and therefore I have spoken'.[179]

Soon after Forbes had submitted his defence Wordsworth offered yet another means to avoid a trial. On 20 January 1860 he wrote to Forbes proposing that Forbes publicly withdraw his charge and state his desire to avoid giving offence in the future. In return, Wordsworth said he would attempt to persuade the bishops to withdraw all the parts of the Pastoral Letter which censured the charge. Wordsworth felt the presenters would find this acceptable and therefore the presentment would not be prosecuted. Forbes was constrained to reply, 'to withdraw my charge would be to withdraw my whole teaching on the subject of the Holy Euch. and I am sure you cd. not ask me to do what wd. be agst. my conscience'.[180] It was anomalous that Wordsworth should propose such an arrangement when he was presumably one of those who terminated Terrot's former negotiation by arguing they could not, by private correspondence, set aside a legal presentment.

With the trial now imminent Pusey begged off attending as he was afraid Wordsworth's antagonism towards him would not help. He also thought that 'the Scottish Bishops dislike what they call English influence, which is what most of them (being Englishmen) are using against the poor Scotch Church'.[181] The use of the same influence could also be

[177] Forbes, *Theological Defence*, 230
[178] Ibid.
[179] Ibid. 233–4.
[180] A. P. Forbes to C. Wordsworth, draft letter n.d., BrMS 1. 2. 340.
[181] E. B. Pusey to A. P. Forbes, n.d., PK v.

charged to Forbes, only his English Tractarian friends were not as influential, nor as numerous, as the High Church contacts of the other bishops. Pusey proposed that Forbes should contact him by telegraph if he needed to consult him during the proceedings. Keble however thought otherwise. He 'could not be happy', he wrote to Forbes, with the thought of the bishop being left 'unsupported by us, who have brought you in the way of trouble'. Keble still felt responsible for encouraging Forbes's charge in the first place, so he travelled up to Edinburgh and arrived on the morning of the trial.[182]

On 7 February 1860, a very cold winter's morning, Forbes's trial began in the Freemasons' Hall in Edinburgh. It was snowing when Forbes, Keble, and two others (probably his lawyers, Grub and Forbes Irvine) had earlier gone to celebrate Holy Communion in the chapel of the House of Mercy in Lauriston Lane.[183] Henderson advised the bishops sitting as judges that he was acting on behalf of the other two presenters who had asked to be excused; David Smith because of illness in his family, and Patrick Wilson due to his advanced age making a journey in winter inadvisable.[184] The primus asked if the remarks by Forbes in his written defence about the extra-judicial involvement of the bishops meant he questioned the competency of the court. Forbes replied that he wanted these things to be known, but made no formal objection. When the court resumed in the afternoon the bishops said they did not believe that acting in their diocesan role precluded them from doing so in their judicial capacity, as they had both jurisdictions. They therefore directed that this part of Forbes's defence be omitted as irrelevant.[185] Bishop Eden then questioned his own impartiality and his right to judge. He said he had not changed his mind since he had agreed to the Pastoral Letter, which declared Forbes's teaching erroneous, and therefore considered he had prejudged the case. But Forbes did not object to Eden since the majority of the bishops had decided they were not so disqualified and Eden consequently decided to continue.[186] Forbes now read his *Answers* to the presentment, which went on though the afternoon of the 7 February, until the end of the following day.

[182] J. Keble to A. P. Forbes, 4 S[unday] after Epiphany, BrMS 1. 4. 820.
[183] Perry, 97.
[184] David Smith and Patrick Wilson to W. Wilson, 6 Feb. 1860, 'Documents in the Appeals of Aitchison . . . Cheyne . . . Smith & in the Presentment Henderson and Others v Bishop of Brechin', SRO CH 12. 60. 10 (iv).
[185] REC II, 7 Feb. 1860, SRO CH 12. 60. 3, 435–440.
[186] Ibid. 440–5.

During all of 9 February, the third day of the trial, the bishops listened to Henderson's *Pleadings against the Answers*. His presentment, Henderson said, was an act of 'strong necessity', only taken after the failure of his request for another bishop than Forbes to administer confirmation at Arbroath. It was only then, claimed Henderson, that Forbes's teaching directly clashed with his own at Arbroath.[187] He went on to allege that Forbes had contradicted Article 31,[188] because to speak of the Eucharist as a sacrifice 'identical' to the cross meant the cross was perpetuated, salvation was incomplete, and Christ's sacrifice was insufficient for atonement. The basic question to be proved, according to Henderson, was 'not whether the doctrine propounded be in accordance with Scripture and the Fathers, but whether it was agreeable or repugnant to the Articles', and he dismissed Forbes's arguments from sources other than the Articles as strictly irrelevant.[189] Henderson repudiated the argument about the sacrifice of Christ being perpetuated through memorial as a contradiction. A memorial, Henderson claimed, was a 'remembrancer' or a reminder of something and not the thing itself. Forbes's distinction between an 'active' and a 'passive' sacrifice amounted to little or nothing. Calvary and the Eucharist both involved Christ so Henderson concluded there was, in Forbes's terms, an active identity, so that the Eucharist became a repetition of Calvary, contrary to Article 31. Regarding Eucharistic adoration, Henderson alleged that Forbes taught the worship of the external bread and wine, because he used 'the blessed sacrament' and 'the Body and Blood of Christ' as interchangeable terms.[190] He then undermined the basis of his own argument that he needed to prove Forbes contrary to the Articles alone, by taking the trouble to allege Forbes also contradicted the catechism and the rubrics of the Prayer Book.[191] Henderson charged that Forbes's teaching led to Roman Catholic devotions, although the 'more extravagant Romish demonstrations are to be prudently withheld in the meantime'.[192] Clearly concern about the Roman Catholic direction of Forbes's theology was uppermost in Henderson's mind. 'In these days of Romanising propensities', he complained, the clergy had a right to expect of a bishop a 'ringing

---

[187] W. Henderson, *Pleadings in the Case Henderson and Others v. the Bishop of Brechin*, (1860), 4–5.

[188] 'The Offering of Christ once made is that perfect redemption, propitiation, and satisfaction, for all the sins of the whole world, both original and actual; and there is none other satisfaction for sin, but that alone. Wherefore the sacrifices of Masses, in the which it was commonly said, that the priest did offer Christ for the quick and the dead, to have remission of pain or guilt, were blasphemous fables, and dangerous deceits.'

[189] Henderson, *Pleadings*, 18.   [190] Ibid. 43.

[191] Ibid. 46.   [192] Ibid. 59.

protest' against this Eucharistic doctrine, which in Roman Catholicism had led to what Henderson called 'idolatry'.[193] He asserted that Forbes contravened the plain sense of Articles 28 and 29, by teaching the wicked do receive Christ in Holy Communion, and charged Forbes with twisting the formularies of the Church to suit his own teaching.[194] Henderson concluded by accusing Forbes of duplicity in not giving an honest assent to the theological standards of the Church because he taught Roman Catholic doctrine and therefore threatened the Church with Roman error. Henderson considered that Forbes's devoted work in Dundee, and his episcopal position, enabled him to enforce these Roman Catholic heresies. The Church therefore had to prevent Forbes's error from spreading. 'It is when the promulgator of unsound doctrines, while gifted with genius and eloquence is adorned with piety and virtue, and invested with official authority and influence to enforce the opinions which he sincerely holds as of essential importance, that the truth really is in danger, and interference on the part of its Guardians imperatively called for.'[195]

At the end of 9 February (no doubt to the relief of the bishops), Forbes asked for two weeks to prepare his reply. The court was adjourned to 14 March, and Forbes was to lodge his rejoinder by 23 February.[196] During the adjournment Boyle gave Pusey an impression of events so far. 'The influential laity of the "Protestant" school have no relish for *individual severities and proscriptions*.' But he hinted that Forbes's defence had not had the immediate impact they hoped, while Henderson's *Pleadings* had produced a 'great impression'.[197] This suggests Henderson's theology was more representative of Episcopalian belief than was Forbes's. Pusey thought Forbes was still worrying about acting the part of a modern Liberius, and was 'terribly afraid of inconsistency'.[198] Then Joseph Robertson, curator of the historical department at Register House, the national archives of Scotland, and a close friend of Forbes, wrote to Pusey on 27 February with news of another attempt at an out-of-court settlement. One of the bishops (he did not disclose who) had written to him, asking if Forbes would repudiate transubstantiation and consubstantiation, and declare that his theological language was to be understood in terms of the seventeenth-century High Church divines. In return the Episcopal Synod would merely pass a sentence of exhortation against

[193] Ibid. 60.   [194] Ibid. 72.   [195] Ibid. 88.
[196] REC II, 9 Feb. 1860, SRO CH 12. 60. 3, 445–7.
[197] G. F. Boyle to E. B. Pusey, 'Eve of S. Mathias' [23 Feb.] 1860, PK v.
[198] E. B. Pusey to J. Keble, n.d., PK v.

polemical discussion or dubious phraseology. There would also need to be some temporary arrangement made concerning Arbroath, and Forbes was also asked to distance himself from 'Unionism'[199] Given the implacable opposition of Wordsworth, and the lack of previous initiative by Suther and Wilson, this approach probably came from either Eden or Terrot. Eden had already expressed personal disquiet about his position as a trial judge. But Terrot delivered the most sympathetic judgement on Forbes at the end of the trial. As primus, he had already demonstrated a desire for reconciliation, and he was in the most advantageous position to convince the others in any second attempt. Ewing seems to have been too ill to take any immediate part in the proceedings. Pusey forwarded the proposal to Forbes, commenting that it seemed a sort of 'feeler' as to whether the bishops could pass a non-coercive sentence. Forbes's reply to the bishop has not been found, but he mentioned his response in a letter to William Bright (who had returned to Oxford in December 1859, where he became Professor of Ecclesiastical History in 1868). He told Bright he had determined to have no negotiation except with the college as a whole, because after his previous experience with the primus he did not want 'another case of W[ordsworth] putting his foot through the negociation'. The only solid basis for a negotiated settlement he would now accept would be 'the Bishops tolerating the *matter* of my teaching, with as much abuse of the *manner* as they think fit'. As to Arbroath, Forbes said he 'and my clergy would thankfully give over Mr Henderson'. But Forbes was not sure what the repudiation of Unionism meant. If by it the bishop meant, 'my strong sympathies for Corporate Reunion and my hatred of the Donatistic attitude of Anglicanism and the duty of all to minimize the differentiae of the three Churches' [Anglican, Roman and Orthodox], then he could not repudiate that. If, however, the bishop meant the *Union* newspaper's controntational attitude to Anglican Protestantism, what Forbes called 'the waving the red flag in the face of dear old foolish Protestant John Bull', then Forbes agreed he was against the *Union*.[200]

It was also during this adjournment that Forbes received the address of 5,386 working men in Dundee. A deputation waited on Forbes on 28 February 1860, to give him the address which read:

We, the undersigned operatives and work-people of Dundee, of all denominations, desire, at this particular time, to express our sincere respect for you,

[199] J. Robertson to E. B. Pusey, 27 Feb. 1860, PK v.
[200] A. P. Forbes to W. Bright, n.d., PK v.

and our gratitude for all your numerous acts of kindness and charity to so many of our suffering brethren, while in sickness and distress, during the twelve years you have laboured among us. May God bless and reward you for such disinterested zeal for our and our childrens' welfare; and may your future exertions among us be still further rewarded, by the conscientious testimony and esteem of every class of the community.

To this address the leader of the deputation added:

And I am respectfully requested to convey to your lordship, the sincere hope and desire of the parties subscribing the address, that you will be victorious over your adversaries, and that you will continue to pursue with increased vigour and success that Christian line of conduct of doing good to all, which you have hitherto so piously and devotedly pursued, nothwithstanding the calumnies of those who, for their own convenience, follow a different and a lukewarm course of conduct.[201]

Signed by men of various denominations, the address is a further indication, along with the infirmary admissions in Dundee, that Forbes was respected by the working-class population in the city beyond those calling themselves Episcopalians. Such a widespread public demonstration of working-class sympathy must have been an invaluable boost for Forbes. What other bishop, on either side of the border, could have boasted such working-class support? It may have disappointed Forbes a little that it came because of his pastoral work, and not because these men understood or necessarily sympathized with his teaching. But it emphatically demonstrated to Episcopalians that the bishop was a singular figure whose work in Dundee was valued by large numbers of the industrial working men. Forbes called his reception of this address one of the proudest moments of his life.[202]

Meanwhile, Joseph Robertson had assured his correspondent that Forbes's friends would not stage any public humiliation of the bishops should Forbes's sentence be lenient. This, Robertson informed Forbes on 27 February 1860, had assisted those bishops counselling moderation, and the outcome now looked likely to be a censure and nothing more. However, he could not be certain of this as Wordsworth still desired Forbes's suspension and could yet prevail. Robertson also reported that Forbes's *Reply* to Henderson's *Pleadings* was 'telling in more quarters than one', which was not surprising as it was shorter and more succinct than his voluminous and scholastic *Defence*. The working men's address was also having an 'excellent effect', according to Robertson.[203]

[201] Mackey, 116.   [202] A. P. Forbes, n. d., BrMS 1. 2. 388.
[203] J. Robertson to A. P. Forbes, 7 Mar. 1860, BrMS 1. 2. 389.

But Forbes continued to be anxious about succumbing to any temptation to moderate his teaching.[204] English Anglo-Catholic interest in the trial was now intense. The wealthy Anglo-Catholic member of Parliament, A. J. Beresford-Hope, was writing of Forbes's predicament in acerbic letters of support to the *Guardian*. In London W. Upton Richards, priest of All Saints, Margaret Street, wrote to Boyle asking for immediate notification when the verdict was delivered.[205]

When the trial resumed on 14 March, Bishop Ewing was absent because of illness. Keble again came to Edinburgh to offer personal support. Forbes's *Reply* was held as read. In it he challenged Henderson's claim that the Thirty-nine Articles were the standard theological authority of the Episcopal Church. They had, in any case, been variously understood throughout Anglican history. But, evidently Forbes felt the force of Henderson's claim for he devoted his rejoinder to disproving that his teaching was contrary to the Articles. He said he had repeatedly acknowledged the all-sufficiency of the cross as atonement, as in Article 31, and that the Eucharist was not something distinct from that. Forbes claimed Article 31 used 'sacrifice' only in the active sense of 'the *act* of offering', and he affirmed that this was indeed 'finished' on the cross, but that its application (the passive sacrifice) went on in each generation of believers through the Eucharist.[206] Regarding Henderson's contention that the distinction between active and passive sacrifice was meaningless, Forbes asked if it followed that Christ's offering in heaven and on Calvary was also the same. Forbes categorically denied that in his charge he had advised his clergy gradually to introduce Roman Catholic devotions.[207] About reception of the Eucharist by the unfaithful, he reiterated his distinction between a beneficial reception by the faithful and a real but judgemental one by the unfaithful, and maintained that Article 28 made a similar distinction.[208]

In the *Reply* Forbes became most personal when defending himself against the accusation that he had disparaged the Episcopal Church, which had evidently stung him. He revealed something of his particular motivation in the controversy when he asked, 'whether the tone and spirit of the Presenters is likely to foster any genuine reverence for the authority of the Church as a practical guide of belief and a check to modern individualism?'[209] This was the fundamental purpose for Forbes's

[204] E. B. Pusey to J. Keble, 8 Mar. [1860], PK v.
[205] W. U. Richards to G. F. Boyle, 10 Mar. 1860, BrMS 1. 7. 109.
[206] A. P. Forbes, *Reply to the Pleadings* (1860), 18.
[207] Ibid. 32–3.   [208] Ibid. 37.   [209] Ibid. 38.

own teaching and his motivation for his primary charge. He believed Henderson's theology was neither exact enough, nor did it uphold a presence of Christ definite enough, to claim the allegiance of the indifferent or disbelieving.[210] Again he asserted that his teaching was within the traditional toleration of the Anglican Church, and said that as a bishop he did not enforce his teaching but acted in accordance with that tradition. 'The Anglican Church since the settlement of 1558 has confessedly and advisedly allowed a great diversity of statement upon the mystery [of the Eucharist], and I as an individual Bishop should not be justified in breaking in upon that arrangement. Even though I did not take this view of a Bishop's duty, I have a great horror of invoking the coercive judgement of the Church, in behalf of a doctrine so intimately connected with the devotional life of faithful souls.'[211] Instead Forbes sought to disparage the Anglican credentials of the old High Church theology of his presenters by identifying their theology with what he called 'the Puritan school of theology'. If the bishops found for them they would not only be authorizing a theology antagonistic to the Church, but would also endorse a theological system that had been 'unable to stem the rationalism of Germany and the impiety of Geneva'. If the trial had such an outcome, Forbes drew a picture of the Church losing the more zealous clergy, and being unable to recruit others of such quality, especially for the 'towns containing such degraded populations'.[212]

The trial then adjourned to the following day, 15 March 1860. That morning the bishops delivered their opinions in order of seniority. Terrot considered Forbes's language censurable as being prima facie inconsistent with the Articles. He found the presentment proved in regard to the first charge, but not the second, or the third where he considered Forbes's interpretation of Article 29 an acceptable one. Eden found likewise, but he particularly criticized Forbes's charge for giving the impression of *ex cathedra* teaching. Forbes's theory of presence could result in the Episcopal Church teaching the same 'idolatry' as the medieval Church fell into. Wordsworth found Forbes guilty on all charges, and he condemned Forbes's theory of presence as a forsaken medieval one only renewed by Newman's Tract 90. Wordsworth as usual upheld virtualism as being the only authorized teaching of the Church on Eucharistic presence, and asserted Forbes's teaching was not appropriate in a Church that should be thankful for the blessings of the Reformation. Suther and Wilson merely confined themselves to agreement with these opinions.[213] The formal

[210] Ibid. 42.   [211] Ibid. 43.   [212] Ibid. 45–6.
[213] *SEJ* (Mar. 1860), 52–5.

judgement and sentence followed. The bishops found the presentment *'relevant and Proven'* in regard to the first and second charges, in that Forbes's teaching was *'unsanctioned by* the Articles and Formularies of the Church and is to a certain extent inconsistent therewith'. They found the third charge 'not proven'. The judgement continued:

But in consideration of the explanations and modifications offered by the Respondent in his answers in reference to the first charge, and in consideration also that the Respondent now only asks for toleration for his opinions, and does not claim for them the authority of the Church, or any right to enforce them on those subject to his jurisdiction—We the said College of Bishops feel that we shall best discharge our duty in this painful case by limiting our sentence to a Declaration of *Censure and Admonition*, and we do now solemnly admonish and in all brotherly love entreat the Bishop of Brechin to be more careful for the future, so that no further occasion may be given for trouble and offence such as has arisen from the delivery and publication of the Primary Charge to his clergy complained of in the Presentment.[214]

A copy of a letter from Bishop Ewing was entered into the record. Ewing stated he could not have agreed to any sentence which went beyond exhorting Forbes to abstain from 'speculative teaching' on the Eucharist. Even then, Ewing said, he remained dubious about any verdict against Forbes, because he felt the bishops bore some responsibility in encouraging such speculation in the Church.[215] Beresford-Hope sent Forbes a jubilant note on 16 March, '10,000 congratulations. Benedictus! soft words butter no parsnips, ergo, censures break no bones.'[216] But Forbes confided in George Boyle that he felt 'decidedly unstrung' in reaction to the end of the tension of the last months. His nerves were very shaken and, he said, he could find no comfort save in plunging into his parish work at Dundee.[217]

Unfortunately this was not the conclusion of Forbes's ordeal, because he now came under pressure from supporters dissatisfied with the judgement. William Bright, for instance, wanted Forbes to do something about the bishops' statement that his teaching was unauthorized by the Church. Bright was particularly concerned that Forbes was being beaten to the public relations punch by Wordsworth, who had already had his trial opinion privately printed for distribution.[218] Bright's argument was

[214] REC II, 15 Mar. 1860, SRO CH 12. 60. 3, 449–50.
[215] Ibid. 450–1.
[216] A. J. Beresford-Hope to A. P. Forbes, 16 Mar. 1860, BrMS 1. 7. 109 (vii).
[217] A. P. Forbes to G. F. Boyle, 28 Mar. [1860], BrMS 1. 7. 110.
[218] W. Bright to A. P. Forbes, 'St. Cuthbert's Day' [20 Mar. 1860], BrMS 1. 2. 398; 18 Apr. [1860], BrMS 1. 2. 415; 19 Apr. [1860], BrMS 1. 2. 416.

reiterated by various writers in the *Union*, who were unhappy at the difference in the lenient judgement passed on Forbes compared to that in the Cheyne case. A loosely co-ordinated campaign of correspondence to various publications was conducted by Forbes's friends, seeking to interpret the judgement favourably. Bright, Liddon, Beresford-Hope, Upton Richards, and others, all wrote or instigated such letters to the *Guardian* and the *Union*, or wherever they thought they could reach uncertain Anglo-Catholics.[219] Forbes himself was growing increasingly annoyed with some of his more zealous supporters, particularly the clergy of St Ninian's, and the *Union*.[220]

Forbes intended to give a charge to the Brechin synod in August 1860 as his reply to the judgement. It was, he believed, the most natural and least provocative way of expressing his opinion on the trial's outcome. But he was also weary of controversy by now, and wary of anything that could rekindle the fire of theological argument. He was, Pusey told Keble, 'disappointed as to the small amount of faith in what we believe on the Holy Eucharist in the Scotch Church'.[221] Forbes addressed his synod at its meeting on 1 August, and gave his explanation of the various expressions in the formal judgement that had been troubling some Tractarians and Anglo-Catholics, including Bright and Pusey. The words that worried them were those that said the bishop had made modifications in his teaching; that the word 'now' (as in: 'the respondent now only asks for toleration of his opinion, and does not claim for them the authority of the Church') implied that he had shifted his ground; and the use of the word 'opinions' to describe his teaching. Forbes told his clergy that his explanations subsequent to his primary charge were for the sake of clarity and precision, and emphatically were not modifications. Nor had he shifted his ground, he said, through fear of the consequences.

I maintain what I have taught, rightly understood, is in conformity with the Word of God, and with our own Formularies as interpreted by the light of the early Church; that is a part of the primitive deposit witnessed to by the liturgies and individual fathers of the earliest ages . . . I claim, then, the right to consider this doctrine as the expression of the true mind of the Church; but, inasmuch as in the Anglican Church there has always been allowed great latitude of belief on this most mysterious subject, I have not claimed the dogmatic sanction of the

[219] W. Bright to A. P. Forbes, 18 Apr. [1860], BrMS 1. 2. 415; W. U. Richards to A. P. Forbes, 23 Apr. [1860], BrMS 1. 2. 419.
[220] A. P. Forbes to G. F. Boyle, 'Easter Day' [8 Apr.] 1860, BrMS. 1. 7. 111; and postmarked 21 July 1860, BrMS 1. 7. 117.
[221] E. B. Pusey to J. Keble, 1 July 1860, PK v.

Church in the sense that she would require my statements to be believed as a term of communion. From this position I have never swerved.[222]

This, he felt, was not a claim for toleration as popularly understood, nor was it a disclaimer of the authority of the Church for his teaching, but only to the Church's 'dogmatic sanction'. 'I claim the authority of the Church in the sense that the Church freely allows the teaching of what I have taught.' As regards his teaching being referred to as his 'opinions', he said he had more often used the word 'belief'. This, he considered, expressed his meaning that these doctrines were part of 'the central truth' which the Church always held. Forbes then recommended prayer, the daily office, frequent communion, and retreats as a remedy to the relaxation of effort that often resulted from the aftermath of controversy. Finally, he reminded his clergy and wider audience of the needs of the cities, and the necessity of unity among themselves if the Episcopal Church was adequately to provide urban mission.

In the great towns it cannot be denied that there is growing up a generation much less under religious influences than the last, while the statistics of the rural districts exhibit to us a most deplorable picture of the morals of the peasantry. Whatever be the causes of this unhappy state of things, it is plain what our duty is . . . we must hold together. [Such] steady adherence to our principles, with a large minded regard for our brethren, cannot but be blessed by God.[223]

The synod passed a motion petitioning the bishops to reconsider the restoration of Patrick Cheyne. Henderson was the sole dissenter.[224]

Forbes was still seeking a resolution to Henderson's refusal to have him confirm at Arbroath, proceeding gently, he said, because of the illness of Henderson's wife.[225] Relations between Henderson and Forbes were further soured, if possible, by Forbes receiving an address from eighteen members of the Arbroath congregation, expressing their 'unabated affection, respect, and esteem', and desiring him to come to Arbroath.[226] Relations between the two men remained estranged, and the confirmation at Arbroath at an impasse, for the rest of the year. But Forbes's problems with the other divided congregation, at Brechin, resolved themselves in October 1861 when Dean Moir resigned to accept the charge of the congregation at Jedburgh.[227]

---

[222] Brechin Diocese Synod Minutes, 1 Aug. 1860, BrMS 4. 1. 3., 81.
[223] Ibid. 83. [224] Ibid. 83–4.
[225] A. P. Forbes to E. B. Ramsay, n.d., BrMS 1. 2. 409.
[226] BrMS 1. 2. 441.
[227] J. Moir to A. P. Forbes, 'St. Simon & Jude's Day' [28 Oct.] 1861, BrMS 1. 3. 540.

After his synod Forbes took up his clergy's petition concerning Patrick
Cheyne, as a mandate to pursue a resolution to the old priest's situation.
But Cheyne's refusal to explain his teaching in similar terms to Forbes
made it difficult for Forbes to support the Brechin resolution at the
Episcopal Synod with anything new.²²⁸ His fears about the outcome of
his diocese's petition proved correct. At the synod meeting on 4 October
the bishops stuck to the letter of the canon, and replied that until Cheyne
sought restoration they could not act.²²⁹ There was one last gasp of the
Eucharistic controversy at this synod. The bishops received memorials
from Sir Thomas Gladstone and from laymen at Brechin, objecting to
Forbes's recent synod address as a repudiation of the trial verdict.²³⁰ But
the bishops contented themselves with an acknowledgement, declining to
take the matter further as being beyond their immediate jurisdiction.²³¹

By the end of 1860 Keble was particularly worried about Forbes's distress over the lack of belief among Episcopalians in the teaching he had
propounded, which teaching Forbes sincerely believed to be fundamental
to Catholic belief. Pusey, as he had been with Newman prior to 1845, was
less ready or able to see signs of real doubt and uncertainty. He thought
Forbes had been too optimistic about the level of acceptance among
Episcopalians of the doctrines he espoused, and was now having to make
a painful readjustment.²³² But in this instance Keble knew better. At
some time in early December he had received a letter from Forbes which
revealed that the bishop's difficulties were serious. Forbes had told Keble:

One cannot but feel that the beautiful school of thought following from 1833
has done its work and exists but as a phase of mind in the Church. It can in
no sense be said to represent Anglicanism. That the world should oppose it
and allow it to exist as a merely tolerated School of Opinion, I lay no store by,
but religiously it seems to have dried up; both stronger and more sentimental
minds seem to have passed through it in different directions, and it has failed
to touch the more pious souls among the Evangelicals and Weslyans.²³³

Unless the Catholic teaching of the Oxford Movement was affirmed as
the doctrine of the Anglican Church, rather than merely tolerated as one
allowable opinion, Forbes felt he could have no ultimate confidence in
the Catholic nature of his Church. Pusey put the whole thing down to

²²⁸ P. Cheyne to F. G. Lee, 12 Sept. 1860, BrMs 1. 2. 462; A. P. Forbes to G. Grub,
24 Sept. 1860, BrMS 1. 2. 470.
²²⁹ REC III, 4 Oct. 1860, SRO CH 12. 60. 4, 12–13.
²³⁰ SRO CH 12. 12. 2204–7.
²³¹ REC III, 4 Oct. 1860, SRO CH 12. 60. 4, 15–20.
²³² E. B. Pusey to J. Keble, postmarked 4 Dec. 1860, PK v.
²³³ A. P. Forbes to J. Keble, n.d. [Advent 1860], PK v.

neuralgia. But Keble was convinced there was doubt of real substance in Forbes's mind about the claims the Oxford Movement made for the Anglican Church as a part of the Catholic Church, doubt caused by the failure of his teaching to convince many people. The events of the next decade would prove that Keble read his friend's mind more accurately.

The most notable consequence of Forbes's Tractarian teaching in his primary charge of 1857 was the way in which it caused further division within the Episcopal Church. The Church was already broadly diversified into the northern area sympathetic to native nonjuring traditions; and the southern portion more influenced by the Church of England. But the divisions created over Forbes's charge cut across this existing divergence. Opposition to Forbes's Oxford Movement doctrine prevailed in both areas. The majority of the northern clergy were content with their traditional virtualist theology on the Eucharist, and others were unhappy with Forbes's criticism of the Nonjurors. A small number of the northern clergy were sympathetic to the Tractarians, but these were mainly confined to Forbes's diocese, or to a few zealous English Anglo-Catholics. Predominant among the southern clergy and influential laity, who were mostly English High Churchmen or Anglicized Scots, was a sincere and deep regard for the Church of England. These southern Churchmen, along with a small number of northern clergy, were unhappy with any sign of nonconformity with the Church of England, such as Forbes's Tractarianism. What did concern all the opposition, north and south, was the apparent sympathy towards Roman Catholicism among Tractarians, and specifically, the similarity of Forbes's teaching to Roman Catholic doctrine. This gave Forbes's opponents the correct impression that he was antipathetic to the Protestant heritage of their Church, which further alienated their sympathies. The various attempts to have Forbes limit the interpretation of his teaching to the words of the seventeenth-century divines were High Church endeavours to return Forbes's Tractarian teaching to the Reformed tradition of Anglicanism. But by the late 1850s this was impossible as Forbes, like the rest of the Tractarian leadership, distinguished that Reformed tradition from what was truly Catholic according to the early Church. Having narrowly defined Catholicism, so as to exclude the beliefs of the High Church majority of Episcopalians, Forbes became distressed when his teaching failed to secure the support he expected. This lack of approval indicated to him that while Episcopalians were High Church, they were not Catholic according to Tractarian understanding.

At the end of the Eucharistic controversy in 1860 neither Forbes's supporters nor his opponents prevailed. Forbes was not entirely acquitted nor effectively condemned. However the dispute had left the northerners more divided than the south. Ability to resolve the dispute had not been assisted by the vacuum of authority within the Episcopal Church with regard to the determination of doctrinal orthodoxy prior to disputes being tried before the Episcopal Synod. But the controversy, and more especially the trial itself, gained widespread publicity for Tractarian teaching, and for Forbes himself. It was extensively reported in many of the leading Scottish newspapers, including the *Scotsman*. This made Forbes the most well-known Episcopalian figure of the period. Respect for his ministry in Dundee probably gained his teaching a more sympathetic hearing, although the continued opposition to it from Sir John Ogilvie, a parishioner of Forbes's, is a warning against pressing this point too far.

The Eucharistic controversy was a catalyst in making the Scottish Episcopal Church a more theologically tolerant Church. Previously it had espoused a nonjuring High Church theology, and was uniformly opposed to Evangelicalism and Roman Catholicism. Forbes had claimed toleration for Tractarian teaching which many Episcopalians, if not most, regarded as foreign to their Church and as too akin to Roman Catholicism. Yet the survival of that claim—the failure of the trial effectively to condemn Forbes, or to silence him when he later reiterated the sanction of the Church for what he taught—left Tractarianism free to be propagated by Episcopalian sympathizers and the small number of Scottish Anglo-Catholics. However, this third party in the Scottish Episcopal Church could not have known that their leader was beginning something of a crisis of confidence. Evidence for the strain the three years of division and acrimony caused to Forbes himself is scanty during the period of the controversy itself. Much of what does exist is found in the correspondence between Pusey and Keble, and most of this belongs to their letters written during the 1860s. Therefore, the story of Forbes's increasing unhappiness and disillusionment with the Episcopal Church, and his growing attraction towards Roman Catholicism, will be told in the following chapter. The evidence for this shift away from Forbes's previous confidence in the catholicity of his Church may well have been one of the reasons for his destruction of most of his personal papers, mentioned by Perry.[234] While the Eucharistic controversy among Scottish Episcopalians provided Tractarianism with a public platform in Scotland, its adherents there could not have known that the failure of its immediate success had undermined Forbes's confidence in the Oxford Movement, and exacerbated his previous unhappiness with the Episcopal Church's smallness and divisions.

[234] Perry, p. ix.

5

Is the Church of England to be Pope?

In the manner of many mentors schooled at Oxford, Forbes was taking a country walk one day with a young man to talk about the youth's intellectual perplexities. The young man was worried about some of the new scientific theories and thought it possible God had abandoned the universe to run according to its own mechanical laws. Forbes touched a blade of grass with his foot and said, 'I believe that God takes as much individual care of that blade of grass, as if nothing else existed in the universe, and that he does not abandon it to the independent action of any laws whatsoever.'[1] It is not known when this small incident took place, but it could well represent the conflicts Forbes experienced during the 1860s. The younger man was apparently troubled by the new theories of empirical science, and in reply Forbes asserted the traditional doctrine of providence that God was intimately responsible for the existence and growth of all life, no matter how insignificant. Faced with challenges to orthodox Christian belief Forbes's usual response was to assert traditional answers. During the first years of the 1860s he renewed his contact with some of the most important of these new theories in the shape of biblical and historical criticism, and later, with science. He also had to come to grips with the growing force of Anglicization in the Episcopal Church, which reached a climax in this decade. Forbes's answer to all three was to uphold tradition, but with varying degrees of flexibility.

Sometime during 1860, possibly in August, Forbes was informed about the publication of *Essays and Reviews* by William Bright, at Oxford. *Essays and Reviews* was a composite volume of seven essays by Broad Churchmen attempting to address the implications of unrestricted theological enquiry for scripture and Christian belief. The essayists' use of biblical criticism was cautious compared to that in Germany, but for most British Churchmen it was their first introduction to higher criticism. Consequently, the book initiated one of the fiercest religious controversies in Victorian Britain. The reaction of the Church of

[1] F. M. C. Skene, *A Memoir of Alexander, Bishop of Brechin* (1876), 22.

England undermined the Broad Church movement and precipitated a second rise of high church influence. The essayists were not linked by any formal theological agreement, and the unplanned and uncoordinated nature of the book was the source of its troubles. Its lack of an editorial policy made the theological position vague, and haste in assembling the essays also led their writers to unconsidered statements they later regretted or wished to modify. It was published in March 1860 and despite significant differences between the contributors there was a basic theological presupposition that religious belief should be defended by an appeal to morality, rather than to doctrine. The contributors argued for a spiritual religion that did not derive authority from external evidences— either a supposed apostolic clarity in understanding revelation, a literal veracity of scripture, or dogma. Christianity was important as a moral religion and an ethical force rather than as the revelation of supernatural truth. The Church was regarded as the religious expression of the community and this required it to be widely comprehensive. While the essayists saw doctrine as historically conditioned they did not understand the same thing of morality, enshrining the values of Victorian England as timeless truth. But the greatest weakness in the book was that there was no mention of Christology. They revered the historical Jesus as a moral teacher but appealed more fundamentally to the philosophical abstractions of natural theology.[2]

According to the essays' historian, the most provocative and influential review of the book was that of the Unitarian Frederic Harrison in the *Westminster Review* who argued that the essays were a united work, timidly standing between orthodoxy and honest agnosticism, whose writers really espoused the latter position.[3] This common viewpoint was reinforced for many orthodox Churchmen (who generally did not read the liberal *Westminster Review*) by Samuel Wilberforce's anonymous review in the *Quarterly Review*, which largely followed Harrison's analysis. Following the appearance of these reviews the book generated enormous controversy. By the end of 1861 *Essays and Reviews* had gone through ten editions, and by 1865 some four hundred books, pamphlets, and articles had been written on it.[4] The overwhelming proportion of these varied publications came from Churchmen fiercely upholding orthodoxy against the essayists. While the reaction of orthodox Churchmen reveals the intellectual isolation of British Churchmen from their counterparts among German Protestants, the opposition of Tractarians and Anglo-Catholics demonstrated the

[2] I. Ellis, *Seven against Christ* (1980), 87–8.

[3] Ibid. 106–8.   [4] Ibid. 117.

influence of Pusey. Forbes had commented to his brother George, 'it will be very sad if we have to go through such a course as the Lutherans in Germany have had to endure.'[5] This remark about the harm Forbes believed had been done to German Lutheranism by the rationalism of higher criticism was most likely coloured by Pusey's well-known reaction to his earlier acceptance of biblical criticism. By 1840 Pusey had become a scriptural literalist because of his fear that rational criticism threatened acceptance of scripture and the doctrine of the Church as divine revelation.

Bright had told Forbes of the evil the work was doing in a rationalist direction, and Forbes thought the essays needed to be answered. George Forbes suggested Alexander write something on the subject because the bishop had 'much influence with the ultras' and it would 're-unite you with others by the feeling we were all struggling against a common danger'. As a northern Churchman, George saw possibilities in the controversy over *Essays and Reviews* for Alexander to restore his standing among northern Episcopalians which had been damaged during the Eucharistic controversy. His brother thought Forbes could help effect a reconciliation between Tractarian 'ultras' and northern Episcopalians, who had been divided over Forbes's Eucharistic teaching, by uniting them against the biblical criticism that both parties perceived as a threat to orthodox belief.[6]

By November 1860 Forbes, who had been staying at Oxford, wrote to his brother lamenting the predominance of the 'Jowett party' at the university.[7] Benjamin Jowett, Regius Professor of Greek, had contributed one of the most controversial essays in *Essays and Reviews*—'On the Interpretation of Scripture'. Jowett made it one of his life's aims to remould the university into a liberal academic institution, influenced by religion but free from the restrictions of confessional tests. Forbes evidently considered Jowett the leading figure among the liberals in the university, although his description of them as a party was too cohesive a term for such individualistic men.

Forbes neither took up his brother's suggestion to write something against the *Essays and Reviews*, 'nor did he respond to another proposal from Walter Trower, who wrote to him in December asking support for a motion to the Oxford University Convocation repudiating the principles of the book. Trower was especially anxious for Forbes's support because Forbes was both a bishop and an Oxford man.[8] His approach seems to

---

5   A. P. Forbes to G. H. Forbes, n.d., SAUL 19. 2. 239.
6   G. H. Forbes to A. P. Forbes, 30 Aug. 1860, BrMS 1. 2. 459.
7   A. P. Forbes to G. H. Forbes, 10 Nov. 1860, BrMS 1. 7. 132.
8   W. Trower to A. P. Forbes, 10 Dec. 1860, BrMS 1. 2. 497.

bear out George Forbes's idea that opposition to the liberals could unite
the Episcopalian parties previously divided over the Eucharistic controversy. Even the formerly antagonistic Trower apparently thought he could
count on Forbes's support against a common foe, despite their past antipathies. Forbes, although anxious about what he called 'the evils of
Rationalism in the English Church', had read only one of the essays (Mark
Pattison's), but that was sufficient for him to appreciate 'their very unset-
tling tendency'.[9] Pattison's essay discussed the development of eighteenth-
century evidential theology, and applied the principle of development to
show 'there is a law of continuity in the progress of theology'.[10] By this he
meant that the anti-rationalism of the Tractarians was a historical reaction
against eighteenth-century rationalism and not a traditional Catholic trait.
His essay was a plea for critical historical scholarship in theology. No wonder Forbes, who had reacted so strongly to propositions of development in
theology in his primary charge, thought Pattison's essay a disturbing
example of rationalism. However, Forbes hesitated to give his consent to
Trower's resolution because he did not want to give liberal theology in
England further assistance by way of persecution. He alluded to the
Tractarian campaign against the liberal R. D. Hampden at Oxford which
had invested him with the character of a martyr. It was only Hampden's
subsequent appointment as Bishop of Hereford which had, according to
Forbes, divested him of that mantle and thereby 'prevented the formation
of a dangerous school as early as the date of his appointment'. Nor did
Forbes think that any expression of what he called 'the country-parson
mind', or mere reaction, would carry any weight with the government of
Lord Palmerston. As Forbes told Bishop Robert Eden of Moray in February 1862, when defending his decision not to support Trower's proposed
resolution:

In my present state of feeling I am inclined to think that an intellectual error has
to be met intellectually, and I shd be glad to see the Reviews & Essays [*sic*]
crushed by a series of able replies—care however must be taken lest the Defence
of the Truth be committed to such feeble men as Burgon & Gresley . . . Distressing as it is that the rising intellect of the country should be thus perverted, I
cannot believe that the evil will be a lasting one. I do not expect that those
negations of truth will ever take a strong hold on the English mind . . . and so
when the fashion of the moment is passed, [they will] lead to a blessed reaction.[11]

---

[9] A. P. Forbes to R. Eden, 'Xmas Eve' [24 Dec.] 1860, BrMS 1. 2. 499.
[10] Mark Pattison, 'Tendencies of Religious Thought in England, 1688–1750', in
Essays and Reviews (6th edn. 1861), 256.
[11] A. P. Forbes to R. Eden, 20 Feb. [1862], BrMs 1. 3. 567.

But Forbes's failure to take up the challenge of *Essays and Reviews* more directly may well have been due to the fact that his energies were occupied closer to home with a threat to the Scottish Communion Office. At the annual Episcopal Synod on 3 October 1861 the bishops considered a remit from the Diocese of Moray and Ross asking them to take appropriate steps to secure the removal of the Scottish clerical disabilities. Bishop Eden made a lengthy statement on 'certain measures' which he, in conjunction with Alexander Ewing, had taken regarding the disabilities when they had recently been in London. The content of this statement is not reported in the minutes, but it led to the bishops agreeing that a paper should be prepared 'as soon as possible' by Eden. After revision by each of the Scottish bishops it was to be sent to the English bishops.[12] At an episcopal conference held in Edinburgh on 18 December 1861 it was decided to authorize a committee to consider measures expedient to the removal of the disabilities by Parliament.[13]

The bishops' concern for the removal of those legal disabilities which prevented Episcopalian clergy being beneficed in the Church of England had previously caused Forbes some anxiety, because the quid pro quo for their removal looked like being the abolition of the Scottish Communion Office. In March 1857 he had considered the possibility that General Synod might change canon 21 which gave the Office primary authority in the Church. If this happened Forbes asked his brother George if he could see any alternative to either submission or resignation.[14] His anxiety at that time had been caused by the desire of Bishop Ewing to get rid of the Office, and an anticipation of a strong move by the southern clergy to abolish it. He told his brother at the time that he suspected that while the northern clergy would deplore such a move, 'they will not take upon themselves the responsibility of a Schism' which their opposition could well compel them into.[15] Evidently, Forbes was aware of the strength of feeling against the Office in the more Anglicized south, and was concerned that northern opposition would not be determined enough to prevent the Office's demise at a future General Synod. Therefore, at the Episcopal Synod in November 1859 he had moved an amendment against calling a General Synod at that time, which was lost in favour of one establishing a committee to report on the possible revision of the Code of Canons.[16]

---

[12] REC III, 3 Oct. 1861, SRO CH 12. 60. 4, 27.
[13] Ibid., 18 Dec. 1861, 30.
[14] A. P. Forbes to G. H. Forbes, Mar. 1857, SAUL 19. 2. 114.
[15] A. P. Forbes to G. H. Forbes, Mar. 1857, SAUL 19. 2. 113.
[16] REC II, 9 Nov. 1859, SRO CH 12. 60. 3, 433.

Forbes's anxieties over the continued place of the Scottish Office in the Episcopal Church were compounded by his personal reaction to the recent Eucharistic controversy. In May 1861 Forbes was again writing in what Keble called his 'old melancholy strain'.[17] Pusey attributed Forbes's depression to his being 'utterly broken by the Scotch trial'. Reiterating his earlier conclusion that Forbes had been more optimistic than the two of them about Episcopalian belief in the real objective presence, Pusey believed he was suffering a profound disillusionment. Pusey also told Keble, ominously, that contributing to Forbes's difficulties was his 'original bias, that the first deep impressions of religion in Bp. F's life of manhood came through R. C.'s'.[18] Pusey's comment, from one who knew Forbes intimately, indicates that Forbes's disenchantment with the Episcopal Church had grown to such an extent that he was beginning to consider the claims of the Roman Catholic Church. Pusey's reference to religion must surely have meant Catholic religion, but he did not elaborate on this, as it must have been well known to himself and Keble as Forbes's spiritual advisers. Nevertheless this early contact with Roman Catholics evidently made a sufficiently strong impression on Forbes for Pusey to call it Forbes's 'original bias'. As mentioned above this impressionable encounter was probably made in India where personal contact across the Churches was more possible than in Britain.

Forbes responded cautiously to Eden's paper about the disabilities. He considered there was no chance of the Episcopal Church winning parliamentary revocation of them under Palmerston's government while the Evangelicals were politically so influential. Forbes was no doubt aware, through his connection with Gladstone, that since Lord Palmerston's ministry had come to power in 1855 Palmerston had turned to Lord Shaftesbury for advice on church appointments. While Shaftesbury endeavoured to recognize merit wherever he found it, inevitably, as a convinced Evangelical, he favoured men of his own party. This influence resulted in other Evangelicals joining John Bird Sumner, Archbishop of Canterbury, and his brother on the English bench, so that for the first time Evangelicals constituted a majority among the English bishops. By the time Palmerston died in 1865 nineteen English bishops were Evangelicals.[19] Those Evangelicals nominated early in Palmerston's first ministry (1855–8) were more extreme than during his second ministry (1859–65), because Shaftesbury

[17] J. Keble to E. B. Pusey, 2 May 1861, KP iv.
[18] E. B. Pusey to J. Keble, n.d. [3 May 1861], PK vi.
[19] Owen Chadwick, *The Victorian Church*, pt. 1 (1971), 19.

did not expect the ministry to last and was concerned to have godly men elevated while he still retained some influence. The secession of John Newman and other Anglicans to Rome after 1845 had increased Evangelical suspicion of the whole high church party. This did not necessarily mean that all Evangelical bishops were equally opposed to the High Scottish Episcopal Church. But to someone like Forbes, who had closely followed the prosecution of George Denison, which had been backed by the Evangelical Alliance, the connection between Evangelicals and opposition to High Churchmen was established well before 1861. But he thought no harm could come from maintaining the lobbying on the issue, although he did not think relinquishing the Scottish Office would ameliorate Evangelical opposition. 'I am glad', he wrote in a draft letter (words he later crossed out), 'to see that there is no intention of bartering the Office for the Disabilities. I do not believe that even if the Office was given up, the Evangelical opposition would be withdrawn.'[20]

On 7 February 1862 Bishop Terrot forwarded to the bishops a letter he had received from Archbishop Sumner concerning the support of the English bench for parliamentary abolition of the disabilities. Sumner had written that a number of the English bishops had discussed the subject and had directed him to ask, 'whether in your opinion the Consecra[tion] Service which differs from that of the English Church would be authoritatively set aside by your episcopal brethren there having been a general opinion that if that were done a great obstacle would be removed which now stands in the way of the measure you desire'.[21] Sumner's letter made plain to the Scottish bishops that abolition of the Scottish Office was the price to be paid for parliamentary support by the English bishops for any removal of the disabilities.

Forbes denounced the proposed bargain. Whatever they each thought of the Scottish Office he thought that surely 'our reputations will not allow us to give it up as the price of the removal of the disabilities'. To call a General Synod on such a basis, Forbes felt, would be to put temptation in the way of the clergy, 'risking a schism between the north and the south'. He continued to place the blame for such a bargain on the Evangelicals in the Church of England, assessing the situation accordingly:

they [the Evangelicals] fear & dislike the dogmatic teaching, which our very position as an antagonist of the Kirk inclines us to. They will therefore reject us tooth & nail, and if they do so, we may be very sure that they whom we

[20] A. P. Forbes to W. S. Wilson, n.d., BrMS 1. 3. 524.
[21] J. B. Sumner to C. H. Terrot (copy), 5 Feb. 1862, BrMS 1. 3. 561.

sought to conciliate by the abandonment of the Office, will be the first to fling that abandonment in our faces.[22]

Fearful of the lack of support for the Communion Office among the clergy Forbes did not want a General Synod which would only allow the clergy a direct control over developments. Preferring to keep the issue within the ranks of the bishops for the present, he argued for an Episcopal rather than a General Synod.

The bishops met in conference in Edinburgh on 26 February. The primus informed them he had replied to Sumner, stating that it was not within their power to set aside the Scottish Office. This could only be done by a General Synod, and such a synod would probably meet soon to consider a revision to the Code of Canons. However, he would give the archbishop no undertaking regarding the Office. The bishops approved the reply, which was sent on 27 February. Eventually it was decided to permit the appointed committee on the disabilities to consult widely on possible further action, and also to call a General Synod for 8 July 1862 for the purpose of canonical revision.[23] In a letter to Bishop Tait of London the following day Terrot explicitly mentioned that the canon about the Scottish Office would come up for debate at the prospective General Synod.[24]

A few days later Forbes informed Gladstone about the calling of a General Synod which he claimed was ostensibly about revision of the canons but, in fact, was really 'to get rid of the Scottish Office', as preparation for the campaign against their legal disabilities. As he stood alone in deprecating the move, Forbes said he feared nothing could be done.[25] This attempt to enlist Gladstone's powerful political influence succeeded in raising the statesman's indignation against the possible bargain. Gladstone replied on 3 March saying he thought such a scheme 'inadmissable, nay even despicable'. According to Gladstone, it was the reversal of religious principles for an essentially civil advantage. Gladstone also assured Forbes that Sir William Heathcote, the other member for Oxford University, supported him in this understanding.[26] Forbes lost no time in sending a copy of Gladstone's letter to Robert Eden, whom he saw as an ally in any campaign for the Scottish Office.[27] Eden responded quickly, saying he was relieved by the attitude of the two MPs although he still

[22] A. P. Forbes to W. S. Wilson, n.d., BrMS 1. 3. 561.
[23] REC III, 26 Feb. 1862, SRO CH 12. 60. 4, 35–9.
[24] C. H. Terrot to A. C. Tait, 27 Feb. 1862, Tait Papers, LPL 79, fo. 271.
[25] A. P. Forbes to W. E. Gladstone, 1 Mar. 1862, Gladstone Papers, BL 44154, fo. 274.
[26] W. E. Gladstone to A. P. Forbes, 3 Mar. 1862, BrMS 1. 3. 572.
[27] A. P. Forbes to R. Eden, n.d., BrMS 1. 3. 575.

thought that, even with such support, they would make little impression on the other bishops. Indignantly, Eden (an Englishman) asked, 'is the Church of England to be Pope? Is she to be the judge of what is and what is not a National Church? & is she to dictate to other Churches what their rites, forms & ceremonies may be?'[28] Forbes's securing of Gladstone's political support against the possible trade-off was further strengthened when Gladstone told Eden he would feel himself at liberty to propose an amendment to a disabilities removal bill if it should come tied to such a bargain, or 'to oppose it altogether in Parliament'.[29]

Before the battle could be properly joined, or perhaps because of its prospect, Charles Terrot notified the bishops of his intention to resign as primus. The election of a new primus became a crucial issue because of the division over the Scottish Office. Although the primus's role was largely confined to chairing the Episcopal and General Synods, it lay in his power to call the General Synod and it was within that arena that the conflict over the Office would be focused, centring on the revision of the canons, and particularly any amendment to canon 21 which gave the Scottish Office 'primary authority' in the Church. The proposed revision would be fought in a succession of General Synod meetings where the primus, as chairman, was influential. This made the role of the primus more important to both antagonists and supporters of the Scottish Office than it might otherwise have been, and a lot of lobbying went on among the bishops to secure a favourable candidate.

Wilson of Glasgow was Forbes's initial candidate. Forbes had sounded him out in a conversation in the Caledonian Hotel in Edinburgh, presumably during the last meeting of the bishops in February 1862. Wilson, however, drew attention to his being the junior among the bishops, as the most recently consecrated.[30] Terrot asked Forbes on 20 March 1862 if he had also received 'a letter from the North' (presumably from Eden) suggesting Wordsworth for primus on the grounds that he was a scholar. The primus was disturbed about this possibility for he thought 'a clear head, habits of business, freedom from crochets, a cool temper, & civil (if we cannot have a conciliating) manners' more important for the position of primus than scholarship. Terrot evidently considered these qualities lacking in the belligerent Wordsworth, and agreed with Forbes in supporting Wilson.[31] After receiving a letter of support from the primus, Wilson

28 R. Eden to A. P. Forbes, 6 Mar. [1862], BrMS 1. 3. 576.
29 W. E. Gladstone to R. Eden, 2 Apr. 1862, Lathbury, i. 435–6.
30 W. S. Wilson to A. P. Forbes, 19 Mar. 1862, BrMS 1. 3. 585.
31 C. H. Terrot to A. P. Forbes, 20 Mar. [1862], BrMS 1. 3. 586.

indicated to Forbes that he would consider offering himself if a majority supported him, but that he did not want a contest.[32] Wilson's candidature, however, began to founder on the opposition of Eden who thought him too conservative and said he had been particularly struck by 'the tone of almost ridicule with wh he treated the notion of our Church's *nationality*'. If Eden was so opposed to Wilson it raises the question of why Forbes did not support Eden from the beginning. Eden was surely the better candidate from Forbes's point of view as he had already expressed his support for the Scottish Office. But Forbes probably had a personal reason for not preferring Eden. In a letter in April 1865 to his chaplain Roger Lingard, Forbes said he felt that Eden had betrayed him over the judgement on his primary charge. Eden, Forbes thought, had initially favoured him but had allowed himself to be overruled at the trial by Wordsworth. Forbes commented, 'I have never quite got over that.'[33] If Forbes felt betrayed by Eden in 1865 then he was obviously still strongly ambivalent towards him three years earlier. Eden was someone Forbes needed as a fellow supporter of the Scottish Office, but he also felt injured by him. It was this emotional ambivalence that prevented Forbes from supporting Eden as his first choice for primus. Forbes must have understood he stood no chance of election himself so soon after the Eucharistic controversy, with the strong antipathies he had aroused among the bishops, especially in Wordsworth and Suther. But the prospect of Wilson as primus was not gaining ground, so by April 1862 Forbes was having to consider supporting Eden. On 10 April Eden was telling him he thought Forbes's vote for him would be thrown away because, personal unworthiness aside, Eden emphasized he was an Englishman.[34] Eventually the choice began to resolve itself as one between Eden and Wordsworth, with Eden having the stronger support. At the Episcopal Synod on 5 July 1862, held in conjunction with the General Synod, Terrot formally resigned as primus and Eden was elected in his place.[35]

During this lobbying the manœuvring over the Scottish Office and the clerical disabilities went on. Terrot was particularly worried about the lack of competent clerical applicants for congregations in his diocese, and thought the removal of the disabilities would encourage candidates from England to be ordained into the Episcopal Church.[36]

[32] W. S. Wilson to A. P. Forbes, 26 Mar. 1862, BrMS 1. 3. 594.
[33] A. P. Forbes to R. Lingard (-Guthrie), 30 Apr. 1865, SPC.
[34] R. Eden to A. P. Forbes, 10 Apr. [1862], BrMS 1. 3. 612.
[35] REC III, 5 July 1862, SRO CH 12. 60. 4, 44.
[36] C. H. Terrot to A. P. Forbes, 20 Mar. [1862], BrMS 1. 3. 586.

Gladstone's letter of support for the Office was now causing concern to Ewing, its principal episcopal opponent.[37] Forbes admitted to Ewing that he had circularized the letter so the bishops could become aware of the opinions of such influential figures as Gladstone and Heathcote.[38]

But Forbes was having difficulty in rousing supporters of the Communion Office, even among northern Churchmen who could be expected to support this exemplar of their own traditions. Some of his difficulties were indicated in a letter he received from Robert Thom, a prominent northern Churchman in his own diocese. Forbes had sent him a letter from Terrot, who had said the southern clergy believed that to retain the Office while removing the disabilities was to attempt the impossible. Thom thought that there was much to be said for Terrot's observations. England and Scotland seemed to be growing into a closer unity, which made it increasingly difficult for the Episcopal Church to justify a different ritual from the Church of England. He said he did not want to be understood as being personally inclined to relinquish the Scottish Office, and added that for him the removal of the disabilities was 'a matter of utter indifference'. Thom's main concern was what he referred to as 'the settlement of our own Church on a united Catholic basis, which will allow her to pursue with undivided energies the work of winning back to the Unity of the One Body & Faith of Christ a lost people'. But this, he thought, could never be accomplished while Episcopalians were still wrangling among themselves over two *'equally modern forms'* of liturgy. As long as the unity, catholicity, and independence of the Episcopal Church was maintained Thom would be content with the English Office, although he would personally prefer the Scottish one. Thom claimed he would never surrender the Scottish Office on the grounds of its teaching erroneous doctrine, but neither would he maintain it as the cost of the Church's unity.[39]

Thom's letter must have been discouraging to Forbes, coming as it did from a northern Churchman willing to concede the possibility of the Scottish Office's demise. It was hardly the sort of determined opposition to the Office's abolition Forbes needed. Against fierce antagonism to the Office Forbes needed equally convinced defenders, rather than a willingness to compromise too soon. Perhaps his difficulties in stimulating enthusiastic protagonists brought on further personal depression for Forbes. In March 1862 Keble received what he called 'a sad letter' from

[37] A. Ewing to A. P. Forbes, 21 Mar. 1862, BrMS 1. 3. 587.
[38] A. P. Forbes to A. Ewing, 22 Mar. 1862, BrMS 1. 3. 587.
[39] R. Thom to A. P. Forbes, 22 Mar. 1862, BrMS 1. 3. 590.

Forbes. Evidently, Forbes was still uncertain about Anglicanism, for
Keble advised him that while he was still doubtful 'he should not decide
against us', and he urged Forbes to further prayer and meditation for
guidance.[40]

Both Keble and Pusey were opposed to the loss of the Scottish Office
and advised Forbes accordingly. Pusey considered it would disgrace the
Episcopal Church, alienate the Church's friends in England, and be a
sacrifice of belief.[41] Keble told Forbes the abandonment of the Office
would appear to be a desertion of the 'high and primitive truth' of the
early Church. He was hopeful of finding enough support for the Office
among English Churchpeople so as to lessen the effect of the English
bishops' demand for abolition. In offering this encouragement Keble had
regard for Forbes's own spiritual indecision. He was hoping Forbes
would not give in to the 'desponding thoughts which I know are too
likely to come thronging upon you in such an emergency'.[42]

Early in April 1862 Gladstone advised Eden to postpone lobbying
for any bill on the removal of the disabilities if there was any intention
on the part of the Scottish bishops to alter the position of the Scottish
Office. As a counter to the demands of the English bishops for the
Office's abolition, Gladstone downplayed their parliamentary influence.
He considered that they were more effective in preventing measures
than in advocating them. Therefore any bill proposed by the Episcopal
Church needed their support, but such support did not necessarily
guarantee success.[43]

The draft revision of the code of canons had finally been completed
by the appointed committee and was sent to the various dioceses for consideration by their synods. There appears to be no record of this draft in
the General Synod papers, but it must have severely threatened the place
of the Scottish Communion Office if the consternation of Forbes and
Eden is any measure. On 9 April, Eden wrote to Forbes hoping that a
decided expression of opinion in favour of the Office from Moray and
Brechin synods would increase the pressure to maintain the Office.[44]
Forbes replied with an outline of proposed campaign tactics. He wanted
to encourage Gladstone and other friendly members of Parliament to
delay supporting any bill for the removal of the disabilities until the

40 J. Keble to A. P. Forbes, n.d. [*c.* 27 Mar. 1862], PK vi.
41 E. B. Pusey to J. Keble, n.d., PK vi.
42 J. Keble to A. P. Forbes, 1 Apr. 1862, BrMS 1. 3. 600.
43 W. E. Gladstone to R. Eden, Lathbury, i. 436–7.
44 R. Eden to A. P. Forbes, 9 Apr. [1862], BrMS 1. 3. 632.

Office was secured. Forbes believed that if such a commitment could be brought to the attention of advocates of the bargain it would influence their policy. As well, Forbes intended at his diocesan synod that year to encourage the Brechin clergy to vote for a canon allowing the Office in new congregations.[45] It may have been these suggestions of Forbes that caused Gladstone to contact Ewing expressing his opposition to the loss of the Scottish Office. Gladstone reminded Ewing of his influence within the Episcopal Church by stating that if the proposed bargain had been advocated at the time of building Trinity College the college would not have been built.[46]

Despite the apparent success of Forbes's political strategy he remained anxious. A possible revision of the *epiclesis* in the Scottish Office's Eucharistic prayer worried him particularly.[47] As Forbes no doubt knew, this proposal originated with Bishop Wordsworth, who raised it publicly at his diocesan synod in September 1862. In reaction to a suggestion from George Forbes (to alter the *epiclesis* according to the wording of the eastern Liturgy of St James), Wordsworth proposed an alteration to use the words of the 1549 edition of the Book of Common Prayer—that the bread and wine 'may be unto us' the body and blood of Christ. Such a change, according to Forbes, would have made the presence of Christ in the sacrament rest on the subjective grounds of the worshipper's faith. Given his position in the recent Eucharistic controversy, Forbes viewed such a threat to the objectivity of the real presence very seriously. But his commitment to the objectivity of sacramental grace was not his sole reason for supporting the Scottish Communion Office. To Forbes, the Office was also a sign of the Episcopal Church's attachment to the Catholic authority of the early Church, because he understood that rite as being closer to the liturgies of the patristic Church than was the English liturgy. Indeed, the Scottish Office was one of the few things keeping Forbes from converting to Roman Catholicism. It was this personal need of the Office as a sign of the Catholic nature of the Episcopal Church that caused Forbes to fight so strenuously for its continued retention. Few on either side of the struggle can have realized that the demise of the Scottish Office could also have meant the scandal of the conversion of a bishop to Rome, a conversion that would have approached Newman's in its effect on the confidence of Anglo-Catholics.

[45] A. P. Forbes to R. Eden, n.d., BrMS 1. 3. 632.
[46] W. E. Gladstone to A. Ewing, Lathbury, i. 437–8.
[47] A. P. Forbes to G. H. Forbes, n.d., SAUL 19. 2. 303.

Pusey wrote to Forbes on 2 May 1862 trying to put the revision of the canonical place of the Office on a less exalted plane than Forbes understood it to be. The revision was not a change in doctrine, contended Pusey, but only an ecclesiastical or institutional one. He also pointedly claimed it was not divisions within the Church that most hurt the faith of Churchpeople, but rather secessions from it.[48] Forbes was planning to spend some time with Pusey in Oxford, and in order to prepare for the visit Pusey asked Keble for advice about Forbes's contention that opposition to the Office was a denial of divine truth.[49] Keble replied on 4 May pointing out that many convinced Tractarians or Anglo-Catholics actually disliked the Scottish Office, believing it to be more dissimilar to the Roman rite than the Book of Common Prayer. But Forbes's identification of Catholic truth with similarity to the early Church had convinced him that the alteration of patristic features of the Scottish Office such as its *epiclesis* (not part of the Eucharistic liturgy of the Book of Common Prayer), or the Office's total abolition, would be a departure from Catholic truth. The fact that Forbes's understanding was not shared by other leaders of the Catholic revival is an indication of just how personally attached he was to the Office. It had become his lifeline to Anglicanism.

But in May 1862 that lifeline had become very fragile. Forbes now intended to call on Newman at the Birmingham Oratory during his trip south to Oxford. This markedly increased the anxiety of the English Tractarian leaders. Pusey feared that the Birmingham visit could have only one end—the bishop's secession.[50] Keble referred to Forbes's 'temper and excitement', and suggested that Forbes was insufficiently aware of God's *'fatherly* love'.[51] Forbes intended to give Newman no prior warning of his impending visit, claiming to see divine guidance in whatever eventuated when he arrived at Birmingham.[52] Meanwhile, Pusey and Keble maintained a vigil of prayer, anxiously awaiting Forbes's arrival at Oxford.

Forbes called on Newman at the oratory in Edgebaston on 15 May but found him away from home. When Forbes arrived at Christ Church that evening a relieved Pusey told Keble that 'the immediate peril is past', but added that Forbes remained despondent about the Church and fearful of death. Presumably, Pusey meant Forbes feared the possibility of his dying outside the Catholic Church while he was

[48] E. B. Pusey to A. P. Forbes, 2 May [1862], BrMS 1. 3. 613.
[49] E. B. Pusey to J. Keble, n.d., PK vi.
[50] E. B. Pusey to J. Keble, n.d., PK vi.
[51] J. Keble to E. B. Pusey, 9 May 1862, KP iv.
[52] E. B. Pusey to J. Keble, 14 May [1861], PK vi.

still unsure just where that was to be located.[53] Keble was thankful for
'the reprieve', but grieved at his own inability to do anything to help.
He asked that Forbes be assured of his own 'deep, deep love'.[54]

Accepting for the present the failure to see Newman in Birmingham
as God's will, Forbes worked with Pusey in Oxford to draft a new canon
on the Scottish Office, which he then sent to Eden.[55] By now support
for the proposed trade-off between abolition of the Scottish Communion
Office and removing the disabilities had grown. Supporters of the tran-
saction included such influential figures as Bishop Samuel Wilberforce of
Oxford and Dean Ramsay in Edinburgh. However, Gladstone continued
to exercise his powerful influence against the bargain. He wrote to
Wilberforce on 28 June warning that if such an arrangement was concluded with Wilberforce's approval 'the relations between us are new
relations', and that Gladstone would have to 'consider my course afresh
upon many matters'.[56] Gladstone wrote in the same uncompromising vein
to his friend Ramsay.[57] Writing to Forbes on 5 July, the day the Episcopal Synod met to elect a new primus, Gladstone harked back to the
days when he and James Hope founded Trinity College. At that time, it
seemed to Gladstone, the English Office of the Book of Common Prayer
was the preference only of wealthy Episcopalians as a result of their
contact with England. But he had been confident of the continuing place
of the Scottish Communion Office because it was dear to 'native and
poorer' Episcopalians, and the bishops of the period 'prized that office
. . . at least as dearly as their own lives'. To eliminate the use of the
Scottish Office Gladstone considered an act of bad faith to the agreement
given to the college founders. With the next General Synod meeting
three days away, Gladstone authorized Forbes to bring his letter to the
notice of the other bishops.[58]

The General Synod met in Freemasons Hall, in George Street,
Edinburgh, on 8 July 1862, to proceed with the most extensive revision of
the Code of Canons in the Episcopal Church to that time. After intensive
consideration for eight days the revised draft was sent back to the diocesan
synods for further consideration, and the synod adjourned until 30
September 1862.[59] In so far as the Scottish Office was concerned the

[53] E. B. Pusey to J. Keble, n.d., PK vi.
[54] J. Keble to E. B. Pusey, 17 May 1862, KP iv.
[55] E. B. Pusey to J. Keble, n.d., PK vi.
[56] W. E. Gladstone to S. Wilberforce, 28 June 1862, Lathbury, i. 438–9.
[57] Ibid. 439.
[58] W. E. Gladstone to A. P. Forbes, 5 July 1862, Gladstone Papers, BL 44154, fo. 278–82.
[59] REC III, 8–16 July 1862, SRO CH 12. 60. 4, 55–62.

General Synod went badly for Forbes. The proposed canon 36 declared it
was expedient to have as little diversity as possible between the Episcopal
Church and 'sister Churches' of the United Kingdom. In consequence, the
English Book of Common Prayer was to be adopted as 'the only service
book of this Church'. The proposed canon 37 allowed existing congregations to continue using the Scottish Office if they presently did so, but all
new congregations had to adopt the English Prayer Book.[60] Pusey
described Forbes as returning to Dundee 'half-dead', and 'sickened at the
miserably low religious tone of the Synod, the hopes of twenty years
blighted'. Appalled at the strength of opposition to the Scottish Office
Forbes developed a nervous tic at nights worrying over what he understood to be a betrayal of apostolic truth.[61] Forbes may also have feared the
personal consequences of losing his Anglican lifeline. He would have
known that his secession to Rome would have resulted in the loss of many
valued friendships and relationships. Especially for a celibate, such friendships were an important source of personal comfort and self-esteem. If this
was a component of his fretfulness it was not without foundation. In 1851
Gladstone had cut off his closest friends, James Hope and Henry
Manning, when they became Roman Catholics. Forbes must have known
he could expect no less.

But the battle for the Scottish Office would not be over until the revision of the canons was finalized at the forthcoming meetings of the
General Synod beginning in late September. Forbes now proposed a
compromise solution, in his annual address to his diocesan synod which
was held on 27 August 1862 (later than usual in order to give the clergy
time to consider the redrafted canons from General Synod). He devoted
his address to the two 'great questions' still outstanding at General Synod,
namely the Office and admission of laity into synods. Forbes reiterated his
usual objection to the Book of Common Prayer. He understood the
authorized liturgies of the Church to be transmitters of its doctrine.
Therefore, to displace the Scottish Office was to question the Episcopal
Church's faithful transmission of the faith. Changing liturgies, he believed,
also changed the symbolic representation of the Church's doctrine. While
he was prepared, he said, to relinquish the description of the Office under
the old canon 21 as having 'primary authority', he would not agree to any
canonical change which did not explicitly describe the alteration as a
matter merely of ecclesiastical organization and not of doctrine. Regarding

    [60] 'Proposed Code of Canons of the Episcopal Church in Scotland' (1862), unlisted
papers in Scottish Record Office, to be added to CH 12.
    [61] E. B. Pusey to J. Keble, n.d., PK vi.

proposals to alter the Office itself, Forbes argued these would be a surrender to the schismatic Drummondites, who had separated themselves
from the Episcopal Church precisely because they objected to the Scottish
Office. According to Forbes the present was a period of poor faith due to
growing religious doubt, and was therefore an unsatisfactory time to
change a liturgy that had proved itself capable of sustaining the faith of
Episcopalians during the persecutions of the previous century. He warned
that any alteration to the formularies of the Church would reopen the
Eucharistic controversy. The present formularies, he maintained, were
capable of being interpreted favourably by either side in the recent
controversy, but any new formula would be unlikely to satisfy all parties
and could well result in schism. Forbes also objected to a fundamental
change in the place of the Office being carried in General Synod by a
simple majority. Then he outlined his proposed conciliation. Supporters of
the Office would concede its primary authority and allow the Book of
Common Prayer to enjoy equal authority. In return, Forbes suggested,
there should be a canonical preamble stating that the change in the
Scottish Office's position was simply a matter of discipline. Congregations
presently using the Office should be permitted to continue doing so, and
new congregations be allowed its use also if so requested by a majority of
the congregation. A change to either liturgy from an existing use should
be permitted only if desired by two-thirds of regular communicants in a
congregation. If such conditions were granted, Forbes believed Scottish
Office supporters could 'rest content, if not satisfied'. Forbes then said
briefly he accepted the canons regarding lay involvement in the election of
bishops in so far as they accorded the laity their ancient right to accept or
reject such an election. But he was against the laity becoming part of
normal synods as this meant they became part of the teaching authority of
the Church which, he believed, was limited to the clergy.[62]

According to Pusey, Forbes's proposals in his synod charge were
indicative of the calm of one who had made up his mind about what he
should do. Forbes had told Pusey he expected his course of action to be
clear by the end of the year but for now he awaited events, by which
Pusey took him to mean that if there was an improvement in the position
of the Scottish Office he would stay on; if not he would resign and
possibly even secede, or what Pusey referred to as 'leave everything'.[63]

But Forbes was not content merely to await developments. During
August 1862 he approached Gilbert Rorison, a senior priest of Aberdeen

[62] Brechin Diocese Synod Minutes, 27 Aug. 1862, BrMS 4. 1. 3, 102–5.
[63] E. B. Pusey to J. Keble, n.d., PK vii.

diocese and a leader among those planning to adopt the Book of Common Prayer in place of the Scottish Office. Forbes wrote to him on 11 August to recommend the compromise he had advocated in his synod charge. He warned that if the present draft canon about the Scottish Office were carried it would leave 'a sense of intolerable wrong' among supporters of the Office that would only lead to further agitation. Supporters among the clergy, he warned, might petition Parliament not to revoke the disabilities. Such a petition would have been fatal to any bill for their removal as suggesting that Parliament was involving itself in a religious controversy. Forbes affirmed that such a petition would have his own support which was not without important influence. 'And I may say for myself, that I shd use my endeavour to induce Mr Gladstone, Lord Robert Cecil & Mr Lygon[64]—as well as any other friends I had in Parliament, *to delay* their support of any bill until our grievances were redressed.' Having threatened real political consequences for any disabilities bill Forbes went on to hold out a carrot as well as a stick. He said supporters of the Office accepted they were in a minority and would not ask the earth. However, they did demand as the basis of a compromise that the Office be permitted in new congregations, and that either liturgy could be adopted by any congregation where two-thirds of the people and their clergyman wanted it; also, that there be a preamble in the canon to 'preserve in some shape the dogmatic authority of the Office'.[65] Forbes endeavoured to back up his presage to Rorison by asking his brother George if some of his fellow supporters of the Office among the clergy in Scottish orders would write to Rorison, threatening to petition Parliament against the removal of the disabilities if the Scottish Office were not granted toleration.[66] Forbes's campaign was boosted on the day he wrote to Rorison by a letter of support from the Earl of Morton, who wanted to have the Scottish Office used in the chapel he was building at his highland seat.[67]

Rorison responded to Forbes on 16 August claiming he did not fear the tactics of any clerical opposition. The present contest was, Rorison believed, between those to whom the Scottish Office was paramount to any other consideration, and those—'an immense majority'—to whom other issues, such as the peace of the Church and the development of a cultivated native clergy, were more important than questions about

[64] Frederick Lygon (1830–91) Tory MP for Tewkesbury and then for West Worcestershire until 1866 when he succeeded as sixth Earl Beauchamp. *DNB* xxxiv, 324–5.

[65] A. P. Forbes to G. Rorison (copy), 11 Aug. 1862, BrMS 1. 3. 633.

[66] A. P. Forbes to G. H. Forbes, n.d., SAUL 19. 2. 306.

[67] Earl of Morton to A. P. Forbes, 11 Aug. 1862, BrMS 1. 3. 634.

liturgies. But he was willing to accommodate the minority if such an adjustment could be consistent with the consciences of the majority. Rorison had most misgivings about the use of the Office in new congregations. He might accept alternate use of both liturgies in new congregations, but in existing congregations he would not concede that the Scottish Office might be permitted to supplant the Book of Common Prayer. This was the maximum concession Rorison said he would support. But he would only support it if he could alter the Scottish Office's *epiclesis* according to Wordsworth's proposal. Further, he would only press for such a compromise 'on the understanding that Mr Gladstone & others will in that case be prepared to throw their whole influence to the minimizing of that opposition which concession may tend to stimulate'.[68]

Forbes wrote back to Rorison on 18 August to say that all negotiations must be founded on an unaltered Scottish Office. In this, Forbes said, he was confident he could also speak for Gladstone.[69] The threat of Gladstone's disapproval again did the trick. Rorison agreed the next day not to demand any change to the Office, and to propose the conciliation on the terms he had originally outlined to Forbes.[70] But this counter-proposal was not satisfactory to Forbes, who opposed alternate use of both liturgies in a single congregation. Writing to Rorison on 21 August Forbes outlined the compromise as he saw it. Supporters of the Office would agree not to petition Parliament against the disabilities bill, and Forbes and others would use their influence with Gladstone and other parliamentarians to support the bill. In return, Rorison and his supporters would accept an unaltered Office; support a canonical preamble that the liturgical change was merely disciplinary while giving 'honourable mention to the Scottish Office'; and accept Forbes's proposal for liturgical use in new or existing congregations. If this was acceptable to Rorison, Forbes would send their correspondence to Gladstone for his response.[71] Rorison still wanted to take further counsel on the matter of the congregations, and stressed again that his ability to promote the conciliation would depend on its having Gladstone's support.[72]

Gladstone's response was sent to Forbes on 30 August 1862, stating that Gladstone considered himself technically a 'stranger' to the Episcopal Church, residing as he did outside Scotland. Therefore, should the

[68] G. Rorison to A. P. Forbes, 16 Aug. 1862, BrMS 1. 3. 641.
[69] A. P. Forbes to G. Rorison, 18 Aug. 1862, BrMS 1. 3. 642.
[70] G. Rorison to A. P. Forbes, 19 Aug. 1862, BrMS 1. 3. 643.
[71] A. P. Forbes to G. Rorison (copy), 21 Aug. 1862, BrMS 1. 3. 644.
[72] G. Rorison to A. P. Forbes, 23 Aug. 1862, BrMS 1. 3. 646.

canon about the Scottish Office pass he would simply withdraw all support for the Scottish Episcopal Church, 'except with particular persons or institutions'. Having thus indicated his continued support for Forbes no matter what happened to the Scottish Office, Gladstone gave him what he wanted in agreeing that the cardinal point at issue was the liberty of new congregations to adopt the Scottish Office if they wished, and that he would 'value no other concession'. Gladstone then backed up Forbes's threat about political influence. 'To any Bill in name or substance founded on a theological bargain between the Scottish Episcopal Communion and the English Bishops I should be opposed,' he affirmed, and agreed that any opposition to a disabilities bill by a portion of the clergy or laity of the Episcopal Church would prove fatal to such a bill.[73]

Faced with Gladstone's overwhelming endorsement for Forbes's plan Rorison agreed on 9 September that if he could get his bishop's permission, he would then move at the Aberdeen synod that their delegate to the General Synod be instructed to support the compromise. But Rorison still hoped to retain something of his own proposal, and so wanted to ask Gladstone if he would support alternate use in new congregations. Rorison had a healthy respect for Gladstone's political influence, maintaining that he was 'the *virtual controller* of such personal hostility in the one quarter [Parliament] where it would be fatal to us'.[74] On 15 September Gladstone observed to Forbes that Rorison's suggestion only gave congregations an option between the exclusive use of the English office and the alternate use of it and the Scottish, which was not an equitable choice.[75] Having no possible doubts now about the strength of Gladstone's support for Forbes's political threat Rorison capitulated, and on 25 September agreed to the compromise as Forbes understood it.[76]

During this time Forbes was seeking further support for his proposed settlement. He had evidently sent copies of his last synod charge outlining his proposals to various people as a means of garnering support for his compromise. Eden wrote to him on 3 September saying that the Moray synod had agreed almost unanimously to the points Forbes had suggested in his charge.[77] Forbes had sent his charge to George Boyle, the most influential layman in the Diocese of Argyll and the Isles. But Boyle had to report that a motion based on Forbes's compromise was defeated in that

[73] W. E. Gladstone to G. Rorison, 30 Aug. 1862, BrMS 1. 3. 650.
[74] G. Rorison to A. P. Forbes, 9 Sept. 1862, BrMS 1. 3. 657.
[75] W. E. Gladstone to A. P. Forbes, 15 Sept. 1862, BrMS 1. 3. 658.
[76] G. Rorison to A. P. Forbes, 25 Sept. 1862, BrMS 1. 3. 663.
[77] R. Eden to A. P. Forbes, 3 Sept. [1862], BrMS 1. 3. 654.

synod.[78] Pusey also received a letter from Forbes, probably in September, asking him to write to the *Guardian* against Wordsworth's proposed alteration to the *epiclesis* of the Communion Office.[79]

But the General Synod meeting, which reconvened on 30 September, did not tackle the canon concerning the Scottish Office. It only passed those permitting lay representatives at the election of bishops and then adjourned until 3 February 1863.[80] Pusey and Keble, meanwhile, were growing more and more anxious about the effect of the battle on Forbes's uncertainty about the Episcopal Church. Pusey had observed that the canonical revision had stimulated the bishop's doubts 'into a fever'.[81] In October, their concern increased when Forbes appeared favourably impressed by something Cardinal Manning had written on the infallible *magisterium* of the papacy, possibly *The Temporal Power of the Pope* published that year. Forbes had thought the argument logical and so Pusey had sent a long letter in refutation. Pusey observed that underneath his outward calm Forbes was in a 'terrible panic', and that he had once again been worried by the debates at General Synod. This time Forbes was 'cast down' because the clergy had refused to be bound by a proposal that the Church accept as a theological standard the decisions of the first four General Councils of the early Church.[82] There is no record of the debates in the minutes of the General Synod, but a proposal about the General Councils possibly came from Forbes or some other Tractarian among whom such Councils were generally regarded as theologically authoritative for the contemporary Church.

Joseph Robertson in Edinburgh was keeping Forbes informed about developments in the south. He believed what pressure for revision of the Scottish Communion Office there was came either from a small group, prompted by George Forbes, who wanted it revised in a high direction, or from Wordsworth, who was threatening to resign if the Office was not revised in a low direction.[83] Forbes wrote to his brother in November 1862 arguing that an unrevised Office had the best chance of securing toleration. He also continued to be worried about the dismissal of the authority of the four General Councils by members of the General Synod, stating, 'I cannot trust my soul in a Church which ignores them'.[84]

[78] G. F. Boyle to A. P. Forbes, 5 Sept. 1862, BrMS 1. 3. 655.
[79] E. B. Pusey to J. Keble, n.d., PK vi.
[80] REC III, 30 September to 4 Oct. 1862, SRO CH 12. 60. 4, 76–7.
[81] E. B. Pusey to J. Keble, 29 Sept. 1862, PK vi.
[82] E. B. Pusey to J. Keble, n.d., PK vi.
[83] J. Robertson to A. P. Forbes, 28 Oct. 1862, BrMS 1. 3. 681.
[84] A. P. Forbes to G. H. Forbes, Nov. 1862, SAUL 19. 2. 299.

During the past two months Forbes had been unsettled by clergy refusing to acknowledge the authority of the General Councils, and by Manning's argument for an infallible papacy. The Eucharistic controversy had previously disrupted Forbes's confidence in the catholicity of Anglican divines and in Episcopalian belief in an objective Eucharistic presence of Christ. Now he was hoping to see the General Councils acknowledged by the Episcopal Church as having doctrinal authority and discovered this also was unacceptable. It would appear that Forbes was engaged at this time in a desperate search for an objective authority for Christian doctrine on which he could confidently rest his belief that the Anglican Church was Catholic. The lack of acceptance for those authorities he did propose made it all the more necessary to secure the one that some agreed about, and which had traditional authority within the Episcopal Church—the Scottish Communion Office. It was not only a matter of the intellectual basis for faith but, as he told his brother, a concern for the salvation of his soul within the Catholic Church. If Forbes could not be sure where that Church was, then he could not be confident of his salvation.

Resignation was once more in Forbes's thoughts, and Joseph Robertson endeavoured to keep him from it by persuading the bishop that he was the only link between the present Episcopal Church and that of the nonjuring days.[85] Robertson asked Forbes to remember the fiery example of his predecesssor in Brechin, Bishop Walter Whiteford, 'who is said to have read the Service Book of 1638 in his cathedral church with a pair of pistols on the desk beside him'. '_He_', said Robertson pointedly, 'went to England and ended his days there . . . but it was not until he had been excommunicated in Scotland, and driven from it by brute force.'[86]

The possibility of alteration to the Communion Office now came to dominate Forbes's anxieties. At the beginning of 1863 Forbes believed that the bishops who stood for non-alteration of the office were Terrot and his new coadjutor, Thomas Morrell,[87] Wilson, and himself.[88] Writing

[85] Robertson was not just being rhetorical, for some leading northern Churchmen were deserting the Scottish Office in preference for the English. Included among them was John Torry, son of Bishop Patrick Torry and Dean of St Andrews, Dunkeld, and Dunblane. He expressed his desire that nothing should be done to support the Scottish Office and the hope it would soon die out. _SEJ_ (Feb. 1863), 25.

[86] J. Robertson to A. P. Forbes, 1 Dec. 1862, BrMS 1. 3. 684.

[87] Charles Terrot had reluctantly bowed to pressure from his diocese and the other bishops and accepted the election of a coadjutor because of his increasing paralysis. Thomas Morrell, at the time of his election in January 1863 incumbent of Henley, was the first bishop to be elected under the new canons at a synod involving lay representatives. REC III, 2 Feb. 1863, SRO CH 12. 60. 4, 86–90.

[88] A. P. Forbes to E. B. Pusey, 25 Jan. [1863], PP 5. 40.

to Pusey from Dublin, where he was engaged in historical research, Forbes said those in favour of revising the Office were Wordsworth, Eden, and Ewing, while Suther was doubtful. He believed there was a good chance of his position gaining majority support at the next meeting of the General Synod, but suspected revision would win in the lower house of the clergy. Pusey still feared the effect on Forbes of the debate at the next General Synod meeting, namely, that the mundane language and lack of acknowledgement of divine guidance of synods would make Forbes feel 'that they and he belong to different systems, i.e., that they have not the Catholic faith'.[89] Pusey's anxiety grew when he did not hear from Forbes concerning his invitation to come to Christ Church that January. He knew Forbes did not like travelling in winter, but even more he did not like coming to see Pusey while he was still harassed. Pusey now opened every letter of Forbes's dreading its news. Once again, looking towards the outcome of the General Synod in February, the two Tractarian leaders feared the worst for their friend.

The General Synod resumed its sittings on 3 February 1863 and continued to meet until 13 February. Most of the time was spent making small alterations to the proposed Code of Canons according to various amendments voted for at the diocesan synods. But the major event was the debate on the Scottish Office which continued from 10 to 12 February. On 10 February the primus, Robert Eden, tabled various petitions and memorials concerning the Office. Included among them was a petition from the 'Clergy & Laity of the Church of England' against giving up the Scottish Communion Office in return for the removal of the disabilities. It contained 311 signatures, including Pusey, Keble, and all the leading Tractarians and Anglo–Catholics.[90] Eden then moved that the Book of Common Prayer be used in all new congregations, unless the incumbent and the majority of communicants desired the Scottish Office. Forbes supported this only with reluctance, probably because it still left the Book of Common Prayer as the authorized service at diocesan level, namely at all consecrations, ordinations, and synods. Eden's motion passed in the upper house, and was successful in the lower house of the clergy on 11 February with only slight amendment. The clergy then returned the amended motion to the bishops, who considered it for the last time in a tense debate on 12 February. Eden thought the canon now represented compromise by both sides. He said it gave the Book of Common Prayer

[89] E. B. Pusey to J. Keble, 'Eve of the Epiphany' [5 Jan. 1863], PK vi.
[90] Bundle of petitions concerning possible abolition or alteration of the Scottish Communion Office, 1863. Unlisted papers in the Scottish Record Office to be added to CH. 12.

canonical acceptance, and disallowed departure from it except in the case of a majority of communicants in new congregations, while for the Scottish Office it meant toleration. He therefore proposed they accept the canon as sent back to them by the lower house. Forbes seconded the motion as being the best the majority would grant, and if this proposal was not passed then that majority would hold out for more stringent terms. Ewing proposed they adhered to the canon as originally drafted in July 1862, and this was seconded by Suther. Wilson, as usual, had difficulty making up his mind. Eventually, the primus moved the canon be adopted, with the further amendment of giving the bishop power to refuse the use of the Scottish Office if he considered undue influence had been put on the requesting congregation. Aware of the reluctance of three of their number Forbes seconded this as the best deal obtainable and it passed, reluctantly supported by Suther but opposed by Ewing. It was sent back to the clergy who again passed it with minor alteration, and the canon was finally agreed to by both chambers on 12 February.[91]

Forbes's immediate reaction was relief at having secured toleration for the Scottish Office. So strong was this feeling that, on 12 February, he wrote Pusey a note from the synod room itself, giving his quick assessment of the gains and losses, and believing that on the whole things had gone better than expected. The gains as far as Forbes was concerned were that there was no revision of the Scottish Communion Office, no discussion on doctrine, toleration of the Office, and no vote for the laity in synod but only at the election of bishops. The losses were that Eucharistic vestments were disallowed (in canon 32), and the General Councils not admitted to be authoritative in the Episcopal Church.[92] He had another opportunity to express his feelings during the speeches on the final day when the two chambers met together. Forbes said he felt a 'deep thankfulness to Almighty God' for what had happened at the synod. Considering the differences of opinions and the strong views of synod members he thought the unanimity they had found was 'something very remarkable'.[93]

Following the General Synod of February 1863 Forbes went to the continent on holiday and returned in June feeling better in health and

[91]   *SEJ* (Feb. 1863), 22–30. See appendix for the final wording of the canon.

[92]   A. P. Forbes to E. B. Pusey, 'Synod Room, Thursday' [12 Feb. 1863], PK vi.

[93]   *SEJ* (Feb. 1863), 30. One who could not reconcile himself to the Scottish Office's demotion was George Forbes. He appealed against the 1863 canons to the Episcopal Synod and, having his appeal turned down, took the issue into the civil courts, as far as the House of Lords. In March 1867 his case (that the Episcopal Church was acting *ultra vires* in revoking the primary authority of the Scottish Office), which he ably defended himself, was rejected, compelling George to submit to the 1863 Canons. W. Perry, *George Hay Forbes* (1927), 94–103.

more relaxed about his spiritual difficulties.[94] This feeling of confidence was evident in his address to the Brechin synod that year where he allowed himself a little optimism in reviewing the Church's contemporary outlook, and brought together his concern about *Essays and Reviews* and the divisions over the Scottish Office under the theme of Church unity. Speaking about 'the very remarkable exhibition of skepticism in religion which has occurred lately in this country', Forbes believed that religious faith was currently retreating before the advance of empirical science, German thought, *Essays and Reviews*, and Bishop Colesno's work on the Old Testament incorporating higher criticism.[95] He expected things to get worse if they were not remedied. But among remedial signs he referred to the rise of a 'truer metaphysical science' which accepted the existence of the supernatural, by which he possibly meant the revival of scholasticism under way in Italy during the early 1860s.[96] Forbes could well have known of this from his travels in Italy and his contacts in the Church there. Alternatively, he may have meant the renewal of interest in metaphysical philosophy created by F. D. Maurice's *Moral and Metaphysical Philosophy*, published in 1861. But because he recognized that philosophy may only address intellectual difficulties without touching inner conviction he returned to the remedy of authority. The 'essence of justifying faith', he said, 'is that it is belief upon authority . . . for all belief implies a certain submission of the soul to an external authority, inwrought by the Holy Ghost, and intimately affected by the moral condition of the believer in the sight of God'. For Forbes this external authority was the Church, as a sort of sacrament of Christ, the outward and visible form of Christ as the divine truth. Therefore, anything which harmed the authority of the Church was a threat to faith. Such a threat, he believed, came from the Church's disunity. Christian unity was a witness to the truth of Christianity, while disunity threatened the Church's authority. Forbes criticized two bases for unity—what he called latitudinarianism and syncretism. These positions meant Christianity 'contains no one definite message, creed or system'. Nor did Forbes hold any brief for those who argued for belief only in 'essentials' because he thought it was impossible to define just what these were, and finite beings had no right to so classify a divine message. Finally, he spoke about the

[94] E. B. Pusey to J. Keble, 26 June 1863, PK vi.

[95] John William Colenso, *The Pentateuch and Book of Joshua Critically Examined* (1862–3).

[96] Joseph Louis Perrier, *The Revival of Scholastic Philosophy in the Nineteenth Century* (1909).

other form of unity—the Church of Rome—and said, 'No one can deny that the aspect she presents in this respect [unity] is striking, claiming as she does, her subjects in every clime, race and civilization.' But imposing as this was to Forbes he still considered it an imperfect unity because it did not comprehend the Orthodox Church, nor the Anglican Church, nor (surprisingly) 'all that is good and pious in the Protestant bodies'. However, he hoped that as transport developed, wearing away isolation and differences of opinion, there would be a General Council to bring about Christian unity as a testament to belief, a Christianity which would be 'organized, hierarchical, and dogmatic'.[97]

The final resolution of the canonical authority of the Scottish Communion Office and the Book of Common Prayer meant the bishops could return their attention directly to the campaign for the legal removal of the Scottish clergy's disabilities in England. By February 1864 the Duke of Buccleuch and Queensberry had agreed to introduce a bill to this effect in the House of Lords. Forbes wrote to Gladstone on 8 February to ask if the time was propitious for the bill in the House of Commons. What particularly worried him was opposition from members from the Church of Scotland and the Free Church. These, Forbes said, 'wd risk their seats if they supported us, in view of the increasing jealousy of the Established and Free Churches. That jealousy is undeniable and arises mainly from the gradual loss of the younger members, [to the Episcopal Church] which both these bodies, especially the former, are sustaining.'[98] By April a petition to Parliament for removal of the disabilities had been organized among Episcopalian congregations.[99]

Pusey and Keble may have been hoping from Forbes's relief at the toleration granted the Scottish Office at the 1863 General Synod, and his critical comments about the Roman Catholic Church in his synod charge that year, that his spiritual indecision was over. But by 1864 he was once again on the see-saw of his religious doubts. While staying with Pusey in June Forbes asked him to write to Keble about his predicament before he went on to visit him at Hursley. Forbes was now thinking he had deliberately deluded himself into remaining a bishop, and was also speaking of having no faith in 'his system'. Pusey thought this could be a fear that the Anglican Church would not last. Alternatively, Forbes could have been referring to his own Tractarianism. Forbes's intermittent ill health

[97]   Brechin Diocese Synod Minutes, 5 Aug. 1863, BrMS 4. 1. 3, 113–16.

[98]   A. P. Forbes to W. E. Gladstone, 8 Feb. 1864, Gladstone Papers, BL 44154, fo. 288.

[99]   SPC 'Vestry Minute Book, St Paul's Episcopal Church, Dundee, 1852– ', 23 Apr. 1864.

contributed to the rise of such fears, according to Pusey. But he thought the point that most worried Forbes now was whether he was right in continuing as a bishop feeling as he did. When Pusey pointed out to him the fruitfulness of his ministry Forbes could only fasten upon intermarriages taking Episcopalians out of their Church. This, presumably, for Forbes, was an indication that some Episcopalians did not see any important difference between their Church and others.[100] After talking with Forbes at Hursley Keble felt more hopeful. He was reassured by the fact that Forbes had preached there on the Sunday morning, which was something Keble had not been able to get him to do before. Keble also felt Forbes needed rest 'rather than intellectual conviction that Rome is right', and he begged him to 'think of the terrible consequences of such moves as he is tempted to, I mean on others in prompting unbelief'.[101]

The Scottish Episcopal Clergy Disabilities Removal Bill was introduced into the House of Lords by Walter Scott, the Duke of Buccleuch, on 10 May 1864.[102] Although an Episcopalian, Buccleuch was a believer in Established Churches and a known benefactor of the Church of Scotland. He was the ideal figure to allay Church of Scotland anxieties about the measure signifying a threat to the Scottish Establishment. Buccleuch deliberately took steps to mollify such fears by circulating copies of the bill at the General Assembly of the Church of Scotland which met in mid-May. The Assembly remitted the bill to a committee which reported it did not affect the Church of Scotland but was a matter only for the Church of England and Ireland. The General Assembly's acceptance had an important effect in favour of the bill's support in Parliament.[103] The bill had its second reading in the Lords on 26 May when the Scottish bishops' fears about opposition from the English bishops were partly justified. Although the bill received judicious support from Archbishop Longley of Canterbury, it was only reluctantly supported by one Evangelical—Charles Baring of Durham—and was opposed by another—Samuel Waldegrave of Carlisle. The first believed the two Churches differed in doctrine and feared hordes of Romish clergy invading the Church of England from Scotland, while the second believed the bill would support 'an extreme party' in the Episcopal Church. Even bishops who supported the bill, such as Tait of London,

[100] E. B. Pusey to J. Keble, n.d., PK vi.
[101] J. Keble to E. B. Pusey, 14 June 1864, KP iv.
[102] Hansard, 175, c. 257.
[103] REC III, Account of the passing of the Disabilities Removal Bill by Robert Eden at the Episcopal Synod, 6 Oct. 1864, SRO CH 12. 60. 4, 320–30.

regretted the Scottish Office had not been got rid of by the recent General Synod.[104] Eventually the bill passed the Lords on 16 June.[105] It was introduced into the Commons the next day by Sir William Heathcote.[106] Despite some opposition, Heathcote piloted the bill to a successful conclusion in the Commons on 21 July 1864.[107] It received the royal assent on 29 July 1864.[108]

Forbes gave the news to his brother with the humour he could use between intimates. 'Ewing is now eligible for the see of Canterbury. Dr. Rorison for the Mastership of the Temple. The Bp. of Glasgow will immediately be made Court Chaplain with the Deanery of Windsor in commendam; but her Majesty has not yet determined what honour she is to heap on Dr. Alexander.'[109] A more serious appreciation of the Act came in his synod address on 3 August 1864. Forbes believed the disabilities had discouraged men of a good social class from entering the ministry of the Episcopal Church, and he now thought numbers of clergy would increase. He commented on the tolerant attitude of the Church of Scotland towards the bill, which, when he considered the numbers of Episcopalian landowners who financially supported the Church of Scotland, was only to be expected. However, Scotland, he feared, was still a country 'where there is so much religious prejudice'.[110] In October Forbes assured Gladstone that they were beginning to feel the good effects of the measure, but, characteristically, he prayed that 'we do not become more secular under the influence of the world's smiles'.[111]

His continued admiration for Gladstone had brought about a change in Forbes's political allegiance. Although raised a Tory, Forbes remained loyal to Gladstone when, in the 1860s, the statesman made his way into the Liberal party. In 1864 Frederick Lygon solicited Forbes's vote against Gladstone at the forthcoming Oxford University election. But Forbes said he had been satisfied with the explanations Gladstone had given regarding his position as member for the university and with his loyalty to the 'Church Cause', that he trusted Gladstone as a 'highsouled man & a Christian', and therefore he did not feel justified in voting against

[104] Hansard, 175, c. 617–31.
[105] Hansard, 175, c. 1824.
[106] Hansard, 175, c. 1939.
[107] Hansard, 176, c. 1408–31; c. 1610–11; c. 1874–6.
[108] 27 and 28 Victoria, cap. xciv.
[109] A. P. Forbes to G. H. Forbes, n.d. SAUL 19 3. 163. 'Dr Alexander' was John Alexander, incumbent of St Columba's, Edinburgh.
[110] Brechin Diocese Synod Minutes, 3 Aug. 1864, BrMS 4. 1. 3, 119–22.
[111] A. P. Forbes to W. E. Gladstone, 18 Oct. 1864, BL 44154, fo. 294.

him.[112] In the 1865 election, when Gladstone finally lost the university seat because he had forfeited the confidence of many Churchmen, Forbes still voted for him, despite disagreeing with Gladstone's support for Jews being admitted to Parliament and his campaign for the laity to be represented in synods of the Episcopal Church.[113] Forbes's willingness to vote for Gladstone as a Liberal was primarily based on his personal admiration for Gladstone, rather than a fundamental commitment to Liberalism. During the same time as he was supporting Gladstone politically, Forbes was defending conservatism, advocating in 1867 the High Church Tory Lord Salisbury for chancellor of Oxford University as a means of retaining the religious tests there.[114]

During the 1860s, and for most of his life, Forbes devoted his recreation to scholarship. He was elected a fellow of the Scottish Society of Antiquaries in 1870.[115] Principally interested in the history of liturgy and hagiology, his major works in these areas were the edition of the *Arbuthnott Missal* he published with his brother in 1863; his *Kalendars of Scottish Saints* (1872); and his edition of the *Lives of S. Ninian and S. Kentigern* (1874). The Arbuthnott Missal represented the only surviving example of medieval Scottish liturgy, and the editing of it stimulated Forbes's interest in the hagiology of Scotland which reached its climax in his *Kalendars*. In this latter work Forbes demonstrated a critical use of his sources, although he was inclined to support traditional beliefs about the saints concerned. But certainly by the 1870s Forbes had begun to acknowledge the validity of the modern critical basis of ecclesiastical history, which was the result of the influence of German historiography upon British historians in the later nineteenth century. In 1871 he observed to Gladstone, 'I feel increasingly the importance of the historical involvement of Theology, a lesson which we have been too slow in learning from the patient & accurate Germans.'[116] It was probably through his friendship with the German historian Ignaz von Döllinger that Forbes encountered German historical thought. According to this German historiography, the miraculous lay outwith the judgement of history, and therefore the history of the Church was considered from a purely natural, rather than supernatural, perspective. The action of God within the Church, and the validity of miracles, was understood as lying within the

[112] A. P. Forbes to F. Lygon (copy), 12 July 1864, Gladstone Papers, BL 44154, fo. 291.

[113] A. P. Forbes to W. E. Gladstone, 27 May [1865], Gladstone Papers, BL 44154, fo. 303.

[114] W. R. Ward, *Victorian Oxford* (1965), 258.

[115] *Proceedings of the Scottish Society of Antiquaries*, viii (1869–70), p. xxiii.

[116] A. P. Forbes to W. E. Gladstone, 19 Oct. 1871, Gladstone Papers, BL 44154, fo. 316.

province of theology rather than history.[117] Theologically, Forbes was as attached as ever to the reality of miracles, but he recognized that doubt about them existed among educated men because of the influence of biblical criticism and empirical science. Forbes still endeavoured to claim a place for miracle stories as valuable evidence for what would now be called social history, but he accepted that many such stories were becoming regarded in historical circles as the stuff of humorous legends. As he said in his *Lives of S. Ninian and S. Kentigern*, 'a historical work like this is not the place to enlarge on its [St Ninian's life] religious aspect'.[118] But his theological resistance to a full acceptance of the critical basis for history is evident in this work also, in his disposition to accept as history all the miracles of St Martin recorded in a contemporary source.[119] But, for Forbes, history served a higher purpose than merely a critical study of the evidence. His understanding of history was fundamentally romantic and theological, in which the past was seen to be a record of 'Providence shaping our ends'. 'No one', he felt, 'can stand within the precincts of the ruined priory of Whithern [*sic*], or look out to sea from the roofless chapel at the Isle [of Iona], without emotions which are difficult to describe. He stands on a spot where the ancient civilization of Rome, and the more ancient barbarism of the Meatae, alike gave place to the higher training of the gospel of Christ.'[120]

Forbes's concern about the influences of contemporary thought upon religious belief had their most public expression in his support for the annual meeting of the British Association for the Advancement of Science held in Dundee in 1867. Unlike his hostile reaction to biblical criticism in *Essays and Reviews* in 1860, he actively supported this event and did not appear to regard science as having quite the same threatening potential for religion as did criticism of scripture. When Dundee was accepted by the Association for its 1867 meeting a massive campaign of support and organization went on in the city to ensure its success. Civic pride was at stake. The bishop subscribed £3 towards the £4,000 considered necessary for a successful show, and various other societies agreed to participate, including the Working Men's Flower Show Society. Forbes became one of the sixty-four members of the Local Executive Committee in overall charge of the event. But he became most involved in a subcommittee, organizing an Art and Industry Exhibition in connection with the

---

[117]   A. P. Forbes (ed.), *Kalendars of Scottish Saints* (1872), p. xlv.
[118]   A. P. Forbes, *Lives of S. Ninian and S. Kentigern* (1874), p. x.
[119]   Ibid., p. xxxviii.
[120]   Ibid., p. lx.

Association's activities.[121] The influence of Forbes and Lord Kinnaird was regarded as having been crucial in getting the local nobility and gentry to offer their artworks to this grand event.[122] Forbes himself loaned a painting by Samuel Bough, a drawing by Overbeck, and a Limoge enamel of St Augustine.[123]

Along with the Art and Industry Exhibition Forbes was also concerned with the Sunday services held during the course of the Association's meeting. On 8 September 1867 he preached at St Paul's in one of the Sunday services advertised as part of the Association's meeting. Forbes made a high claim for the providential involvement of God in all areas of life and the material universe, otherwise, he declared, humanity was at the mercy of a mechanical universe. Life then lost its 'moral significance', because the diverse vicissitudes of life were impossible to explain.[124] The union of God with matter in the incarnation of Christ, Forbes asserted, was the basis for involvement of the supernatural in all facets of physical life, including science, the Church, history, and individual life.[125]

The British Association meeting was held on 4 to 12 September 1867. Forbes's only other public connection with it occurred at the closing ceremony of the art exhibition on 30 September, following the conclusion of the Association's meeting. He was one of the speakers asked to address that public gathering on the relation between art and civilization. His ideas were fairly commonplace aesthetics, pointing to art as the highest expression and measure of any civilization. Upholding the rise of neo-gothic architecture as an expression of medieval principles of 'authority and tradition', he argued, counter-balanced 'the mighty spirit of Democracy' predominant in the nineteenth century.[126]

Faced with threats to tradition from new thought, or from revived older pressures such as Anglicization, during the 1860s Forbes demonstrated a varying degree of flexibility, and, in at least one case, an alteration in his intellectual understanding. He remained fundamentally opposed to biblical criticism, although he believed it needed to be met intellectually and not by the mere exercise of ecclesiastical authority. He

---

[121] *Meeting of the British Association for the Advancement of Science in Dundee, September 1867* (1868), pp. vii–xii.
[122] Ibid. 51.
[123] Ibid. 79, 86.
[124] A. P. Forbes, *Our Lord: The Sufficing Manifestation of the Eternal Father in Nature and in Grace* (1867), 10.
[125] Ibid. 15–16.
[126] *Meeting of British Association in Dundee 1867*, 57–60.

refused to endorse a plan to attack the contributors to *Essays and Reviews* through the Convocation of Oxford University because it would have given the appearance of persecution. The experience of his trial during the Eucharistic controversy had made him more cautious towards institutional authority as a means of dealing with divergent theological positions. However, by 1870, his own historical works reveal he was more amenable towards historical criticism than he had been in 1860. But this applied only in non-biblical areas, and even in these subjects he retained a disposition to understand history as a record of divine providence. Forbes was more positive towards the rise of experimental science, at least in the later 1860s. At the British Association meeting in 1867 he demonstrated a Victorian enthusiasm for the achievements of science and technology, although he was also keen to defend the reality of the invisible, supernatural realm which he knew numbers of his countrymen had difficulty believing in. But his most inflexible opposition came in a stand against the pressures of Anglicization in so far as they posed a threat to the Scottish Communion Office. The resulting demotion of the Scottish Communion Office and the superiority of the Book of Common Prayer did represent 'the anglicising of Scottish Episcopacy'.[127] The weight of the Church of England's power and wealth proved overwhelming to many clergy in the Scottish Episcopal Church, especially as significant numbers of them in the south were English anyway. But it was not only the English who supported Anglicization, because support for the English Prayer Book also came from clergy in Scottish orders. Nor was Anglicization a desire only of southern Churchmen. Gilbert Rorison of Aberdeen had many sympathizers among the clergy of that diocese in his campaign for the Book of Common Prayer. Some Episcopalian clergy wanted to be able to move into the English Church with its greater social advantages. Others believed assimilation to an Established Church gave the Episcopal Church greater legitimacy. Some, like Charles Terrot, hoped to attract Englishmen into the Episcopal ministry. But even supporters of the Scottish Office like Robert Thom thought diversity from England would be difficult to maintain now that railways and industrialization had brought the two nations closer together, increasing the influence of the larger over the smaller neighbour. Further, the clergy increasingly depended on upper- and middle-class support for church extension, and these were the Scottish social orders most in favour of Anglicization during the nineteenth century. Inevitably, the

[127] Christopher Knight, 'The Anglicising of Scottish Episcopalianism' in *RSCHS* 23 (1989), 361–77.

wealth of these members of congregations made them supporters clergy were reluctant to antagonize, and whose enthusiasm for uniformity with the Church of England many clergy shared.

However, the prevailing influence of Anglicization did encounter some important checks or modifications among Episcopalians. Not all Episcopalians of the middle and upper classes were so enthusiastic about England that they neglected their native traditions. The Earl of Morton, George Boyle, and Forbes himself were among an important minority who believed some Scottish traditions superior to their English counterparts. In a number of instances, like that of Forbes, family background or personal contact with the Scottish Office could engender support for the Scottish Office. So also could contact with Scots Episcopalians of the lower classes in traditional Episcopalian areas of the north-east. Nor did cross-cultural influence work only in one direction, from south to north. Robert Eden of Moray is an interesting example of an Englishman who developed an appreciation for Scottish traditions, who resented being dictated to by the bishops of the Church of England over the Scottish Office. Probably being bishop of the most northern diocese had a lot to do with his new outlook.

In so far as Forbes's life provides an illustration of the effect of Anglicization within the Episcopal Church, the principal modification to its influence came from his Tractarianism. The Oxford Movement had taught Forbes to appreciate examples of catholicity wherever they were to be found. This meant he valued such Catholic indicators more than he did national distinctions. He was also less amenable to the influence of the powerful Church of England because Tractarian theology, and experiences such as the Denison case or his own trial, had convinced him that might was not always right, especially in matters of Catholic truth. Such truth, for Forbes, was not necessarily a matter of what the majority believed in the contemporary Church, but was found in those elements of the present-day Church that resembled the patristic Church. One of the most significant of these examples of Catholic truth, according to Forbes, was the Scottish Communion Office. It is true that Tractarianism did not necessarily lead to an appreciation of the Scottish Office—many English Tractarians preferred the Book of Common Prayer as being closer to the Roman liturgy—but it did cause Tractarians to value the Catholic Church above nationalism or uniformity with Established Churches. In this way Tractarianism helped some Scots Episcopalians, like Forbes, to keep Anglicization at a critical distance. As well, by the 1860s, Tractarians had experience of organizing in defence of the Catholic faith—against the state (the Gorham case) and even against the Church (the Eucharistic controversy). Such experience meant that Forbes was able to provide valuable leadership and recruit influential support for those northern Churchmen who, like Robert Thom, valued the Scottish Office, but were often reluctant to defend it vociferously. Forbes's campaign for the Scottish Communion Office enabled him to recapture some of the support among northern Churchmen he had previously alienated in the Eucharistic controversy—men such as his brother George for example. His Tractarianism gave him an appreciation of the Office for its similarity to patristic liturgies, causing him to value it above considerations of closer connection with the Church of England. However, because the pressure on the Scottish Office was also a threat to Forbes's own commitment to the Anglican Church he defended the Office with all the resources at his disposal, leading a campaign of opposition to its probable demise that included a willingness to compromise as well as the use of political muscle. It is ironic that Forbes, fundamentally a religious and political conservative, should have needed the influence of an increasingly Liberal Gladstone to secure the place of Scottish traditions in the Episcopal Church. Forbes's vindication of the Scottish Office was his most entrenched defence of tradition, and was principally motivated by his uncertainty about the Catholic nature of the Episcopal Church. That uncertainty, still finally unresolved in 1864, made him increasingly appreciative of the doctrinal authority and unity of Roman Catholicism, and brought him, by the time of his synod address in 1863, to a realization of the importance of Catholic unity. It is therefore necessary to consider Forbes's involvement with other Churches, and the final outcome of his spiritual indecision.

6

Reunion

On 8 September 1857 a small group of enthusiasts met in the London chambers of the Revd F. G. Lee to vote into existence the Association for the Promotion of the Unity of Christendom.[1] The Association was dedicated to the corporate reunion of the so-called Catholic branches of the Church—Roman, Orthodox, and Anglican—and would survive until the 1920s, although its membership was always predominantly Anglican rather than Roman Catholic or Orthodox. In 1865 it was condemned by Rome, and Roman Catholics forbidden to join. Although Forbes was not present at the original meeting, he did play a major role in the new initiatives; indeed, the formation of the Association was the consequence of an earlier conversation in July 1857, also in London, between Forbes, the Roman Catholic layman Ambrose Phillipps de Lisle, and the ritualist priest F. G. Lee. Forbes's involvement marked the beginning of an intense personal concern for Catholic reunion that would be one of the driving forces of the rest of his life. At various times during the final two decades of his life he would also demonstrate an awareness of the Orthodox Churches and, on one occasion, a passing interest in the high church movement in Denmark. But the central focus of his attention remained reunion with Rome, a concern which reached a climax with the First Vatican Council. His disappointment over the result of that Council caused him to redirect his attention towards the emerging Old Catholic movement, and to come to a resolution of his doubts about Anglicanism.

Forbes had always been conscious of the Catholic nature of the Eastern Orthodox Churches. In 1858 there had been a possibility that he would go to Russia, taking J. M. Neale as his chaplain, to confirm among the families of the British diplomatic community there.[2] The possibility of a trip to Russia also arose in 1873, but again fell through, probably because of Forbes's uncertain health.[3] He had a mixed attitude to the Orthodox. In 1865 he had translated the Scottish Office into Greek as a contribution towards greater understanding with the Eastern Christians, and he was

---

[1] APUC minutes, PH.   [2] Eleanor Towle, *John Mason Neale* (1907), 272.
[3] A. Thomson to A. P. Forbes, 15 Feb. 1873, BrMS 1. 4. 789.

prepared to be more positive than Pusey regarding the Orthodox opposition to the *filioque* clause in the Nicene Creed.[4] But in 1866 he told Gladstone he thought the acceptance of the seventh Ecumenical Council by the Orthodox, sanctioning the veneration of icons, stood in the way of closer relations.[5] In 1870 he severely criticized the response from Archbishop Tait to a synodical letter from the Greek Church, in which Tait said the Church of England did not sanction prayer for the dead.[6] Forbes was committed to recognizing the Orthodox Churches as indispensable components of Catholic Christendom, but his experience, and therefore his attention, remained primarily with the Church in the west.

Despite Forbes's fervent Catholic beliefs and his serious consideration of conversion to Roman Catholicism, during 1852 he fleetingly became interested in an attempt to Anglicanize the high church movement in the Lutheran Church of Denmark, a movement which had originated in the influence of the Danish theologian Nicolai Grundtvig. Forbes's involvement came about through his friend, the Anglo-Catholic MP Alexander Beresford-Hope who, in February 1852, asked his advice about a Danish pastor who was considering episcopal reordination. Beresford-Hope's interest was stimulated by Nugent Wade, vicar of St Anne's, Soho, who had visited Denmark and had been impressed with Grundtvig. Beresford-Hope decided that Anglican links with the high church group in the Danish Church could be established more easily through the Scottish Episcopal Church than through the established Church of England.[7] He was therefore in touch with the Scottish bishops about this prospect during February and March 1852, receiving encouraging replies from both Ewing and Eden.[8] Forbes advised him to secure a Danish deputation to the Episcopal Synod of 1852.[9] Forbes also suggested translating the *Tracts for the Times* into Danish. Wade's zeal had convinced him that the Danish high church movement might be encouraged by an Anglican mission to Denmark that summer led by a Scottish bishop—a position he had in mind for Forbes.[10] But Forbes failed to express any interest in this Anglo-Catholic evangelism to Denmark, despite Beresford-Hope's wish to see Scandanavians being ordained in St Ninian's, Perth.[11]

[4] A. P. Forbes, *An Explanation of the Thirty Nine Articles* (1867), i. 81–2.
[5] A. P. Forbes to W. E. Gladstone, 3 July [1866], Gladstone Papers, BL 44154, fo. 301.
[6] A. P. Forbes to A. C. Tait, 8 Oct. 1870, Tait Papers, LPL 167, fo. 298.
[7] A. J. Beresford-Hope to A. P. Forbes, 22 Feb. 1852, Eeles Papers, LPL 1543, fo. 75.
[8] A. J. Beresford-Hope to A. P. Forbes, 14 Mar. 1852, Eeles Papers, LPL 1543, fo. 81.
[9] A. J. Beresford-Hope to A. P. Forbes, 18 Mar. 1852, Eeles Papers, LPL 1543, fo. 85.
[10] N. Wade to A. J. Beresford-Hope (copy), n.d., Eeles Papers, LPL 1543, fo. 87.
[11] A. J. Beresford-Hope to A. P. Forbes, 26 Mar. 1852, Eeles Papers, LPL 1543, fo. 91.

Forbes's personal priority was not with the Lutheran Churches, but was rather Anglican reunion with Rome. Following the July meeting with Lee and de Lisle he had written to Lee outlining his position. Excited by the prospects for reunion work engendered by their conversation Forbes nevertheless stressed the need for caution, because he felt it needed only an inopportune phrase to set off the usual British no-popery. He there-fore counselled limiting the objectives of the Association to prayer for unity, and submitting to the Roman Curia relevant documents in sup-port of the validity of Anglican orders. But he re-emphasized his belief that less haste, more speed, was the way forward for such an unprece-dented step as a public organization bringing together Anglicans and Roman Catholics dedicated to reunion between their Churches.

With regard to my own immediate part in this business, I feel that I must proceed with great caution. The object in view is one that I have prayed for for many years and therefore I am willing both to act and to suffer in the cause—at the same time a false step on my part, may both do the cause harm, and be a scandal to those whose souls are immediately entrusted to me. I shall probably do nothing in public without consulting the Bishop of Moray, Mr Keble and Mr Justice Coleridge. You will, I am sure, see the wisdom of this caution. In a matter of such unexampled moment and difficulty one cannot be too circumspect where one acts officially.[12]

The foundation of the Association for the Promotion of the Unity of Christendom (APUC) was the work of three men devoted to the cause of Roman Catholic-Anglican reunion. F. G. Lee, although an ardent ritualist, was not a follower of the Oxford Movement, having come to a Catholic position independently through his own thinking, which was dominated by aesthetic ritualism and a desire for reunion with Rome. He had moved to London after having been dismissed from Oxford diocese by Samuel Wilberforce in 1856 for ritualism. Eventually, after appointments in London and Aberdeen, Lee became vicar of All Saints, Lambeth, in 1867.[13] Ambrose Phillipps de Lisle was a wealthy squire who had con-verted to Roman Catholicism from the Church of England when he was just 15. He founded the Cistercian monastery of Mount St Bernard on his land and, after the foundation of the APUC, the monastery enthusias-tically supported their patron by becoming a member of the Association, at which time Forbes and Lee were welcomed as visitors to the abbey.[14]

---

[12] Henry R. T. Brandreth, *Dr Lee of Lambeth* (1951), 77–8.
[13] Ibid. 48.
[14] E. B. Stuart, 'Unjustly Condemned? Roman Catholic Involvement in the APUC 1857–64', in *Journal of Ecclesiastical History*, 41 (1990), 49.

De Lisle was a romantic Tory who believed in established Churches. The Oxford Movement had convinced him that the Church of England was becoming more sympathetic towards Rome but was also forsaking establishment, which threatened to leave the country at the mercy of dissent and revolution. He therefore believed that reunion could save England from disintegration by allying the Church of England with Rome, which would then support establishment.[15] Both Lee and de Lisle were ardent advocates of reunion who brought little discretion to their cause, being temperamentally disinclined to heed Forbes's more cautious counsel.

Forbes's suggestion about presenting the case for Anglican orders to Rome was briefly taken up. The responsibility for its formulation was given to George Boyle who, in September 1857, sent his work to Forbes for endorsement.[16] But by October Forbes had become cooler towards the proposals about Anglican orders. Boyle observed to Lee that 'certain very recent circumstances make him [Forbes] deem it better not to give them the *formal imprimatur* which I solicited'. This was clearly a reference to the beginning of the Eucharistic controversy in Scotland—a controversy which served to increase Forbes's wariness about the Association. Aware that much of the opposition to his teaching on the Eucharist derived from its similarity to Roman Catholic doctrine, he became understandably reluctant to lend his name to a defence of Anglican ordination to the Vatican. Therefore, on 19 October Forbes advised adoption of de Lisle's suggestion not to continue seeking a formal vindication from Rome, and Forbes's obvious reluctance to proceed caused the abandonment of the project.[17]

Despite the fact that historians who mention the APUC consider Forbes to have been a founder member, he, in fact, never joined the Association. In a letter of welcome to Lee after the latter had accepted the appointment of an Aberdeen congregation in 1859 Forbes said, 'You will recollect that tho' generally sympathizing I have never enrolled myself as a member.'[18] At first Forbes intended to be formally connected with the Association. But his caution was awakened by the intemperate enthusiasm of Lee and de Lisle, which intensified his emerging decision not to join. This decision was initially due to the intervention of the growing Eucharitic controversy in Scotland after September 1857.

To be sure, the publication of the *Union Newspaper* as the official organ of the Association must have confirmed Forbes in his decision.

[15]   Ibid. 45.   [16]   Brandreth, *Dr Lee*, 79.
[17]   Ibid. 79–80.
[18]   A. P. Forbes to F. G. Lee, n.d., Lee Papers, LPL 2074, fo. 129.

The paper quickly established itself as the journal of the most pro-Roman elements among Anglicans and alienated conservatives such as Keble, who resigned from the APUC because of it. Alarmed at the tone of the *Union* Forbes wrote to Lee, probably in late 1857, criticizing the wholesale endorsement of Roman Catholicism and disparagement of Tractarian moderation in the paper's early issues.

> The articles against Tractarianism have driven back and alarmed many of your general well-wishers, and those who have hitherto opposed the paper now point triumphantly to these papers as the best vindication of their hostility. Others object to many puerilities which I confess I cannot defend, e. g. though one must admire the grand features of the Roman system, one is not the better for holding up for imitation every little discipline and use.[19]

But Forbes's decision not to join the APUC in 1857 did not mean he had given up hopes of the corporate reunion of Catholic Christendom, and he maintained many personal links with Roman Catholics. A letter to Lee in 1859 demonstrates that Forbes maintained a detailed knowledge of contemporary European Roman Catholicism. He asked Lee if he had seen the new periodical edited by Abbé Guettée, *L'Union Chrétienne*, and offered to send Lee the first issue. Guettée was a leading writer of Gallican views who was eventually condemned by the French bishops. His journal became influential among pro-reunion circles in England and he actively solicited letters and articles from Anglicans for it.[20] Forbes seems to have served as a conduit through which Guettée's Gallican views became known in Anglican circles. Nor was Guettée the only Roman Catholic connection Forbes had made by the beginning of the 1860s. He was by then a frequent traveller to the continent, especially to Italy and France, for the sake of his health. His brother George was a useful source of introductions as he had lived in France for some years in his youth, under the care of a French specialist for his polio. Included among George's acquaintances was the patristic scholar Jean Baptiste Pitra. Pitra was prior of the new monastery of St Germain-des-Prés in Paris when Forbes called on him while visiting France in July 1857.[21] He was subsequently made a cardinal in 1861, and became Vatican librarian in 1869.[22]

[19] Brandreth, *Dr Lee*, 93.
[20] Henry R. T. Brandreth, *The Œcumenical Ideas of the Oxford Movement* (1947), 34.
[21] J. B. Pitra to G. H. Forbes (translated copy of a letter in French), 2 July 1857, SAUL 19. 2. 146 (b).
[22] *New Catholic Encyclopedia (1967)*, xi. 390.

The Eucharistic controversy continued to divert Forbes's attention from plans for reunion during the early 1860s, although he maintained his European contacts through his continental visits. However, the resolution of the controversy, and the following campaign over the Scottish Office and the clerical disabilities in 1864, left Forbes more free to turn his attention back to his earlier hopes for corporate reunion. But this time he offered support to Pusey's reunion dialogue with French Roman Catholic bishops.

Pusey's theology had become more favourable towards Rome as he came to accept the early Church as normative in doctrine and practice. Pusey also rationalized Newman's secession in 1845 as a divine means of bringing the Anglican and Roman Churches closer together, and from that time began to involve himself in work for reunion. He believed that the Church of England had a duty to conform itself to what was held in common by the other two 'branches' of the Catholic Church—Roman and Orthodox. This common faith was what constituted Catholic Christianity for Pusey. However, he thought the Anglican Church's first duty was towards reunion with Rome as the other western Catholic Church. In August 1845, in a letter to Henry Manning, Pusey was already proposing reunion on the basis of the decrees of the Council of Trent.[23] In response to an attack on the Church of England in 1864 by the now-Roman Catholic Manning,[24] Pusey published in September 1865 *The Church of England, a Portion of Christ's One Holy Catholic Church and a Means of Restoring Visible Unity. An Eirenicon in a Letter to the Author of 'The Christian Year'*. This was the first of three books published separately but regarded by Pusey as comprising three connected instalments of his *Eirenicon*, his plan for reunion between Rome and the Church of England. Pusey made a distinction between official Roman teaching and popular piety, arguing that many of the objections to Roman Catholicism belonged to the latter area and not to the former. It was on this basis that Pusey began to canvas support for his proposal for reunion.

Forbes wanted him to have the work translated into French and German so as to be read by influential Roman Catholics, and Pusey agreed. He told Gladstone that he and Forbes hoped 'to have a hearing with the non-extreme party before the Synod at Rome'.[25] This was a

---

[23] Robert Harvie Greenfield, 'Such a Friend to the Pope', in Perry Butler (ed.), *Pusey Rediscovered* (1983), 174.

[24] H. Manning, *The Workings of the Holy Spirit in the Church of England: A Letter to the Rev. E. B. Pusey, D. D.* (1864).

[25] H. P. Liddon, *The Life of Edward Bouverie Pusey (1897)*, iv. 112.

reference to the synod of bishops convened by Pope Pius IX on 26 June 1867 for the eighteenth centenary of the martyrdom of SS Peter and Paul. Pusey's comment illustrates that he and Forbes were working together in considering an approach to the less ultramontane Roman Catholic bishops. Pusey had already implemented this idea by visiting France to present his book personally to some of the French bishops, leaving for the continent on 11 October 1865 and returning to England on 20 October.[26] He considered the trip to have been very satisfactory, singling out especially the 'extreme sympathy and largeness of view of the Abp of Paris'. He sent a long letter reporting the trip to Forbes which he hoped would be 'very encouraging to him'.[27] The archbishop's attitude encouraged Pusey to think that reunion on the basis of an elaboration of the Council of Trent was feasible. The archbishop had proposed a continued correspondence, and recommended Newman as one suitable to frame terms of reconciliation.[28]

Georges Darboy had become Archbishop of Paris in 1863 and his Gallican tendencies were strengthened in a controversy with the Vatican over jurisdiction in his diocese. He was an extremely intelligent man, withdrawn in temperament but favourable towards moderate liberalism in France, later becoming a senator. Along with Bishop Dupanloup of Orleans he would lead a minority of the French bishops in their opposition to the decree of papal infallibility at the Vatican Council. Both he and Dupanloup had a rare positive perception of Protestantism (which to them included the Church of England) and were among those who regarded any decree of papal infallibility as inopportune, because it would place a further obstacle in the way of Protestants and Orthodox reuniting with the Roman Catholic Church.[29]

In one of Forbes's few surviving letters about Pusey's reunion campaign he commented to the Tractarian leader, 'You have got more from the ABp of P than I expected you wd get from any R. C. Bishop in view of the terrorism of the Jesuits.' But he regretted that Pusey did not engage the archbishop in correspondence so as to have some written evidence of his position. Pusey characterized Forbes's response as delight over the interview with Darboy.[30] But the evidence for Forbes's views about these French contacts remains slim because not only was most of Forbes's correspondence destroyed after his death, but also the majority

---

[26] Ibid. 113.   [27] E. B. Pusey to J. Keble, n.d., PK vii.
[28] E. B. Pusey to A. P. Forbes (copy), n.d., BpF.
[29] Margaret O'Gara, *Triumph in Defeat: Infallibility, Vatican I, and the French Minority Bishops* (1988).
[30] E. B. Pusey to J. Keble, n.d., PK vii.

of Pusey's letters to Forbes were returned to him on the bishop's death and are mostly no longer extant.

Pusey made a second trip to France, from 19 December to 18 January 1866, which he believed was 'theologically more satisfactory' than the first.[31] Pusey, following Darboy's suggestion that Newman's involvement in the discussions would be useful, contacted his old friend. But Newman was not particularly encouraging, being more aware of the degree of differences between the two Churches than either the optimistic Pusey or the eager Forbes. Pusey wrote to him in March 1867 hoping to get a clear definition of what the Roman Catholic Church officially believed the pope's powers were, as a basis for reunion negotiations. But Newman's reply was disappointing. Newman evidently regarded this approach as coming from both Forbes and Pusey, for he explicitly mentioned he was also answering Forbes in his reply to Pusey. Newman criticized their search for an official minimum of belief. Using a similar argument to his published reply to Pusey's *Eirenicon* he dismissed the distinction between declared and popular belief as artificial, which would only restrict the doctrinal development of the Church.[32] According to Newman, the two were merely aspects of the one faith of the Church—the one explicit and the other implicit—the latter of which may be required to be declared formally in the future.[33]

In the course of the reunion campaign prior to 1867 Pusey had kept Forbes informed of his initiatives towards reunion with the French bishops, while Forbes took an active interest without any direct involvement. Despite Forbes's concern for Catholic reunion stretching back to 1857 his energies at that time were almost entirely taken up with the threat to the Scottish Office. But from 1867 until 1870 Forbes increasingly became a partner in Pusey's promotion of corporate reunion with the Roman Church.

On 27 March 1866 John Keble died and Forbes and Pusey went to Hursley for the funeral. Although the termination of the correspondence between the two oldest Tractarian leaders also meant the end of their invaluable direct evidence for Forbes's internal struggles, the conclusion of this evidence did not mean the cessation of Forbes's indecision. This continued past his successful defence of the Scottish Office in 1864. After 1866 there is some indirect evidence for Forbes's continued attraction towards the Roman Church, and for his uncertainties about Anglicanism.

---

[31] Liddon, *Life of Pusey*, iv. 133–4.
[32] J. H. Newman, *A Letter to the Rev. E. B. Pusey, D. D., on his Recent Eirenicon* (1866).
[33] J. H. Newman to E. B. Pusey, 22 and 23 Mar. 1867, BpF.

Meanwhile, Forbes's efforts towards Catholic reunion were again interrupted. Later in 1867 he became concerned about the first Lambeth Conference of Anglican bishops due to be held in September. On 25 March 1867 Forbes had replied affirmatively to Archbishop Longley's invitation to the Conference. However, he expressed his regret that the meeting was not to concern itself with any definition of doctrine but would only concentrate on practical issues.[34] The declaration of doctrine by the bishops acting as a pan-Anglican council was favoured by high churchmen as a means of opposing doctrinal liberalism, such as that contained in Bishop Colenso's book on the Pentateuch. But conscious of the opposition to anything resembling a dogmatic council by many English bishops, Longley was determined the meeting would be informal.

Tractarians and Anglo-Catholics were also anxious over the possible involvement in the first Lambeth Conference by the episcopal Church of Sweden, which was Lutheran. Some High Churchmen, with a more positive attitude to the Reformation than was common among the Oxford Movement party, had asked Longley to invite the Swedish Church.[35] Pusey deprecated any such recognition of the validity of the orders of the Swedish Church, in a letter to the *Guardian* on 29 July 1867. He felt that any such recognition of the Swedish Lutheran episcopate would unsettle the confidence of Tractarians and Anglo-Catholics in the catholicity of their own Church—Lutherans being regarded by them as heretical.[36] A correspondence was engendered in the *Guardian* to which Forbes contributed in support of Pusey. Forbes upheld his argument against the legitimacy of the Swedish episcopal succession by citing the high frequency of illegitimate births in Sweden as proof of the poor spread of the gospel in that country![37] In a further letter to the *Guardian*, Forbes pointed to the Prayer Book injunctions to reject heresy, and to avoid the company of 'fornicators', adding that this was 'a very difficult task indeed in Stockholm'.[38] But the Oxford Movement party need not have worried themselves with Swedish faith and morals because the Anglican bishops had their minds preoccupied with Bishop Colenso's book, and nothing was done about the Swedish Church.

Forbes was one of those who wanted the Lambeth Conference to act as a sort of general council, which would also serve as a final Anglican

[34] A. P. Forbes to C. T. Longley, 25 Mar. 1867, Longley Papers, LPL 6, fo. 57.
[35] Alan Stephenson, *The First Lambeth Conference 1867* (1967), 213, 221.
[36] *Guardian*, 31 July 1867, 823.
[37] *Guardian*, 28 Aug. 1867, 933.
[38] *Guardian*, 11 Sept. 1867, 971.

court of appeal in matters of doctrine. Forbes believed such a council to be necessary because the present condition of Anglicanism was 'not only essentially provisional, but universally perilous'. He regarded the era of established Churches as now over, leaving Anglicans the alternative of either rationalism or Catholicism.[39] Nevertheless, he was also worried that if Anglican bishops were invited to the forthcoming Vatican Council, they might be compromised by something previously defined at the Lambeth Conference.[40] In considering in which direction the Lambeth Conference would take Anglicanism Forbes remained 'profoundly anxious' about the theological expertise of the bishops who, he felt, 'know so little of precise theology that one cannot tell what they may do', while he was also concerned that there was 'no provision for the presence of learned theologians, as there ought to be on such occasions'.[41] But Longley's determination not to make the Conference a doctrinal synod triumphed, and he thereby secured the attendance of Liberal and Evangelical bishops in the Church of England. The Lambeth Conference's historian maintains that, in 1867, the move away from the Conference becoming a doctrinal authority prevented the Anglican Church from committing itself to a statement against Colenso and biblical criticism. Although desired by the majority of American and colonial bishops, such a decision would have become outdated and untenable within a few years.[42] In the event, Forbes's ill health prevented his attendance at the Conference in London.[43]

Throughout 1867 Forbes was engaged on his major theological work, *An Explanation of the Thirty Nine Articles*. It was his primary contribution to Pusey's campaign for reunion. The intention of the work was to provide a Catholic interpretation of the standard Anglican theological formularies in the light of the prospective Vatican Council formally announced by Pius IX on 26 June 1867, but anticipated for some time before that. It followed the lines of Tract 90, and Pusey gave Forbes unstinting assistance in researching patristic sources and even in writing whole sections.[44] The book also gave Forbes an opportunity to acknowledge his debt of discipleship to Pusey. In a dedicatory letter to Pusey at the beginning of the book he wrote:

[39] A. P. Forbes to W. E. Gladstone, 15 Aug. 1867, Gladstone Papers, BL 44154, fo. 305.
[40] A. P. Forbes to W. K. Hamilton, 29 May [1867]; and 18 July 1867, PH Hamilton correspondence, 3. 14. 65; 6. 59. 4.
[41] A. P. Forbes to W. E. Gladstone, 20 Aug. 1867, Gladstone Papers, BL 44154, fo. 307.
[42] Stephenson, *Lambeth Conference*, 328.
[43] A. P. Forbes to W. E. Gladstone, 22 Sept. 1867, Gladstone Papers, BL 44154, fo. 309.
[44] Liddon, *Life of Pusey*, iv. 145–6.

This enables me to express, in however inadequate terms, the veneration in which I hold you; and to acknowledge the deep debt of gratitude which I owe you, for the many benefits which you have bestowed upon me, during a friendship which has lasted for more than twenty years, and which has been one of my greatest earthly blessings. To have been trained in your school of thought has been the best discipline for the discharge of the onerous duties of the Episcopate.[45]

But Pusey was concerned that the unsure Forbes would be overly biased towards Roman Catholicism, using only Roman books and 'meagre on anything but the Roman side'.[46] He remarked to his son Philip that Forbes was 'specially sensitive' on the subject of the Primacy of Peter, which indicates Forbes was still strongly attracted to the Roman Catholic claims to authority when he wrote the book.[47]

The book was Forbes's theological *magnum opus* and it included many of his favourite themes. He proposed to offer a presentation of the 'positive doctrines' of the Anglican Church by supplying an 'accurate theology', because he believed the 'want of clear-headedness and precision' in contemporary theology contributed to the present imperfect understanding of Christian truth and thus to doubt and disbelief.[48] He therefore continued to make wholesale use of the specific categories of scholastic philosophy. More understanding of historical criticism of scripture than he had been earlier in the 1860s, he now accepted that the historical truth of what the Church asserted 'must be submitted to the severest historical criticism'. However, he remained overly confident about its effects on traditional exegesis, asserting that higher criticism had failed to find in the gospels any 'contradiction such as can destroy their historic worth'.[49] Forbes continued to assert traditional Catholic teaching that the Bible was the inspired product of the inspired Church and, accordingly, required to be authoritatively interpreted by the Church.[50] Forbes remained unconcerned about the effects of biblical criticism because of his understanding of revelation. He considered it was fundamentally impossible for God to transmit mistaken or imperfect information, and therefore Forbes laid before his readers a stark and simplistic choice—'either the Bible must be true in every respect, or not the word of God at all'.[51] The communication of these inspired truths Forbes left entirely to the clerical hierarchy, as compromising the

---

[45] A. P. Forbes, *Explanation of the Thirty Nine Articles* (1867–8), vol. i, p. iii.
[46] E. B. Pusey to P. Pusey, 2 Aug. 1867, PH Philip Pusey correspondence, v. iii.
[47] E. B. Pusey to P. Pusey, 3 Jan. 1868, PH Philip Pusey correspondence, v. iii.
[48] A. P. Forbes, *Explanation*, p. vi.   [49] Ibid. i. 65.
[50] Ibid. i. 95.   [51] Ibid. i. 92–3.

teaching Church.[52] Essentially this meant the diocesan bishops, each the equal of the other as the direct successors of the apostles.[53] Forbes continued to oppose theological liberalism because it provided the basis for the abnegation of all revealed dogmatic truth.[54] To undermine revealed truth, authoritatively encapsulated in the dogma of the Church, was also to undermine the basis of morality. Like all the Tractarians, Forbes retained his belief in the essential connection between the teaching of the Church and moral life.

In the present day there is a great jealousy of the principle of dogma. It is imagined that a true Christian morality, a holy Christian sentiment can exist without it; that Creeds, professing to give us very definite statements on supernatural subjects, are by the very imperfection of language and thought, only trammels to the soul, which is thereby kept from aspiring to the indefinite. Yet this is unreasonable, for there can be no Christian morals without Christian definite faith. Dogma is to morals as cause to effect, will to motion. Christian morality is dogma in action, or practical faith. Indeed, to make men receive and practice a morality severe and painful to human nature, one must give great and positive reasons for so doing: when the morality is superhuman, the motives must be also. Virtues imply beliefs. Nay more, the very fact of Christian morality and its realization in the world implies a set of dogmas at its back, perfect like unto itself.[55]

But his greater caution since the heady days of his 1857 diocesan charge was revealed on the topic of the worship of Christ in the Eucharist. He claimed it was 'unnecessary' to go into this question since the 'exhaustive' treatment of the subject by Keble, and he simply referred the reader to Keble's *On Eucharistical Adoration* of 1857.[56] But he continued to criticize virtualism, and endeavoured to explain transubstantiation as simply being the means by which the Roman Church interpreted with greater definition the words of Jesus at the Last Supper.[57]

Forbes established the basis for his Catholic interpretation by asserting that to understand the Articles correctly it was necessary to remember the 'organic unity of the Church of England before and after the Reformation'. Using this historiography Forbes felt free to assert the similarity of the teaching of the Articles with Roman Catholic doctrine. His concern to promote reunion as a Christian defence against infidelity and secularization was plain in his final words in the preface; while his limiting the Catholic Church to the Romans, Orthodox, and Anglicans (usual among Tractarians and Anglo-Catholics) was evident in his description of the Protestant Churches as 'bodies' rather than as Churches.

52 Ibid. i. 268.   53 Ibid. i. 289, 423.   54 Ibid. i. 259–60.
55 Ibid. i. 132–3.   56 Ibid. ii. 571.   57 Ibid. ii. 557.

Lastly, convinced that a divided Christendom will not be able to stand the assaults of infidelity, as a house divided against itself cannot stand, I therefore, in all that I have written, have had in view the future reunion of the Church. Recognizing the providential position of the Anglican Church, as stretching forth one hand to the Protestant bodies, and the other to the Latin and Greek Churches, I have tried to do justice to that position . . . The basis of reunion must be on what is ruled as *de fide*, and of this nothing is assumed as such, but the contrary of what is published under anathema. This reduces the difficulty, and leaves a wide margin for negociation and explanation.[58]

Forbes was adopting Pusey's distinction between official and popular belief, hoping there could be the basis for reunion negotiations on the foundation of the former rather than the latter. However, conscious of the impending Council at the Vatican, Forbes spent some time addressing infallibility and the papacy. Inerrancy, he maintained, was not the gift of any individual Church, but belonged to the whole Church. Therefore, until the Orthodox Churches were reunited with the west this faculty was in suspension. In the mean time the Church may witness to truth previously declared, but was not in the position to sanction new dogma. 'While the schism lasts, we must be content with this.'[59] The proper vehicle for an infallible declaration of dogma was an Ecumenical Council of a reunited Church, but even then the test of infallibility would not be the claims of any council itself but its universal reception by the faithful.[60] At the conclusion of the book Forbes asked what was to be done about growing unbelief and secularization. He believed they could be addressed by a general council, and the only power able to convene such a council was the papacy. He therefore made an eloquent plea for a more ecumenical attitude on the part of the pope and the forthcoming Vatican Council.

Let the successor of St. Peter . . . only rise above the miserable triumph of an immediate Ultramontane success . . . [and be] the principle of reunion in Christendom. Let him send forth his invitation, not merely to all the Bishops of his own subjection . . . but let him invite first his own to testify to tradition and to judge freely in matters submitted to him. Then let him invite the ancient Eastern hierarchies . . . Let him summon the Anglican prelates, not prejudging the doubts of their jurisdiction, but accepting them as they are historically, the occupants of the chairs of St. Austin and St. Paulinus. Let him call to himself all that is still sound in the Lutheran and Calvinist bodies . . . so shall the great cause of reunion be promoted.[61]

[58] Ibid., pp. xxx–xxxi.
[59] Ibid. i. 207.
[60] Ibid. i. 297.
[61] Ibid. ii. 812–14.

Such a plea, given the character and experience of Pius IX, was always bound to fall upon deaf ears. Pio Nino had become pope in 1846 with a reputation as a liberal, and amidst great expectation among Italians that he would support the cause of the unification of Italy. But the revolutions of 1848, which caused the pope to flee for his life from Rome, provoked a reaction in Pius's attempt to place himself at the leadership of European liberalism. His experience in the tumult of 1848 convinced Pius that in liberalism, popular sovereignty and human reason combined to threaten the faith of the Church. Henceforth, he regarded the maintenance of his temporal power as the security for his spiritual independence, and turned his back on liberalism in politics and in the Church. By 1860 Pius IX regarded the Italian *Risorgimento* and its liberal principles as based on the atheistic principles of the French Revolution and consequently as the enemy of the Church. Therefore, under his leadership the Roman Catholic Church was placed on the defensive against what was perceived as the threat from modern thought and politics. This attitude was reflected in the introduction of the Syllabus of Errors in 1864. It was unlikely that such a reactionary pope, committed to the defence and assertion of the Roman Church, would have been prepared to countenance the sort of ecumenical role Forbes requested of him.

An indication that Forbes's book was less than likely to have the impact he desired in Roman Catholic circles came in Newman's response to the copy Forbes sent him. In April 1868 Newman said he thought Forbes's reduction of the anti-Roman aspect of the Thirty-nine Articles would only increase the demand for their abolition as a theological standard. Nor was he overly optimistic about the book attracting the attention of Roman Catholic theologians, although he expressed the polite hope that it would.[62] Forbes did receive a more enthusiastic response from the German historian Ignaz von Döllinger who considered it was 'the best and certainly the most Catholic commentary' on the Articles. Like Newman, Döllinger also thought such an interpretation of the Articles would lead to the reduction of their role as a theological standard for Anglican clergy, but imagined this would leave the clergy freer to adopt theological views more favourable to future reunion. Döllinger mentioned his concern about the influence of the ultramontane party at Rome as prejudicial to Forbes's hopes for the Vatican Council, but hoped that 'a small but resolute knot of Bishops' would be able to oppose the

[62] J. H. Newman to A. P. Forbes, 6 April 1868, in *The Letters and Diaries of John Henry Newman*, ed. C. S. Dessain *et al.* (1973), xxiv. 58.

ultramontanists.[63] Döllinger was a Roman Catholic priest and professor of church history at the University of Munich who had broken away from a previous ultramontanist position under the influence of his historical research. By 1868 he had developed an intense dislike for what he considered was the historically unjustified autocracy of the papacy, which one historian has attributed to his 'Germanic contempt for all things Roman or Italian'.[64] Forbes had visited Döllinger in Munich in 1863 and a friendship of mutual respect had developed. Forbes became one of Döllinger's primary sources of information concerning English developments and religious views, which he greatly admired since his visit to Oxford in 1836. His British sympathies, and friendship with men such as Lord Acton and Gladstone, had converted Döllinger to a Whig view of history, in which he sided with the liberals.[65] Döllinger's hostility to Rome was increased when he was not invited to Rome to take part in the preparatory commissions for the Vatican Council. This slight intensified his arguments against infallibility and in favour of independent national Churches.[66]

At the beginning of 1868 Forbes travelled to Italy to canvas the prospects for reunion in the light of the approaching Vatican Council, and to make various presentations of his book. He took with him a letter of introduction from Pusey to Archbishop Darboy and, visiting the archbishop in February 1868, found him affectionate and friendly towards the Catholic revival in the Church of England. Darboy also gave him a letter of introduction to the French ambassador in Rome as a means of gaining a papal audience. Forbes was anxious because he would not go to Rome as any sort of official representative. The archbishop, however, thought this informality the safest basis for any negotiations as failure would not leave anyone compromised. Forbes was still troubled by Anglican incohesiveness and diversity of doctrine.[67] It was this lack of doctrinal authority in Anglicanism that he thought a major contributor to contemporary difficulties of faith. The restoration of a greater standard of ecclesiastical authority, resulting from reunion with Rome, would prevent the Anglican Church being criticized by the sceptical for lack of doctrinal definition.

Forbes's visit to Rome in 1868 was not his first visit to Italy. He had made the trip for reasons of health on a number of occasions in

---

[63] I. von Döllinger to A. P. Forbes, 5 Oct. 1868, BpF.
[64] E. E. Y. Hales, *Pio Nino* (1954), 286.
[65] Mathias Buschkühl, *Great Britain and the Holy See 1746–1870* (1982), 134–41.
[66] Ibid. 139.
[67] A. P. Forbes to E. B. Pusey, 20 Feb. 1868, BpF.

past years, and had developed especially close relations with the monks of the Benedictine abbey of Monte Cassino, to whom he had been introduced by Gladstone.[68] In 1865 he had spent a 'delightful' week at the monastery before going on to Munich to see Döllinger.[69] His experiences among the Benedictines had stirred him deeply.[70] He told the monks he would retain 'the happiest memories of this visit & the infinite courtesy received' throughout his life and, in a burst of romantic medievalism, he prayed, 'may the Venerable House of Monte Cassino thrive for long as the true Sinai of the Middle Ages'.[71] In February 1866, the community reciprocated Forbes's interest. While acknowledging the copy of one of Forbes's devotional works, one of the monks remarked, 'We are troubled a little by the fear of the imminent general suppression of the monasteries.'[72]

The unification of Italy, proclaimed in 1861, had brought into sharp relief the conflict between Pius IX's distrust of liberalism and the new Italian government. Unwilling to take Rome from the papacy by force the capital of the new Italian state was established in Florence. In 1865 a new civil law code was passed which included suppression of various religious institutions. The money raised from the sale of suppressed institutions was then used to increase the stipends of poor clergy. But underlying the apparent utilitarianism of the law was an anti-Catholicism, which was strengthened by the papacy's hostility to the liberal state.[73] This hostility was compounded by the pope's refusal to recognize the Italian government because of Pius's antagonism to the loss of the Papal States, which had been annexed by the new Italian state. Papal control of Rome and its vestigial territories was only maintained by a French army of occupation sent by Napoleon III, which remained in place until the outbreak of the Franco-Prussian War in 1870.

Forbes became active in the attempt to save Monte Cassino from secularization. Knowing of his friendship with Gladstone, who was influential with the Italian government, the monks of Monte Cassino endeavoured to cultivate Forbes's support. In March 1866, when he was about to leave for another trip to Italy, Forbes had approached Gladstone about the campaign to save Monte Cassino. Gladstone had already told

[68] A. P. Forbes to W. E. Gladstone, 18 Oct. 1864, Gladstone Papers, BL 44154, fo. 294.
[69] A. P. Forbes to W. E. Gladstone, 8 May 1865, Gladstone Papers, BL 44154, fo. 296.
[70] A. P. Forbes to R. Lingard (-Guthrie), 30 Apr. 1865, SPC.
[71] A. P. Forbes to Monte Cassino abbey (translated copy of a letter in Italian), n.d. [1865], BrMS 1. 4. 5. 894.
[72] Bonifacio Ma Krug to A. P. Forbes, 28 Feb. 1866, BrMS 1. 4. 5. 897.
[73] A. C. Jemolo, *Church and State in Italy 1850–1950* (1960), 11–12.

him that, as a member of the British government, he could not act publicly, but that he was prepared to act in his private capacity. Therefore, Forbes offered himself as a messenger for any correspondence Gladstone might care to send the monastery.[74] Forbes visited the abbey that April but his stay was cut short by ill health. One of the monks kept him informed of subsequent developments, acknowledging the support of 'kind and distinguished friends in England, who exert themselves in our behalf', although the abbot now believed the monastery would be suspended eventually.[75] On 11 April 1866 a flattering article by Forbes about his visit to Monte Cassino a year before appeared in the *Guardian*. It was designed to elicit public sympathy for the monastery. Forbes stressed its continuous history and its contribution to European civilization and scholarship, as well as the warmth and reasonableness of its occupants.[76] In June his Benedictine correspondent informed Forbes that the law of suppression of monasteries, including Monte Cassino, had been passed in the Chamber of Deputies and only required to be passed by the Senate and to receive the royal assent. While the monk did not think that a proposed petition from leading British universities and other academic bodies could be prepared before the Italian legislation was passed, he did feel that if it could be sent in time such a petition could possibly prevent them from being evicted from the monastery.[77]

The Italian government secularized Monte Cassino, along with other religious houses, in 1866, and it eventually became a national monument with the monks as its guardians. Forbes maintained his contacts with monastery for the rest of his life.[78] In August 1868, one of his monastic correspondents told him they still knew nothing of the conditions the government wished to impose on their remaining in the abbey.[79] Forbes's last surviving letter concerning Monte Cassino was written in 1873 when he approached Gladstone about using the diplomatic bag to send copies of his *Kalendars of Scottish Saints* to the monastery and to Döllinger.[80]

Therefore, when Forbes went to Rome in 1868 in pursuit of the campaign for reunion, he was neither unfamiliar with the city nor

[74] A. P. Forbes to W. E. Gladstone, 8 Mar. 1866, Gladstone Papers, BL 44154, fo. 299.
[75] Bonifacio Ma Krug to A. P. Forbes, 8 Apr. 1866, BrMS 1. 4. 5. 898.
[76] *Guardian*, 11 Apr. 1866, 381–2.
[77] Bonificio Ma Krug to A. P. Forbes, 18 June 1866, BrMS 1. 4. 5. 901.
[78] Bonificio Ma Krug to A. P. Forbes, 27 Apr. 1867, BrMS 1. 4. 5. 904; L. Tosti to A. P. Forbes (translated copy of letters in Italian), 2 May 1867, BrMS 1. 4. 5. 906; 12 June 1868, BrMs 1. 5. 970.
[79] Bonificio Ma Krug to A. P. Forbes, 8 Aug. 1868, BrMS 1. 4. 5. 909.
[80] A. P. Forbes to W. E. Gladstone, 27 July 1873, Gladstone Papers, BL 44154, fo. 319.

without his contacts in the Italian Church. Forbes went with offers from
Bishop Dupanloup to take Pusey's propositions about reunion to Rome
himself, and from Archbishop Darboy to send such propositions to Rome
in his own name. But despite this encouragement from the French bishops Forbes met with disappointment. In newly unified Italy, with a
secularizing government and only French troops preventing Rome from
being incorporated into greater Italy, the Church was on the defensive. In
reaction to the secularism of the Italian government even his Benedictine
friends had become ultramontanes. Few Churchmen in Italy were disposed to relax the Church's resistance, and Forbes was met with demands
for his own submission as the sole response to his request for the consideration of Pusey's reunion proposals. Forbes therefore chose not to take
the preparation of theological propositions any further and persuaded
Pusey accordingly.[81]

Newman was not surprised at Forbes's reception when Pusey notified
him of it in May 1868. As Newman observed, 'the central authority cannot *profess* to relax'. He believed Forbes and Pusey should have approached the English Roman Catholic bishops before Forbes went to Rome. But
even then Newman would not have expected anything to come of it
because of the predominance of the ultramontanists, led by Manning, in
the Roman Catholic Church in England. Rome, said Newman, would
make concessions on the application only of representative bodies, and not
of individuals.

The Bishop of Brechin, represented nothing tangible. He did now [*sic*] show a
list of Anglican Bishops, 'Lordi', Members of Parliament, country gentlemen,
farmers and labourers, who, he could pledge himself, would one and all sign
the Creed of Pope Pius and hold the later decisions of Rome including the
Immaculate Conception, on condition they might hold an Ecumenical Council
was the one and only seat of Infallibility.[82]

Newman explained that only the expectation of a large body seeking
reconciliation would cause the Roman authorities to moderate the
normal requirements of submission. Newman, in short, could offer
little encouragement to Pusey and Forbes in the present conditions
prevailing at Rome and in England.

By the end of 1868 Forbes's hopes for an reunionist initiative at the
Vatican Council were fading. In a letter to Döllinger, written after the

[81] E. B. Pusey to H. P. Liddon, 6 Oct. [1869], PH Liddon correspondence.
[82] J. H. Newman to E. B. Pusey, 24 May 1868, *Letters and Diaries of John Henry Newman* (1973), xxiv. 78–80.

announcement of the Council in June 1867, he revealed his increasing distrust of ultramontanism and his continuing thoughts of secession.

> I need not say how profoundly anxious we are about the coming Roman Council. Many of us who have practically to choose between Anglicanism and Ultramontanism (for secessions in this country amount to this) were in hopes that the questions at issue between the Churches would be submitted to careful analysis and that as a result the way would be made clear to us. As it is, it all seems to point to a stereotyping of the present dominant notions and to an aggravation of the consequences of the fatal divorce between Historic Truth and Dogma, to my mind one of the most dangerous conditions of these Times.[83]

History, according to Forbes, demonstrated that the papacy had not always professed or exercised the infallibility claimed by the ultramontanists, and therefore any dogmatic definition of papal infallibility had to ignore the facts of history. Forbes held no truck with the idea of doctrinal development which allowed Newman and others to accept both the facts of the Church's past and the definition of new dogma. He had hoped the Vatican Council would be more conciliatory to the Anglican position, and be reluctant to proclaim new doctrine if Anglican negotiations were demonstrably serious. If this happened then he, and presumably those others he described as having 'practically to choose between Anglicanism and Ultramontanism', would have had the knowledge that Anglican claims had been examined thoroughly by an Ecumenical Council. If these claims were then found wanting, Forbes and the like-minded would have been able to secede from the Anglican Church in good conscience. This letter, in which Forbes implicitly includes himself among those still having to chose between Canterbury and Rome, is another indication that his own doubts about the matter were not yet resolved, although he was growing increasingly critical of the Roman position.

In late 1868 Forbes had good reason for his pessimism about the Vatican Council. By September of that year the pope had issued an invitation to the Orthodox bishops to attend the Council. Anglicans, however, were presumed to have been included in his encyclical of 13 September 1868 addressed to '*Omnibus Protestantibus aliisque Acatholicis*' inviting them to join the one fold.[84] Pusey thought this encyclical indicated that Rome had 'prejudged' Anglican orders as invalid.[85] It would also have been disheartening to Pusey and Forbes not to have Anglicans acknowledged by the papacy as part of Catholic Christendom,

[83] A. P. Forbes to I. von Döllinger, n. d. BpF.
[84] Liddon, *Life of Pusey*, iv. 159.
[85] Ibid. 158.

and unbearable to have been lumped with Protestants. By dismissing
their most cherished desire for the Anglican Church to be regarded as a
branch of the Catholic Church, the encyclical demonstrated that Anglicans
were unlikely to receive any conciliation from the Vatican.

But Pusey and Forbes could still cling to the hope that the Council
itself would bring forth other, more ecumenical voices. This hope
received encouragement when, in January 1869, Forbes began a secret
correspondence with the Belgian Jesuit Victor de Buck, who had
favourably reviewed the first part of Pusey's *Eirenicon* in the journal
Etudes religieuses, historiques et litteraires in March 1866.[86] De Buck was a
Bollandist, a group dedicated to the critical study of hagiology, and his
studies inclined him to more liberal sympathies than were usual among
his ultramontanist order. He was also a friend of such leading liberal
Roman Catholics as Dupanloup. In 1864 de Buck had written a pamphlet
reconciling the liberal Belgian constitution with Catholic principles.
These mild liberal inclinations and his natural optimism had led de Buck
to take an early interest in the Oxford Movement, and in 1854 he published a sympathetic article on Anglicanism.[87] However, his liberal views,
historical criticism, Anglican sympathies, and inopportune expression in
writing about popular piety brought him into disfavour at Rome. By 1865
the suspicion he was under in Rome meant that de Buck could not allow
his name to be associated publicly with the cause of Anglican reunion.
He did, nevertheless, continue to correspond with a number of English
contacts favourable towards Anglican-Roman Catholic reunion, including
Richard Simpson, a liberal Roman convert who was sanguine about
reunion with the Anglo-Catholics, and Richard Littledale, a ritualist
priest and writer, who was a friend of Forbes.[88]

De Buck had known of Forbes's prominence among Anglo-Catholic
circles from these and other contacts in England but did not make direct
contact with the bishop until the beginning of 1869. In early January
1869, responding to a letter from John Stuart,[89] a Scottish genealogist,
written on 29 December 1868, about Forbes's research for his prospective
Kalendars of Scottish Saints, de Buck offered Forbes his assistance in his

---

[86] James P. Jurich, 'The Ecumenical Relations of Victor de Buck, S. J., with Anglican
Leaders on the Eve of Vatican I', Doctor of Sacred Theology thesis (Catholic University of
Louvain, 1988), 271ff.
[87] Ibid. 245.
[88] Ibid. 112–13, 378–9.
[89] John Stuart was a friend of Forbes from a nonjuring Episcopalian family in
Aberdeenshire. He was interested in reunion, and he and de Buck had corresponded on
hagiographical and reunion matters since 1866. Jurich, 'Victor de Buck', 381.

research.[90] On 19 January 1869 the Belgian wrote another letter to Stuart, intended to be also seen by Forbes, which this time related to reunion matters. In it he mentioned for the first time an argument he would later use repeatedly with Forbes—that if Anglican bishops regarded themselves as Catholics they were bound to come to the Vatican Council. Their presence in Rome, de Buck believed, would lead directly to a debate about the validity of Anglican orders and other matters of doctrinal dispute, which would be easily resolved. De Buck also mentioned that he would be present at the Council as the personal theologian of the Jesuit superior general.[91] Forbes now wrote directly to de Buck, sending him a copy of his book on the Thirty-nine Articles as an illustration of the position of Anglican reunionists. Forbes drew attention particularly to those parts of the book on the validity of Anglican orders. He implied that Roman doubts about Anglican orders were detrimental to the cause of reunion, in part because of the influence of the Anglican clergy in English society.[92]

In a letter which has not survived except as an incomplete draft among de Buck's papers, the Jesuit wrote in early February, endorsing Forbes's call for an Ecumenical Council to forward reunion.[93] Forbes's reply on 24 February indicated the continuing strength of his attachment to Anglicanism. Despite his existing uncertainties, he fastened on the devoted lives of many he knew, and on the response of people to the Catholic revival—which seemed to him signs that divine grace was within the Anglican Church. Forbes was not prepared to reveal his own anxieties about his Church to the Jesuit, and preferred instead to emphasize Anglican strengths to an outsider. Remarking on the irony of this correspondence between a Jesuit and a representative of his Society's oldest foes Forbes continued:

Your tradition therefore must be hostile to us [the English Church], whereas we who have been brought up within the pale of Anglicanism, (while we do not fail to confess & deplore many grievous blots & scandals, yet) have brought home to our convictions in many wonderful ways that Christ is indeed within her. You cannot know the beautiful lives of many who profess her tenets. The strong virile piety of her men, the unspeakable purity of her women. So good are they that if their lives are not the fruit of the grace of the sacraments, the natural conclusion is, that people can do very well without sacramental grace at all. Then think of the later movement—the thousands of churches built &

[90] *DNB* (1889), lv. 102; Jurich, 'Victor de Buck', 441–2.
[91] Jurich, 'Victor de Buck', 443ff.
[92] A. P. Forbes to V. de Buck (translated copy of a letter in French), 'Septuagesima' [24 Jan.] 1869, BpF.
[93] Jurich, 'Victor de Buck', 461–4.

endowed by private munificence—the development of the religious life, and the high standard of attainment of the younger clergy.[94]

Meanwhile, Bishop Dupanloup was encouraging de Buck to endeavour to attract Anglicans to the Vatican Council.[95] Presumably, Dupanloup hoped that the presence of Anglicans in Rome would impress others there with the possibility of reunion. This, in turn, might convince the Council that the definition of papal infallibility would be inopportune at that time. Accordingly, de Buck wrote Forbes an extremely long letter on 8 March 1869 attempting to convince him to attend the Council with Pusey as his theologian, regardless of any formal invitation. De Buck was flattering about the degree to which the Oxford Movement had moved the Anglican Church towards an understanding with Rome, and about Forbes's personal Catholicism. 'You are much more Catholic than you think,' he assured Forbes, and promised him an honourable reception if he or Pusey came to the Council, again suggesting dogmatic differences could be resolved without too much difficulty. De Buck begged him to seize the historic opportunity for reunion presented by the Council. 'Never will there be an occasion like the Council for realizing this end. You, a Scotch Bishop are more free than any other. You have expressed more than any other the desire for the union . . . More than any other you are bound to go to the Vatican Council.' He again tried to convince Forbes that he was in fact included in the papal invitation to all Catholic bishops, citing the example of an Orthodox archbishop who attended the Council of Trent unannounced and was admitted. All Forbes would be asked to do, claimed de Buck, was to profess the creed of Pope Pius.[96] If Forbes came de Buck was convinced others would follow and reunion could proceed on the basis of an elaborated creed of Pius. But if Forbes could not come, then de Buck hoped to secure another indication of Anglican desire for reunion by proposing that Forbes prepare a paper giving a positive summary of Anglican doctrine which the Jesuit undertook to communicate to Rome.[97] The characteristic optimism of the Belgian, or his comparative isolation from Britain and Rome (for he hardly ever left Belgium in his life), caused him to play down, or perhaps

[94]   Ibid. 467.

[95]   Liddon, *Life of Pusey*, iv. 174.

[96]   This was published by Pius IV in 1564 and was imposed on all holders of major ecclesiastical office in the Roman Catholic Church. It contained a summary of the doctrines promulgated at the Council of Trent including the relation of scripture and tradition, original sin and justification, the mass, the seven sacraments, the saints, indulgences, and the primacy of the Roman see.

[97]   V. de Buck to A. P. Forbes (translated copy of a letter in French), 8 Mar. 1869, BpF.

to fail to realize, that ultramontanists in the Vatican and Britain were generally unwilling to countenance anything beyond individual submissions to Rome, lest corporate reunion negotiations concede too much.

In his reply to de Buck, on 13 March 1869, Forbes protested against a common accusation that he and other leaders of the Catholic revival met from Roman Catholic clerics—namely, that it was the wealth of their livings that kept them within the Anglican Church. For his part, Forbes observed that his private fortune brought him 'very much' more than his stipend, and that he remained an Anglican because of 'the love I bear to my Flock' and the dread he had of destroying his work among them, presumably through the consequences of his conversion.[98]

It was up to Pusey to inject a bit of practical reality into de Buck's overly optimistic outlook on the consequences of an Anglican presence at the Vatican Council. He pointed out to Forbes that subscription to the creed of Pius IV would be taken by many Anglicans to mean that Forbes had ceased to be an Anglican, and had vacated the see of Brechin. Pusey instead proposed that an appeal to the Council by Forbes could be effected more satisfactorily by sending a theological defence than by appearing in person at Rome. He reminded Forbes that their object was not simply individual reconciliation but reunion between Churches, and that Anglicans would require some time before they became sympathetic to reunion. Pusey suspected that de Buck's purpose was not so much reunion as to overwhelm any Anglicans, such as Forbes, who went to Rome, with the scale and grandeur of the Roman episcopate, thereby causing their submission. 'You are impulsive,' Pusey concluded sharply, 'and I should think that he did not miscalculate about you.'[99] Pusey's impatience with Forbes's over-eagerness to trust de Buck's proposals was manifest in his comments to Liddon that Forbes 'harps always upon that string "we represent no one" or "a handful". I say we represent a large number, but we cannot tell whom we represent until we have definite papers formalized by us, accepted by them.'[100] The differences in Pusey's and Forbes's assessments of how much support they had for their reunion plans indicated a difference in their respective perceptions of Anglicanism. Forbes continued to be uncertain about the Anglican position and keen to resolve this by a submission to an appropriate Catholic authority. He was therefore more inclined to trust de Buck's sincere, but optimistic, representation of the reunion position in Rome. Pusey, whose

---

[98] Jurich, 'Victor de Buck', 493–4.
[99] E. B. Pusey to A. P. Forbes, n.d. [Mar. 1869], BpF.
[100] E. B. Pusey to H. P. Liddon, n.d. [Mar. 1869], PH Liddon correspondence, fo. 220.

Anglicanism remained unshakeable, was less concerned about the official nature of their approach to Rome and more inclined to scepticism about these motives. While Pusey probably misunderstood these motives, his close friendship with Forbes meant he was only too familiar with Forbes's precipitate desire for reunion to become a reality.

This dose of ecclesiastical realism from his oldest and most trusted adviser prompted Forbes to write again to de Buck on 10 April 1869. He now backed off from attending the Vatican Council, and injected a more cautious tone into his correspondence by outlining some of the problems he thought Anglicans had with Roman Catholicism. Forbes believed there was an uncompromising attitude on both sides, and said he could in no way construe the invitation to the Council as including either himself or the Anglican bishops. If he came as an individual bishop he feared he would expose himself to recriminations on the part of his own 'protestant-minded laity'. All he would represent would be the 'Unionist School of thought' in the Anglican Church, and as this was neither a cohesive nor formal group, it could hardly be a satisfactory category for the Roman authorities. He concluded that formal theological propositions were the way forward for the reunion movement and he would endeavour to present these, using the good offices of Dupanloup. Among the aspects of Roman Catholicism difficult for Anglicans Forbes specified compulsory confession, Marian devotions and dogmas, the denial of the chalice to the laity, and the veneration of the cross. In any reunion, he observed, Anglicans would need guarantees from Rome that they would be permitted to proceed along their more 'sober way' in doctrine and liturgy. Referring to the issue of doctrinal development Forbes added: 'I suppose our standing point must be that Christianity is ever regarded as . . . a definite depositum once for all bestowed, not a philosophy capable of infinite elucidation and varying in its essential forms according to the action of the human spirit.'[101]

On 19 April de Buck hastened to assure Forbes that, far from a hardline attitude predominating among Roman Catholics, counsels of reconciliation were prevalent in many European Roman Catholic minds, as opposed to those in England. He asserted further that reconciliation with 'the High Church of England' was one of the motivations of the Vatican Council, and that in the deliberations prior to the meeting of the Council 'no person has had more influence with the pope . . . than Mgr. Dupanloup'. This was unlikely as the central concern of

---

[101]   A. P. Forbes to V. de Buck, 10 Apr. 1869, BpF.

Dupanloup's life—the continuing relationship between the Church and modern society—was diametrically opposed to that of the pope, and, once the Council began, Dupanloup quickly became the spokesman for the opposition French minority bishops.[102] In fact, at the Council Dupanloup promptly distanced himself from papal desires for a decree of infallibility, declaring on 11 December 1869 that it was inopportune.[103] De Buck again asked Forbes to understand himself as included in the papal invitation if he was indeed a Catholic bishop, and urged him to disregard anti-papal protests and do his duty, even if this meant a sort of martyrdom. Regarding Forbes's claim that he would represent no one if he came to the Council, de Buck said that as a diocesan bishop he would be on the same standing as the other Council Fathers. But if Forbes declined to come, de Buck asked if he could use his influence to ensure that 'a respectable number of Doctors authorized by the English Church Union' attended. De Buck went on to answer most of Forbes's concerns on doctrine and liturgy, arguing that the Marian cultus could be toned down by restrictions and there would be no intention by Rome to turn reunited Anglicans into Spanish or Italian Catholics.[104]

Pusey, who Forbes kept informed about his correspondence with de Buck, remained unsatisfied with the Jesuit's suggestions. On 3 May he assured Forbes that the submission of a theological defence could only be a beginning and that they would still have to inculcate Anglican sympathy for reunion. For this they would require authoritative statements from Rome on the contentious subjects. Dissatisfied with de Buck's position on Anglican orders and with his urging of conditional reordination, Pusey said he preferred to wait until such time as they could receive 'more consideration' from Rome.[105]

Pusey's attitude finally convinced Forbes he could not go to the Vatican Council. On 5 May 1869 he wrote de Buck to say he felt 'more and more hopeless about any *immediate* fruit as to reunion' coming from the Council, as he could not discern any readiness on either side to take genuine steps towards reunion. Had the terms of the Council accorded with those expressed in his *Explanation of the Thirty Nine Articles* Forbes would have felt bound to go, even at the risk of losing his see. But as they did not, he decided he could not go to Rome because to do so would be to sever his communion with Anglicanism.

[102] O'Gara, *Triumph in Defeat*, 10.
[103] Friedrich Heyer, *The Catholic Church from 1648 to 1870* (1969), 190.
[104] V. de Buck to A. P. Forbes (translated copy of a letter in French), 19 Apr. 1869, BpF.
[105] E. B. Pusey to A. P. Forbes, 3 May [1869], BpF.

As it is, I am morally free to act as I think right, and at this moment I do not see how I should be able to appear without breaking with those with whom I am in Communion. To sign the Creed of Pope Pius even with explanations would be virtually to renounce Communion with England—for this reason signature of that Creed has always been the type of individual submission. I should not, believe me, fear the protestant howl, but I have to consider the many tender and holy souls committed to me, who would be scandalized by the act.[106]

Forbes therefore intended to proceed by way of the theological proposi-tions. It appears that this letter of 5 May was not sent at that time because, on 20 May, he added a postscript expressing the 'greatest alarm' over the possibility of a definition of papal infallibility at the Council. This, he feared, would bring an end to hopes for reunion between the high church party and Rome. 'The English High Church party', Forbes stressed, 'have been so trained to believe in Tradition, and to appeal to the Early Church, that they look upon this doctrine with the utmost dis-like.' Advised again by de Buck, in a letter of 15 May, that he was going to the Council as the personal theologian to his general, Forbes declined de Buck's offer of acting as a channel of communication to Rome, believing this was best left in the hands of Pusey and Dupanloup.[107]

This May letter indicates that by this time, at the latest, Forbes had finally resolved his uncertainties, in so far as remaining within the Anglican Church went. His theology, like that of other Tractarians and Anglo-Catholics, was rooted in the normative standard of the early Church. He therefore could not ultimately countenance what he regarded as unjustified innovations to the criterion of patristic worship and doc-trine. Forbes remained unhappy with much of the Marian cultus of the Roman Church which had developed after the patristic era, and found the dogmatic definitions of the immaculate conception of Mary (1854), or the impending promulgation of papal infallibility, even harder to stomach. He could not bring himself to accept the theory of doctrinal development, nor could he believe that these later dogmas formed part of the original deposit of the faith. Theological objections aside, Forbes was also con-strained, as always, by his pastoral responsibility to his congregation and diocese. He felt bound to reject a step (secession) that his people would find so objectionable as to constitute a threat to their continuing in the faith. By 1869 Forbes's search for a basis of doctrinal authority had been subsumed under the wider hope of corporate reunion. He was therefore no longer interested merely in resolving his personal need for a Catholic

[106] A. P. Forbes to V. de Buck, 'Eve of the Ascension' [5 May] 1869, BpF.
[107] A. P. Forbes to V. de Buck, 5 May and 20 May 1869, BpF.

authority—he now desired a corporate reunion of Catholic Christendom as a bastion against doubt and disbelief. But his own uncertainty had made him too eager to trust de Buck, and uncritical about the Jesuit's over-optimistic presentation of the desire for reunion within Rome. It was his friendship with Pusey which kept Forbes in touch with a more critical viewpoint. Pusey's greater pessimism in 1869 regarding the reunion aspirations of the papacy and the Vatican Council convinced Forbes to decline de Buck's pressing invitation to come to Rome for the Council.

Forbes now agreed with Pusey in proceeding with the preparation of theological propositions to be forwarded to Rome through the agency of Dupanloup. At the beginning of July de Buck returned to Brussels from Rome where he had been one of the theologians working in the preparatory commissions for the Council. From Brussels he advised Forbes that various leading figures in the Roman Curia had responded favourably when he reported, without divulging any names, the negotiations between them. He had in fact received a letter from Forbes, dated 6 June, when he was in Rome and had taken the liberty of showing it (having first cut off the signature) to his interlocutors as an earnest of Forbes's proposals for reunion. Confident of the reception his reporting had received in Rome, de Buck urged that Forbes's theological exposition be ready in time for the commencement of the Council, which would be in December 1869. He concluded by telling Forbes he had prayed for him at the tomb of St Peter in Rome and felt it would not be too long before Forbes could reciprocate.[108]

Forbes now began to disagree more freely with de Buck. That summer he had made a three-week visit to the continent, and he told the Jesuit that his contact with diplomatic sources there had convinced him of the ascendancy in Rome of the ultramontanist programme. Forbes had spent much of his holiday in Bavaria where he had stayed with Döllinger in Munich. There he had learned of the plans of the ultramontanists for the Council, what he called 'the tactics of the extreme party'.[109] He also heard of the Bavarian foreign minister's letter to his ambassadors about the political ramifications of the approaching Council. This dispatch mentioned the probability that papal infallibility would be declared a dogma, and also that the propositions of the Syllabus of Errors would become dogmatically infallible statements.[110] Forbes mentioned this communiqué in his letter to de Buck as confirming what he now

---

[108]   V. de Buck to A. P. Forbes (translated copy of a letter in French), 7 July 1869, BpF.
[109]   A. P. Forbes to V. de Buck, 10 July 1869, BpF.
[110]   C. Butler, *The Vatican Council 1869–70* (1962), 77–8.

expected from the Council. Personally, Forbes believed there was something to be said for the pope's reactionary politics which 'in view of the present advance of democracy' would act as a 'judicious drag-wheel' on contemporary democratic development. Nevertheless, regarding the Syllabus's condemnation of liberalism, Forbes considered that to make any political theory a matter of dogma was against the teaching of Christ. He believed the assumption of Mary was a legend, and he could not abide infallibility. At a time when the educated classes of Europe often could not accept the doctrines already proclaimed by the Church Forbes censured Rome for seeking 'to cram against the stomach of the sense these additional burdens'. Regarding de Buck's prayers for him at St Peter's tomb, Forbes responded with acerbity, saying, 'I doubt not that they are heard but not perhaps in the sense that they were offered.'[111]

Döllinger's increasing antipathy to Rome had evidently shattered Forbes's illusions about the Council, especially concerning papal infallibility, and Forbes had now come to believe there would also be an attempt to obtain a formal condemnation of Anglican orders. He anticipated there would be no change in the attitude towards Anglicanism from that expressed in the condemnation of the APUC by the Holy Office. Forbes now looked forward to the Council with 'simple dread', and he believed Anglicans had a legitimate grievance towards the papacy—that it had 'exercised a tyranny instead of such a Primacy as belonged to the Divine Constitution of the Church'.[112] Forbes's disappointment at the ultramontanist ascendancy in Rome had finally soured his attitude to the papacy, which he previously regarded as a source of ecclesiastical authority to which Anglicans could possibly submit if the Vatican had been prepared to be conciliatory.

Referring to his own experiences in Rome, de Buck once again played down the possibility of the ultramontanist programme predominating at the Council. In July 1869 he urged Forbes to complete the projected doctrinal exposition, observing that one of the four prominent Roman Churchmen he had spoken to about it had advised him that, if the exposition arrived in Rome in time, it could 'prevent disagreeable questions being raised' at the Council. 'Once more', said de Buck, 'let us not recoil before certain difficulties which perhaps are only imaginary and which even were they real could not prevent us in doing our duty.'[113] But Forbes now said he would not sign Pius's creed, even with

[111] A. P. Forbes to V. de Buck, 10 July 1869, BpF.
[112] A. P. Forbes to G. Cobb, 12 July 1869, BpF.
[113] V. de Buck to A. P. Forbes (translated copy of a letter in French), 16 July 1869, BpF.

explanations, 'as long as it is regarded as the symbol of *individual submission* not *corporate reunion*' and that there were, anyhow, real doctrinal difficulties in it. Yet despite believing the Vatican Council was not going to be the sort of Ecumenical Council he had called for in his book Forbes was still working on the Anglican rule of faith, but with less and less hope of any good result deriving from it.[114] De Buck promptly responded by claiming that the creed was not a symbol of individual submission but was rather an expression of the faith of the Catholic Church, and he defended the ecumenicity of the Council.[115]

That September Newman wrote to Pusey also encouraging him to go to Rome as it would be the best way to learn just how the various bishops regarded reunion. If Pusey could not go he should suggest someone else, but Forbes would not do because, as a bishop, he was too official a figure.[116] But by the end of 1869 Forbes was too thoroughly disillusioned about the ecumenical prospects of the Vatican Council in the light of the ultramontanist ascendancy to want to go to Rome. Immediately prior to the first formal session of the Council he told de Buck that he expected the Council would only 'stereotype [fix] the Ultramontane pretensions'. Still he hoped the Holy Spirit would keep the Council from 'pernicious action', and that de Buck would do his best as an attending theologian to insert into Council documents the 'complementary truths' held by all Christians.[117]

De Buck was now pressing for Forbes's individual conversion. On 13 December 1869 he wrote from Rome saying he was 'embarrassed' by Forbes's indecision, and that his contact with Forbes was bringing him into suspicion at Rome, presumably among the dominant ultramontanists who demanded personal submission, not negotiation, with Anglican enquirers. He cited Manning's nomination as a cardinal 'as a sort of earnest of what awaits you if you decide finally of making the definitive step', and he encouraged Forbes to believe that in doing so he would 'be made *effectively* part of the Catholic Church'.[118] On 20 December de Buck wrote again, not having given up hope that Forbes would still come to the Council where, he said, Forbes would be received on the basis of the creed of Pius with explanations.[119] De Buck's theological training

[114] A. P. Forbes to V. de Buck, 24 July 1869, BpF.
[115] V. de Buck to A. P. Forbes (translated copy of a letter in French), 27 July 1869, BpF.
[116] J. H. Newman to E. B. Pusey, 16 Sept. 1869, in *Letters and Diaries of Newman*, xxiv. 333.
[117] A. P. Forbes to V. de Buck, 2 Dec. 1869, BpF.
[118] V. de Buck to A. P. Forbes (translated copy of a letter in French), 13 Dec. 1869, BpF.
[119] V. de Buck to A. P. Forbes (translated copy of a letter in French), 20 Dec. 1869, BpF.

disposed him to urge individual conversion where that appeared to be a possibility, and he was never as compelled by the case for corporate reunion as were Forbes and his other Anglican correspondents.[120] In response, Forbes wrote a long letter clearly spelling out what he called the position of the 'Reunionist party in the Church of England'. This letter was the closest Forbes came to producing the sought-after doctrinal exposition. The Reunionist party, he said, looked for the corporate reunion of all Christendom as the remedy to the 'advancing and all devouring Rationalism of the XIX century'. First, they sincerely believed all the statements of faith they were required to sign as Anglicans, interpreting them in a Catholic sense according to the early Fathers. Secondly, they deplored the schism of the Reformation, accepted their isolation from the rest of Catholic Christendom, but believed the Holy Spirit was working in the Anglican Church. Thirdly, they believed salvation was possible in Anglicanism because they had valid sacraments and a Catholic ministry. They particularly pointed to the Oxford Movement which had restored many Catholic practices and produced a higher standard of faith and practice for both clergy and laity. But they had a 'conservative horror' for Roman extremes such as the cult of Mary and exaggerated papal claims, and would desire these to be authoritatively checked in any reunion proposals. Forbes drew particular attention to this point. The Anglican reunionists, Forbes declared, acknowledged that the division of Anglicanism from 'the Great Church of the West' was unsatisfactory. Forbes, however, believed that disestablishment of the Church of England would soon permit the Catholic party to unite with Rome leaving the 'Calvinist element' to join the Dissenters. 'This', he said, 'was what they worked for, even if they did not live to see it.'[121] To ensure that de Buck had got the point that Forbes was acting in the name of such a party, and was not seeking personal submission to Rome, he told him bluntly on 27 December that 'the question is not an individual one but a corporate one'.[122]

On 17 November 1869 the pope sanctioned the decision of the Holy Office that de Buck cease his correspondence with Anglicans. Pusey's biographer, Henry Liddon, believed the correspondence continued into the next year because the Jesuit general was slow in forwarding the decision to de Buck.[123] The personal campaign for reunion conducted by

[120]   Jurich, 'Victor de Buck', 677–8.
[121]   A. P. Forbes to V. de Buck, n.d. [post 20 Dec. 1869], BpF.
[122]   A. P. Forbes to V. de Buck, 27 Dec. [1869], BpF.
[123]   Liddon, *Life of Pusey*, Iiv. 186.

Pusey and Forbes also came to a definite end when, in March 1870, the copies of part three of Pusey's *Eirenicon—Is Healthful Reunion Possible?* which he had sent to Dupanloup were returned, probably also a decision of the authorities in Rome.[124]

When the Vatican Council opened on 8 December 1869 even some Roman Catholics feared it would result in the issuing of dogmas on Mary as Mediatrix of grace, or elevate the anti-liberal propositions of the Syllabus of Errors into dogma.[125] In the event, dogma was proclaimed only on specifically theological matters and issues of Church and state were not included. The decree on the Church became limited to papal infallibility, and has to be seen against the desire by the majority of Roman Catholic bishops to defend the Church from the attacks of modern forces. There were good reasons for this fear, especially in Italy where the liberal government had given ample evidence of its anti-Catholicism. But public opinion in Britain was formed by such Roman Catholics as Lord Acton and Döllinger who were antagonistic towards those who saw a conflict between the Church and modern thought and, unlike Italian Churchmen, were less fearful of the forces of liberalism. The pope also openly favoured the declaration of papal infallibility which made it harder for those opposing the decree, like the French minority bishops, to appear loyal. Therefore, the decree was passed in July 1870 unanimously, after opposition bishops absented themselves so as not to vote against papal wishes. Eventually, however, all the minority bishops conformed and agreed to the decree.[126] Even without the Holy Office injunction to de Buck, the promulgation of papal infallibility by the Council would have terminated the basis for his reunion discussions with Forbes. If de Buck was inclined to be overly optimistic, and too remote from England and Rome to make entirely accurate assessments about the opinions prevailing in each place, he was at least prepared to regard the views of his Anglican correspondents more charitably, and in a more Catholic light, than was common among his contemporaries. Forbes, spurred on by his own anxieties about the Anglican Church, initially shared de Buck's optimism about the Vatican Council and reunion, but his widespread European contacts and Pusey's influence eventually convinced him that de Buck's hopes were unrealistic. They did, however, continue writing, largely on matters of hagiology, and Forbes visited de Buck in Brussels in 1872.[127]

[124] Ibid. 190.
[125] Hales, *Pio Nino*, 277.
[126] Ibid. 310.
[127] Jurich, 'Victor de Buck', 664.

The First Vatican Council fuelled British anti-papalism and was almost universally condemned in Britain. It was understood by most Anglicans to be the victory of ultramontanists like Manning, and moderate voices within English Roman Catholicism became quiet. Forbes himself made a stinging attack on the Council which occupied the whole of his diocesan charge in August 1871, and which he later published as a separate pamphlet. In it he reiterated and developed the objections he had made to de Buck in his letter of May 1869 when he expressed his resolution to remain an Anglican. He even used the same phrase, that the Council had 'stereotyped a false view of history'. Papal infallibility he regarded as without historical precedent or justification; it was a 'denial of history' and left doctrine resting upon a 'new dogmatic basis'—meaning that 'the appeal to history is now heresy'. According to Forbes, the doctrine of papal infallibility was not part of the original deposit of revealed truth communicated by Christ to the apostles. The dogma was therefore an innovation in the historic belief of Church and consequently illegitimate. The Council, he believed, had exceeded its authority by creating 'new objects of faith'.[128]

Throughout the 1860s Forbes had attempted to discover a concrete Catholic authority which might form a bastion against the disbelief and doubt of the nineteenth century. In the case of the Vatican Council, Forbes recognized that papal infallibility was the answer of the Roman Church to the 'infidelity and materialism of the age', but because it was illegitimate it would not succeed. Forbes, who had long been concerned about the growing disunity of British society, feared that the dogma was a new threat to the social cohesion of Europe. He told his clergy that educated people were having difficulty believing the truths the Church already proclaimed. Papal infallibility would only add to the difficulties of faith for them, while it would be accepted by the poor and ignorant. Thereby it would increase social and religious divisions.

Correspondingly, Forbes maintained that the Anglican Church could have an important role in the future as a unifying force because it included, he said, both Protestantism and Catholicism. But he also pointed to some dangers facing the Anglican Church. The theological liberalism of many of the clergy he equated with 'unfaithfulness to truth'. Liberalism, he said, was the consequence of uncertainty about religious truth, and it resulted in the destruction of every basis for belief but emotionalism. Nor could liberalism provide the social cohesion Forbes

---

[128] A. P. Forbes, *The Church of England and the Doctrine of Papal Infallibility* (1871).

expected of religion. It merely criticized belief based on authority, leaving each individual to judge for himself. But, in proposing a basis for religious certainty other than mere individual judgement, Forbes recognized that contemporaries now had a more positive outlook towards human faculties, and a growing abhorrence of the concept of damnation. Therefore, he believed, Evangelicalism, with its theology of the total corruption of humanity, was not a viable alternative for the maintenance of belief. What was needed, Forbes affirmed, was 'a more scientific spirit among our clergy', by which he meant a systematic theology. Such theology, he thought, would be more in keeping with the ethos of the time. As examples of what he meant he commended the German historical theologians such as Döllinger. If the clergy learned their theology in this more scientific way, Forbes thought it would help the laity meet the difficulties of science and biblical criticism by creating a firm religious conviction that 'certain things have by legitimate authority been defined to be true'.[129] In pointing to the German historians Forbes was reinforcing his criticism of the Vatican Council for promulgating dogmas which he felt were without historical precedent. He had learned from the Germans, he told Gladstone, the lesson of 'the historical involvement of Theology'.[130] Forbes was advancing the claim that theology and Christian dogma could find a solid basis for truth in the facts of the Church's history. Such facts, critically established in the way German historians had demonstrated, could provide the scientific basis for religious truth demanded by the educated opinion of the day. It was an extraordinary claim because, in making it, Forbes showed no awareness of the propensity for historical criticism to raise doubts about the historical claims of scripture. He still thought history would merely vindicate scripture. But his solution for educated doubters of an Anglican systematic theology, based upon the historical claims of the Church's teaching as established by historical criticism, revealed how Forbes had refined his old argument from authority for the truth of the Church's doctrine. By 1871 he understood that the teaching of the Church could no longer be upheld by a crude resort to established authority if that authority was itself the object of doubt to intelligent people. He had criticized the Vatican Council for this sort of argument—that a doctrine was true just because the Church said so. He had used the same argument himself in the past. But now he no longer believed it was strong enough to withstand the doubts and disbelief of Victorian men and women. A critical historical basis for

129 Ibid.
130 A. P. Forbes to W. E. Gladstone, 19 Oct. 1871, BL 44154, fo. 316.

doctrinal truth also suited Forbes's theory of an original deposit of revelation. It meant he had only to argue that anything not held by the early Church was an illegitimate innovation. This supported his Tractarian theology in which the faith and practice of the early Church was normative. In turn, this meant that the norm of the early Church could continue to provide Forbes with the theological basis for Catholic reunion. But he was not sufficiently aware that the same historical criticism could also undermine the apparent unanimity of the early Church, making it more difficult for that historical period to provide a theological standard for the contemporary Church. Understanding the early Church as the passive recipient of a complete deposit of supernatural truth may have been too static a model of history, exhibiting over-confidence about the recovery of historical evidence for all Catholic doctrines, but it was the means by which Forbes recovered his intellectual confidence in Anglicanism, and came finally to reject contemporary Roman Catholicism as being a historically illegitimate development.

Forbes's hopes for Catholic reunion came closest to being realized in the formation of the Old Catholic Church, whose development he kept in close touch with through his friendship with Döllinger. In 1873 he pressed the Episcopal Synod for an expression of sympathy towards the Old Catholics, whose movement had first developed as a protest among German intellectuals to the definition of papal infallibility.[131] The movement was led by professors from German Roman Catholic universities who, in July 1870, began a series of protests against the Vatican Council as neither ecumenical nor valid. By the end of 1870 they became disappointed in their hopes of the protest being led by the bishops. After being suspended from their posts, some professors conformed. But Döllinger did not, and in April 1871 he was excommunicated for his failure to submit to the Council decrees. The following June, some 18,000 Roman Catholics petitioned the German government to grant them civil recognition as Old Catholics and, in September, they held their first Old Catholic Congress. The German chancellor, Otto von Bismarck, supported the Old Catholics as a means to weaken the Roman Catholic Church in the ongoing *Kulturkampf* between the Church and German nationalism.[132] This first Old Catholic Congress established the doctrinal basis for the movement, with participants from Germany, Austria, Switzerland, and also the Church of Utrecht, which had separated from Rome in the seventeenth century over the controversy surrounding

---

[131] Handwritten agenda, 18 Nov. 1873, BrMS 1. 4. 805 (ii).
[132] Bruschkühl, *Holy See*, 170.

Jansenism. The Congress also included some Anglican observers. It repudiated the Vatican Council, and maintained its faith on the basis of the creed of Pius IV and the Council of Trent. The Old Catholics upheld the primacy of the Roman bishop but rejected his jurisdiction and claim to independent infallibility, while they demonstrated some liberal sympathies by protesting against the Syllabus of Errors. The Congress also expressed a desire for Christian reunion. While some of this programme, especially with regard to Trent, was transitional, the 1871 Congress established the Old Catholic Church as an independent, though very small, minority in the countries in which it existed. A second Congress also gave greater attention to reunion by forming a reunion committee under Döllinger's chairmanship. In 1873 the Old Catholics accepted episcopal ordination from the Church of Utrecht, although the two Churches remained formally separate until 1889.[133]

In September 1874 an Old Catholic reunion congress was held in Bonn. Forbes did not think his doctor would let him travel to Germany, and he was unsure about the conference programme. The Scottish bishops were prepared to be encouraging, and at the Episcopal Synod in November 1874 they passed a motion of support and thanksgiving for the Bonn conference, with Forbes as its seconder. The motion expressed agreement with those 'who adhere closely to the form of doctrine which was delivered by Apostolic teaching, and held by the Primitive and Undivided Church'.[134] The Bonn conference was one of a number of conferences exploring the question of reunion on the basis of the early Church. It provided for a different model to that of corporate reunion, proposing instead the search for intercommunion on the basis of '*unitas in necessariis*', leaving aside those tenets of individual Churches which were not regarded as essential.[135] The Bonn conference concentrated on relations between the Old Catholics and Anglicans, and led to an agreement on some fourteen points. The reunion conferences, however, did not continue after 1875.[136] Forbes drew attention to the Old Catholics in his final synod charge in 1875, maintaining it was a testimony to Anglicanism that the Old Catholics were forming a similar system—combining an appeal to history with respect for nationalism. He was delighted when his synod, a few days before his death, passed a motion supporting the Bonn reunion conference.[137]

[133] C. B. Moss, *The Old Catholic Movement* (1977), 191ff.
[134] REC IV, 18 Nov. 1874, SRO CH 12. 60. 6, 46–8.
[135] Moss, *Old Catholic Movement*, 260.   [136] Ibid. 262–9.
[137] Brechin Diocesan Synod Minutes, 5 Oct. 1875, BrMS 4. 1. 3, 195–7.

The Old Catholic movement as it stood in the early 1870s was the encapsulation of Forbes's hopes for Christian reunion. The influence of Döllinger in these early years committed the Old Catholics to a Catholicism that increasingly looked to the early Church as paradigmatic, and energetically worked for reunion upon that basis. The Old Catholics adopted Döllinger's historical outlook, which was Forbes's also, that what was not explicitly taught by the patristic Church was doctrinal innovation and therefore illegitimate. It is no wonder, therefore, that Forbes supported the Old Catholics so whole-heartedly. Indeed, it may be said that, lacking a Protestant element the Old Catholics upheld, for Forbes, a Catholicism more complete than that of the Church of England. While the Old Catholics and the Scottish Episcopal Church were alike committed to the early Church as normative, the Old Catholic Church also embraced the Catholic ritualism that Forbes desired, but was pastorally too cautious to promote in his own Church.

7

Tractarianism Revived

BY 1870 Forbes had resolved his doubts about Anglicanism and recovered his whole-hearted commitment to the Anglican Church. Freed from the counter-attractions of Roman Catholicism he once again became an enthusiastic proponent of Tractarianism, advocating sacerdotalism and the religious life, and upholding the independence of the Church in education and public worship. He regained that confidence in the Tractarian vision of the Church that he nearly lost during the 1860s.

During the 1870s Scottish society was relatively stable and confident about future progress. The passing of the second Reform Act in 1867 had widened the franchise to include most middle-class and skilled working-class men, and this expanded electorate had swept Gladstone's Liberal Party to power the following year. The Liberals had overwhelming support in Scotland and Gladstone became a sort of 'household god' to many working-class families.[1] The confidence of Scottish Episcopalians in their Church was also high. Divisions within the Episcopal Church created by the debate over the Communion Office had been settled, and the second half of the nineteenth century was a period of unprecedented growth for the Scottish Episcopal Church. During the first half of the century the Church had begun to move into the cities and southern lowland areas from the rural north. This enabled it to take advantage of both English and Irish immigration into Scotland, and rural migration into the towns. According to the 1851 census, Episcopalians numbered 43,000. By 1877 membership had risen to 56,000, and by 1879 to 63,000, according to the Church's official returns. For the rest of the century membership continued to rise steadily.[2] The Church also benefited from conversions by middle-class members of the Church of Scotland who desired a more liturgical and aesthetically pleasing worship. By the late nineteenth century the Episcopal Church had become a respectable part of Anglicized Scottish society, at least in the lowland south.

[1] W. Ferguson, *Scotland 1689 to the Present* (1968), 325.
[2] R. Currie *et al.*, *Churches and Church-Goers* (1977), 219, 132–3.

As with most late Victorian Churches, the Episcopal Church experienced pressure from the laity for a greater involvement in ecclesiastical government. This engendered the final crisis of Forbes's life, which centred on the question of lay representation in diocesan and general synods. The issue had been simmering throughout the 1860s. In 1863 the General Synod had given the laity a vote in the election of a bishop. The question of further lay participation came before the Episcopal Synod in 1867 on a remit from the Diocese of Aberdeen. This called for lay involvement in temporal matters, but proposed that the laity be excluded from synodical discussion of doctrine and discipline.[3] On that occasion the remit apparently failed to gain sufficient support from the other dioceses to proceed further. But in 1869 the matter again became a serious possibility.

In November 1869 the primus, Robert Eden, received resolutions from all dioceses except Brechin requesting a General Synod to consider lay representation. Forbes was opposed to the move, considering it contrary to the constitution of the Church and 'exceedingly dangerous'. It was an issue on which, he told the bishops at the Episcopal Synod on 16 November, he felt 'very strongly'. Notwithstanding Forbes's objections, the bishops referred the matter back to special diocesan synods to determine the exact extent of the lay representation they desired. The bishops sought widespread debate of the prospective innovation, requesting that various lay office-holders be asked to attend and to speak at the special synods.[4]

Before the special synod of the Diocese of Brechin met in June 1870 Forbes issued a Pastoral Letter to the clergy and laity of his diocese on the subject of lay representation. Once again he referred to his concern over widespread uncertainty about religious truth, and said he believed the desire for lay representation to be a symptom of this religious restlessness. He disavowed any intention to unchurch the laity, or to grant the clergy overweening power, but claimed it was the prerogative of the clergy to formulate and teach doctrine, as a consequence of their ordination and theological training. Forbes understood this authority to be threatened by lay representation in synods, because it would involve theologically untrained laity in the decisions of the only bodies in the Episcopal Church capable of formulating doctrine into a canonical, binding form. 'The faith is as dear to the layman as to the clergyman. He has the same interest in it. The *depositum* has been consigned to the body of the faithful. It rests in the Church; and the Church is not the clergy,

[3] REC III, 20 Nov. 1867, SRO CH 12. 60. 4, 374–5.
[4] REC III, 16–17 Nov. 1869, SRO CH 12. 60. 4, 389–93.

but the clergy and laity together, the body, the members of Christ. Nevertheless, while the faith reposes in the body, the power to determine and judge of it has ever been held to rest in the hierarchy.'[5] Forbes understood the synods of the Church to be the highest enunciators of the content of the Christian faith. Such doctrinal responsibility could not be given to the laity who were uneducated in theology, which he thought to be a technical science. For the laity to have such responsibility was also a usurpation of the clergy's divine commission of ordination. What was true of doctrine for Forbes was also true of discipline and ritual in the Church. Both of these were the prerogative of the clergy because they were consequences of doctrine—with discipline the 'practical aspect' and ritual the 'devotional aspect'.[6] Forbes's objections continued to be about the laity being involved in the formulation of doctrine. While this lay in the hands of the clergy, he also believed the clergy should consult the laity about doctrinal matters prior to a synodical decision; in fact, he held the consent of the laity to be necessary in matters of faith and morals.[7]

On 1 June 1870, the special synod of the Diocese of Brechin met to discuss lay representation. The majority of the Brechin clergy favoured a resolution which envisaged General Conventions involving lay and clerical representatives, in addition to the diocesan clergy continuing to meet separately in synod. Such Conventions would not be free to initiate action on doctrinal matters but would have to consent to any canon for it to be binding. Trials for heresy would remain the prerogative of the synod, but the Convention could deal with trials for immorality. Following the debate Forbes opined that 'from the very beginning of my Episcopate, I have always entertained the greatest dread of this lay movement'. Referring obliquely to the constitutions of some Anglican Churches in the colonies (such as in New Zealand) which gave the laity a place in synod, Forbes said he thought it a consequence of the 'democratic spirit apparently inseparable from English colonial life'. In addition to the objection he had raised in his Pastoral Letter he now said he also opposed the move because there was no precedent for it in the early Church, and it would involve the laity in questions which would 'agitate and unsettle their faith'. So strongly did Forbes feel upon this question that, in an unprecedented action, he used his canonical power to refuse to give effect to the synod's resolution.[8]

---

[5] A. P. Forbes, *Pastoral Letter of the Bishop of Brechin on the Admission of the Laity into Synod* (1870), p.xxxi.

[6] Ibid., p. xxxii.   [7] Ibid., p. xviii.

[8] Brechin Diocesan Synod Minutes, 1 June 1870, BrMS 4. 1. 3, 152–5.

Understanding lay representation as a threat to the Church's doc-trine, Forbes could not be otherwise than deeply perturbed about it. All through his episcopate he had strongly defended the Tractarian con-nection between doctrine and divine revelation, and he believed a precise and systematic exposition of doctrine by the Church to be its best defence against religious uncertainty. Now he saw these cherished beliefs at risk if theologically illiterate laity appropriated the spiritual authority of the clergy. It would result, he assumed, in poor, or even incorrect, doctrinal definition. It would also represent a submission to prevailing democracy which would destroy the divinely ordained hierarchy of ecclesiastical society. In Forbes's argument, Tractarian sacerdotalism also upheld the bishops' control of the Episcopal Church, already maintained by the old nonjuring tradition of monarchic episcopacy. It was a hierarchy of authority, not of privilege, that Forbes was concerned to defend. He held the laity to be as much a part of the Church as the clergy. But if the clergy's authority over doctrine was lost then the connection between doctrine and its divine source, via doctrine's teachers, would be severed. Forbes therefore became anxious to avoid a General Synod which, as the highest authority in the Episcopal Church, could allow the laity to be represented in synods if that so pleased a majority. If this happened, Forbes felt he would have to resign, so seriously did he regard the issue, and so much did it threaten his beliefs.[9]

At the Episcopal Synod in November 1870, the primus reported that all the dioceses were in favour of increasing lay involvement, most of them by simply admitting laity to the present synods. Brechin and Aberdeen, however, wanted separate General Conventions. Except for one, all dioceses wanted restrictions on lay participation in matters of doctrine, discipline, and worship, and all dioceses but Brechin (because of Forbes's refusing his synod's resolution) resolved to request a General Synod to determine the question. None the less, by a majority of three to two, a motion proposed by Forbes—that the bishops were not prepared to call a General Synod at that time—succeeded. Because of insufficient agreement among the dioceses about the exact nature of lay participation, a majority of the bishops decided to postpone further action.[10]

In 1873, while the matter was still under discussion by the bishops, Forbes reissued his Pastoral Letter in a pamphlet, now raising further objections to the innovation. This time Forbes largely turned his objec-tions on the existing influence of the laity in the Episcopal Church, which

---

9 A. P. Forbes to R. Thom, n.d., BrMS 1. 4. 846.
10 REC III, 16 Nov. 1870, SRO CH 12. 60. 4, 398.

he described as already predominant because of the clergy's inferior social position. He also drew attention to the role of many Episcopalian landowners who were heritors in the Church of Scotland by virtue of their role as feu holders. This, Forbes argued, gave them divided ecclesiastical loyalties. The increasing numbers of converts from the Church of Scotland also meant many new Episcopalians had not sufficiently absorbed the ethos of their new Church. He feared the Church would be 'affected by the great tide of democracy, which is sweeping every institution into the hands of the proletariat'. On the one hand he thought the teaching of the Church suffered from the overly influential upper classes with their connections to the Established Church. On the other, he was anxious lest the determination of doctrine be exposed to the theologically illiterate masses. Such a *magisterium* of the doctrinally unconcerned laity, he believed, would only result in the breakdown of the 'dogmatic basis of the church' and the triumph of the 'lax popular undogmatic Christianity' of the liberal theologians.[11] In the same year Forbes also issued, in conjunction with the Bishops of Aberdeen and Glasgow, who favoured the status quo, a pamphlet claiming that there was no historical or theological evidence for the synodical representation of the laity.[12]

In the event, although the issue came up for discussion at Episcopal Synods in succeeding years, no General Synod was called before Forbes's death. In fact, nothing further was done about lay representation in synods by the Episcopal Church until the twentieth century.

The effective stalling of a General Synod in November 1870 ended the last controversy of Forbes's life. His remaining energies were directed less towards defending the Catholic faith, and more towards its extension within the Church and its promotion outside it. Chief among such enterprises was his founding in 1871 of a religious sisterhood in Dundee, known as the Community of Saint Mary and Saint Modwenna.[13] In 1861 Forbes had invited Mrs Frances Bolland, a wealthy English clergyman's widow, to work in Dundee as a district visitor. Two years later Forbes, as Bishop of Brechin, was bequeathed a house at 10 King Street, Dundee, plus £800 to use at his discretion. With Forbes's encouragement, Mrs Bolland decided to test her vocation to the religious life. She and another woman went to the Community of All Saints, in Margaret Street,

---

[11] A. P. Forbes, *The Claims of the Laity* (1873).

[12] *May Laymen have Decisive as well as Consultative Votes in the Sacred Synods of the Church: A Case for the Bishops of Brechin, Aberdeen and Glasgow* (1873).

[13] Modwenna was an Irish nun who lived in the ninth century and founded two nunneries in Scotland, at Stirling and Edinburgh, before departing for England in *c.*840.

London, for their novitiate, with the intention of returning to establish a
sisterhood in Dundee.[14] Forbes drew up a rule for the community and,
on 18 August 1870, laid the foundation stone of a chapel at the King
Street premises.[15] The following year he consecrated the chapel and
installed Frances Bolland as Superior of a community with nine nuns.[16]
The sisters concentrated on pastoral work in the five city congregations of
Dundee, among mill girls, the aged, and the house-bound; and later they
ran a home for incurables and a small orphanage.[17]

The sisterhood was the most tangible fruit of Forbes's long interest in
the religious life which stretched back to his days as an Oxford undergraduate when he joined the quasi-monastic Brotherhood of the Holy
Trinity. In 1849 he had published a pamphlet on the religious life for
women entitled *A Plea for Sisterhoods*, arguing that such communities
were a means of meeting the ever-growing social and religious needs of
the towns, especially as trained nurses and prison visitors. Emphasizing
their utilitarian work, Forbes argued that sisterhoods could provide an
alternative to marriage and motherhood for women who could not find
fulfilment in this way. The promotion of the religious life for women was
a Tractarian challenge to the Victorian ideal of the gentlewoman, whose
function was solely that of wife and mother. This social expectation left
middle- and upper-class women who did not marry little prospect of
useful lives other than doing genteel charitable work. Forbes asked
rhetorically if the usual activities regarded as accomplishments for gentle-
women, such as painting, music, and languages, could be regarded as *'the*
occupation of life'. He believed many educated women, faced with only
this future, became weary of life, and that such frustration was the cause
of unhappy marriages and 'lifelong sorrow'. He also advocated the religious life to women from the poorer classes, for whom it could offer a
better and more purposeful life.[18]

Nor was Forbes's understanding of religious life for women limited
solely to the theoretical. There is evidence for his connection with the
Park Village sisterhood (the Sisterhood of the Holy Cross) established by
Pusey in 1845, which was the first Anglican religious community. Among
its initial members was Mary Bruce who, after she left the community

[14] 'The Community of S. Mary and S. Modwenna'. A short typewritten account of the
Community by Sister Constancia who attempted to revive the Dundee community in the
1870s. Included in the Community's records in the keeping of St Mary's, Broughty Ferry.
[15] Perry, 153.
[16] Marion Lochhead, *Episcopal Scotland in the Nineteenth Century* (1966), 133.
[17] Constancia, 'Community'.
[18] A. P. Forbes, *A Plea for Sisterhoods* (n.d. [1849]).

because of ill health, went to work in Dundee to manage the training school for schoolmistresses founded by Forbes.[19] Forbes also gave extreme unction to one of the dying sisters of the Park Village community in 1850, in what is generally regarded as the first recorded instance of unction administered in the Church of England (other than the Nonjurors) since the Reformation.[20] One historian of Anglican religious communities connects Forbes also with the Society of the Most Holy Trinity, the second Anglican sisterhood to be established (in 1848). He claims that the original rule of this community envisaged a bishop other than the diocesan Bishop of Exeter as visitor and that this 'could only have been Forbes'.[21] In 1848 no other bishop in England or Scotland was as amenable to the vowed religious life as Forbes so this judgement is probably correct. This early connection of Forbes with English sisterhoods further illustrates the importance Tractarians in the Church of England placed on having one of their own in the episcopate.

In addition to Forbes, a number of Tractarian parish priests established sisterhoods to assist in parish work. They included Thomas Chamberlain, J. M. Neale, and T. T. Carter, another friend of Forbes's who, in 1852, founded the Community of St John the Baptist, Clewer, and whom Forbes consulted when he was establishing his Dundee community.[22] Carter, an experienced priest and spiritual director, was one among many contemporaries who felt the force of Forbes's attractive personality. Recalling his conversations with him concerning the prospective sisterhood, Carter observed:

Even in those short interviews one could not but be deeply struck with the clear, bright single-hearted devotion, the immistakeable [*sic*] piety, the gentleness & refinement of his mind, the accomplished talents, the delightful & genial tone of intercourse, which made his society so charming, & the grace of his manner so attractive. I know no one who left on me the impression so strongly as he did, & that quite unselfconsciously, of a pure devotion & a high sense of duty, & this, in the most engaging manner, united with high intellectual gifts.[23]

These religious communities owed their existence to the influence of the Tractarians on responsive women, so that the institution of the religious life was one of the most characteristic and enduring facets of

---

[19] Constancia, 'Community'.
[20] Thomas Williams and Allan Campbell, *The Park Village Sisterhood* (1965), 69.
[21] Peter Anson, *The Call of the Cloister* (1955), 279 n. 2.
[22] Mackey, p. xxx.
[23] Biographical note on Forbes by a Miss French, Bodleian, Ms. Eng. misc., d. 1096, fos. 13–24.

the Oxford Movement. It was an encapsulation of the Oxford Movement's desire for holiness within the Church.[24] Therefore, signs of this
pursuit of holiness through the religious life constantly surfaced during
the course of the Oxford Movement—in the translation of the Sarum
Breviary in the *Tracts for the Times* as an inducement to the clergy to
recite the daily office; in Hurrell Froude's proposals for colleges of
unmarried priests; in the mooting of sisters of mercy by Pusey and
Newman; and in Newman's quasi-monastery at Littlemore.

Forbes's interest was not restricted to the religious life for women. He
was associated with two of the more successful nineteenth-century efforts
to establish the religious life for men in the Anglican Communion. The
first of these was the Society of the Holy Cross, a devotional society for
priests founded in 1855 by Charles Lowder, the famous slum priest of
east London. The Society's original rule envisaged that some members
would take traditional monastic vows, although they would not live in
community. Although never a member, Forbes was used by the Society
as an adviser on various occasions, and when the Society introduced
retreats into the Church of England Forbes made his first retreat with
the members, in 1859.[25] His experience of these retreats with the Society
of the Holy Cross encouraged Forbes to introduce them for his own
clergy from 1867, making him one of the first Anglican bishops to do so.
George Grub, his curate during the 1870s, described his experience of a
retreat given by Forbes in which the bishop gave the addresses dressed in
purple biretta, surplice, and stole.[26]

The first permanent religious community for men in the Anglican
Communion was the Society of St John the Evangelist (SSJE) founded in
1866, and Forbes came very close to joining as one of its founding members. By the time of the first meeting in the summer of 1865 to consider
the possibility of establishing the community, Forbes had been favourably
impressed by his experience of visiting at least two monasteries—the
Benedictine abbey at Monte Cassino, and the Cistercian abbey founded at
Mount St Bernard by Ambrose Phillipps de Lisle. This initial meeting to
discuss the foundation of the SSJE included Forbes, as well as Richard
Benson, one of his friends from his Oxford days, who was Vicar of
Cowley, Oxford, and the leader of the group. Two of the group,

---

[24] Benedicta Ward, 'A Tractarian Inheritance', in Geoffrey Rowell (ed.), *Tradition
Renewed* (1986), 218.

[25] T. Embury, *The Catholic Movement and the Society of the Holy Cross* (1931), 93;
Mackey, 143.

[26] G. Grub, *My Years in Dundee with Bishop Forbes* (1912), 40.

including Benson, had already decided to proceed and the meeting adjourned to give Forbes time to consider his position. At the next meeting Forbes decided not to join because of his uncertain health and his diocesan commitments. However, he continued to interest himself in the project and, along with Pusey, advised Benson first to establish the community before seeking support from ecclesiastical authority.[27] Both men must have feared that otherwise the plan for a community with formal religious vows would be mitigated by English bishops, to whom vows smacked of Roman Catholicism.[28]

Along with his attraction towards religious life, Forbes's enduring interest in spirituality was also manifest in 1872, when he gave a paper entitled *Of the Deepening of the Spiritual Life* to the Church Congress held that year in Leeds. The Church Congresses had begun in 1861 as unofficial gatherings of Anglican clergy and laity which met to discuss contemporary issues. The 1872 venue enabled Forbes to return and stay for a few days in his old parish of St Saviour's.[29] In this paper, his most mature writing on spirituality, he understood the spiritual life for all Christians to be, like religious life, a training in spiritual discipline. Presupposing an Augustinian necessity for grace to initiate any human response to God, Forbes concerned himself in the paper with the human dimension of spiritual growth. While most of what he said were commonplaces of ascetic theology, it was no doubt reasonably new to his audience as this theological discipline had only recently been revived in the Church of England by Pusey's translations of Roman Catholic works from the 1840s. Basically, Forbes adopted the classical model of western Christian spirituality which understood the spiritual life as proceeding through three stages regarding the effect of God on the soul—purgation, illumination, and union. However, in the paper he almost completely devoted his comments to the purgative way, or the need for purification of the soul as the first step towards perfect union with God. This emphasis gave the paper an overly scrupulous slant, the continuing legacy of Pusey's grim spiritual influence on Forbes's natural conscientiousness. But his emphasis may also have been determined by Forbes's desire to be relevant to the needs of his audience, for whom comments on the beginning stages of the spiritual life would have been most pertinent.

[27] Allan Cameron, *Religious Communities of the Church of England* (1918), 164–5; M. V. Woodgate, *Father Benson Founder of the Cowley Fathers* (1953), 61–3.
[28] Anson, *Call of the Cloister*, 280, 300; Woodgate, *Father Benson*, 66.
[29] Mackey, 192.

Forbes's basic theme was the need of sorrow for sin. 'Life', he said, 'is in the long-run, at its brightest, a period of sorrow.'[30] Proceeding from this understanding, probably born in the dour conditions of Dundee, he concentrated on the influence of sin in human life and proposed various spiritual remedies such as the need for self-knowledge, control of the passions, and avoidance of sinful pursuits. He referred to some of the problems created for spiritual growth by contemporary life, singling out ritualism and 'busyness' which could lead to a concentration on external life rather than the inner life of the soul. To balance this emphasis on the negative effects of life he recommended developing a recollection of the presence and love of God. Particularly he advocated meditation, the recitation of the daily office, and understanding the Eucharist as the expression of the condescending love of Christ. He encouraged his hearers to believe in one of the elementary truths of the spiritual life—that it is in whatever occupation of life they found themselves that God willed their sanctification.[31] He also reassured them that, despite the problems of spiritual development, they had received sufficient grace for such growth in baptism, and that any additional sin could be dealt with by forgiveness through confession.[32] Forbes ended on his favourite theme of the need for an accurate theological understanding of Christ. The worship of Christ as God and man, he said, 'is the Christian life', and this especially entailed having a right conception of Christ as he has revealed himself—'for only that accurate Truth is the Truth which will make us free and save us'.[33]

In the same year as his address to the Leeds Church Congress, on 28 October 1872, Forbes was guest of honour at a luncheon in Dundee given by the Diocese of Brechin to celebrate the twenty-fifth anniversary of his consecration as a bishop. Robert Thom gave an address on behalf of the diocese, and Forbes was presented with a pastoral staff for his use and that of his successors in the diocese. In reply, Forbes said that he had not in the past 'been used to overmuch praise, and therefore you may believe it is very sweet to me'. 'This is', he added, 'one of the most gratifying events that have ever taken place in my life.'[34] He said he had always attempted in Dundee to combine the definite message of the Church with a concern to promote the 'social and industrial civilization of the country'. Confident that the Episcopal Church was now becoming 'emphatically expansive', Forbes saw his Church taking a more prominent

---

[30] A. P. Forbes, *Of the Deepening of the Spiritual Life* (1884), 59.
[31] Ibid. 39.   [32] Ibid. 58.   [33] Ibid. 66.
[34] Mackey, 185.

position in Scottish society than it had when he first came to Dundee. The Episcopal Church in Dundee had, he claimed, 'with great self-sacrifice, gone out into the lanes and streets of the city, and dealt with a population, which would not have been dealt with otherwise'.[35]

But Forbes's efforts to promote the Church's involvement in the civic affairs of Dundee had not been without strain. The promotion of their narrow class interests by the Liberal bourgeoisie of Dundee had often conflicted with Forbes's Tory paternalism, old-fashioned social benevolence, and distrust of emerging democracy. By the early 1870s, Forbes could no longer accept the sectional politics of Dundee middle-class Liberalism, despite his personal admiration for the Liberal party leader, and his political allegiance to Gladstone when he was the member for Oxford University. In August 1873 he wrote to Gladstone to say that he was reverting to his traditional Conservative loyalties. He claimed that 'twenty years collision with the selfish democracy of Dundee has thrown me much back upon the Tory traditions in which I was bred & from which for a time I confess I swerved under the charm of your eloquence and character'.[36]

In 1874, Forbes's health, never robust, seriously failed. In May of that year, he was invited to represent the Scottish Episcopal Church at the first Church Congress held in Scotland, which met in Edinburgh. He was to give a sermon in St John's, Princes Street, but a few days before he collapsed and the sermon had to be cancelled, although he later recovered.[37]

Forbes was well enough to give his synod address on 1 October 1874. It was largely concerned with the Scottish Education Act which he understood to herald 'an epoch in the intellectual history of Scotland'.[38] The Act of 1872, which paralleled the English Act of 1870, was designed to provide a new national, undenominational, elementary education system by establishing state schools managed by elected school boards and funded by rates. Under the Act, attendance at either a board school or an independent school was compulsory for children between the ages of 5 and 13, while those too poor to attend the board schools would receive assistance from the Poor Law. All three Presbyterian churches were in agreement with the board schools, which provided religious instruction on the basis of the Shorter Catechism.[39] Forbes was not persuaded that the

[35] Ibid. 186–9.
[36] A. P. Forbes to W. E. Gladstone, 3 Aug. 1873, Gladstone Papers, BL 44154, fo. 312.
[37] Mackey, 200.
[38] Brechin Diocesan Synod Minutes, 1 Oct. 1874, BrMS 4. 1. 3, 186.
[39] S. and O. Checkland, *Industry and Ethos: Scotland 1832–1914* (1984), 112–13.

Act was necessary in rural areas where it would bring increased taxation, and where the transfer of schools from heritors and presbyteries, he suspected, would not be an 'unmitigated advantage'. Presumably, Forbes was anxious about the social consequences of a reduction of the traditional influence of the established Church and the principal land-owners in these areas. But whatever his worries about the country areas, Forbes was convinced that the Act was 'absolutely necessary' in the towns, where the population had outgrown the old system. Personally, he would have preferred the denominational system to have been continued, with a conscience clause allowing parents to remove their children from religious instruction. He thought such a system would have been fairer to taxpayers (possibly on the basis of user pays) and that the denominational system, with state support, could have met projected needs. A system of religious instruction based upon the Presbyterian and Calvinist Shorter Catechism was not acceptable to the Episcopal Church, since Calvinism had been rejected by that Church after 1689. Forbes therefore defended the action of the Episcopal Church in not transferring their schools to the control of school boards. The bishops had sought to secure the continuation of government grants for Episcopalian schools, while at the same time supporting board schools by acquiescing in school rates and agreeing to serve on school boards. Forbes pointed to the schools established by the Episcopal Church as one significant means by which Scottish prejudice towards his Church had been mitigated. But he thought Episcopalian Church schools in country areas would be difficult to maintain after the Act because of the higher salaries for teachers in board schools. Therefore he urged richer Episcopalians to be generous in maintaining their rural schools. He ended by defending Church schools precisely because they permitted denominational teaching, or the 'dogmatic teaching of the faith', as a necessary alternative to the non-denominational board schools which would, he thought, only teach 'a vague, sentimental Christianity'.[40]

One historian of Scottish education in the nineteenth century has pointed to the influence of secularization as providing one of the keys to understanding the growing role of the state in establishing non-denominational education. In Scotland the historical precedent of an existing national, albeit denominational, system under the old parish schools predisposed public opinion to favour a non-denominational national system of education.[41] By the 1870s, with a greatly increased population, Scotland

---

[40]   Brechin Diocesan Synod Minutes, 1 Oct. 1874, BrMS 4. 1. 3, 186.
[41]   R. D. Anderson, 'Education and the State in Nineteenth-Century Scotland', in *Economic History Review*, 2nd ser. 36 (1983), 525.

could maintain a national system of elementary education only with the resources of the state, and that inevitably meant secular pressure for a reduction in denominational teaching in public education. But the resulting non-denominational religious instruction enacted in the board schools was too unspecific to suit Forbes because, he believed, morality was based upon definite Christian beliefs as opposed to the 'latitudinarian spirit which prevails extensively in the literature of the day'.[42]

In many respects, Forbes was increasingly out of step with British society in the 1870s. His paternalism towards the poor was being challenged by the hardening of class divisions, and by movements which sought greater autonomy and less dependence for the working class. One of Forbes's curates during this time recalled that whereas previously 'a well-known clerical collar' ensured a welcome among Dundee's tenements, this began to change in the later 1870s under the influence of anti-religious socialism.[43] Forbes's paternal charity, aimed at alleviation of the poor rather than social change, began to strike less of a chord among the labouring poor than previously as the 1870s witnessed a change among some sections of the urban poor—from religious indifference or residual respect, to increasing antagonism towards religion. Forbes's attachment to a society united in bonds of hierarchical dependence no longer corresponded to the new democracy emerging with the development of Gladstonian Liberalism in the late 1860s and early 1870s. Towards the new democratic society Forbes continued to be unsympathetic, largely because he thought it a threat to the Church and to the maintenance of Christian belief. A democratic society would cut the lower orders loose from the Christian influence of the upper classes. As he had perceived in Dundee, increasing democracy would disintegrate society into sectional interests, antagonistic to one another, which would imperil society's weakest members—the poor. Democracy would also bring the laity into ecclesiastical government, threatening the precision of doctrine under the influence of theological ignorance. Forbes knew he was living in a time of social transition, but regarded most of the changes as leading to a more divided, less caring society where the influence of Christianity was endangered. So, for example, with regard to the 1872 Education Act: he appreciated the need for state involvement in education for the new urbanized society, but would have preferred state subsidy of denominational schools rather than non-denominational state education. State involvement was necessary to meet the need for popular

---

[42] Brechin Diocesan Synod Minutes, 1 Oct. 1874, BrMS 4. 1. 3, 186.
[43] Grub, *My Years in Dundee*, 12–13.

education, but Church schools remained the best means of ensuring specific Christian teaching.

Forbes's concern for the establishment and maintenance of independent Episcopal elementary schools was motivated by his Tractarianism. Believing that individual and social morality was fundamentally motivated by the beliefs a person held, he desired denominational teaching for children free from the influence of the liberal state. Independent Church schools were an expression of the spiritual independence of the Church from the Erastian state. His Tractarian dislike of Erastianism also activated Forbes's opposition to the attempt to curb ritualism in the Church of England by parliamentary legislation, in the passing of the Public Worship Regulation Act in 1874. The Act had been drafted by Archbishop Tait of Canterbury who hoped it would be a means to securing the internal unity of the Church of England, currently divided over ritualism, and, at the same time, help to retain the Church's links with the state. Parliamentary legislation to enforce liturgical uniformity became possible in 1874 because of increasing Protestant anger towards ritualist clergy who had alienated moderate opinion by their refusal to obey the admonitions of their bishops. A recently elected Conservative government, with little else on its legislative programme, was also susceptible to pressure from Tait for a statute. When passed in August 1874, the Act provided for the appointment of a barrister or ex-judge, rather than the diocesan bishop, to try ritual cases. It was the one of the last attempts by Parliament to impose legislation on the Church of England against the opposition of a substantial party of that Church's members. But the Act was unworkable when the defiance of Anglo-Catholic clergy became apparent in the imprisonment of four priests for contumacy between 1877 and 1882.[44]

In a letter to Pusey during 1874, Forbes said he thought the Public Worship Act made a *reductio ad absurdum* out of the establishment of the Church of England, because it had reduced the Church's most solemn institutions to the level of 'playthings of . . . the House of Commons'. He believed the English bishops had acted precipitately in agreeing with Tait on the need for legislative coercion. He was, moreover, convinced that the ritualist movement would be strengthened by what it perceived as persecution.[45] Forbes's further opinion on the Act, and ritualism in general, came in his 1875 synod charge. He first welcomed the relaxing of

[44] P. T. Marsh, *The Victorian Church in Decline* (1969), ch. 7.
[45] A. P. Forbes to E. B. Pusey, n.d. [1874], PP 5. 40.

ties between the landowning classes and the Church of Scotland after the abolition of lay patronage in that Church by the Church Patronage (Scotland) Act 1874. Forbes welcomed the Patronage Act as likely to increase the attachment of Episcopalian landlords towards their own Church by diminishing their responsibilities to the established Church. Forbes noted with approval the increased interest in the external beauty of worship in the Church of Scotland. This, he believed, was creating a taste for aesthetic worship which only the liturgical worship of the Episcopal Church could satisfy. While he thought the Episcopalian laity needed to be protected against clergy unilaterally introducing liturgical ritual 'disproportionate' to their congregation's religious life, he disparaged the English Public Worship Regulation Act as pandering to the 'prejudices of the British Phillistine'. Forbes believed that because this Act was opposed by many sincere and zealous clergy in the Church of England it was doomed to fail. But he also expressed his conviction that ritualism had its limitations. Both the emotional religion of the ritualists and the widespread desire for decent order in the Church, he asserted, were insufficient without first 'securing the intellectual position of the Anglican Church' upon teaching with a historical and dogmatic basis.[46] Forbes was demonstrating a characteristic Tractarian emphasis on the priority of Catholic doctrine and teaching over ritualism.

Forbes was not present at the 1875 synod because of a severe gastric illness, and his charge was read by the synod clerk. At first Forbes, with his history of sickness, was not thought to be seriously unwell, but on 7 October an English priest[47] who was staying with him heard his confession and administered the last rites of the Church. The following day, 8 October 1875, just after 8 o'clock in the evening, aged 58, Forbes died, while attended by James Nicolson and three nuns of his community.[48] His body lay in state, dressed in his episcopal robes, in the Castlehill clergyhouse. Some 5,000 people came to pay their last respects.[49] The funeral was held in St Paul's, Dundee, on 15 October, having been preceded by five celebrations of Holy Communion. It was estimated that between two and three thousand lay admirers of all classes attended, as well as clergy from England and Scotland, who processed to the church from the school in the Seagate.[50] Forbes's body, vested as a bishop and

[46] Brechin Diocesan Synod Minutes, 5 Oct. 1875, BrMs 4. 1. 3, 194–5.
[47] The Revd R. S. Hunt, Vicar of Markbeech, near Edenbridge, had attended Forbes during a previous illness. Mackey, 206.
[48] Mackey, 206–7.
[49] *Guardian*, 13 Oct. 1875, 1286.
[50] *Scottish Guardian*, 22 Oct. 1875, 219.

enclosed in three coffins, was finally laid to rest in a vault under the chancel of St Paul's, as he had requested.[51]

Pusey did not attend the funeral, telling James Nicolson that it had been 'sometime since I ceased to be able to be present at the last sad office'. The shock of his younger friend's death grieved Pusey greatly, and he choked when he tried to speak of him.[52] But, by December, Pusey was able to pen a portrait of Forbes for Henry Liddon, in which he remarked on Forbes's revived spirits in the final years of his life, after the trauma of his heresy trial.

What strikes me most about the dear Bishop in looking back are his great love, tenderness, simplicity, and self-forgetfulness, and his sensitiveness about whatever bore on doctrinal truth. That trial was like the piercing of a sword to him, for fear the truth should be compromised, or in defence lest he should any way compromise it. He did not recover the physical effects of it, in any degree, for two years . . . His happiest time was that which he spent in the hospitals by the sick, or in the alleys of Dundee, if so he might minister to souls or bodies. Then there was his utter want of self-consciousness. He had, as you know, brilliant conversational talents, yet no one could ever detect the slightest perception that he was aware of it. So also as to his theological knowledge. He had a large grasp of mind, devoted loyalty to truth, sorrow for those who had it not, tender feeling for them; but for himself utter unconsciousness of his gifts.[53]

Tributes came from many quarters. Some of those who memorialized Forbes's death found it apposite that his last-attended diocesan function—on 21 September 1875—had been the laying of the foundation stone of a new church at Stonehaven, his very first charge in the Episcopal Church. Gladstone expressed his respect and admiration for Forbes as 'a man of devoted life and labour, of wide learning, of balanced mind, uniting with a strong grasp of Catholic principles the spirit of a true historic student and a genuine zeal for literary culture'.[54] The primus, Robert Eden, commented that the history and traditions of the Episcopal Church were 'entwined with his very heartstrings'. Eden believed that Forbes's piety and 'uncompromising adherence to dogma', had restrained many people unsettled by liberal theological speculation or the prevalent Erastianism in England from seeking shelter within Roman Catholicism.[55] Newman, surprised at Forbes's death, feared for its effect on Pusey and said a mass

[51] Mackey, 208–11.
[52] Biographical note by a Miss French, Bodleian, Ms. Eng. misc., d. 1096, fos. 13–24.
[53] H. P. Liddon, *Life of Pusey* (1897), iv. 296.
[54] *Scottish Guardian*, 15 Oct. 1875, 192.
[55] *Scottish Guardian*, 22 Oct. 1875, 220.

for Forbes's soul.[56] James Nicolson, who had the task of notifying friends and acquaintances of the death, gave his opinion of his close friend in a sermon preached the Sunday after the funeral. He remarked on Forbes's delightful conversation, impressive personality, and 'deep and unaffected' piety. He recalled that when Forbes said his daily office he seemed 'penetrated through and through with religion'. Nicolson, however, did not overlook the harsher side of Forbes's character, and observed that he was often considered 'uncharitable in his judgements'. But he noted that Forbes avoided expressing judgements against those outside the Church; they were 'left in God's merciful hands'.[57] Nicolson evidently believed that Forbes's severest judgements were reserved for those within the Church who he believed were maligning or distorting dogmatic truth.

Forbes's death attracted widespread attention. A United Presbyterian minister in Dundee, George Gilfillan, referred to Forbes in a sermon as one very well known in the city. Gilfillan believed Forbes's views were, in many respects, 'exceedingly narrow', but added, 'his heart was broad. He might be called, indeed, the father of the poor in his locality, and he was unwearied night and day in his attentions to the outcast, the destitute, and the forlorn.' Recounting one incident that particularly impressed him, Gilfillan referred to a Dr George Aspinall who had come to Dundee to be the clergyman for a group of Low Church Episcopalians disaffected by Forbes's teaching (probably the Northern Irish from St Mary Magdalen's, Blunshall Street). Soon after his arrival Aspinall was stricken with paralysis and sent for Gilfillan, who was a previous acquaintance. However, when the minister arrived he found Forbes already by Aspinall's bedside. Forbes continued to care for his erstwhile opponent thoughout his illness, raised money for his needs, and petitioned the Archbishop of Canterbury on his behalf. Unfortunately, the clergyman died before something could be done. Gilfillan concluded, Forbes was 'a gentleman, a scholar, and a Christian'.[58] One of the ministers of the Church of Scotland in Dundee spoke of Forbes as a man of 'conciliation and highest Christian courtesy, by which he always disarmed prejudice and opposition'.[59] But the Evangelical *Record*, while acknowledging Forbes's 'self-denying labours', nevertheless asserted these were

---

[56] J. H. Newman to J. Nicolson, 11 Oct. 1875, *Letters and Diaries of John Henry Newman* (1975), xxvii. 366.

[57] J. Nicolson, *In Memoriam: A Sermon Preached in S. Salvador's Church, Dundee, On Sunday the 17th October, 1875, being the Sunday after the Funeral of the Right Rev. A. P. Forbes, D.C.L., Bishop of Brechin* (1875), 7.

[58] *Scottish Guardian*, 15 Oct. 1875, 192.

[59] Ibid. 192.

'calculated to exercise over others an ensnaring influence'—a recognition
of the evangelistic motivation of his Catholic piety and philanthropy
which Forbes would no doubt have been happy to acknowledge.[60] The
Daily News believed that Forbes's decision not to remain in the Church
of England, but to accept a bishopric in his native Scotland, had restricted his wider influence. At the same time, the paper admitted, 'with
the clergy of his school his name was a power'.[61] Perhaps the most
balanced tribute to Forbes came from the *Dundee Advertiser*:

> Whatever may be thought of his ecclesiastical views, his earnestness, his bene-
> volence, and his piety will long be cherished in remembrance. While naturally
> aristocratic in his tone, Bishop Forbes keenly sympathised with the masses, and
> showed this not only by his readiness to further every benevolent movement, but
> by his anxiety to heal the breaches between the divided classes. He was the first
> to call upon us during the recent strike to suggest mediation between the
> employers and employed; and in various instances when the poor were suffering
> greatly from want of employment his appeals on their behalf opened the fountains
> of public liberality.[62]

The *Guardian*, the weekly Anglican newspaper, made the perceptive
social comment that Forbes was 'more popular as a rule with the
extremes of society at each end of the social scale than with those of
the intermediate class'.[63]

   Shortly before his death, Forbes had expressed the wish for a
purpose-built episcopal residence. He said he had been feeling the effects
of living in the unsalubrious centre of Dundee for twenty-eight years
and, as the next bishop would not be incumbent of the St Paul's congregation, there was no need for his successor to live there. Forbes,
however, died before the plan could be implemented.[64] At a public meeting in Dundee on 23 October to discuss a memorial to Forbes it was
resolved that money be raised to build a house for the Bishops of
Brechin, complete with private chapel, and that another suitable memorial should be placed in St Paul's.[65] A month later subscriptions totalled
nearly £4,000, led by £500 from Forbes's beloved nephew, George
Boyle, now the sixth Earl of Glasgow. Other close friends also gave

---

[60] Quoted in ibid.
[61] Quoted in ibid.
[62] Quoted in ibid.
[63] *Guardian*, 13 Oct. 1875, 1286.
[64] *Scottish Guardian*, 10 Dec. 1875, 321.
[65] Eventually the episcopal residence was built at Broughty Ferry, but it was sold by the
diocese earlier this century. The memorial in St Paul's, Dundee, in the form of a recum-
bent statue of Bishop Forbes in his episcopal robes, still survives in the cathedral's chancel.

generously, including £100 each from Lord Kinnaird, Forbes's former chaplain Roger Lingard-Guthrie, and Forbes's eldest brother William. Other English and Scottish Churchmen who contributed included the primus, James Nicolson, Canon Henry Liddon, his old vicar Thomas Chamberlain, and the Brotherhood of the Holy Trinity.[66] Gladstone gave £150.[67] Another meeting to foster the memorial was held in the chapter house of St Paul's Cathedral, London, in early December 1875. Canon Henry Liddon, the leading Anglo-Catholic, in proposing the resolution to support the Scottish memorial fund, said he had known Forbes as a close friend for many years. As a man, Liddon said Forbes was distinguished by qualities of tenderness and moral courage. As a bishop, Liddon recalled his first visit to Dundee, where he was surprised by the experience of having all the men they passed take their hats off to Forbes. Referring to the respect accorded to the Episcopal bishop, Liddon remarked that it was 'almost impossible for me to believe that I was in a Presbyterian city'. When Liddon observed to Forbes that he seemed to have a very large flock, Forbes dismissed the acknowledgements with a modest remark, 'Oh! they are very good natured'. Liddon was none the less convinced that the people of Dundee recognized Forbes as a 'great chief of the Church of Christ' despite their Presbyterian prejudices against bishops.[68] But Liddon believed that Forbes's greatest significance was as a theologian. Here, Liddon believed, Forbes's fondness for a priori reasoning and fine distinctions was restrained by his dedication to what was historically true. 'He wished to be true', affirmed Liddon, 'to all that the undivided Church had really taught, and to nothing whatever beyond.' Dean Richard Church of St Paul's, however, remembered the far-off days when the Tractarians were ascendent at Oxford, and he recalled seeing Forbes there for the first time as an undergraduate in Newman's company. Perhaps of all the obituaries it was Church who encapsulated all that Forbes, as a rejuvenated Tractarian, would most have valued, when he described him as 'one of those who received and maintained in their purest form the best influences of the great movement with which Dr Newman's name was associated'.[69]

---

[66] *Scottish Guardian*, 19 Nov. 1875, 273.
[67] *Guardian*, 8 Dec. 1875, 1568.
[68] Ibid. The doffing of hats may have had more to do with respect for Forbes's philanthropy than for his episcopal rank.
[69] Ibid.

EPILOGUE

FOR all his significant influence in his own day Alexander Forbes has been largely overlooked by historians. Not only is the historiography on Forbes meagre, but so is that on the Oxford Movement in Scotland. Most of the research into the Oxford Movement in Britain has focused on the Church of England. This was inevitable given that the Catholic revival begun by the Movement originated there and, being the largest single Christian body in Britain during the nineteenth century, the revival had its widest ecclesiastical and social impact in England. Aside from the works referred to below, and William Perry's biography of George Forbes, virtually the only published work primarily on the Oxford Movement in Scotland is an essay published by A. MacLean in 1984 about the changes wrought by the Catholic revival on Episcopalian worship during the past two centuries.[1] The Scottish Episcopal Church during the nineteenth century has also attracted little contemporary historical research, apart from two articles from the 1960s.[2] More recently, some invaluable attention has been paid to the Episcopal Church as a consequence of scholars researching old High Churchmanship in the Church of England. The thesis of Dr Peter Nockles points to the discontinuities between the northern High Churchmanship and the Tractarians, while Professor Frank Mather's monograph on Bishop Samuel Horsley reveals the strength of pre-Tractarian support for the Scottish Episcopal Church by English High Churchmen.[3]

Perhaps the comparative paucity of research into the Scottish Episcopal Church owes something to historians' preferences. A Church

---

[1] A. MacLean, 'Episcopal Worship in the Nineteenth and Twentieth Centuries', in D. Forrester and D. Murray (eds), *Studies in the History of Worship in Scotland* (1984), 96–112.

[2] R. Foskett, 'The Episcopate of Daniel Sandford 1810–30', in *RSCHS* 15 (1966), 141–52; and 'The Drummond Controversy 1842', in *RSCHS* 16 (1969), 99–109. There are also two recent theses on the 19th-c. Episcopal Church, but these contain little original research. They are: D. W. T. Crooks, 'The Effects of the Oxford Movement in the Scottish Episcopal Church in the Nineteenth Century', BD thesis, (Trinity College, Dublin, 1983); and A. E. Nimmo, 'Charles Wordsworth, Bishop of St. Andrews 1853–1892: Reconciler or Controversialist', M.Phil. thesis (University of Edinburgh, 1983).

[3] Peter Nockles, 'Continuity and Change in Anglican High Churchmanship in Britain 1792–1850', D.Phil. thesis (University of Oxford, 1982), ch. 7, 529–601; F. Mather, *High Church Prophet: Bishop Samuel Horsley (1733–1806) and the Caroline Tradition in the Later Georgian Church* (1992), ch. 7, 117–38.

commonly regarded as largely upper-class has not attracted the attention of modern historians of the nineteenth century, who have been generally oriented towards working-class movements. But even a small, predominantly upper-class Church was influential in nineteenth-century Scottish society and deserves more attention than it has hitherto received. Nor did the Episcopal Church's aristocratic and landed connections mean that it was without allegiance or contact among the lower orders, even the very lowest, as Forbes's ministry indicates.

However, while social factors are very important in ecclesiastical history, E. R. Norman's caution about judging the Churches only by their social engagement needs to be heeded. In the nineteenth century, the social dimension of Church work was, for most Churchmen, only a consequence of what Norman calls their 'pursuit of eternity'.[4] It would be an anachronistic distortion to focus on Church ministry to the labouring poor in that century (or lack of it) without understanding that it was a consequence of Christian belief. In Forbes's case, this would be to highlight his ministry in the urban slums of Dundee without also giving priority to the major event of his ecclesiastical life—his being tried for doctrinal error. To understand nineteenth-century Churchmen (including Forbes) in their own terms, it is necessary to appreciate the fundamental importance they ascribed to doctrine and correct belief.

The most negative historical opinion of Bishop Forbes is that of Andrew Drummond and James Bulloch who consider that his influence was confined to the Episcopal Church, having 'no more effect on the average Scot than had Pusey, let us say, among English Methodists'.[5] The most laudatory opinion is that of Forbes's earlier twentieth-century biographer, William Perry. The first begs the question about just who constituted 'the average Scot', seeming to exclude Episcopalians, or non-Presbyterians, by definition. The second, by equating Forbes with Edward Pusey in England, has given him far too much prominence within the Scottish nation. The truth may lie, as so often, between the two extremes. Forbes, as bishop and worker among the labouring poor, was neither so unknown to Scots as Drummond and Bulloch assert, nor so influential within Scotland as Perry believed. Certainly Forbes was significant in both the Episcopal Church, the Church of England, and the working classes of Dundee, as the most important leader of early Tractarianism in Scotland.

Perry found Forbes to be 'the Scottish Pusey', and his Church, at least in its northern areas, to be 'by conviction and sympathy Tractarians

---

4 E. R. Norman, *Church and Society in England 1770–1970* (1976), 5.

5 A. Drummond and J. Bulloch, *The Church in Victorian Scotland 1843–1874* (1975), 212.

long before the Tracts for the Times were written'.[6] Perry, Dean of
Edinburgh and a convinced high churchman, was writing in the 1930s,
the decade in which the centenary of the Oxford Movement (1933) was
celebrated. It was a period when the Anglo-Catholic party was predomi-
nant in British Anglicanism (except in the Church of Ireland), and when
Anglo-Catholicism had virtually captured the Scottish Episcopal Church.
Consequently, Perry believed the influence of Forbes and Anglo-
Catholicism upon the Episcopal Church to be entirely benign. The
Tractarians were regarded as the revivifying heirs of the northern High
Churchmen. It was this old northern nonjuring tradition that Perry
regarded as a precursor to the Oxford Movement, and, therefore, he
held the Oxford Movement as essentially continuous with that older
Episcopalian High Churchmanship. 'To the Churchmanship of the
north', asserted Perry, 'the Oxford Movement could contribute nothing
in the shape of Christian doctrine.'[7] For Perry, this harmony of northern
Episcopalianism with Tractarianism stood in contrast with the south of
Scotland where Episcopalians were unable to stomach that epitome of the
northern tradition, the Scottish Communion Office, because 'it was too
strong [i.e. Catholic] for their spiritual constitutions'.[8] Southerners preferred instead the more moderate Churchmanship of the Book of
Common Prayer and the Church of England. Perry believed Forbes to be
the personification of this northern Episcopalian-Tractarian continuity,
whose Tractarian beliefs were therefore welcomed by the northerners for
re-energizing their tradition, and opposed only by the Anglicized southerners. It was this Scottish–English conflict that Perry saw lying behind
the Eucharistic controversy and the condemnation of Forbes's 1857
diocesan charge.

This interpretation stressing the continuity between Scottish Episcopalianism and Tractarianism, and the beneficial effect of the later
tradition upon the earlier, continues to prevail in more recent historical
works. The only other modern monograph on the nineteenth-century
Episcopal church, by Marion Lochhead, inclines to the hagiographical
and the anecdotal. But Lochhead is reliant upon Perry for her understanding of the Oxford Movement in Scotland and also sees Forbes as
responsible for adding Tractarian vigour to the nonjuring heritage.[9] Two
articles have lately also perpetuated this historiography whereby the
Oxford Movement is hailed as the successor and resuscitator of

   [6] W. Perry, *The Oxford Movement in Scotland* (1933), 37.
   [7] Ibid.   [8] Ibid. 38.
   [9] M. Lochhead, *Episcopal Scotland in the Nineteenth Century* (1966), 106.

Episcopalianism. Gavin White sees Tractarianism in Scotland as simply a 'new name' for an 'old thing', and confines opposition to the Oxford Movement largely to separated Evangelical congregations.[10] Gibb Pennie in his work on the trial of Patrick Cheyne maintains that the Oxford Movement in Scotland was 'responsible for helping to rescue the Scottish Episcopal Church from years of gloom and depression', and was therefore welcomed by the northern Episcopalians.[11]

This prevailing historiography might be described as Anglo-Catholic as it first emerges in the various histories of Scottish Episcopalianism written by Tractarians and Anglo-Catholics, supremely by Perry, but stretching back to include Forbes's nineteenth-century memorialist D. J. Mackey.[12] Its earliest expression is found in J. P. Lawson's *History of the Scottish Episcopal Church from the Revolution to the Present Time* (1843). Lawson, writing during the Oxford Movement itself, is concerned to refute contemporary accusations of Romanism levelled at the Oxford Movement by stressing Tractarian sympathy for the Nonjurors.[13]

Although it has had a lengthy life this Anglo-Catholic historiography needs to be extensively revised. Outside the Church of England, Scotland was one of the first countries the Catholic revival migrated to after England and where there had been for centuries an Episcopalian presence. During the seventeenth century that tradition was maintained within the Church of Scotland by royal government. Following the overthrow of the Stuart James VII and II in 1688, proscription of Episcopalians as Nonjurors, and the consequent triumph of Presbyterianism in the Church of Scotland, there arose a distinct Episcopal Church with a developing nonjuring High Church theology. What then happened when the Oxford Movement encountered the Scottish Episcopal Church which, unlike the Church of England, was, by the nineteenth century, more uniformly High Church in its theology and outlook? As Forbes was the outstanding exponent of the Oxford Movement in the Scottish Episcopal Church from 1847 until 1875 his life offers a challenge to the standard answer of Anglo-Catholic historiography in two major areas— the continuity between northern Episcopalianism and Tractarianism, and the revitalizing of Scottish Episcopacy by the Oxford Movement.

---

[10] G. White, 'New Names for Old Things: Scottish Reaction to Early Tractarianism' in D. Baker (ed.), *Renaissance and Renewal in Christian History* (1977), 329–37.
[11] G. N. Pennie, 'The Trial of the Rev. Patrick Cheyne for Erroneous Teaching of the Eucharist in Aberdeen in 1858', in *RSCHS* 23 (1987), 77–93.
[12] D. J. Mackey, *Bishop Forbes: A Memoir* (1888), pp. xxiff.
[13] J. P. Lawson, *History of the Scottish Episcopal Church from the Revolution to the Present Time* (1843), pp. viiiff.

Forbes was more confident in his earlier life of the fundamental
similarity between the old nonjuring theology of the Episcopal Church
and Tractarianism than he became later. In his novella of 1846 he had
affirmed that it was this nonjuring High Church theology and the
Scottish liturgy which maintained 'the harmonies of Catholic truth' when
England was captivated by Protestant Latitudinarianism during the
eighteenth century. But because of the polarization of the Eucharistic
controversy, Forbes began to identify this Catholic truth with the new
Tractarian doctrine of the real, objective presence of Christ in the
Eucharist. Under the influence of his developing Tractarianism the claims
of the northern tradition to the fullness of Catholic faith began to appear
more dubious. Forbes believed Tractarian theology was a rediscovery of
the Catholic theology of the Fathers of the early Church, and therefore
that patristic teaching had also to be Episcopalian theology in order for
the Episcopal body to be a part of the Catholic Church. But the
Eucharistic virtualism of most Episcopalians, which was representative of
the mainstream of northern theological tradition, was understood by
Forbes and the Tractarian leadership as a dangerous compromise with
Catholic truth.[14] It was Forbes's Tractarian Eucharistic theology, unprecedented in Scottish High Churchmanship, which provoked the Eucharistic controversy by its similarites to Roman Catholicism. That quarrel was
not between a more Catholic northern tradition versus a moderate
English Anglicanism as Perry claimed, but between Tractarianism represented by Forbes, and the virtualistic High Church theology common to
both Scottish (northerners and southerners) and English High Churchmen. By the end of the Eucharistic controversy Forbes, disillusioned by
the amount of opposition to his signs of catholicity among Churchmen he
had previously regarded as inheritors of Catholicism in Scotland, was
equating the Episcopal attitudes to Tractarianism with the Anglican
Church's belief in the mediation of the Blessed Virgin Mary! If this belief
was true, then the Anglican Church differed from the other two branches
of Catholic Christianity and was consequently 'heretical on the point'. Or
it was false, in which case Anglicanism still differed from the other two
Churches which meant that 'any other doctrine they held in common was
no guarantee for sound doctrine'.[15] Forbes's inference was that the
Anglican Church either accepted the Tractarian standard of Catholicism
as equated with the faith of Rome and Constantinople and was thus
Catholic herself, or that there was no practical standard of Catholicism

[14]   E. B. Pusey to J. Keble, 29 Sept. 1862, PK vi.
[15]   A. P. Forbes to J. Keble, n.d. [? Advent 1860], PK vi.

available. Either way, it appeared to Forbes by 1860 that the Episcopal Church had largely rejected Catholicism according to the Tractarian ideal, a rejection caused in part by the Eucharistic theology and practice predominant in the northern tradition. By 1860 Forbes could no longer confidently assert that Episcopalianism and Tractarianism were two sides of the same Catholic coin. This belief was substantiated by the lack of support for his Eucharistic doctrine among northern Churchmen during the controversy, and also for the Scottish Communion Office during his campaign in the 1860s. If even northern clergy were not prepared to uphold Forbes's two major indicators of Catholic faith—the Scottish Office and the objective Eucharistic presence—then how could the Episcopal Church be completely Catholic? It did not occur to Forbes that in regard to Eucharistic presence he was being anachronistic, demanding that Episcopal tradition espouse a Eucharistic theology that Church had not known until it was set forth by the Tractarians. Therefore by the time of the Eucharistic controversy and the fight over the Communion Office Forbes was expressing his equivocations about the harmony of Tractarian belief with that of the northern tradition, a disharmony that was epitomized in the divergence of himself and his brother George during the Eucharistic controversy.

The more militant and dismissive attitude of the few Scottish Anglo-Catholics towards Anglicanism during the Eucharistic controversy, as compared with Forbes and the Tractarian leadership, is a further indica-tion of the discontinuity of the Oxford Movement and High Church Episcopalianism. According to the most vocal exponent of this small group centred around St Ninian's cathedral, Canon Henry Humble, 'truth will not coalesce with error' as regards Eucharistic doctrine, by which Humble meant Tractarian truth would naturally prevail over High Church error. Humble therefore desired the perpetuation of divisions rather than peace based on a compromise with untruth, especially when such a reconciliation would have for its object 'the termination of distur-bances which have arisen in trying to teach the Catholic Faith'.[16] During Forbes's negotiations with Terrot, Keble and Pusey drew Forbes's attention to the way in which such Anglo-Catholics disparaged Anglican tradition as a watered-down Catholicism. Pusey, for example, believed the final position of Forbes in this conciliation would be dismissed only by those 'who wish to force on in the Tridentine language'; those who would 'of course, call us Anglicans, in contempt'.[17]

[16] H. Humble to A. P. Forbes, 5 Jan. 1860, BrMs 1. 2. 325.
[17] E. B. Pusey to A. P. Forbes, n.d. [Dec. 1859], BrMs 1. 2. 292.

Far from Tractarianism reviving a moribund Episcopal Church, with which it was in fundamental theological agreement, the Eucharistic controversy demonstrates the degree to which Tractarianism was a source of division among Episcopalians, not just through English Anglo-Catholic imports into Scotland, but also among Scottish clergy. When Forbes and Patrick Cheyne attempted to proclaim the harmony of Tractarianism with Episcopalian tradition, by interpreting Episcopalian Eucharistic doctrine according to Tractarian theology, they were condemned. Cheyne's condemnation by the bishops brought a strong reaction from among a significant minority of northern clergy of whom twenty-four were present at the Stonehaven protest meeting to hear with approval a letter from Pusey and Keble.[18] These included an even smaller but fervent group of younger clergy, like Daniel Sandford of Edinburgh diocese who, agreeing with Henry Humble, wanted a more confrontational approach to what they perceived as Episcopalian compromise with truth. Sandford expressed views indicative of Tractarian divisiveness within the Episcopal Church when he told Forbes following the Stonehaven meeting, 'I confess I am beginning to feel strongly the strange nature of a Communion which claims your Lordship on the one hand—& the Bps. of Glasgow and S. Andrews on the other—as exponents of its theology. I dont know whether it serves the cause of Truth that two opposite religions shd. thus be forced into an external semblance of harmony & union.'[19] Evidently, during the controversial years of the later 1850s and early 1860s, Forbes's Tractarianism was a divisive innovation in the Episcopal Church, rather than a revitalizing restatement of Scottish High Churchmanship.

This revision of early Scottish Tractarianism as initially a source of contention within the Episcopal Church needs to be set alongside its propensity to be both a force for and against Anglicization in Scotland. On the one hand, in the case of the St Ninian's clergy, Anglo-Catholicism was an English standard of Catholicism which found Scottish High Churchmanship wanting. Forbes's Tractarianism also came to the same conclusion regarding Eucharistic doctrine. However, on the other hand, his Tractarianism could also come to the defence of native Scottish tradition in the form of the Scottish Communion Office. This is clear, despite a recent article in which Christopher Knight argues that Forbes exacerbated Episcopalian divisions by being one of the Anglicizing influences within his Church.[20] Although, as Dr Knight

[18] J. Moir to A. P. Forbes, 19 Nov. 1858, BrMs 1. 1. 13 (i).
[19] D. Sandford to A. P. Forbes, 24 Nov. 1858, BrMs 1. 1. 16.
[20] C. Knight, 'The Anglicising of Scottish Episcopalianism', in *RSCHS* 23 (1989), 361–77.

points out, Forbes was critical of the inadequacy of Scottish nonjuring Eucharistic theology, Knight fails to make clear that Forbes very much preferred the Scottish Communion Office to the English Book of Common Prayer when it came to expressing his Eucharistic theology. He was also partial to the native liturgy precisely because it was the worship of earlier Scottish Episcopalians who had borne the distress of illegality and persecution in the eighteenth century. To forgo the nonjuring Office in the 1860s seemed to Forbes too much like a betrayal of these hard-pressed forebears in the faith. Despite the undoubted Anglicizing influences in his own life—his education, the Oxford Movement and his English friends, and his early ministry in the Church of England—Forbes retained all his life his family's affection for, and belief in, the superiority of the Scottish liturgy to its English counterpart. This was not a common belief among all Tractarians, among whom many in England preferred the Book of Common Prayer for what they believed to be its greater similarity to the Roman missal. But Forbes's family background combined with his Tractarianism to decide in favour of the Scottish liturgy. It was, ultimately, his Tractarian theological convictions that found the Scottish Communion Office to be more explicitly Catholic in its liturgical form and theological expression than the English rite, and these caused Forbes to defend the Office so vehemently in the early 1860s. Without that campaign led by Forbes the Episcopal Church would have succumbed to a greater degree of Anglicization than it did in the later nineteenth century. Forbes therefore enabled the Scottish Communion Office, a significant representation of Scottishness in Episcopalianism, to be retained in the use of the Episcopal Church until it could be revalued as a major heritage by a succeeding generation of Episcopalians led by John Dowden, Bishop of Edinburgh from 1872 until 1910.

In contrast with Forbes's emphasis on the value of these national Episcopalian traditions was the importance he placed on the Scottish Episcopal Church being a part of the universal Catholic Church. In fact these local traditions he valued only because he regarded them as authentic manifestations of the Church Catholic. This link between local or national Church and the universal Church led Forbes and other Anglo-Catholics to seek for what they called 'corporate reunion' with the Churches they identified as the other branches of Catholicism— the Orthodox and the Roman Catholic. Forbes was particularly drawn into this intermittent campaign by his appreciation of the tiny size of the Scottish Episcopal Church, which made it more difficult for him to rest content with his own Church as a branch of the Catholic tree. Forbes found it, at times, more of a twig compared with the great trunk of the Roman Church he knew intimately from his European travels and contacts.

The Anglo-Catholic desire for institutional union with Rome was, of course, very divisive within the Church of England and the Episcopal Church. It could hardly be otherwise given the traditional mutual enmity between these Churches since the sixteenth century which was still prominent in nineteenth-century Anglicanism. Nevertheless, despite the divisiveness it created at the time, Anglo-Catholic corporate reunionism does represent a pioneering ecumenical endeavour, albeit a restricted one. Anglo-Catholics and Tractarians, like Forbes, had little time for the Protestant Churches which they generally regarded as outside the Catholic Church, and were sometimes rather fixated on Rome.

For Forbes the Church of Rome became increasingly attractive throughout his personal and ecclesiastical battles of the late 1850s and early 1860s. These conflicts did not initiate his desire for Catholic reunion, which dated back at least to his involvement with the Association for the Promotion of the Unity of Christendom in 1857. But his ensuing anxieties created by the Eucharistic controversy and his defence of the Scottish Communion Office made Rome desirable to Forbes personally in comparison with his own Church. Rome represented to him a Catholicism unmixed or untainted by the Protestantism and Erastianism he ascribed to his opponents. Rome was also a powerful example of ecclesiastical unity and authoritative doctrine which mightily appealed to Forbes, who felt he was a victim of Anglican divisions and diversity of doctrine in his disputes. He was teaching and upholding the Catholic faith and was being condemned for it by those who also drew support from Anglican formularies and the example of the Church of England. He believed no such confusion over essentials like Eucharistic doctrine and liturgy existed in the life and *magisterium* of Roman Catholicism. So, in 1862, Forbes came extremely close to turning his back on the old hopes of corporate reunion between the Anglican and Roman Churches, and opting instead for his own individual conversion. However, once the Scottish Communion Office had secured a continuing place in the Episcopal Church Forbes returned to his earlier reunion aspirations, although his own uncertainties continued for a while. It was Forbes's increasing involvement in Pusey's reunion campaign between 1867 and 1869 which eventually disabused him of his Roman fever. Paradoxically, it was precisely those things which Forbes most admired about the

Roman Church which caused his disillusionment with it. The Roman Catholic unity and teaching authority to which Forbes was drawn were just those qualities which were defended by the prevailing Ultramontanism. As Forbes discovered in his 1868 trip to Rome, and his correspondence with Victor de Buck, the predominant ultramontanists had no time for anything less than Anglican submission to the existing Roman Church, and certainly did not intend to enter into modifications to Roman teaching just to appease what they regarded as a Protestant heresy. As de Buck focused more and more on Forbes's personal conversion, so he insisted on corporate reunion. In Forbes's case reunion languished with the promulgation of the decree of papal infallibility at the Vatican Council in 1870. But by then his distaste for ultramontane Catholicism had reawakened Forbes's appreciation of the effects of the Oxford Movement in the Anglican Church, especially in regard to the increased Catholic piety of many Anglicans, higher standards of clerical life among the younger clergy, and the restoration of religious life. These, he felt, were signs of divine grace which demonstrated that God was surely blessing the Anglican Church. He also believed that, while his own Church was grievously divided from the rest of Catholic Christendom, it was at least without the illegitimate additions to the faith of the early Church found in Roman Catholicism-papal infallibility and the 'excesses' of the Marian cult.

Forbes's untimely death in 1875 cut off what may have become an even more prominent leadership in the Scottish Episcopal Church. The 1870s was a period of renewed high church predominance in the Church of England, and Anglo-Catholicism was beginning its lasting rise within the Scottish Episcopal Church. Also, by 1875 Forbes had been joined by one or two like-minded men among the Scottish bishops. Given his preeminence, these factors would possibly have furthered Forbes's influence which may, in turn, have increased the Episcopal Church's social involvement. But, in one important respect, it would have made the Episcopal Church a hostage to the future. Dogmatic theology was not the solution for religious doubt that Forbes believed it to be. The future of Anglicanism lay with an acceptance of biblical criticism, and that of Anglo-Catholicism with the liberal Catholicism of men like Bishop Charles Gore. These both impacted upon Anglicanism in the essays of *Lux Mundi* in 1889. Forbes's attachment to a pre-critical dogmatic theology would have led the Episcopal Church into a historical dead-end, and only increased its difficulties in accepting the insights of the *Lux Mundi* school.

Yet there is some truth in the old Anglo–Catholic historiography, even though its claims for Tractarianism were excessive. As represented by Forbes Tractarianism made a gainful impact upon the Scottish Episcopal Church in addition to bringing division. As the first Tractarian bishop, he was an inspiration and a leader to many in his lifetime, both within his own Church and in the Church of England. Forbes sought to uphold the independence of the Church against Erastianism and secularism by promoting within the Episcopal Church the rising influence of Tractarianism. His Tractarian commitment to the labouring poor was an admirable initiative difficult to make for a man of his refined sensibilities. Yet it was this sacrificial personal example among Dundee's slums, more than his Tractarian doctrine, that did most to legitimize and encourage the Catholic revival in the Scottish Episcopal Church. Forbes was a fundamental catalyst both in making the Episcopal Church more responsive to the needs of Scottish society, and in making Scotland more aware of the Episcopal Church. He brought a breadth and depth of theological and pastoral vision to the small Episcopal Church unequalled by his peers among the Scottish bishops. Being at the forefront of early ecumenical initiatives by Anglicans of the Catholic revival made Forbes's name familiar to many influential European Roman Catholics. His widespread connections in England and Europe helped to make the Scottish Episcopal Church known far beyond Scotland, and exposed that Church to various religious movements beyond its borders. Yet for all his national and international involvement in his own day, it is the example of Forbes's sacrificial and unstinting work among the poor of Dundee's streets and tenements which most endures to this.

APPENDIX CANON XXX

The final Canon XXX read as follows:

Of Holy Communion

1. Whereas the Episcopal Church in Scotland, under the guidance of divers learned and orthodox Bishops, has long adopted and extensively used a Form for the celebration of the Holy Communion, known by the name of the 'Scotch Communion Office', it is hereby enacted that the adoption of the Book of Common Prayer as the Service Book of this Church shall not affect the practice of the Congregations of this Church which now use the said Scotch Communion Office. In such congregations the use of the said Scotch Communion Office shall be continued, unless the Incumbent and a majority of the Communicants shall concur in disusing it.

2. The Office of the Book of Common Prayer shall be used in all new Congregations, unless the majority of the applicants mentioned in Canon XX, section 1, shall declare to the Bishop at the time of sending their resolutions to him that they desire the use of the Scotch Office in the new Congregation, in which case the Bishop shall sanction such use. The use of the said Office shall be continued in such Congregation, unless the Clergyman and a majority of the Communicants shall concur in disusing it.

3. Whenever it may appear to the Bishop that any undue influence has been exercised in an application for the use of the Scotch Office, it shall be in his power to refuse such application, subject to an appeal to the Episcopal Synod.

4. At all Consecrations, Ordinations, and Synods, the Communion Office of the Book of Common Prayer shall be used.

5. In every Congregation the Holy Sacrament of the Lord's Supper shall be administered on the Great Festivals of the Church, and at least once in every month, except under special circumstances, to be approved of by the Bishop.

6. In the use of either the Scotch or the English Office, no amalgamation, alteration, or interpolation whatever shall take place.

7. Every Clergyman shall observe the Rubrics applicable to the Office used.

8. When persons join a Congregation, with the intention of remaining therein, they shall, previously to receiving Holy Communion, produce, if required by the Clergyman, from the Incumbent of the Congregation to which they previously belonged, or, in the event of the Incumbency of the

[*Code of Canons of the Scottish Episcopal Church* (1863), 29–31.]

Congregation being vacant, from a Communicant of this Church, an attestation that they are Communicants in the Episcopal Church.

BIBLIOGRAPHY

1. Works published as A. P. Forbes

Forbes, A. P., 'On Religious Guilds', *Ecclesiastic*, 1 (1846), 49–53.

'Parochial Work in France', *Ecclesiastic*, 1 (1846), 81–9.

'The Revolution and the Nonjurors', *Ecclesiastic*, 1 (1846), 213–22.

A Catechism to be Learnt before the Church Catechism (London, n.d.).

A Companion to the Altar, Adapted to the Office for the Holy Communion According to the Use of the Scottish Church (Aberdeen, 1847).

Questions for Self-Examination for the Use of the Clergy (London, 1848).

Jesus our Worship: A Sermon Preached at the Consecration of St. Columba's Church, Edinburgh (Edinburgh, 1848).

The Cry of the Prophet: A Sermon Preached in St. Mary's, Montrose, on the Occasion of the Death of the Rev. Leonard Morse, B. A. Oxon. (Montrose, 1848).

A Plea for Sisterhoods (London, n.d. [1849]).

Haggai's Mission: A Sermon (Edinburgh, 1849).

The Christian's Foundation: A Sermon Preached in St. John's Chapel, Aberdeen, on the Occasion of Laying the First Stone of a New Church under the Same Dedication (Aberdeen, 1849).

The Christian's Converse: A Practical Treatise (London, 1849).

(ed.), *Meditations on the Suffering Life on Earth of our Lord and Only Saviour. From the French of Pinart* (London, 1850).

A Commentary on the Te Deum (London, 1850).

A Short Explanation of the Nicene Creed, for the Use of Persons Beginning the Study of Theology (Oxford, 1852; 2nd. edn. 1866).

Cantus [A. P. Forbes], *A Letter to the Right Reverend Father in God, William Skinner, D. D., Bishop of Aberdeen, and Primus of the Church in Scotland, on the Subject of the Rt. Hon. W. E. Gladstone's Proposal to Admit the Laity into the Synods of that Church* (Edinburgh, 1852).

The Prisoners of Craigmacaire: A Story of the '46 (London, 1852).

(ed.), *The Nourishment of the Christian Soul: or Mental Prayer Rendered Easy by Meditation on the Passion of our Lord Jesus Christ. With Exercises and Prayers. From the French of Pinart* (London, 1852).

A Commentary on the Canticles, Used in the Divine Service (London, 1853).

'Go thy way, shew thyself to the priest'. *An Earnest Exhortation to Confession* (London, 1853).

The Holiness of the Human Body (London, 1853).

The Duties of Society (London, 1853).

(trans. and adapted), *Memoriale Vitae Sacerdotalis or Solemn Warning of the Good Shepherd Jesus Christ. A Work of Devotion for the Use of the Clergy. From the Latin of Arvisinet. Adapted to the Use of the Anglican Church* (London, 1853).

Suffering; the Great Earthly Sanctifier: A Sermon Preached in St. Paul's Church, in Behalf of the Dundee Royal Infirmary, on the Fifth Sunday in Lent, 1853 (Dundee, 1853).

A Memoir of the Pious Life and Holy Death of Helen Inglis (London, 1854).

A Commentary on the Litany (London, 1855).

Are You Being Converted? A Course of Sermons on Serious Subjects (London, 1856).

A Commentary on the Seven Penitential Psalms (London, 3rd. edn. 1857).

Sermons on the Amendment of Life (London, 1857).

Primary Charge to the Clergy of his Diocese at the Annual Synod (London, 1857).

Opinion in the Appeal of the Rev. Cheyne against the Sentence of the Bishop of Aberdeen (Edinburgh, 1858).

A Letter to the Congregation of S. Paul's, Dundee (1859).

Answers for the Right Rev. Dr. Alexander Penrose Forbes, Bishop of Brechin to the Presentment against Him at the Instance of the Rev. William Henderson, Incumbent of St. Mary's, Arbroath, and Patrick Wilson and David Smith, Vestrymen of Said Church (Edinburgh, 1860).

Theological Defence for the Right Rev. Alexander Penrose Forbes, D. C. L., Bishop of Brechin, on a Presentment by the Rev. W. I . Henderson, and Others, on Certain Points Concerning the Doctrine of the Holy Eucharist (London, 1860).

Reply to the Pleadings in the Case Henderson and Others versus the Bishop of Brechin, before the Episcopal Synod of the Scottish Episcopal Church (Edinburgh, 1860).

The Waning of Opportunities and Other Sermons, Practical and Doctrinal (London, 1860).

A Charge Delivered to the Dundee, on the 27th of August, 1862 (Dundee, 1862).

Sermons on the Grace of God and Other Cognate Subjects (London, 1862).

The Sanctity of Christian Art: A Sermon Preached at the Reopening of the Chapel at Roslin on Easter Tuesday, 1862 (Edinburgh, 1862).

A Sermon Preached at the Chapel Royal, Savoy Street, Strand, before the Church Penitentiary Association on Thursday, May 12, 1864 (London, 1864).

The Notes of Unity and Sanctity in Reference to Modern Scepticism (London, 1864).

'Account of a manuscript of the Eleventh Century by Marianus of Ratisbon', in *Proceedings of the Society of Antiquaries in Scotland*, 6 (1864), 33–41.

and Forbes, G. H. (ed.), *Liber Ecclesiae Beati Terrenani de Arbuthnott: Missale Secundum usum Ecclesiae Sancti Andreae in Scotia* (Burntisland, 1864).

Η ΘΕΙΑ ΛΕΙΤΟΥΡΓΙΑ: *The Scottish Office Done into Greek* (London, 1865).

The Seal of the Lord: A Catechism on Confirmation (London, 1866).

ed., *Meditations on the Passion of our Lord Jesus Christ, According to the Four Evangelists, by the Abbot of Monte Cassino* (London, 1866).

Our Lord; The Sufficing Manifestation of the Eternal Father in Nature and in Grace: A Sermon (Dundee, 1867).

An Explanation of the Thirty Nine Articles (2 vols., Oxford, 1867–8).

'Some Account of Robert Watson, with Reference to a Portrait of him, Painted by Professor Vogel von Vogelstein, now Presented to the Museum', in *Proceedings of the Society of Antiquaries in Scotland*, 7 (1867–8), 324–34.

'On Greek Rites in the West', in O. Shipley (ed.), *The Church and the World: Essays on Questions of the Day* (London, 2nd. edn. 1868).

'Notice of the Ancient Bell of St. Fillan', in *Proceedings of the Society of Antiquaries in Scotland*, 8 (1869–70), 265–76.

Draft of the Order for Evening Prayer on Sundays, in Addition to that Provided in the Book of Common Prayer (London, 1870).

Notes of Eight Meditations Given at a Retreat for Clergy Held in Dundee by the Bishop of Brechin in November 1869, ed. J. Nicolson (Dundee, printed for private circulation, 1870).

The Body is for the Lord. The Substance of a Sermon Preached . . . in Behalf of the Church Penitentiary Association, on Thursday, May 4th, 1871 (London, 1871).

The Church of England and the Doctrine of Papal Infallibility (Oxford, 1871).

(ed.), *Kalendars of Scottish Saints* (Edinburgh, 1872).

The Claims of the Laity to Vote as Constituent Members of Synod Practically Considered: A Charge Delivered to the Synod of Brechin on the 2d of October 1873. To which is Appended a Pastoral Letter on the Same Subject Issued in 1870 (Dundee, 1873).

Lives of S. Ninian and S. Kentigern (Edinburgh, 1874).

The End of the Way, the Beginning of the Life (Dundee, 1874).

Letter to the Congregation of S. Paul's, Dundee (1875).

(ed.), *Remains of the Late Rev. Arthur West Haddan* (Oxford, 1876).

Of the Deepening of the Spiritual Life (Edinburgh, 1884).

2. Manuscripts

Aberdeen Papers, BL MS 43247.

Baldoven Institute minute books, DUL THB 8. 3. 1–3.

Blackwood Papers, NLS MSS 4061, 4186, 4192, 4209.

Blomfield Papers, LPL v. 39.

Brechin Diocese Papers, Dundee University Library.

Brotherhood of the Holy Trinity Papers, Pusey House, Oxford.

Burton (John Hill) Papers, NLS MSS 9397, 9398, 9399.

De Buck, Forbes and Pusey correspondence, Pusey House, Oxford.

Devine Papers, NLS MS 1273.

Dowden Papers, NLS MS 3560.

East India Company Papers, IOR O 1. 97; L AG 20. 1–4, L AG 23. 8. 1.

Educational Returns, Scottish Episcopal Church, SRO CH 12. 64. 15

Eeles Collection, LPL MSS 1524, 1543.

Forbes, (Bishop) correspondence, Pusey House, Oxford.

Forbes (A. P.) Papers, St Paul's Cathedral, Dundee.

Forbes (A. P.) miscellaneous papers, Bodleian Library, Oxford, MS Eng. misc. d. 1096.

Forbes (A. P.) Trial documents, Scottish Episcopal Church, SRO CH 12. 60. 10 (iv).

Forbes, A. P., 'The Anglican Theory of Absolution', MS sermon (1875), Coates Hall Library, Edinburgh, pXLVII (19).

Forbes (A. P.), 'Let me die the death of the Righteous and let my last end be like his', MS sermon (1875), Coates Hall Library, Edinburgh, pXLI (i).

Forbes (George Hay) Papers, SAUL MS 19.

Forbes (William) Journal, NLS MS 1539–45.

correspondence, SRO CH 12. 12. 2412.

Gladstone Papers, BL MSS 44763, 44154.

Haileybury College Papers, IOR MSS J 1. 52, 94, 99, 104.

Hamilton Papers, Pusey House, Oxford.

Jenkins Papers, LPL MS 1604.

Jolly (Alexander) Letters, SRO CH 12. 30. 97, 151, 171, 194, 150; CH 12. 14. 150

Keble correspondence, Pusey House, Oxford.

Laing Papers, EUML MSS La. IV. 17.

Lee (F. G.) Papers, LPL MS 2074.

Longley Papers, LPL MSS vv. 6, 7.

Minto (third Earl of) Papers, MS 12346.

Minutes of Episcopal Conferences, Scottish Episcopal Church, SRO CH 12. 60. 9.

Miscellaneous pamphlets and letters, previously in black trunks at the General Synod Office, Scottish Episcopal Church, awaiting cataloguing at the Scottish Record Office under CH 12.

Miscellaneous Papers, LPL MS 3417.

Morton Papers, NLS MS 81. 1. 17.

Pusey correspondence, Pusey House, Oxford.

Pusey Papers, Pusey House, Oxford.

Register of the College of Bishops, Scottish Episcopal Church, SRO i (1743–1819), CH 12. 60. 1; ii (1822–60), CH 12. 60. 3; iii (1860–72), CH 12. 60. 4; iv (1872–99), CH 12. 60. 6.

Royal Infirmary (Dundee) Papers, DUL THB 1. 4. 1–4; 1. 1. 3–5.

Rutherfurd Letters, NLS MS 9718.

St Columba's church, Edinburgh, correspondence and histories, SRO CH 12. 5. 34, 45, 74, 81.

St Paul's Cathedral records, Dundee.

Scott Papers, Pusey House, Oxford.

Selbourne Papers, LPL MS 1895.

Tait Papers, LPL vv. 79, 81, 142, 167, 199, 420.
Torry (Patrick) Letters, SRO CH 12. 12. 2412; GD. 2. 173.

3. Books, Pamphlets, Articles Published before 1900

ALISON, A., *A Sermon Preached in The Episcopal Chapel, Cowgate, Edinburgh, November 16, 1806, The Day after the Funeral of Sir William Forbes of Pitsligo, Bart.* (Edinburgh, 1807).
ANDERSON, W., *The Scottish Nation; or the Surnames, Families, Literature, Honours, and Biographical History of the People of Scotland* (3 vols., Edinburgh, 1859–63).
BALL, T. I., 'Recollections of Bishop Forbes and of Dundee Two and Thirty Years Ago, in *Scottish Standard Bearer*, 9 (1898), 74–5, 116–17, 140–1, 155–8.
—— *The Bishop of Brechin and his Flock or the War in Blinshall Street. By an Observer* (Dundee, 1868).
BUCKLAND, C. T., *Social Life in India* (London, 1884).
BURGON, J. W., *Lives of Twelve Good Men* (London, 1891).
CHAMBERS, W., *A History of Peebleshire* (Edinburgh, 1864).
CHESNEY, G., *Indian Polity: A View of the System of Administration in India* (London, 1894).
CHEYNE, P., *The Authority and Use of the Scottish Communion Office Vindicated* (Aberdeen, 1843).
—— *Six Sermons on the Doctrine of the Eucharist* (Aberdeen, 1858).
CHURCH, R. W., *The Oxford Movement: Twelve Years 1833–1845* (London, 3rd edn. 1892).
COCKBURN, H., *Journal of Henry Cockburn* (2 vols., Edinburgh, 1874).
—— *Memorials of his Time* (Edinburgh, 1856).
—— *Circuit Journeys by the Late Lord Cockburn* (Edinburgh, 1889).
The Code of Canons of the Episcopal Church in Scotland, as Revised, Amended, and Enacted, by an Ecclesiastical Synod, Holden for that Purpose, at Edinburgh, on the 29th Day of August, and Continued by Adjournment till the 6th of September, Inclusive, in the Year of our Lord MDCCCXXXVIII (Edinburgh, 1838).
—— *Code of Canons of the Scottish Episcopal Church* (Edinburgh, 1863).
COLERIDGE, J. T., *A Memoir of the Rev. John Keble* (Oxford, 1869).
DANVERS, F. C., Monier-Williams, Sir W. *et. al.*, *Memorials of Old Haileybury College* (Westminster, 1894).
Documents Relative to the Proceedings of the Special Meeting of the College of Bishops Held at Edinburgh on May 27 1858 (Edinburgh, 1858).
DREXILIUS, J., *The Heliotropium; or, Conformity of the Human Will to the Divine Expounded in Five Books*, transl. by Reginald N. Shuttle with a Preface by the Bishop of Brechin (London, 1863).

Dundee Lodging House Association (Dundee, 1848).

Dundee Directory (Dundee, 1850–75).

[Edinburgh Academy] *Prize List of the Edinburgh Academy* (Edinburgh, 1831, 1832).

The Edinburgh Almanac or Universal Scots and Imperial Register for 1836 (Edinburgh, 1836).

FORBES, G. H., 'Eucharistical Adoration', *Panoply*, 2 (n.d.), 263–314.

FORBES, J. H., *A Short Account of the Edinburgh Savings Bank* (Edinburgh, 1815).

—— *Observations on Banks for Savings; to which is Prefixed a Letter to the Editor of the Quarterly Review* (Edinburgh, 1817).

—— *On English Episcopal Chapels in Scotland* (Edinburgh, 1846).

—— *Address to the Members of the Episcopal Church in Scotland* (Edinburgh, 2nd. edn. 1847).

FORBES, W., *Narrative of the Last Sickness and Death of Dame Christian Forbes*, ed. Alexander P. Forbes (Edinburgh, 1875).

FOSTER, J. (arr. and ann.), *Alumni Oxonienses: The Members of the University of Oxford 1715–1886* (4 vols., Oxford, 1887).

FROUDE, R. H., *Remains of the Late R. H. Froude* (2 vols., London, 1838).

GRUB, G., *An Ecclesiastical History of Scotland* (4 vols., Edinburgh, 1861).

HENDERSON, W., *Pleadings in the Case Henderson and Others v. the Bishop of Brechin before the Episcopal Synod of the Scottish Episcopal Church* (Edinburgh, 1860).

HUMPHREY, W., *Recollections of Scottish Episcopalianism* (London, 1896).

KAY, J., *A Series of Original Portraits and Caricature Etchings by John Kay* (Edinburgh, 1877).

KAYE, J. W., *The Administration of the East India Company: A History of Indian Progress* (London, 1853).

KEBLE, J., *On Eucharistical Adoration* (Oxford, 1857).

KEENE, H. G., *A Servant of John Company: Being the Recollections of an Indian Official* (London, 1897).

KINLOCH, M. G. J., *A History of Scotland: Chiefly in its Ecclesiastical Aspect, with an Introduction by A. P. Forbes* (2 vols., Edinburgh, 1874).

LATHBURY, T., *A History of the Non-Jurors* (London, 1845).

LAWSON, J. P., *History of the Scottish Episcopal Church from the Revolution to the Present Time* (Edinburgh, 1843).

LEWIS, G., *The State of St. David's Parish; with Remarks on the Moral and Physical Statistics of Dundee* (Dundee, 1841).

LIDDON, H. P., *Life of Edward Bouverie Pusey* (4 vols., London, 1893, 1894, 1897).

MACKEY, D. J., *Bishop Forbes: A Memoir* (London, 1888).

May Laymen have Decisive as well as Consultative Votes in Sacred Synods of the Church: A Case for the Bishops of Brechin, Aberdeen and Glasgow (Edinburgh, 1873).

Meeting of the British Association for the Advancement of Science in Dundee, September 1867 (Dundee, 1868).

NEALE, J. M., *The Life and Times of Patrick Torry, D. D.* (London, 1856).

NEWMAN, J. H., *Arians of the Fourth Century* (London, 3rd edn. 1871).

—— *A Letter to the Rev. E. B. Pusey, D. D., on his Recent Eirenicon* (London, 1866).

—— *Apologia Pro Vita Sua*, ed. M. J. Svaglic (Oxford, 1967).

—— *The Letters and Diaries of John Henry Newman*, ed. C. S. Dessain *et al.* (Oxford, 1961–).

New Statistical Account of Scotland, (vol. xi, Edinburgh, 1845).

NICOLSON, J., *In Memoriam: A Sermon Preached in S. Salvador's Church, Dundee, on Sunday the 17th October, 1875, being the Sunday after the Funeral of the Right Rev. A. P. Forbes, D. C. L., Bishop of Brechin* (Dundee, 1875).

PATTISON, M., 'Tendencies of Religious Thought in England 1688–1750', in *Essays and Reviews* (London, 6th. edn. 1861).

—— *Memoirs* (London, 1885).

PITLIGO, Lord Alexander, *Thoughts Concerning Man's Condition and Duties in this Life, and his Hopes in the World to Come, with a Biographical Sketch of the Author by Lord Medwyn* (Edinburgh, 1834).

POLLEN, J. H., *Narrative of Five Years at St. Saviour's, Leeds* (Oxford, 1851).

Prospectus of St. John's Agricultural Home, Drumlithie, in the Diocese of Brechin, for the Sons of Farm Labourers, with Explanation, and Illustrative Letters (Montrose, 1853).

PUSEY, E. B., *The Real Presence of the Body and Blood of our Lord Jesus Christ: The Doctrine of the English Church, with a Vindication of the Reception by the Wicked and of the Adoration of our Lord Jesus Christ, Truly Present* (Oxford, 1857).

—— *The Church of England, a Portion of Christ's One Holy Catholic Church, and a Means of Restoring Visible Unity. An Eirenicon, in a Letter to the Author of 'The Christian Year'* (London, 1865).

RATTRAY, T., *An Essay on the Nature of the Church* (Edinburgh, 1728).

ROBERTSON, Joseph, *Scottish Abbeys and Cathedrals, Incl. a Biography of the Author* (Aberdeen, 1893).

RUSSELL, E. F. (ed.), *Alexander Heriot Mackonochie: A Memoir* (London, 1890).

The Scottish Ecclesiastical Journal (Edinburgh, 1851–63).

The Scottish Guardian (Edinburgh, 1875).

SIMEON, A. B., *A Short Memoir of the Rev. Thomas Chamberlain M. A.* (London, 1892).

SKENE, F. M. C., *A Memoir of Alexander, Bishop of Brechin* (London, 1876).

SKINNER, J., *Annals of Scottish Episcopacy, from the Year 1788 to the Year 1816 Inclusive* (Edinburgh, 1818).

STEPHEN, W., *History of the Scottish Church* (2 vols., Edinburgh, 1896).

STEPHENS, W. R. W., *The Life and Letters of Walter Farquhar Hook D. D.* (London, 1880).

THOMSON, T. (ed.), *A Biographical Dictionary of Eminent Scotsmen, Originally Edited by Robert Chambers* (London, 1875).

268 Bibliography

TORRY, P., *A Pastoral Letter to the Clergy and Laity of the United Diocese of St. Andrews, Dunkeld, and Dunblane, from their Bishop* (Edinburgh, 1846).

Tracts for the Times (6 vols. in 5, London, 1834–41).

TULLOCH, J., *Movements of Religious Thought in Britain during the Nineteenth Century* (Leicester, 1971 repr. of 1885 edn.).

WALKER, W., *Life of the Right Reverend Alexander Jolly and the Right Reverend George Gleig* (Edinburgh, 1878).

—— *Three Churchmen: Sketches and Reminiscences* (Edinburgh,1893).

WORDSWORTH, C., *Notes to Assist towards Forming a Right Judgement on the Eucharistic Controversy* (1858).

—— *Proposals for Peace or a Few Remarks on The Eucharistic Doctrine of Bishops Taylor, Ken, and Wilson with Reference to the Recent Pastoral of the Bishop of Brechin* (Edinburgh, 1859).

WORDSWORTH, J., *The Episcopate of Charles Wordsworth* (London, 1899).

4. Books, Pamphlets, Articles Published since 1900

ALLCHIN, A. M., *The Silent Rebellion: Anglican Religious Communities 1845–1900*, (London, 1958).

Alexander Penrose Forbes: The Search for Integrity (Dundee, 1977).

ALTHOLZ, J. L., 'The Warfare of Conscience with Theology', in J. L. Altholz (ed.), *The Mind and Art of Victorian England*, (Minneapolis, 1976).

ANDERSON, R. D., 'Education and the State in Nineteenth-Century Scotland', in *Economic History Review*, 2nd ser., 36 (1983), 518–34.

ANSON, P. F., *The Call of the Cloister : Religious Communities and Kindred Bodies in the Anglican Communion* (London, 1955).

ARCHIBALD, J., *A Ten Year's Conflict and Subsequent Persecutions; or, a Struggle for Religious Liberty* (Dumfries, 1907).

AVIS, P., 'The Shaking of the Seven Hills', in *Scottish Journal of Theology*, 32 (1979), 439–55.

BEST, G., *Mid-Victorian Britain 1851–1875* (London, 1971).

BORSCH, F. H., '"Ye Shall be Holy": Reflections on the Spirituality of the Early Years of the Oxford Movement', in *Anglican Theological Review*, 66 (1984), 347–59.

BRANDRETH, H. R. T., *The Œcumenical Ideals of the Oxford Movement* (London, 1947).

—— *Dr Lee of Lambeth* (London, 1951).

BRILIOTH, Y., *The Anglican Revival: Studies in the Oxford Movement* (London, 1933).

BROWN, C. G., *The Social History of Religion in Scotland since1730* (London, 1987).

BROXAP, H., *The Later Non-Jurors* (Cambridge, 1924).

BUSCHKÜHL, M., *Great Britain and the Holy See 1746–1870* (Blackrock, Co. Dublin, 1982).

BUTLER, C., *The Vatican Council 1869–70* (London, 1962).

BUTLER, P., *Gladstone: Church, State and Tractarianism. A Study of his Religious Ideas and Attitudes, 1809–1859* (Oxford, 1982).

CAMERON, A. T., *Religious Communities of the Church of England* (London, 1918).

CASHDOLLAR, C. D., *The Transformation of Theology, 1830–1890: Positivism and Protestant Thought in Britain and America*, (Princeton, NJ, 1989).

CHADWICK, O., *The Victorian Church* (2 vols, London, 3rd edn. 1971).

—— *The Mind of the Oxford Movement* (London, 1960).

—— *The Secularization of the European Mind in the Nineteenth Century* (Cambridge, 1975).

—— *The Spirit of the Oxford Movement: Tractarian Essays* (Cambridge, 1990).

CHECKLAND, O., *Philanthropy in Victorian Scotland: Social Welfare and the Voluntary Principle* (Edinburgh, 1980).

CHECKLAND, S. and O., *Industry and Ethos: Scotland 1832–1914* (London, 1984).

CHEYNE, A. C., *The Transforming of the Kirk: Victorian Scotland's Religious Revolution* (Edinburgh, 1983).

COBB, P. G., 'Thomas Chamberlain: A Forgotten Tractarian' in *Studies in Church History*, ed. D. Baker, 16 (Oxford, 1979), 373–87.

CURRIE, R., *et. al.*, *Churches and Church-Goers: Patterns of Church Growth in the British Isles since 1700* (Oxford, 1977).

DAVIE, G. E., *The Democratic Intellect: Scotland and her Universities in the Nineteenth Century* (Edinburgh, 2nd edn. 1964).

DAWSON, C., *The Spirit of the Oxford Movement* (London, 1933).

DELEHAYE, H., *The Work of the Bollandists through Three Centuries 1615–1915* (Princeton, NJ, 1922).

DOWDEN, J., *The Scottish Communion Office 1764* (Oxford, 1922).

DRUMMOND, A. L., and Bulloch, J., *The Church in Victorian Scotland 1843–1874* (Edinburgh, 1975).

—— *The Early History of the Church of St. Columba by the Castle* (Edinburgh, 1927).

The Edinburgh Academy Register (Edinburgh, 1914).

EDWARDES, M., *Raj: The Story of British India* (London, 1969).

ELLIOT-BINNS, L. E., *English Thought 1860–1900: The Theological Aspect.* (London, 1956).

ELLIS, I., *Seven against Christ: A Study of 'Essays and Reviews'* (Leiden, 1980).

ELLSWORTH, L. E., *Charles Lowder and the Ritualist Movement* (London, 1982).

EMBURY, J., *The Catholic Movement and the Society of the Holy Cross* (London, 1931).

FARRINGTON, A., *The Records of the East India College Haileybury and other Institutions* (London, 1976).

FERGUSON, W., *Scotland 1689 to the Present* (Edinburgh, 1968).

Forbes of Brechin: An Unofficial Patron Saint of the Scottish Episcopal Church (Company of the Servants of God, n.d.).

FORRESTER, D., *Young Doctor Pusey: A Study in Development* (London, 1989).

FOSKETT, R., 'The Episcopate of Daniel Sandford 1810–30', in *Records of the Scottish Church History Society*, 15 (1966), 141–52.

—— 'The Drummond Controversy 1842', in *Records of the Scottish Church History Society*, 16 (1969), 99–109.

FRANKLIN, R. W., 'Pusey and Worship in Industrial Society', in *Worship*, 57 (1983), 386–412.

FRAPPELL, L., '"Science in the Service of Orthodoxy": The Early Intellectual Development of E. B. Pusey', in P. Butler (ed.), *Pusey Rediscovered* (London, 1983).

FULLER, R. H., 'The Classical High Church Reaction to the Tractarians', in G. Rowell (ed.), *Tradition Renewed*, (London, 1986).

GARDNER, B., *The East India Company* (London, 1971).

GAULDIE, E. (ed.), *The Dundee Textile Industry 1790–1885* (Edinburgh, 1969).

—— 'The Middle Class and Working Class Housing in the Nineteenth Century', in A. A. MacLaren (ed.), *Social Class in Scotland: Past and Present* (Edinburgh, n.d.).

GIFFORD, J., *et.al.*, *Edinburgh* (Harmondsworth, 1984).

GILBERT, W., *Edinburgh Life in the Nineteenth Century* (Glasgow, 1989 repr. of 1901 edn.).

GILLEY, S., *Newman and his Age* (London, 1990).

GLADSTONE, W. E., *The Gladstone Diaries*, ed. M. R. D. Foot and H. C. G. Matthew (9 vols., Oxford, 1968–).

GOLDIE, F., *A Short History of the Episcopal Church in Scotland* (London, 1951).

GREENFIELD, R. H., 'Such a Friend to the Pope', in P. Butler (ed.), *Pusey Rediscovered* (London, 1983).

GRIFFIN, J. R., 'The Radical Phase of the Oxford Movement', in *Journal of Ecclesiastical History*, 27 (1976), 47–56.

GRISBROOKE, W. J., *Anglican Liturgies of the Seventeenth and Eighteenth Centuries* (London, 1958).

GRUB, G., *My Years in Dundee with Bishop Forbes of Brechin 1871–1875* (Edinburgh, 1912).

HALES, E. E. Y., *Pio Nono: A Study in European Politics and Religion in the Nineteenth Century* (London, 1954).

HARDELIN, A.; *The Tractarian Understanding of the Eucharist* (Uppsala, 1965).

HEYER, F., *The Catholic Church from 1648 to 1870* (London, 1969).

HIMMELFARB, G., *The Idea of Poverty: England in the Early Industrial Age* (London, 1984).

HINCHLIFF, P., *Benjamin Jowett and the Christian Religion* (Oxford, 1987).

HOUGHTON, W. E., *The Victorian Frame of Mind 1830–1870* (New Haven, Conn., 1957).

HYLSON-SMITH, K., *Evangelicals in the Church of England 1734–1984* (Edinburgh, 1988).

INGLIS, K. S., *Churches and the Working Class in Victorian England* (London, 1963).

JEMOLO, A. C., *Church and State in Italy 1850–1950* (Oxford, 1960).

JOHNSTON, J. O., *Life and Letters of Henry Parry Liddon* (London, 1904).

JONES, O. W., *Isaac Williams and his Circle* (London, 1971).

KER, I., *John Henry Newman: A Biography* (Oxford, 1988).

KITSON CLARK, G., *Churchmen and the Condition of England 1832–1885* (London, 1973).

KNIGHT, C., 'The Anglicising of Scottish Episcopalianism', in *Records of the Scottish Church History Society*, 23 (1989), 361–77.

LATHBURY, D. C. (ed.), *Correspondence on Church and Religion of William Ewart Gladstone* (2 vols., London, 1910).

LATOURETTE, K. S., *A History of the Expansion of Christianity*, vol. vi: *The Great Century in Northern Africa and Asia A. D. 1800–A. D. 1914* (London, 1944).

LENMAN, B., 'The Scottish Episcopal Clergy and the Ideology of Jacobitism', in E. Cruickshanks (ed.), *Ideology and Conspiracy: Aspects of Jacobitism, 1689–1759* (Edinburgh, 1982).

LOCHHEAD, M., 'The Christian Sacrifice: The Eucharistic Tradition of the Scottish Episcopal Church', in *Theology*, 67 (1964), 388–94.

—— *Episcopal Scotland in the Nineteenth Century* (London, 1966).

McCULLOCH, J. H., and Stirling, K. J., *The Edinburgh Savings Bank 1836–1936* (Edinburgh, 1936).

MacLAREN, A. A., *Religion and Social Class: The Disruption Years in Aberdeen* (London, 1974).

—— (ed.), *Social Class in Scotland: Past and Present* (Edinburgh, n.d.).

MacLEAN, A., 'Episcopal Worship in the Nineteenth and Twentieth Centuries', in D. Forrester and D. Murray (eds.), *Studies in the History of Worship in Scotland* (Edinburgh, 1984).

MAGNUSSON, M., *The Clacken and the Slate: The Story of Edinburgh Academy 1824–1974* (London, 1974).

MARSH, P. T., *The Victorian Church in Decline: Archbishop Tait and the Church of England 1868–1882* (London, 1969).

MARTIN, B. W., *John Keble Priest, Professor and Poet* (London, 1976).

MATHER, F. C., *High Church Prophet: Bishop Samuel Horsley (1733–1806) and the Caroline Tradition in the Later Georgian Church* (Oxford, 1992).

MATTHEW, H. C. G., 'Edward Bouverie Pusey: From Scholar to Tractarian', in *Journal of Theological Studies*, N.S. 32 (1981), 101–24.

—— *Gladstone 1809–1874* (Oxford, 1988).

MECHIE, S., *The Church and Scottish Social Development 1780–1870* (London, 1960).

MIDDLETON, R. D., *Dr Routh* (Oxford, 1938).

MILLAR, A. H., *Jubilee of the Albert Institute 1867–1917* (Dundee, 1917).

MOSS, C. B., *The Old Catholic Movement, its Origins and History* (Hillspeck, Ariz., 2nd edn., 1977).

MOWAT, J. D., *Bishop A. P. Forbes* (Edinburgh, 1925).

NEALE, J. M., *Letters of John Mason Neale D.D. Selected and Edited by his Daughter* (London, 1910).

NEWSOME, D., *Two Classes of Men: Platonism and English Romantic Thought* (London, 1974).

NOCKLES, P., 'The Oxford Movement: Historical Background 1780–1833', in G. Rowell (ed.), *Tradition Renewed* (London, 1986), 24–50.

NORMAN, E. R., *Church and Society in England 1770–1970* (Oxford, 1976).

O'DONNELL, G., 'The Spirituality of E. B. Pusey', in P. Butler ed., *Pusey Rediscovered* (London, 1983).

O'GARA, M., *Triumph in Defeat: Infallibility, Vatican I, and the French Minority Bishops*, (Washington, DC, 1988).

OVERTON, J. D., *The NonJurors: Their Lives, Principles, and Writings* (London, 1902).

PARRY, J. P., *Democracy and Religion: Gladstone and the Liberal Party 1867–1875* (Cambridge, 1986).

PECK, W. G., *The Social Implications of the Oxford Movement* (New York, 1933).

PENNIE, G. N., 'The Trial of the Rev. Patrick Cheyne for Erroneous Teaching of the Eucharist in Aberdeen in 1858', in *Records of the Scottish Church History Society*, 23 (1987), 77–93.

PERRIER, J. L., *The Revival of Scholastic Philosophy in the Nineteenth Century* (New York, 1909).

PERRY, W., *George Hay Forbes: A Romance in Scholarship* (London, 1927).

—— *The Oxford Movement in Scotland* (Cambridge, 1933).

—— *Alexander Penrose Forbes: Bishop of Brechin, the Scottish Pusey* (London, 1939).

PHILIPS, C. H., *The East India Company 1784–1834* (Manchester, 1940).

PREBBLE, J., *Culloden* (London, 1961).

PRESTIGE, L., *Pusey* (London, 1933 repr. 1982).

PRIMROSE, J. B., 'The Pitsligo Press of George Hay Forbes', in *Edinburgh Bibliographical Society Transactions*, 4 (1962), 55–89.

PURCELL, E. S., *Life and Letters of Ambrose Phillipps de Lisle* (2 vols., London, 1900).

REARDON, B. M. G., *From Coleridge to Gore: A Century of Religious Thought in Britain* (London, 1971).

—— *Liberalism and Tradition: Aspects of Catholic Thought in Nineteenth-Century France* (Cambridge, 1975).

ROWELL, G., *The Vision Glorious* (Oxford, 1983).

—— (ed.), *Tradition Renewed: The Oxford Movement Conference Papers* (London, 1986).

SELBY, R. C., *The Principle of Reserve in the Writings of John Henry Cardinal Newman* (Oxford, 1975).

SHANNON, R., *Gladstone 1809–1865* (London, 1982).

SHARP, R., 'New Perspectives in the High Church Tradition: Historical Background 1730–1780', in Geoffrey Rowell (ed.), *Tradition Renewed* (London, 1986).

SHEPHERD, D., *Alexander Penrose Forbes, Bishop of Brechin, 1847–1875* [a brief biographical pamphlet], (Dundee, 1975).

SIKKA, R. P., *The Civil Service in India: Europeanisation and Indianisation under the East India Company 1765–1857* (New Delhi, 1984).

SMOUT, T. C., *A History of the Scottish People 1560–1830* (London, 1972).

—— *A Century of the Scottish People 1830–1950* (London, 1986).

SOLOWAY, R. A., *Prelates and People: Ecclesiastical Social Thought in England 1783–1852* (London, 1969).

SQUIRES, T. W. (ed.), *In West Oxford: Historical Notes and Pictures concerning the Parish of S. Thomas the Martyr, Oxford* (London, 1928).

STEPHENSON, A. M. G., *The First Lambeth Conference 1867* (London, 1967).

STUART, E. B., 'Unjustly Condemned? Roman Catholic Involvement in the APUC 1857–64', in *Journal of Ecclesiastical History*, 41 (1990), 44–63.

TAYLOR, B., 'Bishop Hamilton', in *Church Quarterly Review*, 155 (1954), 235–48.

THOMAS, I., *Haileybury 1806–1987* (Haileybury, Herts., 1987).

THOMPSON, F. M. L., *The Rise of Respectable Society: A Social History of Victorian Britain 1830–1900* (London, 1988).

THOMPSON, K. A., *Bureaucracy and Church Reform* (Oxford, 1970).

TOWLE, E. A., *John Mason Neale: A Memoir* (London, 1907).

WALKER, W. W., *Juteopolis: Dundee and its Textile Workers 1885–1923* (Edinburgh, 1979).

WARD, B., 'A Tractarian Inheritance: The Religious Life in a Patristic Perspective', in G. Rowell (ed.), *Tradition Renewed* (London, 1986), 214–25.

WARD, W. R., *Victorian Oxford* (London, 1965).

WATERMAN, A. M. C., 'The Ideological Alliance of Political Economy and Christian Theology 1798–1833', in *Journal of Ecclesiastical History*, 34 (1983), 231–44.

WEBB, C. C. J., *A Century of Anglican Theology and Other Lectures* (Oxford, 1923).

—— *Religious Thought in the Oxford Movement* (London, 1928).

WHITE, G., 'New Names for Old Things: Scottish Reaction to Early Tractarianism', in D. Baker (ed.), *Renaissance and Renewal in Christian History* (Oxford, 1977).

WILLIAMS, T. J., and Campbell, A. W., *The Park Village Sisterhood* (London, 1965).

WITHRINGTON, D. J., 'Non-Churchgoing *c.*1750–*c.*1850: A Preliminary Study', in *Records of the Scottish Church History Society*, 17 (1972), 99–113.

—— 'The Churches in Scotland, *c.*1870–*c.*1900: Towards a New Social Conscience', in *Records of the Scottish Church History Society*, 19 (1977), 155–68.

WOODGATE, M. V., *Father Benson Founder of the Cowley Fathers* (London, 1953).

YATES, N., *The Oxford Movement and Parish Life; St. Saviour's, Leeds 1839–1929* [Borthwick Papers, 48] (York, 1975).

YATES, N., *Leeds and the Oxford Movement: A Study of 'High Church' Activity in the Rural Deaneries of Allerton, Armley, Headingly and Whitkirk in the Diocese of Ripon, 1836–1934* [Thoresby Society Publications, 55] (Leeds, 1975).

5. Theses

CROOKS, D. W. T., 'The Effects of the Oxford Movement in the Scottish Episcopal Church in the Nineteenth Century', BD thesis (Trinity College, Dublin, 1983).

JURICH, J. P., 'The Ecumenical Relations of Victor de Buck, S. J., with Anglican Leaders on the Eve of Vatican 1', Doctor of Sacred Theology thesis (Catholic University of Louvain, 1988).

NIMMO, A. E., 'Charles Wordsworth, Bishop of St. Andrews 1853–1892: Reconciler or Controversialist', M.Phil. thesis (University of Edinburgh, 1983).

NOCKLES, P. B., 'Continuity and Change in Anglican High Churchmanship in Britain 1792–1850', D.Phil. thesis (University of Oxford, 1982).

INDEX